R. Gomal

Gul Kach

Mugł

Sambaza

Takht-e- Sul

ez

R. Kundar

HAN

Manikhwar

Mughal Kot

U

L

SAN

Fort Sandeman

Kapip

D

E

A

I

R

Shaighalu

M

A

Mina Bazaar

R. Zhob

Lakaband

A

J

zai

N

OB VALLEY

A

Murgha Kibzai

T

R

A

Mekhtar

Kingri

N

ralai

G

E

D.G. KHAN

Manzai

Ruckni

Chotiali

Sakhi Sarwar

Kohlu

Barkhan

Fort Munro

OF PAKISTAN

Scale = 0   20   40   60 miles

Sturrey Masheh

Sturrey Masheh

*Wanderings Along the Afghan Borderlands
Over Forty Years*

A. F. M. Burdett

Butleigh & Barton

Copyright © A. F. M, Burdett 2011
First published in 2011 by Butleigh & Barton
70 Barton Road, Butleigh, Somerset, BA6 8TL

Distributed by Gardners Books, 1 Whittle Drive, Eastbourne, East Sussex,
BN23 6QH
Tel: +44(0)1323 521555 | Fax: +44(0)1323 521666

www.amolibros.com

British Library Cataloguing in Publication Data
A catalogue record for this book is available from the British Library.

ISBN 978-0-9563401-0-8

Typeset by Amolibros, Milverton, Somerset
This book production has been managed by Amolibros
Printed and bound by T J International Ltd, Padstow, Cornwall, UK

Contents

Maps & Charts

List of Illustrations

Section One

Section Two

Section Three

shortly after being escorted out of Waziristan to Bannu in 1971.

6) The author briefly resting on the last range of the Torr Ghar before Kakar Khorrasan and the Afghan border.

7) Mair Jan, a Mahsud refugee from Waziristan because of a feud with a larger family, working on Hashim Khan's (Luni not Jogezai) at Manzai, eighty miles east of Tarawal.

8) Wali Jan (Shinwari) and two relatives, from Chagchalan in Afghanistan, camped for the winter at Ghabar Ghar.

Section Four

Section Five

FACING PAGE 306

1) Breaking camp shortly after dawn with the peak, Yau Harsk, looming behind.
2) Bibi Ruziamat milking a sheep while Ziauddin holds it, plus one or two others.
3) Ruziamat filling our water bags at a spring as the next camp further on was a dry one.
4) The family threading its way up and out of a deep gorge.
5) Part of the main bazaar at Badani on the Afghan border as locals warm themselves in the early morning sun. The place is not marked on any map.
6) A cool early morning and Ruziamat and Malanga warm themselves by the meagre fire.
7) The main street in Kila Saifulla, now tarred, looking east towards the small strong point built during the last war, presumably against the axis party that eluded the British to gain entry into Afghanistan.
8) Humayun et al praying in the small Sanzar Nika Ziarat, near Kot. Sanzar is the putative ancestor of the largest and dominant section, the Sanzar Khel, of the Kakars.
9) Border post at Ghazluna by the frontier with Afghanistan.
10) The baker at work in Kila Saifulla, his oven being a bee-hive shaped cavity in the earthen plinth. He is shown hooking out a naan at lunchtime.
11) The huge ancient mound situated ten miles east of Duki, called Dubbr Kot or the Thal Shahghullai.
12) The way we travelled in 1959 and the 'sixties.

Preface

Since the last world war the usual custom of a preface to a book on travel or exploration or adventure seems to have died, such earlier writers being usually retired military men or colonial administrators or even missionaries in some far-flung country who wrote their memoirs after retirement. Today most writers on travel or exploration have journeyed simply in order to gather material for a planned or commissioned book and, instead of a preface, there is a brief c.v. of the author on the dust cover. This book, however, is by accident rather than by design and one or two explanations are needed.

When heading from India back to Chaman on the border with Afghanistan in 1958 I may or may not have managed to go into the Toba Kakar hills along the Afghan – Pakistan border to stay with the Achakzais as invited, for martial law had been declared recently and a newspaper report said that one of the tribe's 'sardars' or leaders had been imprisoned for his support of the Pashtunistan movement; and I had no idea if he was the one that I had met earlier on my way overland to India. However, as one door possibly closed another opened and I was enormously fortunate in my chance meeting with Ahmad Yar Khan Jogezai of the Kakar tribe at the road-rail bridge over the Chenab River near Muzaffagar. Thereby I was introduced to his brothers and extended family and the many of the tribe as a whole, but also in him I chanced to meet someone unusually well versed in tribal lore and custom. Further, in the fullness of time, he became the next best thing to a real brother when I had none of my own.

The Kakars may not rank so valiantly as the Wazirs and Mahsuds in the area's turbulent history but neither did they torture their captured or wounded enemies. Above all I have come to regard them as 'my tribe', warts and all, though I met very few 'warts' in my travels among them. Tribalism has gained a poor reputation in recent years, invariably when egged on by those with political ambitions or mullahs with a thirst for power, but it lays down strict ground rules. For example, in the past, when embarking on a raid or foray, the Kakar young bloods were urged by the elders not to harm old men, women and children or Hindus.

Since the Second World War, books on Afghanistan have dealt largely with the Russian invasion and the mujahudin, revealing little of the normal, everyday life in the area. Since my first contact with the Kakars of northern Baluchistan in 1958, life has changed greatly and needs recording before too much of the traditional way of life and local events are lost. In addition I was fortunate to come upon Afghanistan in its innocence, before the ugly actions of some hippies began to change local attitudes and then its ruination by the Russians, the local warlords and the Taliban in turn. The legacy of the involvement by Britain, America and others remains to be seen.

No one coming in contact with the Pashtu/Pakhtu speakers, be they Afghan, Ghalzai or Pashtun can be unaffected by them and I still recall a twelve-hour, jolting bus journey from Kandahar to Kabul in 1960, when the road was still a narrow gravel track winding through seemingly endless semi-desert mountains. Cramped next to me was an elderly Afghan in threadbare cotton clothes: he probably had only a small handful of Afghani coins to his name. Around mid-day he fumbled in his shawl and drew out a piece of dry 'naan': carefully breaking it into two, he offered me a half, and insisted when I politely declined his generous offer. He must be long dead but since then I rarely eat next to someone without offering to share what I have.

While Farsi (= Persian) is spoken in the west of Afghanistan and Dari, a dialect of Farsi is prevalent in the south-east, Dari is also the official or state language. Further north along both sides of the Pakistan border, Pashtu in the south or the hard variant Pakhtu further north is spoken by the eastern Afghans, by some Ghalzai and by the Pashtun tribes. Its alphabet has forty letters, its grammar is complicated, while some of its sounds are difficult for us to pronounce. Converting such words and names into the Roman alphabet is often a problem and combinations of letters are sometimes necessary:

'kh' is like 'ch' in Scottish *loch*
'gh' is a strange guttural from the back of the mouth not met in any European language so far as I know
'zh' is like the **soft 'j'** in French
'a' is as in *far* but shorter
'eh' like the **French 'é'** or a short 'ay' in English
'i' is like **'ee'**
'o' as in *sow* or *hoe*
'u' is usually **as 'oo' in *boot*** but the title of the book is an exception, the 'u' in that case pronounced as in *hurry*. Otherwise the remaining letters are much as we use them. As for the many names in the text, all are actual but two men are referred to as X and Y to protect their professional positions.

Apart from Ahmad Yar Khan, two of his brothers deserve special thanks: the late Jehandar Shah for his endless hospitality whenever I was in Quetta and for copying various documents and large tracts from the Zhob Gazetteer of 1907, all unasked; and Mohammad Hassan for introducing me to a nomad family of the Shahizai clan on their spring migration back to Badani on the Afghan border. Ruziamat Shahizai and his family deserve thanks for their tolerance and good humour when I was literally thrust upon them and for letting me share their lives for a month or so and thus realise an ambition of thirty years. My thanks are also due to the late Nasserullah Khan of the Luni tribe who, ignoring a government ban, welcomed me to his home at Manzai near Duki and took me to the nomad wintering ground at Ghabar Ghar to meet Shinwari, Kharoti, Doutani and other nomads wintering there.

So far I have not mentioned the late chief, Nawab Mohammad Khan Jogezai, who was so trusting in allowing me to wander off alone into his wild hills, something that I took for granted at the time with the brash confidence of youth. That our eldest son's third name is Jogezai is a measure of my deep regard and affection for him.

My parents and my landlady before leaving England, Kathie Brown, were very useful by hoarding my letters to them, thereby fixing the chronology of events when I did not keep a diary. However I did record tribal traditions and events told me by Ahmad Yar Khan there and then, at all times. Lastly, my sincere thanks are due to my wife Sheila for her tolerance and faith in letting me go off at intervals on visits and expeditions that could be hazardous, especially when accompanied by one or other of our young sons. Hers was the humdrum task of looking after the family, usually for weeks on end, waiting for reassuring letters and possibly fearing an official telegram or visit.

Chapter One

On To India

During my early teens I avidly read books on Africa and Central Asia, being particularly fascinated by Tibet and when a turbulent engagement finally ended for the third and last time in 1956 I needed a 'walk-about'. So for the next two years I bought equipment, designing and having made a special two-part rucsac to be carried either by a human or a pony, for a solo expedition across Tibet. However, the Chinese then invaded that sad nation and made it clear that they did not want me wandering across the country. With everything ready in 1958, after so much effort, a traverse at high altitude from Kashmir to Assam presented itself as the only possible alternative, a difficult trek that has yet to be made by anyone. My equipment was sent by sea to a contact in Bombay but, as I lacked money for the sea fare, I left England on the 9th April on an aged bicycle bought for ten shillings (but then fitted with new wheels) with a tiny 50cc.motor bolted beneath the pedals. I had just £21.10/- for the journey of around six thousand miles so it would be Spartan.

At Torino the Moto Garelli factory insisted on giving me various spares for the motor to ensure that I reached India come what may, with a result that the Bergans rucsac on my back often topped eighty pounds / thirty-six kilos and was dreadfully painful until I became accustomed to it. Dysentery contracted in northern Italy lead to alarming bleeding for a couple of days in Yugoslavia when I had little money for treatment. In the mountains of southern Yugoslavia, Turkey and beyond, attacks by pairs and trios of fierce sheep dogs were very worrying, especially as treatment against rabies at that time involved fourteen injections in the stomach in as many days, but the row of old-fashioned clinker nails around the soles of my climbing boots worked wonders time after time. When a snarling head was contacted as I desperately fended off my attackers, often in the dark, that one problem at least was over and often the other attackers took heed.

Disaster struck in eastern Turkey as I approached Erzincan when, because no oil was available, the rear hub with its back-pedalling brake seized and was ruined. A train on to Erzerum offered the hope of a spare being flown there but I discovered that it was a hyper-sensitive military zone and I was not allowed to stay there. That left the stark choice of going back to Erzincan or going forwards by whatever means presented themselves in the hope of reaching Tehran. As the motor was covered by an RAC carnet the machine could not simply be abandoned as I would have wished. A worrying gamble paid off: two lorries and two lorry 'buses' took me to the Iran border and from there author Michael Alexander and his friend carried me all the way to the capital in his Landrover. There I was fortunate to be allowed to pitch my tent in the Manzarieh scout camp site near Tadreesh high on the slopes of the Elburz range.

Naively expecting a replacement hub to arrive any day, I turned down a generous offer by Arragh Hatamil, a successful Tehran photographer I chanced to meet, to visit the ruined fortress of Alamut in the Valley of the Assassins because the expedition would have taken a week. In the event the first hub sent out went missing. Realising afterwards that the replacement might not come for weeks, I managed to obtain temporary work teaching English part time for the British Council, prior to which I had already sold a half litre of blood in Istanbul and another unit in Tehran to make ends meet. One day I happened to meet

Bob Chambers, an Australian traveller temporarily working for a local newspaper. A week or two later we joined forces with Pat Morrison an Irish traveller and Carl Zimmerman, an American seconded to work with Radio Tehran, plus a local named Sheikh as a guide to climb Mount Damavand, an extinct volcano nearly 18,000 feet high. Admiring a painting by a local artist in a shop window, Bob and I discovered that not only was it inexpensive but that there was an almost identical copy inside. More importantly, if we bought both paintings, a discount would bring the price down to that of a unit of blood each: thus I sold my third half-litre of blood in ten weeks. After that I took a brief look at Isfahan and the Caspian Sea coast. The frustration of having to wait for the spare part so that I could continue to India was indescribable but, although I failed to realise the importance at the time, I learnt passable Farsi. It radically changed my life. After some eight weeks a second hub sent out from England did arrive and I was free to continue.

The southern route through Qum, Yazd, Kerman and Zahedan was very tempting as it would involve one less visa and less currency changing. That was until I learned that there was no water for one hundred and twenty miles on one stretch of the dirt track and that hot winds tore down from the north but what really decided the issue was hearing about four American oil prospectors in a jeep who decided to shoot it out when accosted by bandits, only to be wiped out to a man. Maybe I had little to steal but for some forgotten reason I had my 16mm cine camera with me and it was essential to my plans. The alternative route, to Mashad and Afghanistan, was along the southern flank of the Elburz. It turned out to be dreadfully corrugated, so much so that I had to stand on the pedals for mile after mile in order to spread the load equally on the wheels lest the rear one collapse under the constant impact. I even saw one abandoned tanker lorry sagging in the middle with its chassis completely fractured due to metal fatigue. It was slow, tiring work even relying on the motor and for considerable stretches it was easier to ride on the desert itself alongside the road.

Late one evening I was suddenly hit by another attack of fever, much worse than usual, and became so weak that I was unable to reach the next small town whose lights seemed so near and inviting in the dark. I had no water at all and just managed to force down a spoonful of oatmeal moistened with some jam before collapsing into my tent. The next morning the groundsheet was wet with condensed sweat but I was well again. A day or two later the vague internal pain that I had suffered in Yugoslavia reasserted itself, possibly due in part from the physical stress of hard travelling: I suspected an infected amoebic ulcer as I was still passing blood at intervals but I lacked the courage to inject myself with the single vial of penicillin that I carried. The antibiotic would not cure the amoebic problem but it might rid me of the secondary infection that I suspected and in those days drug resistance had yet to manifest itself. However, in the middle of nowhere I came upon a small army camp nestling among some low hills not far from the road and the resident medical officer kindly did the job for me. Hours later things improved.

At one stage, after trying to repair the same puncture three times in an hour or so because the searing heat dried the solution too quickly, I paid a lorry driver to take me on to Sabzevar where I could find both shade and water. Entering the caravanserai, and in those days one really did see long strings of camels threading their way across the desert, I filled the enormous glass provided by the small tank of water and gulped it down: it must have held at least a litre. Pausing halfway through my second glass, I saw that the heavenly brew was full of myriads of minute creatures of various shape and size, gyrating and zig-zagging energetically. They were probably no threat in themselves but they had to be feeding on something even smaller and that would mean bacteria as there was no sign of uni-cellular algae to supply their needs. It was by then too late but in the event it didn't matter as no harm befell me. Several caravanserais that I saw were appealingly traditional, entered by a lofty arched gate, single-storied and consisting of perhaps forty rooms, all built of mud brick and arranged around an enormous square or rectangular courtyard. As said earlier, the road surface was often so poor that it was better to travel on the desert instead, and it was such hard going that I did not bother to visit the tomb of Omar Khayyam at Nishapur. In any case the Iranis do not rate him as high as some of their other poets such as Firdausi: simply, the English translation was excellent and caught our imagination. At intervals I saw abandoned villages where the 'qanat' wells had run dry and life had become insupportable.

Upon reaching Mashed, some of the British Council people I had come to know in Tehran welcomed me as a guest at their new branch for a couple of days. In former times the building had been a British Consulate that covered Afghanistan, Baluchistan and Kashmir, when the Consul rode out with an escort of twelve lancers. Whereas my first rear tyre had endured three thousand, two hundred miles, the five hundred or so miles from Tehran had created just as much wear in my second one because the corrugation led to bouncing and scuffing by the drive roller. I had no other spare tyre for the front either, I could find none in the bazaar of the size that fitted and therefore rebuilt the front wheel to use what was available. Although my rear tyre offered little comfort, I pressed on the one hundred and sixteen miles to the Afghan border as my extended visa expired in two days. On the first night a particularly violent skid on loose sand made me decide that enough was enough and I stopped at the tiny 'chai khane' in the village of Sangbast. Around noon on the following day, of necessity as the tiny motor was becoming sluggish again, I carried out a complete decoke by the roadside. Late that night I finally reached the Iranian border post at Taibad-e-Jam. It was closed but they obligingly let me sleep in the large hall.

I entered Afghanistan early the next morning. A dust storm blew up and I had to be careful in following the vague stony track that masqueraded as a road and at one stage I had to push the cycle with its motor running over sand dunes that had overwhelmed it. Dust devils spiralled along at frequent intervals once the sun was high and some were quite powerful. Late in the afternoon, four or five miles ahead of me, I saw an extraordinary village of towers: it was mysterious looking and almost unreal so that I was greatly puzzled. Nearing it half an hour later I saw that the square towers were windmills, each with two slots opposite one another in the wall at the top and aligned along the valley to catch the prevailing wind. However, the creaking vanes revolved horizontally, often at different speeds, each tower producing a different note so that a weird chorus filled the air as they turned. As the sun was going down, I decided to turn off to the village to get water. Upon entering it I was set upon by a trio of fierce dogs but managed to keep them at bay with a barrage of well aimed though small stones until a villager came out to investigate the rumpus. I was in Mimizak I learnt, and was promptly given tea after a generous share of water, then food, and finally offered a room for the night. Official memories still recalled the unfortunate American, Winant, and his Swedish girl companion who disappeared in the country, leading eventually to the resignation of the Afghan Minister of the Interior. Travellers were advised by the British embassies in the area, and by the Afghan authorities themselves, that responsibility for their safety lapsed if they stayed in any place other than an official hotel. Mindful of this, although my hosts appeared to be fine people, and, feeling a little guilty, I slept tightly against the door on their beautiful Turkoman carpet and with my loaded pistol inside the sleeping bag. No one was going to take me by surprise while I slept.

6

On the way to Herat I stopped to help some stranded Afghans in a pick-up, providing them with rubber solution and patching to repair their puncture. The road was rough and stony but at least it was not corrugated and I reached the town after midday. My petrol tank held only half a gallon and I always carried a spare quart in a plastic bottle, the total enough for something like one hundred and fifty miles, depending upon wind and road conditions. Stopping at the filling station just before entering the town, I came upon a group of Afghans inside squatting around a large bowl of stew and torn-up 'naan' or flat bread, their so-called 'shorwa' or soup. I was immediately pulled into the circle and they were visibly pleased at my obvious relish of their food. Afterwards, having filled both tank and bottle with petrol, money was firmly refused in spite of my own insistence. The petrol was Russian, dark and with a very strong odour.

After only a brief stop in a single-storied bazaar to buy a few grapes, shop weights being simply stones or pieces of iron, then admire the great fort that dominated the town, I set out for Shindand, the next town along my route. The rear tyre by now was virtually threadbare so I decided to continue travelling when night fell to give it a better chance. Shortly after dark and a few miles up into the hills from Herat, the tyre exploded like a pistol shot. I parked the cycle by the road and walked ahead to find a gully or small valley sheltered from the headlights of any passing vehicle where I might camp unseen for the night, a wise precaution in not a few places. As I returned to my bicycle a lorry from Heart lumbered up the rise towards me. Without my hailing it, it stopped. Being now fairly fluent in Farsi I explained my problem but before I had finished a host of hands hauled me physically up onto the top of the huge load of grain in sacks and my cycle followed. They didn't ask me: they just did it. I was to find that it was typical of Afghans and I warmed to them even more.

We reached Shindand, referred to as Sabzevar on some maps, at one thirty in the morning and I was exhorted by several people to go to the government hotel. I explained that I lacked funds for hotels and was told that payment didn't matter. However, somewhat bewildered by the situation, I felt obliged put up my little tent on the edge of the tiny town. In the morning a deputation of hotel staff came to see me. Would I please remove to their hotel. I again explained that I had no money for accommodation but just enough for food and petrol. It didn't matter they said. They didn't want any money for staying at the hotel so would I please be their guest. Not used to such commercial altruism and the hotel being a government project, I held out, thankfully, patiently and politely but firmly. I then ate a bowl of yoghurt and 'naan' that had been given to me under the gaze of a crowd of curious tribesmen that included a veritable giant at least six and a half feet tall and massively built. Shindand had one street, a fine fast-flowing river called the Adraskand whose one stone-built bridge had long ago been washed away, and packs of crop-eared curs whose sole pleasure in life lay in fighting one another. Farsi was still the language used and as I sat chatting to various shopkeepers it seemed that all day long the air was rent with wild snarls and scuffles in the dust but the people were wonderful. However, the complete absence of women in the street made one wonder how the population maintained itself.

Drinking water came from a number of wells along the street and was both muddy and foul smelling. The only alternative was tea but I needed to conserve my meagre finances: later I was to regret that economy. The 'naans' here were baked in small ovens built into a plinth or flat platform of dried mud on top of which the baker squatted when baking. The inside of the oven was shaped like an old-fashioned beehive and had its opening at the top. The duly flattened dough would be placed on a small sort of cushion, the baker would thrust his arm into the hot opening, deftly stick the 'naan-to-be' on the wall and withdraw swiftly to avoid being scorched. When ready the 'naans' were tugged from the hot walls of the oven by means of a length of stout wire bent into a hook at its end. They were of wholemeal flour, very tasty and much nicer than the Irani ones but, as in Iran, such baking was done only at meal times, the hot dry climate making such naans barely edible after a couple of hours. The small bazaar had little to offer other than basics but upon admiring a fine rug in one shop it was immediately presented to me as a gift. This was totally unexpected, and equally undeserved in my eyes, but I managed to avoid offence in declining by saying that my cycle could not possibly carry anything more.

That evening another deputation came from the hotel. It was soon evident that to continue refusing would be churlish to the extent of being hurtful and rude so I capitulated, to their considerable satisfaction. I suspect that I may have been their sole guest. The place was quite large, clean if a little threadbare, and I was surprised to find light fittings and plumbed bathrooms with flush toilets. I tried the nearest switch in my room but nothing happened; and in the bathroom, with the same result. I next tried the taps but they were dry. It then dawned upon me that there was neither electricity nor piped water in the town but they were prepared for the day when such things did arrive. I stayed there for two nights and was treated as an honoured guest. I felt that we had something to learn from such people but the Russian invasion, followed by the warlords then the Taliban, has probably changed such fine attitudes for ever.

At last there was a lorry bound for Farah, the next town across the desert. It left in the late afternoon, carrying an enormous load of wheat in sacks, on top of which some forty passengers sat. Mounting the nearby hills I was surprised to find that the area around was comparatively green so that the town lived up to both its names, 'sabz' meaning green in Farsi and 'shin'

9

meaning green in Pashtu. Now, while Farsi is a common language across most of southern Afghanistan, years later I was to learn that the Taimani section of the Kakar tribe of Afghans is settled in the nearby Siahband mountains, nearly four hundred miles from their tribal kith and kin to the east, in the north of Baluchistan Province in Pakistan, hence Shindand no doubt. The road was very bad and once or twice as we lurched along I thought that we were about to topple over as we mounted a lump of bedrock that protruded more that usual. I was quite alarmed at times and glad that I sat on the edge so that, if the worst happened, I might be able to jump clear to avoid being crushed by the load of wheat from the stricken lorry. Just before sunset we stopped to pray and to go to the toilet, spreading out in a great semi-circle facing away from the lorry. While I urinated, as did the rest, a roar of laughter went up and I sensed that I was somehow the focus of their amusement. Sure enough, upon turning around I saw that all eyes were upon me. I asked them what was so funny. "You do it standing up, like a horse," someone helpfully explained to me in Farsi. Of course, as I was to learn later, with the baggy 'shalwar' trousers that they wear such a stance would be disastrous. Anyhow, I retorted that where I came from only women did it that way.

Stopping at some remote 'chai khane' for tea during that night my mouth organ, my dynamo torch, fork, spoon and toothbrush disappeared. I was a bit disappointed but every coin has two sides. After that, with extra passengers, four of us had to cling on to the outside of the truck as best we could but as we rarely topped twenty-five miles per hour it was not really hazardous. Afghans tended not to be used to fragile things and I was nearly frantic at times when some of them clambered over my precious bicycle, dislocating the speedo cable and breaking the throttle one. We reached Farah at three in the morning and I decided to remain on the load until the tiny but comfortable 'hotal' opened. The breakfast menu was dark puffy 'naan' and sweet black tea but the stewed meat at noon was delicious. There was virtually no yoghurt and no white cheese stored in water as in Iran, and the water was both muddy and smelly. During my second night there I woke in the early hours to learn that Afghan bacteria are a far tougher breed than those in Iran and elsewhere and was forced to squat in a secluded corner of the large courtyard at the rear for over three hours. Once dawn broke it was a humiliating experience as men came and went.

Although foreigners were rare in those days and my presence must have aroused considerable curiosity, I was left untroubled until a minor fight developed in the 'hotal' between the proprietor and some other man. The word got around and suddenly I had a plain clothed policeman guarding me. It was well meant but unwelcome. I managed to give him the slip once or twice but I was soon located each time. Baluch rugs were nailed to the mud walls for customers to rest against and above the entrance of the 'hotal' was a strange oil lamp ringed by metal vanes. I thought nothing of it for some time until I noticed a thin wire running from it to the radio that blared away non-stop and realised that the device converted heat into electricity and powered the radio. It was a Russian idea, without any moving parts, using semi-conductors I was told, and very practical as the town lacked an electricity supply.

After a couple of days there a truck was to leave for Kandahar and again we left as sunset to avoid the fierce heat of the day. Here and there we collected extra passengers along the way until it was impossible to count their number. While drinking tea at around midnight at one halt in the middle of the desert there was a distant but loud explosion that reverberated through the ground. As the desert to the south of the road was virtually empty, it was puzzling. Mining or military manoeuvres at that hour seemed highly unlikely. The answer came at our next halt a couple of hours later. A driver there reported that he had earlier seen a large blazing star shoot across the sky so it must have been a sizeable meteorite. We stopped at Girisk at three in the morning. After a sleep on top of the truck an American irrigation expert discovered me and took me for a welcome breakfast in their canteen. I now learnt that the truck was staying and not going to Kandahar after all. However, some time later another came along and it was definitely was bound for that city.

After reaching Kandahar in the late afternoon I was taking a meal in some tiny 'hotal' in the city when an engineering student sponsored by the Ariana Airline joined me. He invited me to stay with his family for a few days but I had to decline as I was so far behind schedule. He wore a white traditional 'camise' or shirt, buttoned to one side on top of the shoulder, with an exquisitely embroidered panel across its front. It had been stitched by his mother and sister. Carelessly, in view of my Shindand experience over the rug, I admired it. Quietly and without explanation he began to take the shirt off and I asked him what he was doing. He explained that as I had admired it I must have it. After considerable argument he put it on again and I was more careful about such things thenceforth. I just hope that he survived the political upheavals and Russian occupation. I left Kandahar just before dark, having put on the extremely worn original tyre in place of the split one but as the canvas was showing through in places there was scant hope that it would get me as far as Chaman in Pakistan, let alone to Quetta. I camped late at night far out in the desert. It was wonderfully quiet and the stars were brilliant.

The next morning, as there were no villages in sight, I did some target practice with the pistol to 'keep my hand in' as they say. Following this I set off, pedalling very steadily and without using the motor. After only a mile or so along the gravel road, the replaced worn tyre burst. I then trudged the sixteen or eighteen miles to the Spin Boldak border post, watching a procession of dust devils created by the heat, pushing the heavy cycle weighing around sixty-five pounds and carrying my heavy rucsac which was probably seventy pounds but I was fortunately able to buy a piece of bread and a few grapes in a hamlet on the way. Over the border at Chaman I soon located the resident missionary but found him to be away. During the following four-hour wait a youngish tribesman passed me three times, and spoke to me on the last occasion. Questioned, I explained that I hoped to leave my useless cycle in the mission and go on to Quetta to collect a new tyre being flown out from England. He introduced himself as Mohammad Sediq, his father was one of the four leading 'sardars' or leaders of the Achakzai tribe, and would I take tea with them at their house nearby? I went with him and discovered that the 'sardar' was entertaining three Achakzai 'maliks' or village headmen down from the Toba-Kakar range of mountains to the north. They were sturdy and bright-eyed, they spoke Dari as well as their own Pashtu, and we hit it off immediately. Soon I was invited to stay with them in their distant villages. However, we were now into September, I was three months behind schedule and very worried about my sea baggage incurring demurrage in Bombay, apart from which I was almost out of money. I said that I would return in December and was given a bed for the night by the 'sardar'.

Having deposited my cycle with the less than warm Padre the next morning, I set off on foot for Quetta as a bus was not due to leave until much later but near the top of the Khojak Pass a lorry bound for Quetta picked me up. In Quetta I became quite despondent upon finding that there was no tyre waiting for me at the post office, although there were several welcome letters. Sitting outside on the veranda were several scribes with typewriters who cater for the illiterates, especially tribesmen in from the hills. Compared with Afghan towns Quetta's Jinnah Road was quite modern, with far more prosperous shops, while the Suraj Ganj and Liaquat Ali bazaars ran a close second and all had tarred roads. Looming over them was the jagged peak of Murdar, approaching twelve thousand feet in height. However, what impressed me most was a huge flock of black kites, numbering perhaps a hundred, swarming over the meat market. I was told that they will even snatch food from the hands of people enjoying a picnic, especially young children who are less attentive, though only in parks or the countryside. By good fortune I was soon aboard another lorry heading back to Chaman and on the way tried to buy the driver a meal but as usual it proved impossible. En route we were stopped at various checkpoints to deter smuggling, and so did not reach Chaman until after midnight but I was allowed to sleep in the cab.

The Padre was in a critical and rather un-Christian mood in the morning when I asked to leave my cycle with him for a month or so, muttering darkly that I had "been brought in from the desert" and that he had heard that I had been "nearly run over in Quetta". It was all news to me but in the end, grudgingly, he agreed. After the endless hospitality and kindness I had met from Muslims along the way, he made me wonder whether their conversion, which seemed extremely unlikely with his attitude, would in fact be a good thing. Returning to Quetta once more, seventy miles away, to my great joy I discovered that a tyre had arrived, sent out by a close friend Hedley Ellis. It was too late that day to return to Chaman to collect and mobilise my cycle and on my way to the town's Dak Bungalow, originally set up for lesser officials of the Raj when on tour I believe, I was approached by a youngish teacher. We chatted and I accepted his offer of shelter in his flat for the night. In the evening we went out and the typical form of entertainment seemed to be a stroll through the bazaars, taking cups of tea at intervals. The next morning I visited the shared toilet in the block of flats. It consisted of a small cubicle with two low brick walls, strategically built so that one could squat on top of them, and a scattering of dry earth in between to catch whatever nature bestowed. There was also a small hole in the wall at the rear in case there was too much liquid. I could not help thinking that Lem in *The*

Specialist by Charles Sale would have made a better job of it. Anyhow, the person who had so obviously preceded me had left there some two dozen large, white tapeworm segments that were still slowly writhing. He must have had the grandfather of all tapeworms inside him and it was rather gruesome. It was not the sort of thing one wants to meet first thing in the morning but at least it had to be a beef tapeworm, which is less troublesome to remove.

Back in Chaman that day, after fitting the new back tyre a persistent puncture in the front one delayed me until dusk and it was only with difficulty that I persuaded the guard at the chain across the road out to Quetta to let me pass. Little kangaroo rats (jerboas) seemed to be hopping everywhere and I re-crossed the Khojak Pass in bright moonlight. The obvious route onwards was down the historic Bolan Pass, one of the great Afghan nomad migration routes to and from the Sinde and Indus Valley, but also favoured by past Persian and Mughal armies, not to mention the British, as it avoided the fierce and more populous tribes that guard the Khyber Pass. However, my now tattered Bartholomew's map revealed a tiny road heading north-east from Kuchlagh, a few miles from Quetta on the Chaman road, to the Zhob Valley and on through an irresistible tangle of wild hills to Dera Ghazi Khan in the Panjab. After collecting more mail in Quetta but not an inner tube as hoped, I returned to Kuchlagh and headed north-east.

Beyond the looming hulk of Takatu with its sheer rock faces to the right or east of the road the long, low, barren pass ahead seemed unforgettably remote until, hours later, in the dark I saw the faint lights of Hindubagh some distance away and below me. When I finally entered the little town I was so dazzled by the Petromax lamps that I failed to see the security chain stretched across the road. I was thrown violently backwards off the cycle onto the road as the chain bounced up off my front wheel and hit my chest and arms but the rucsac broke my fall.

People came to my aid instantly and to my intense relief the cycle was not seriously damaged, though the bruises to the bones in my arms remained for some months. After that I was given food and then a bed for the night. The reason for the chain across the road was then explained to me: it was to prevent vehicles from travelling after dark, when they were more liable to be ambushed by outlaws and were more vulnerable. As I chatted with my host for the night, rustlings and faint whispers from behind the curtain across the other doorway revealed that I was being scrutinised by the womenfolk of the house.

Hindubagh, now renamed Muslimbagh, is at the head of the vast one-hundred-and-twenty-mile-long semi-desert Zhob Valley, each flank being guarded by range after range of arid hills and mountains, some rising to ten thousand feet on the north-west side, while those to the south-east are lower but often with ridges so sharp that one would be forced to walk along them with a foot each side. Today, with the advent of electricity, boreholes powered by Japanese pumps have transformed the valley in some places, there is a tar road of sorts, heavily laden trucks trundle up and down constantly on their way to and from Quetta and Karachi, and the population has at least trebled: but in those days it had an air of utter remoteness. To me it seemed like the far end of the world and was wonderfully exciting.

The next morning I set off down the seemingly endless little dirt road that stretched ahead as far as the eye could see, the great valley continuing over the horizon. Although narrow, the surface of the road was quite good as it bore limited traffic and so was without the dreadful corrugation that one met in Iran. At intervals, to the left, I saw tiny hamlets with a tree or two perched in the mouths of larger side valleys, where either a tiny stream flowed for a few yards from a spring or a small well had been dug, the meagre flow supporting perhaps two or three, maybe four families. Three hours later I reached Kila Saifulla where I had a quick meal in its short bazaar. Europeans other than soldiers hardly ever penetrated the valley and those left before 1947, though there was still a solitary Englishman who ran the chrome mines near Hindubagh I learned later. As I gulped down the sweet, milky 'poi chai' favoured locally since crossing the border from Afghanistan and ate a warm puffy 'naan', costing a few annas, a procession of turbaned tribesmen shuffled by to take a look at the 'ferangai', the European that had appeared out of the blue on a battered old bicycle. They stared long and hard but the act was almost childlike in its innocence and not in the least offensive. However, Darri was no longer used, I was only just getting to grips with the rudiments of Urdu and the locals spoke Pashtu in any case though many shopkeepers were more versatile. I was soon on my way over the hills to Loralai, forty-six miles away, but as I neared that little town hours later, again in the dark, the motor began to fail once more and I had to rely on pedal power for the last few miles though fortunately the dirt road was fairly level.

There I was installed in the dilapidated Dak Bungalow but as an invited guest, being without funds for such luxuries except in extreme emergency. In the morning Mr. Sharif, my benefactor and manager of a local bus service, allowed me to decoke my motor in his small garage. As my shirt was almost in tatters I was forced to buy a new one but before I set off I was mobbed by a crowd of curious, ragged urchins as I prepared to leave. After two or three warnings, one was incautious enough to overstep the mark and I gave him such a slap that he staggered back into the crowd, which then took the hint and moved back a yard or so, allowing me space to adjust my rucsac in reasonable peace. I mention this incident because twenty-five years later I was at the tribal wedding of a friend's son at Pishin, perhaps one hundred and sixty miles from Loralai, when the guest sitting next to me stared at me a great deal. At length, in halting English, he said, "You bit me." I was at a loss to understand. He repeated the charge and gradually it became clear that he meant I had beaten him. Casting my mind back it slowly dawned on me that he had been that small cheeky boy. I asked him, "Loralai ki?" He nodded. Now a grown man, it turned out that he was a magistrate. It's nice to be remembered.

I was pressed to stay in Loralai for a few days but had to hurry on. Before leaving I was variously warned that I was liable to meet bandits, leopards, wolves and bears when I reached the hills ahead. The warning about bears had a very faint element of truth I later discovered for on the Takht-i-Sulaiman peak and its surroundings, eighty miles to the north, a few bears had managed to survive in those days. The leopards and wolves were not so rare but are not usually a threat to humans. As for bandits, I had little that would really interest them, apart from my pistol and that was discreetly out of sight. Even so it was not really the sort of news that a lone traveller on a bicycle wants to hear but I had met similar advice before and seemed none the worse for it. I set off in the late afternoon, the narrow road at first being tarred, with little villages at intervals with irrigated, mud-walled orchards. Soon I saw a impenetrable grey wall approaching rapidly. At first I thought that it was rain but it turned out to be a tremendous dust storm reaching hundreds, if not thousands, of feet into the sky. Luckily I missed the violent rain in its wake but as I reached a stretch of road under a foot of water a bus came from behind and obligingly carried me to the far side of the flood perched with my bicycle precariously on its tiny back step. Later, as it grew dark, I met the bus coming back: the ford in the river ahead was chest deep, the driver told me.

I had little choice but to carry on and, by the time I reached the un-cooperative river, it was pitch dark and the rush of water did little to reassure me. Dumping the cycle on the bank I cautiously entered the flood, to find it halfway up my thighs but I got across without much trouble and left my rucsac and ciné camera on the far bank before returning for the cycle. I entered the water with the cycle on my shoulder and had only gone two or three yards when I heard a strange clonking sound up-river. I realised with considerable alarm that it must be a flash flood coming down. In a second or two the foaming water was up to my waist and only the weight of the cycle with its motor prevented me from being swept away. For a split second I considered returning to the safety of the river bank that I had just left but then I reckoned that as I was setting off from the outside of the river's curve I would be moving into shallower water and a less fierce current if I continued crossing. Above all I was extremely worried at the prospect of being separated from my things left on the far bank and plunged ahead.

Thereafter the gravel road was a shambles, with half-finished bridges over raging torrents, where I was forced to walk across narrow parapets with the cycle and, as the motor was merely idling, the rather dim cycle lamp did little to help. In addition there were numerous detours to cope with and so on. Mindful of the warnings in Loralai I travelled with the pistol in my hand and ready cocked, just in case someone did jump down onto the track with a rifle at the ready. Somewhere along the way a couple of dogs attacked me but sensibly heeded a warning shot under their noses and between their front legs as they reached my rear wheel. I had planned to reach Mekhtar but then came upon a much wider though shallower river also in spate. It was perhaps fifty yards or more wide. Recalling how earlier I had very nearly ended up separated from some of my precious baggage, this time I left cycle, rucsac and cine camera on the high bank before wading across to reconnoitre unencumbered. It was only knee-deep. Reassured, I returned, collected everything and re-crossed to the far bank, the extra weight compensating for the continuous movement of the gravel bottom.

All went well but I could not find the road's continuation and dumped everything on the high bank in order to make a thorough search up and down the river bank. In spite of that I was still unable to find where the road continued on the far side. Returning a second time, unladen, to where I had started my crossing, it was quite clear that the road did enter the water at that point. Baffled, I started back once more to where my things lay on the far side. Moments after entering the water I heard that now familiar clonking of boulders bumping into one another as they were violently rolled along but this time I was dealing with a very much wider river and knew that a deep, dry gully lay ahead, towards the far bank. Desperately I ran through the torrent and as I jumped down into the gully I could just see a four-foot wave of foaming water rushing at me in the gloom. I got clear but from the high bank stared aghast as, within a mere two or three minutes, the river grew into a wild flood that would have swept away a lorry. Fearing that it might rise even higher I chained the cycle to a tamarisk tree, took my rucsac and fled to higher ground, pistol in hand, to set up my tent for the night. I was without food or water but I had survived two serious threats and felt strangely elated.

The next morning was bright and clear, the river was a gentle flow again and I discovered that the road turned sharp right along a gravel bank in midstream then left for the far bank some two hundred yards down-river. Moreover a loop of the road was within a hundred yards of my camp site. Mekhtar's tiny bazaar produced some long overdue 'poi chai' and 'naan' after which I continued. I now knew that every little town put up chains at night to prevent vehicles from travelling and all the little 'pukka' buses plying along the route had to have two armed guards or four in the case of lorry-buses, but I now saw single, armed men in tribal dress standing on various hills near the road and felt a little uneasy. Later I learnt that they were 'khassadars', meaning tribal levies without uniform and with their own rifles, paid a paltry Rs.2 per day to guard the road six days a week. They were not meant to actually fight any marauding gang but were meant to fire a shot to warn them off if possible and to alert other such 'khassadars' in a chain reaction and thus stop any approaching vehicle. They were placed only at strategic points, where ambush was more likely. I spent that night in a diminutive 'hotal' in the village of Kingri, fortified by a delicious meat stew. A misunderstanding over change, when the hotelier virtually accused me of trying to cheat him, made me flare up and almost led to a fight. However, I realized that I had made the mistake and apologised.

The arid hills were a wild jumble, the tallest vegetation being dwarf palms and thorn trees little more than eight or ten feet tall. The winding road was so bad now that I only got as far as the hamlet of Ruckni the following day, in territory inhabited by Khetrans and Baluchis, rather than ethnic Afghans such as the Kakars, Lunis or Tarins around Hindubagh, Kila Saifulla and Loralai. The crowd that immediately gathered upon my arrival noticed my belt full of .222 cartridges and asked to see the rifle, which was among my baggage in Bombay of course. I merely carried the cartridges to prevent the leather belt loops from being crushed and damaged. Realising after a while that they were a good crowd and as a firearm permit was not required in tribal territory, I eventually dug out my pistol and we took pot shots at a road sign some forty yards away, where the road forked. During my forced stay in Iran I had discovered that .22 ammunition was quite cheap and sold without check. Thus I had managed to stockpile a few boxes and could afford to be generous, allowing everyone who wished to have three shots, so that everyone present was happy. My social standing soared further when my group of three shots was judged to be the best, thanks to the hours spent at the Ham and Petersham Rifle Club. I then became the guest of a young Panjabi land surveyor, Mohammad Yaqub Patwari, billeted with his colleague in the tiny redundant gaol there.

During the night I was awakened several times by the blowing of a whistle and an explanation for this was given in the morning. About six years earlier a man from Ruckni, whose clan I forget, had come across a man of the Baluch Gurrchani clan from another village grazing his flock on Ruckni land and therefore trespassing. Hot words led to hotter deeds and the Ruckni man was shot dead for his protest. Under a mixture of civil and tribal law the killer was duly sentenced to seven years and, with remission, had been released after four or five years some months previously. His family would have given some Rs.3,000 compensation to the dead man's family as well. Very unwisely the Gurrchani man had recently come to Ruckni to buy wheat. Amnesia is rare among Afghans and Pashtuns, and quite unknown when it concerns family honour. The opportunity was too good to miss: he did not return to his home and a reprisal was feared. Therefore a boy was paid to roam around all night with the whistle so that men from the other village would believe that the Ruckni men were on their guard and thus be deterred from making a reprisal.

Before leaving I let my host ride the cycle then went on to the levies post at Bewatta, a mere mile or so away. It was a solid, stone-built fort and marked the official boundary between Baluchistan and the Panjab, although an impressive range of mountains lay in the way before the plains are met. As I passed the post I was invited in for a meal by the officer in charge of the border post, Mohammad Dur. Setting off afterwards, my front tyre burst like a shot only a couple of hundred yards on. Returning to the fort, the hospitable man kindly agreed to store the wretched machine in one of the towers until I returned in December or thereabouts to collect it. We then indulged in a bit of pistol shooting with my .22 Star. As we chatted he told me that he had accidentally shot his first wife but I gained the distinct impression that his new, second wife was rather special to him and that few tears had been shed over his first one. However, I try not to be a suspicious man. It was not until the following afternoon that a truck laden with sacks of grain came along, heading for Dera Ghazi Khan, and I was installed on the load.

We stopped briefly at Fort Munro atop the mountains after which the road ran perilously down the side of an immense gorge and I got my first glimpse of the Panjab and Indus Valley, red in the sunset and shrouded in dust. I had almost arrived and felt very excited after so many uncertainties, setbacks and delays, when the sub-continent had seemed so far away. Leaving the serried limestone ramparts behind us and crossing the last few miles of sand desert in moonlight we reached D.G.K., or "dijjikay" as everyone calls it, after dark. Sitting at a small snack stall a rat ran beneath the bench I was on and after a quick meal I was off again but gave up hoping for a lorry northwards after a couple of hours and returned to the bazaar. I was soon given a bed for the night and we slept on the roof, indoors being too warm for comfort. In the morning breakfast included 'double roti', European style bread and my first in many days. However, it tends to be slightly sour tasting in Pakistan and India but it was bought for my benefit and was a kindly gesture. Now Urdu was spoken, with Sindi and Baluchi as well, though my host spoke good English. However, the general poverty, the crowding and dirt everywhere, particularly in towns, came as a tremendous shock both then and in the days that followed. The tribal territory I had just left was just as poor, even poorer, but somehow the impact was not the same; perhaps because its people were so sturdy and independent, believing themselves to be equal to the rest of the world if not actually better. Moreover they could roam almost at will and had an unmistakable elan but here people were hemmed in by private fields and wealthy landlords were powerful. Also there was an element of hysteria in the air and vague talk of war. Things were not going well in the country I was told repeatedly. There was corruption among the police and government officials everywhere, and widespread lawlessness. To my astonishment a number of older men along the way previously, some of whom had served under the British, had said that they wished that the British were back, which was quite the opposite of what I had been told to expect by various people in London. Martial law was thought to be imminent.

The rains were only just over and on the following day I felt the full force of the humid heat. Whereas I had walked nearly thirty miles without much stress in the Kashan desert when the temperature probably topped a hundred and twenty Fahrenheit or fifty Celsius in the shade, and there was no shade, seven miles in that dripping cauldron at a mere ninety or hundred degrees was enough. Unable to buy a passage in a passing truck or get a lift in a car, I tried to sleep under the stars in a field that second night. At two in the morning sweat was still trickling down between my ribs and I gave up, returning to the road in the faintest hope of finding a lift. However, my pessimism was unfounded for a lorry then came along and stopped for me. And the Derajat, that area between the Indus and the tribal hills to the west, was a different world in other ways. Twenty to thirty large vultures roosted in two large trees by the irrigation canal and road just outside D.G.K., croaking hoarsely at one another among the dead upper branches that they had obviously killed; bright green parakeets screeched between slender palms, water buffalo wallowed in ponds formed where the clay had been taken to build the raised road or a village, and yard-long monitor lizards hunted for tiny fish in slimy pools using their long slender tails to flush them out. Flocks of kites floated lazily overhead, jaunty mynah birds strutted everywhere, white egrets mingled with little humped cows browsing on wasteland, small striped ground squirrels scratched for food and mongooses darted across the road at intervals. There were brilliant green fields of young, spiky sugar cane thrusting upwards and the whole place exuded a rather overpowering fecundity. The source of that abundant life is a tremendous canal system, built in the days of the Raj, to use the ample water of the great Indus River: a river dedicated to ruinous flooding at intervals and said to have changed its course by ten miles in a single night. Where these life-giving waters have not been led there is bare, fine soil, today at least, though I suspect that in the distant past thorn scrub probably covered it.

My journey to the north across the depressing flatness of the immense, heavily populated Panjab plain was by lorries and buses. The Indus was in flood so that we had to detour via the Taunsa barrage instead of crossing the endless pontoon bridge over several channels of the Indus directly for Lahore. Multan had a positively evil air about it but in Montgomery street vendors with little handcarts equipped with strong, ribbed steel rollers dispensed juice from freshly crushed sugar cane flavoured with the juice of green limes squeezed on the spot to help combat the oppressive heat. However, I declined the addition of crushed ice, having seen blocks of it resting upon dark, sodden sacking on filthy pavements. Floods near Lahore delayed us for several hours and it was at night three days later that I eventually reached Amritsar, on the Grand Trunk Road that runs from Peshawar to Calcutta.

Buying a ticket in the railway station I was surprised to hear what I took to be a Welsh voice behind a partition, until a turbaned Sikh appeared. In those days there were no less than five different classes on trains: third (incredibly cheap by our standards but with hard benches), second, first, intermediate and air-conditioned. I had little choice anyway. Looking out of the window I noticed lots of 'sparks' at intervals in the dark but then realised that the engine was a diesel: I was looking at fireflies. Stopping at various stations throughout the night one was always met with the repeated dolorous cry: "garrm dood, garrm dood", and when a customer appeared the vendor would draw the warm milk from his little churn and pour it from the measure held high above his head into an aluminium mug held down at arm's length. It was an impressive performance and rarely was a valuable drop spilt. In the cold light of morning, as we passed village after village, rows of bare squatting bottoms presented themselves on the outskirts of each as the inhabitants prepared for the new day. It was almost a ritual and signalled each dawn on those endless plains.

I arrived in New Delhi on the 16th September, long overdue and with the equivalent of £1.75 in my pocket. My original estimate for the journey had been six to eight weeks but I had taken over five months and I had set out with only £23-10, though donating three half-litres of blood in Istanbul and Tehran had maintained my finances. However, the real problem lay in the fact that my one and only contact in the city, in a Quaker Mission, turned out to be away on leave. From the Education Officer in the British Council I learned of the 'dharamsala' or hostel attached to the Birla Mandir temple. It was located in Reading Road but I encountered a lot of difficulty in finding that road. Eventually I realised that everyone pronounced Reading as in the context of books, after which it was speedily located. The 'dharamsala' was beautifully built of white marble, in traditional style, and was spotlessly clean. I and others slept on the cool floor free of charge until I was granted a room with a 'charpai' bed for a few annas after two nights. I had been loaned Rs.30 by the U.K. Citizens Association, a benevolent body set up to help impoverished elderly British people who, having no close relatives in their home country and little or no pension, had remained behind after independence. I spent most of this on sending my c.v. to four large schools in the north and north-west of the country.

I discovered that the Delhi Public School was advertising for a Head of Science with a Ph.D. at a salary of Rs.120 per month plus a 'dearness allowance' to use as a yardstick. The latter might bring the total to Rs.170, and official rate of exchange at that time was Rs.13 per £1 sterling. It was hardly a princely sum in any case but I presumed that the advert was a misprint and that it really meant per week. When I telephoned the school I was dismayed to learn that it really was per month. The sole of my dog-bashing boots (called that from their vital role in fending off numerous attacks by pairs and trios of fierce shepherd dogs in the mountains of southern Yugoslavia and Turkey, especially as rabies was not uncommon in 1958) now had a hole and in any case were far too hot so I purchased a pair of leather 'chapplis' or sandals. Not being used to them, I soon grazed my toe badly whereupon life was not made easier when it went septic, required penicillin and needed lancing. While my accommodation was so cheap as to be almost free, I still had to eat now and again and rationed myself at each meal to a small slice of bread and a fried potato cake served on a fresh pipal leaf, at a little stall on bicycle wheels in the street outside the 'dharamsala'. Being still very warm this was not as hard as it might seem. A group of very pleasant musicians from Radio Calcutta arrived after a couple of days and repeatedly invited me to join them for a meal but as I could not return their hospitality I always made some excuse. Either 'I had already eaten' or 'I was just on my way out'. After some days one of them, whose name took some mastering, Satyanayaran Jhunjhunwala, sensed my position and asked how much money I had. A check revealed that I had just two annas left. He insisted on loaning me thirty rupees until such time as I could repay it and I accepted. There was also an engineer in the 'dharamsala' who was very depressed at having been robbed of all his possessions upon arrival in the capital, and a thin, gaunt 'sadhu' or holy man stayed for a couple of days. Both were poorly off and for the first time since leaving England I was allowed to buy someone else a humble meal or two.

New Delhi itself was a modern city and a bustling one at that. In addition to the ubiquitous single-deck buses and taxis, swarms of three-wheeled motor rickshaws roared everywhere, often belching clouds of blue smoke. These were of two types: the larger ones had a motorcycle front, behind which two pairs of passenger seats faced one another and sideways under a brightly coloured awning. The others consisted of a covered-in Vaspa scooter front with a pair of forward-facing seats behind the driver, also under a gaudy awning. The latter had meters but often these did not work and I soon learned to avoid these like the plague, otherwise there was a dispute over the fee at the end of almost every journey. In the case of those that did function, I frequently found it necessary to trip the meter sideways when the driver 'forgot' to set it. The traffic was chaotic, and the sartorial police on traffic duty with their white uniforms and long white gloves did little to improve matters but, balancing on tiny rostrums in the centre of turbulent crossroads, they moved their arms with the elegance of ballet dancers, blowing their whistles 'when the spirit moved' rather than for any special purpose. In spite of all this I saw only one accident, when a scooter rickshaw just in front of my own tipped over sideways from swerving and braking sharply to avoid another one, at which the passenger got out with the driver, both lifted the thing up, got in and carried on as if nothing had happened.

Another resident at the 'dharamsala' was a wealthy, if rather ferrety, business man wearing a 'dhoti', a sort of loin cloth, who constantly travelled around India. He had a daughter aged sixteen, whom I did not see, and offered me the job of tutoring her on such travels, not only in the academic sense but in Western social graces as well. The salary would be very modest but involve all keep. Above all it offered a way out of my predicament should all else fail. Further, it would show me the real India but also it would delay my proposed expedition. After a couple of days I was on the point of accepting this when an offer, subject to interview, arrived from the Doon School in Dehra Dun, nestling against the Himalayan foothills. Vying with Mayo College in Ajmer to be the most prestigious school in India, it was a wonderful break. Taking a train to Saharanpur and from there the overnight mail bus over the Siwalik hills, I reached the town in late monsoon rain as dawn broke. When a civilized hour arrived, I made my way to the school on foot. As I approached its main entrance I chanced to glance at a small troupe of Rhesus monkeys across the road. Revered by the Hanuman sect of Hindus they tend to be a pampered, arrogant bunch and the large buck amongst them was no exception. He advanced threateningly across the road to within two or three yards of me, baring his impressive canines for my benefit. However, I had not eaten for many hours, I had slept little on the bus, I was rather cold from the rain and not in the mood for such threatricals. I waited for him with murderous intent and he seemed to understand my intentions as I eyed his scrawny neck but from then on we were enemies. My interview with the John Martyn, the Headmaster, ended my worries: or so I thought for the Customs in Bombay would not release my equipment for a further six months and even then only after intervention by Mrs. Indhira Gandhi whose two sons I happened to teach. The Doon pupils were excellent and a far cry from the Barnes' savages. The term seemed to flash by but two letters to Mohammad Sediq Achakzai in Chaman received no reply; in any case I had to retrieve my cycle from the Bewatta border post when term ended.

Chapter Two

Return to Baluchistan

At the Wagga Customs post in Pakistan I spent a couple of hours giving what amounted to a French lesson to one of the officials who was studying the language, though why he was doing that I forget. Being able to do that rested largely upon having done three 'vendages' near Montpellier in the south of France rather that what was reluctantly learnt at school. Having lost over a week of a five-week holiday in going to Delhi to secure the release of my baggage if possible and to collect my pistol from the Customs in the capital as I now had a permit, I was in a hurry and decided to travel at night – that meant by lorry as few buses travelled far after dark. Arriving at the road-rail bridge over the Chenab River near Muzaffagar on the following day, the truck I was in had to wait for a train to cross so I got out to stretch my legs and look around. A large American Chevrolet containing four men, three of whom wore tribal dress and turbans, drew up behind us. Behind it was another car similarly full of tribesmen. The driver of the first vehicle, who was wearing a dark 'karakuli' hat of lambswool instead of a turban, got out and came across to me. He was short but stockily built, direct in his manner, had a firm handshake, looked one in the eye and was obviously wide awake: I took to him instantly. Who was I and where was I going he asked in halting but good English. I explained that I was going to Chaman.

Now, as Chaman is not the sort of town anyone would choose

to visit for its own sake, his next question was to be expected. I then explained the invitation I had to visit the Achakzai 'maliks' in the Kakar Toba hills along the border. But why was I going to visit the 'maliks'? Using the Indian and English word I said that as they were Pathans I was interested in them. He then introduced himself as Ahmad Yar Khan Jogezai, and went on to say that he was a 'Pathan' and that his father was the chief of the Kakar tribe. So why should I waste time going down to Chaman when his tribe was just as good as the Achakzai? The Achakzai plan was fraught with considerable uncertainty: two letters to Mohammad Sediq there had brought no reply and Indian newspapers had reported that an Achakzai 'sardar' had been imprisoned by the new Martial Law administration because of his sympathies with the Pashtunistan movement. That could refer to the Chaman 'sardar' with whom I had briefly stayed on my way to India. If so, then his son would be under suspicion and surveillance. Without hesitation I gladly accepted Ahmad Yar Khan's invitation and he explained how to find his family home in Tarwal village in the immense Zhob Valley. It was just off the one and only road from Kila Saifulla to Fort Sandeman, to the left and about seven miles from the former. I said that I would be there in two days time, after collecting my bicycle at Bewatta. On the far side of the bridge the two cars passed us and some miles further on my truck came to a series of pontoons spanning the several channels of the Indus. As the water level had dropped considerably since last time, a number of other channels were dry and we simply trundled through these, choosing what seemed to be the easiest track.

In Dera Ghazi Khan I filled my quart plastic bottle with petrol, bought some lubricating oil and was then fortunate to be actually sought out in the bazaar by the driver of a bus going to Bewatta but the night would be spent in the little village of Sakhi Sarwar Sultan, set in the miles of sandy waste that lead from D.G.K. to the foot of the mountains. So few Europeans passed that way in those days that they stood out and he had heard on the grape vine that I was heading for Bewatta. I later discovered that he was the brother of Mohammad Dur who was storing my bicycle. Sakhi Sarwar is in a narrow tract of sand desert extending several miles from the plains to foot of the mountains, which rise in a series of spectacular, pinkish limestone cliffs, and when we arrived there its tiny 'caravanserai' was almost full of Baluchi tribesmen plus a few Pathans, or 'Pashtana' as they call themselves ('Pashtun' being the singular), while the name Pathan is an Indian corruption of 'Pakhtana' the northern variant of the language. My only complaint about the tribesmen is their widespread habit of spitting on the floor, especially as one has to sit on it, eat on it and sleep on it. True they do avoid the mats of woven palm or rugs but only just, and of course good manners dictate taking off one's shoes and parking them beside the matt itself.

When passing through Fort Munro atop the hills the next morning Mohammad Dur boarded the bus for a short distance and gave me a note for the man left in charge of the fort, which we reached at midday. A letter that I had posted two or three weeks earlier advising him of my coming had not been delivered. Blessed with a new tyre and inner tube, we got the ageing and battered machine down from the corner tower, topped up the petrol, tightened various nuts and bolts – an essential daily routine on such rough tracks – discarded the old tube with its six-inch split and all was ready. Calling briefly on the Panjabi surveyor at Ruckni a couple of miles on, I found that the road, being of soil rather than gravel, was badly rutted from previous rain and now frozen hard so that I did not reach the hamlet of Kingri until well after nightfall. I paid for my food with some difficulty, the hospitable proprietor not wanting money but I insisted, and a goodly number of us settled down on the floor of the tiny 'hotal' for the night. However, we were soon woken by an influx of passengers from a lorry so the place became literally packed from wall to wall but at least it was wonderfully warm, the frost outside being considerable.

I left early in the morning but carelessly forgot my tent in the crush as everyone else also left. From there on the road / track was generally stony and so not rutted, winding through countless small, arid hills sprinkled with dwarf palms and short thorn trees, which sparse scrub was somehow raised in status to being called 'jangal' locally. On the way a road gang invited me to take tea with them and this I did, although reluctant to delay, as to decline would have been discourteous. After Mekhtar there were black nomad tents scattered everywhere, the country became less hilly and offered a little grazing for the flocks. The two rivers that previously had so nearly swept me away were mere trickles and in the bright sunlight it was difficult to believe just how dangerous they could be. Passing through Loralai I had a quick meal of spinach cooked in oil, for it was the 'meatless day of the week' as decreed by the Martial Law body, to conserve livestock I gathered, and enjoyed the luxury of their special 'paratas'. Usually 'paratas' are no more than somewhat stodgy 'chapattis' cooked with 'ghee', nice enough in their own way and satisfying when hungry, but these Loralai creations were light, beautifully crumbly and golden brown, without doubt the finest 'paratas' in the whole of the sub-continent. Indeed they were so superior to those elsewhere that thenceforth I always made a point of eating in Loralai whenever passing through. One wonders how someone in such a tiny, isolated little town came to discover such a superb recipe or technique; and it is even more surprising that 'hotal wallahs' elsewhere had not discovered the secret and taken it up.

I was surprised to come across Ahmad Yar Khan in Loralai but it was not until well after dark that I covered those last fifty-three miles to Tarwal, corrugation along much of the way slowing me. The village is half a mile off the road, which skirts the nearest rocky ridge, and near the end of the long, gentle, gravel slope where the fine white soil of the valley floor begins. It consisted of fifteen or so randomly scattered houses, all but that of the chief being single-storied and mud built, both walls and roof. With such a gentle slope and a natural torrent bed some way off to divert any flood from the village, one could not foresee that a flash flood from the nearby hills and sharp ridges could pose a threat, yet thirty-five years later, in 1993, when our youngest son Richard returned there on his own to see Mamu Jogezai and others, a flood washed away Nurullah Khan's house completely though not before the family had evacuated. Nearby, after the big gates into the garden had been burst in, Ahmad Yar Khan's house became so threatened that he, with his two resident married sons Saeed and Raza Shah, and Richard had to help the women or carry children through chest-deep swirling water in pitch darkness to the safety of the late chief's stone house nearby. Other houses in the village escaped, the main flood having followed the track down from the main road, now tarred, leading to the Jogezai properties.

Back to 1958: how I located the tiny village in the dark I forget, for no lights showed, but the gravel track lead directly to the chief's house. No one heard me banging on the large front door so I went around to the side of the big house and found another entrance. Going in, I came upon a courtyard dimly lit by a Petromax lamp and full of women and children. I had yet to absorb the importance of 'purdah' for some people and there was consternation, with figures rushing in all directions it seemed. A rabid dog could not have created more panic. Then A.Y.K. appeared and ushered me out with almost indecent haste, installing me in a mud-walled guest room in a courtyard separate from the house itself. An oil lamp was brought, someone collected my cycle for me and within minutes a pot of 'poi chai', that wonderful sweet milky tea that has sustained generations of Pashtuns and Afghans in Pakistan was reviving me. It is far more sustaining that the sweet black tea met in just over the border, in Afghanistan. I had covered one hundred and thirty miles of appalling dirt roads that day and felt a little battered. Soon a much-needed meal of excellent meat cooked in 'ghee' and boiled 'landi' (dried meat) was laid out and A.Y.K. ate with me. After that we talked until it was quite late. Outside there was a deep frost, brilliant stars and an utter silence that one never meets in Britain, broken only by the occasional, muffled bark of a distant dog.

In the morning, after a light breakfast consisting of a pot of 'poi chai' and a biscuit or two, four of A.Y.K.'s younger brothers came to meet me. In order of seniority they were Mohammad Hassan, Nurullah Khan, Ashraf Khan, and Nur Ahmad, all in their twenties and students in college in Quetta but home for the holiday. Very soon, almost needless to say, all were trying out my pistol. Pathans and guns were clearly inseparable. His eldest brother, Temur Shah, was about fifty and lived three or four miles away, out across the great valley floor. There were two other older: Jehangir Shah in Lahore and Jehandar Shah in Quetta I was told. I had yet to learn that there was also another younger but adult brother who lived elsewhere, Mohabat Khan, and twin boys aged about twelve years, Mohammad Anwar and Salim whom I initially thought were grandsons of the chief. Presumably there was a similar number of sisters tucked away but I had guessed by now that it was not the done thing to ask about them, curious though I was.

Most of the men of the village joined us as we sat in the courtyard and enjoyed the warm sun, having heard of my arrival no doubt. There was no electricity and the transistor radio was still uncommon so that the arrival of a stranger, especially on a bicycle all the way from England was not to be missed. After lunch a crowd of us went by car to Kila Saifulla where we met other members of the numerous Jogezai family-cum-clan or section, the chief having two surviving brothers in the area, both with numerous sons and hidden daughters presumably. Sitting on a rickety wooden bench in the sparkling air at five thousand feet, a mud wall prickly with straw at our backs and with the sun to warm us, we drank countless cups of 'poi chai' from miniature bowls while a continual stream of locals shuffled by to take a long look at us. In any case a crowd usually gathered when the young Jogezais arrived in the bazaar but the word soon spread that a stranger was with them, a European, and their number swelled. Many of the passers-by stared long and hard at me, with an innocent, almost child-like curiosity so that it was not in the least offensive or irritating.

Kila Saifulla is on most maps and is named after one Saifulla Khan, long dead, who had built a 'kila' or fort there. Its bazaar boasted a single business street that began about five hundred yards down the slope from the main dirt road along the south-eastern edge of the valley but since those days the original bazaar has extended to the main road and an ever-growing satellite bazaar composed mainly of 'hotals' and small businesses has been established along the main road to cater for the lorries that now pass regularly. It had and still has a sizeable levies' post, which is built of mud mixed with straw except for four steel sentry boxes perched high on the corners, intriguingly termed 'machicoolies'. Also there is a stone-built strong point atop the tiny isolated hill abutting the main road half a mile from the top end of the bazaar. That fortified tower was built in 1942, probably in response to a group of German agents that had managed to evade a British cordon in Persia designed to prevent them from entering Afghanistan in order to foment an up-rising among the tribes. There is also a post office, surrounded by a high stone wall, with its own courtyard and massive double gates. The shops are all single-storied and it is kinder not to describe the open drain that runs along their fronts on either side of the now-tarred but then dusty street. It almost seems that poverty, dirt and tremendous hospitality go hand in hand. However, with tiny villages scattered here and there among the endless ridges and mountains flanking each side of the great valley, and being at that time at the junction of two important nomad migration routes, Kila Saifulla was and still is important.

We had been joined by a lean fellow in a long dark coat who had a black patch over one eye, or eye socket to be more precise. He was introduced to me as 'Charlie Sahib', to the obvious enjoyment of all and Ahmad Yar Khan added with a wicked smile, "Ferarai weh". His real name I soon learned was Sheikh Rahmat Akhtarzai, being of the Akhtarzai clan and not a Jogezai. As well as having been a wanted outlaw or 'ferarai' for a number of years, though now pardoned, he could be relied upon to entertain those present: hence his nickname, the real Charlie Chaplain certainly being unaware of the honour thus bestowed upon him. He was a man of many parts, hardy and resourceful yet not belligerent, and, if someone had a difficult or dangerous enterprise to undertake, Sheikh was liable to be consulted for advice or perhaps asked to accompany the mission. Indeed for many years he was the unofficial right-hand man of the chief. No one held his brushes with authority against him as his wayward years had been forced upon him by circumstances that involved defending his family's honour.

When puzzled he always raised his voice to a falsetto. He wanted to know where I was from: "Da kum zai deh?" he demanded of Ahmad Yar Khan, our unofficial spokesman. In reply A.Y.K. was casual and non-committal: "Ferangai deh," he said, almost implying that Europeans called at Tarwal every day of the week and were of little interest. At a loss as to why anyone should want to visit Zhob, Sheikh's next question was, "Chi shai ghware?" – what did I want? Now A.Y.K. knew his man and was not in a mood for an interrogation, while the true but imprecise explanation that I was simply interested in Pashtuns would only have led to further questions and other listeners might even become suspicious. "Tarikh likka," he replied, casually but impatiently. So I was writing a history, though exactly on what did not seem to matter, and it seemed to suggest that A.Y.K. was in the habit of entertaining historians. Once more Sheikh found a moment to adjust and readjust his grimy black turban for the umpteenth time and drew back for a few moments, somewhat thwarted.

It was then my turn to question A.Y.K. about Sheikh, for he was clearly something of a character and had an alert look about him, but not all that follows was immediately revealed. First of all he had lost his eye in his early twenties when a horse kicked him. More importantly, it was his right eye, the one normally used for aiming a rifle. That, as we shall see, could be no small handicap in that part of the world. Then around 1934, his uncle, Nawab Khan, was shot in the course of a feud by one Dat Karim and Sheikh took it upon himself to help the dead man's brother avenge the family's honour. Dat Karim was in gaol, having been sentenced to seven years, which would work out at four with remission, in addition to which his family would have paid 'blood money' as compensation to the dead man's family under a wise blend of tribal and civil law established by the British. However, it is blood for blood amongst the tribes and as he was out of reach, under tribal custom any close adult male relative was an acceptable substitute.

Having announced that the man's cousin was their target, the pair crossed range after range of mountains to Kakar Khorrasan; a remote, high and barren plateau to the north-west of Zhob and along the Afghan border. Three weeks later, judging that the selected victim and his family would be relaxing their guard, the pair returned secretly to Zhob and crossed by night to Loralai, where they settled themselves in ambush before dawn. As the chosen man and his wife set to work in their field, Sheikh and his uncle fired, hitting the man in the thigh. The luckless man collapsed but his wife was as resourceful as she was brave. Immediately and without pause she threw handful after handful of the white powdery soil into the air, hiding him so successfully

38

that, apart from being further hit in the shin and the hand, and incidentally losing a ploughing ox in the fracas, he survived until family reinforcements arrived to drive off the marauding pair. How the two managed to get away from the new arrivals I do not know but as already said, Sheikh was ever resourceful.

Being outnumbered as a family and having stirred up a hornets' nest, Sheikh retired to Allah Jirga just over the border in Afghanistan where many Kakars still live, being joined by Fukhruddin of the Khodadzai clan who had a similar problem on account of his own uncle's death. The latter's uncle had been accused of adultery and shot, allegedly in compromising circumstances but the erring woman, if she were and if present, had managed to escape so that essential evidence was missing, but more of that later. Unable to find work, without water to irrigate crops and too poor to purchase a flock the pair were forced to rely upon nomad friends from time to time, who in any case had little enough to spare, and a bit of outlawry. So they rustled sheep at intervals and engaged in a bit of armed robbery when the chance arose on the Pakistan side of the border, ever wary of the government militia posts at Ghazluna, Shaighalu and elsewhere. Often they operated with bands of wild Sulaiman Khels, Ghalzai rather than Afghan or Pashtun and notorious as robbers and raiders. In 1996, Fukhruddin died but Sheikh was still very much alive, in his late eighties then and living with his sons on the far side of Kila Saifulla when I was last there in 1999. From the late fifties to the early nineties he lived in Tarwal, maintaining a discreet silence about his activities as an outlaw: enemies are made and both Pashtuns and Afghans have long memories. It is a pity that neither has recorded an account of their exploits for at least one was very daring.

★

About six years after the Loralai episode the Second World War

39

broke out and unrest along the sensitive border with Afghanistan was the last thing the British administration wanted. The First World War had shown them the potential for trouble along the border when Fort Sandeman was besieged and almost overwhelmed by a 'lashkar' of Mahsuds and Wazir, helped by nearby Sheranis, as noted further on. Word was sent out and A.Y.K.'s father, Nawab Mohammad Khan and Major Barnes the Political Agent for Zhob toured the border area, granting amnesties to Sheikh and Fukhruddin, among others, on the condition of surrendering their rifles. Thus in 1941 our two friends returned to Zhob, both discreetly moving their homes to Tarwal and thereby enjoying a good measure of seigneurial protection for the Kakar chief would not tolerate shooting on his own doorstep.

Now some five years earlier a Turraki from Afghanistan, Sher Gul by name, had been wintering in Zunga Walla village near Loralai and hiring his donkeys to a local contractor, Abdul Waheed. Unwisely, he fell in love with his employer's wife and in spite of the extreme danger the woman responded. Finally the lovers eloped one night, the woman disguised as a man. They reached Adwal, a long hog's back of a mountain on the southern edge of the broad Zhob Valley (one which A.Y.K. and I climbed once in search of mountain sheep) just before dawn and decided to remain hidden during the day as many, if not most Kakars would be against them for eloping and pursuit was certain. Having made the same journey on foot myself, it is around thirty-five miles across stony, waterless country and no mean feat for a woman. Moreover, even in daylight the track is difficult enough to follow.

Abdul Waheed, his brothers, relatives and friends had spread out in three parties to hunt the couple, covering the most likely escape routes. Abdul Waheed's own party, numbering about twenty, unknowingly passed the runaways who were hidden above a narrow gorge that cuts the small Adwal range. Story has it that one of the pursuers smelt the 'luwung' twigs (from Burma) that the woman carried on her person for scent, looked back and saw the couple. Whatever the truth of that, Sher Gul was equal to the occasion, or nearly so, for he not only managed to shoot dead two of his pursuers, though not the husband, during the ensuing gun battle but almost miraculously managed to escape across the fifteen or more miles of wide, open Zhob plain to the relative safety of the Spin Ghar mountains and on to his home in Kandahar. There he wisely remained, keeping several fierce dogs as an added precaution. The erring wife, probably exhausted from the night's trek, could not keep up with her lover though she managed to escape as far as Kuli Allahadadzai ('kuli' or 'killi' means village) but was turned over to her husband and promptly shot.

When Sheikh returned to Zhob in 1941, neither he nor his father had money to provide 'wulwer' or dowry for a bride, nor was there a sister whose own 'wulwer' would then permit Sheikh to marry. However, Abdul Waheed was still anxious to wipe out the insult to himself and his family and, having heard of and been impressed by Sheikh's reputation, sought him out. He offered him a thousand rupees if he would bring in Sher Gul's head. Having such poor marriage prospects, this was a tempting offer and enough for a bride in those days, but it transpired that Adul Waheed literally wanted his enemy's head. While Sheikh would have no qualms about shooting such a man who had offended both tribal law and tribal honour, that was a different matter. He had no stomach for that sort of grisly nonsense and offered to take along any relative of Abdul Waheed as witness of the shooting but to no avail. Thus Sher Gul died a natural death around 1968, wisely remaining near Kandahar with his fierce dogs while Sheikh was unable to marry for another twelve years. In 1953, he did and that event involved a bit of outlawry.

★

Sheikh Rahmat was the Nawab's general right-hand-man and unofficial body guard for some time, though there seems to have been little real need for the latter function, but it is an indication of the high regard in which he was held. His last brush with the law was in the 1950s. As said already, he had little money for the usual dowry or 'bride price' and his years were passing when he took a strong fancy to a local girl. She was years younger than he and her parents were unwilling to forego the usual 'wulwer'. Perhaps understandably, they rejected his overtures. Ever enterprising and fearless of the possible repercussions, Sheikh enlisted the support of Fukhruddin, his old crony of many a year, and they hijacked a lorry in Kila Saifulla bazaar. The unfortunate driver was made to drive it along a jeep track through the mountains to Kakar Khorrasan and thence over the border to Alla Jirga, where the pair had friends among the Hushana clan of Kakars that had elected to remain in Afghanistan when McMahon and Nawab Sahib, as the chief's family and friends always addressed him, marked out the Durrand Line as the boundary. While not condoning Sheikh's action the chief sympathised with him and prevailed upon the girl's family to relent. In any case, any other man who had taken a fancy to the girl or was regarded by the parents as a potential husband would now be reluctant to cross Sheikh Rahmat in such a situation, where both affection and honour were involved, and the girl's parents would have been all too aware of this. Whether the chief paid them some 'wulwer' or 'bride price' on behalf of Sheikh, to compensate them for their damaged pride, is unknown as that would be embarrassing to Sheikh but I would be surprised if he had not done so. What ever the case, Nawab Sahib also prevailed upon the District Magistrate to pardon Sheikh for hi-jacking the lorry and all was well. He claimed his bride and I saw her momentarily by chance in 1996 when a guest of Sheikh and his four sons.

Back to my first meeting with various locals in Kila Saifulla bazaar; having dealt with me as we sat against the mud wall, the next topic was Martial Law, which had been imposed shortly after my first journey through the area and all those present seemed to be strongly in favour of its imposition. Law and order was at a very low ebb, corruption was rife and justice depended upon one's bank balance. Things could only get better. That was followed by a discussion on the merits of various pistols and rifles, the tribal factories in Kanigurum and in Durra Adam Khel up north coming into the discussion. The consensus of opinion was that, while guns from the tribal workshops were quite well made, the materials used were unreliable, being old vehicle axles and leaf springs. The AK 47 had yet to arrive and the Lee Enfield .303 was highly regarded, genuine British ones costing ten times those made at in Waziristan or in Darri Adam Khel near Kohat. It was as one would imagine the Wild West in the old days but the players wore turbans instead of a stetson or a feather headdress. I was enthralled by it all.

Abruptly, A.Y.K. decided to visit the District Magistrate at the other end of the bazaar about some matter. During our conversation with that worthy my pistol, a .22 calibre Star with a six-inch barrel, was mentioned in passing by A.Y.K. and, while a permit was not necessary in tribal areas, it certainly was for the settled ones, meaning the Panjab through which I had travelled, the Sinde and others and at that stage I did not have such a permit. This was suddenly very embarrassing but I put on a casual front and produced the weapon for private inspection. To my considerable relief, the D.M. asked no awkward questions and offered to take me to a nomad encampment in the hills bordering the valley where he had to stay that night. It was a tempting proposition but, as I was quite unprepared and had left my camera at Tarwal, I declined the kind offer. Back in Tarwal the village mullah joined me for a meal after dark and A.Y.K. came to my guest room later.

That night there was snow and in Tarwal a sheep was killed

by a wolf, whose footprints were also outside my door. The following morning in a blizzard that was blinding at times I went into Kila Saifulla on my bicycle, often through difficult drifts, to buy a pair of tribal shoes. They were embroidered all over with silver thread and cost me seventeen rupees. This was not just a whim, for our types of shoe let in stones and grit constantly and must be emptied just as often, whereas tribal shoes are boat-shaped and largely avoid this problem and they are not laced. Also, it was the height of bad manners to enter a house or nomad tent without taking off one's shoes, and laces take time to undo. The snag with the pointed tribal shoes, which I had yet to discover, is that they are all made on one last and there is no left or right. Therefore one's feet have to mould them into shape during the first week or so and it tends to be painful. Moreover the leather soles provide little grip on bare rocks.

The alternative type of footwear is the 'sapplai' (Pashtu) or 'chappli' (Urdu), tribal ones having soles made from old car tyres. The best ones, with massive soles made from truck tyres, come from Bannu. Unfortunately, Kila Saifulla bazaar did not have any really good 'sapplai'. They have a different advantage by being open at the toes and the heel so that any sand and stones entering can simply be wriggled out whilst walking. They do have a strap and buckle at the heel but that is easily undone with one hand when entering a house or nomad's tent. As I was soon to realise, the 'sapplai' give a much better grip on rocks than the leather-soled tribal shoes, which advantage could be important if one chanced to meet trouble and needed to seek cover in a hurry, for there was quite a bit of banditry in those days.

I was also having a pair of 'partook' made by the tailor in the village, these traditional baggy trousers being far more practical when sitting cross-legged on rugs or kilims or felts than our European trousers which drag so irritatingly at the knee. A.Y.K. had ordered them fairly wide at the ankle, a current fashion I discovered, but I soon found that undue width there seriously interfered with running as they tended to flap together so I had them altered to be much narrower; like those of the Mahsuds and Wazir, someone commented and who better knows the practicalities of a hardy life? Although made of cotton, the waistline of my pair was thirteen feet and needed seven yards of cloth, so they were quite warm. A tube stitched all round at the top takes the tie-cord or 'wagga', threading which is no easy task, and the top of the 'partook' must be heavily pleated when worn. The alarming thing about 'partook' is that should the 'wagga' become untied and one end of it then retreat into the tube sewn around the top, all control is lost and the 'partook' become temporarily unusable. The prospect of such an event made one very careful when going to the toilet and explains why Afghan and Pashtun men squat to urinate, for to do so standing would be to risk ending up with a mass of cloth around one's ankles and possibly one end of the 'wagga' out of sight and out of reach in the waist tube, quite apart from the other and obvious hazard.

On the third day I had lunch with the chief and his eldest son Temur Shah, a retired officer of the Zhob Levy Corps and very 'pukka'. We sat on an enormous and fine 'kilim' woven by visiting Afghans, and talked, Temur Shah translating. The chief, whose title of Nawab was bestowed upon him by the British, Mohammad Khan Jogezai to do him full justice, was a powerfully built man still in spite of his seventy-plus years, clearly shrewd and obviously of a very strong character: he exuded authority. His father, Bungal Khan, had also been of strong character and defied the British for three years from the seclusion of the wild hills bordering the great valley until he recognized that it was a hopeless struggle, surrendered and was pardoned. Surprisingly, the chief had blue eyes and light brown hair. Everyone addressed him deferentially and I soon noted that anyone with different views from his kept them to themselves. He had two surviving wives and had outlived two others I was told. Each morning he would go riding on his white stallion across the plain, on the way inspecting the orchards that he had planted. I heard that on one such ride another stallion had attacked his, at which he pulled out his revolver and promptly settled the matter. Later, on several occasions I saw him drive off in his big black American car to visit relatives with the two wives chatting amicably to one another in the back seat, and I found it rather intriguing.

The chief enjoyed chess and played a good game so that his sons generally avoided playing with him. On my subsequent visits, having incautiously admitted that I used to play though I had long since lost my enthusiasm for it, after the usual formal greetings the board would be fetched by a servant and we would sit on the steps of his house in the sun. He usually won two of our three games. Even on this first three-week visit he let me wander off alone into the hills, something that I almost took for granted with the confidence and brashness of youth at the time. It was only later that I really appreciated just how generous and trusting he had been. Had anything untoward happened to me, even at the hand of some other tribe such as the Sulaiman Khels, it would have been acutely embarrassing for him. In appreciation of this and his unfailing hospitality, when I later married and our first son James was born, his third given name was Jogezai. Twenty years later, in 1978 I took this son, then aged twelve years, to be introduced to the old man who was in the very twilight of his years, for he was gone just four months later. Aged ninety-three years, he was sitting beneath the great mulberry tree in front of his house with a cluster of grandchildren around him and his faithful 'hookah' or water pipe by him.

After lunch with the chief and Temur Shah I excused myself and made for a pair of jagged peaks three or so miles away, along the southern edge of the valley, running at intervals as I had scant time to complete a brief tour of other hills that I had in mind The two peaks were joined by a sharp ridge and dominated the area quite dramatically. My host had told me that their name was Seerzha, because they were serrated like teeth, the smaller peak being perhaps four or five hundred feet and the main peak eight hundred feet above the valley floor. Nearing the upper slopes of the main peak I was excited to come across a flock of nine wild mountain sheep above me and chased after them from below, hoping to get a closer view. As I crossed a series of very low undulations, I suddenly came upon a magnificent wolf a matter of forty or fifty feet away, in his winter coat with a fine ruff of hair at the neck. He too had been after the wild sheep, though for a different reason, and was as startled as I when we met. For a moment we both paused, then I decided to chase him for a bit of fun but after perhaps three-quarters of a mile, during which he stopped several times to glance back at me, I lost him up some small gully. To cap it all, I saw a pair of enormous lammergeyers floating up and down the endless ridges, scanning for carcasses and bones, their pinions whistling quite loudly in the frosty air so that one could hear them from well over half a mile away. It was the astonishing effortlessness of their search that fascinated me and later I penned a few lines.

> Great wings outspread against the azure sky,
> Their pinions whistled in the frosty air
> As the lammergeyers floated gently by
> And scanned each jagged ridge around their lair
>
> Each day the great birds sought the dead or weak
> From the crags of Seerzha, their abode,
> Among the endless arid hills and peaks
> That guard the eastern flank of distant Zhob.

When I got back to Tarwal I found that my tent, left behind by mistake in Kingri and which I intended to collect upon my return journey, had been delivered by a police bearer who had walked the seven miles from Kila Saifulla. Fortunately the poor man was fed by the Jogezais before returning on foot to the bazaar. This delivery was apparently arranged by Inspector Innes of Loralai, an extremely pleasant and friendly Anglo- Pakistani whom I had met on my first journey through the area. The tent must have been sent to him by the 'hotal' owner. In the evening A.Y.K. related tales of tribal bravery and honour and asked me about England and our customs. Just as we have many misconceptions about them so had they about us. When I mentioned my earlier escape from the two flash floods, he related how a few months previously a party of ten men from Quetta had gone for a picnic in the desert along the road to Zahedan, choosing a wide gravel torrent bed where to enjoy their meal. As was the custom they were without their families. Carelessly ignored or perhaps un-noticed by them, a distant storm in the hills sent down a wild flash flood that swept away the entire party. One man was lucky to be carried into a tamarisk tree and survived but the rest perished, their remains being found miles downstream, some dismembered by the violence of the torrent.

A thing that almost morbidly fascinated A.Y.K. and some of his brothers was the subject of alcohol: did I drink 'sharab'? So I would explain that some people used it moderately, like myself of course, while others became addicted and drank to excess, making their families suffer. Even so my new-found friends were left very worried. Then we would go on to hashish, and of course that had not been proscribed by the Prophet, presumably because it was not to be found in Arabia at the time. However, while not banned in the Quran there was a general feeling that it was not quite respectable. That topic then brought up the story of a young man employed to build an extension to the 'kila' of Sardar Azim Khan, a brother of the Nawab. It seems that the builder did not have a head for heights and began to work very nervously and slowly as the extension grew in height. Anxious about this slow progress and mounting expense, Azim

48

Khan called him down and suggested a few puffs of his pipe, which contained more than mere tobacco, after which the young man was said to have skipped around the roof fearlessly. I in turn was intrigued by the green 'naswar' that quite a few tribesmen carried in a special little tin, putting a pinch of the stuff under the tongue at intervals, a habit which soon made their breath smell like ripe silage. It consists of ground tobacco mixed with lime and I was content not to share that experience.

Tarwal was and still is no more than a scattered hamlet. The houses, except that of the Nawab, were built of mud, had flat, earth roofs and a small mud-walled compound. If there were windows, they faced into the compound and had crude wooden shutters but no glass. Most have changed little since then. Water for everyone came from a distant horizontal well of the Persian type called 'qanat' in Iran and 'karez' in Zhob. The one supplying the village was named Nowi Kashmir Karez, initiated two or three miles away at the foot of Seerzha and coming to the surface one and a half miles or two away. Therein lay a snag, for covering such a distance above ground meant that it was exposed to a rich mix of bacterial and protozoan pollution whenever the wind blew in spore-laden dust. I used to drink the water happily where it issued to the surface when walking to and from Kila Saifulla for mail, but in Tarwal one needed to build up antibodies in order to enjoy it fully. From what I learnt about infant mortality in the area in those days, even among the comfortably off Jogezais, that water was as effective as the 'pill' though less kind. A.Y.K. had lost two sons out of six and two daughters of four born, while Musa Khan Jogezai in Khaisor had lost ten out of sixteen children born I later discovered; and in due course Fukhruddin was to lose eight sons out of twelve and five daughters of nine born and possibly one more. Today deep boreholes served by electric Japanese pumps have taken over and the 'karez', carefully dredged and maintained by Turrakis, Tokhis and others from around Kandahar each winter for longer than anyone could remember are in ruin. Tradition holds that Nowi Kashmir and others in the area were built by the Mughals, but virtually everything older than handed-down memory is regarded as being of Mughal origin.

Once the scant crops had been sown or had been harvested, apart from some weeding there was little to do and life during the intervening periods was leisurely. In winter, while deep frosts ruled the night, during the day the sun was warm and comforting unless a bitter wind blew from the Hindukush far to the north and the men of the village would squat in the shelter of the tiny village shop to chat for hours on end, while rival cocks crowed defiance at one another and the little maize mill filled the air with its peculiar ponk, ponk, ponk until all those who needed their corn ground into flour had been served. But there is a limit to entertaining or interesting conversation and when the day's quota was complete, for those of a competitive nature there were two roundish lumps of rock to act as shot putts and a large mass of iron for weightlifting.

Some time during the middle of the morning, each day a whistle would sound as the little, narrow guage train from Khanai passed slowly by on its way to Fort Sandeman eighty miles down the valley. Linking with the broad guage line at Khanai, between Quetta and Chaman, it was laid to Hindubagh in 1910 to collect chromite ore from small mines nearby, then extended to Fort Sandeman by 1927. It was always full and looked more like a fun fair creation than a serious passenger service. Sadly, since 1987 or thereabouts it is no more, though whether that is because the engine died of old age and no one cared to repair or replace it or whether the frequent breaches of the track by flash floods proved too much in the end I don't know. In any case the road is now tarred, after a fashion, and bulging buses decorated all over with paintings, bright tassels, mirrors and shiny cut-outs have taken over. Another form of public transport are Suzuki and Toyota minibuses, usually so packed that elbows protrude

1) *My second visit in 1958 to Kila Saifulla. With me are L-R: unknown, Hashim Khan, Ahmad Yar Khan, Sarfraz Khan, Abdur Rahman and Sheikh Rahmat (Akhterzai).*
2) *Row of young poplars in patches of snow with Seerzha Peak in the far distance.*

3) Mohammad Khan Jogezai, chief of the Kakars since 1907, enjoying a quiet chat with the village Mullah after the Eid celebrations in 1971.

4) *The male wedding guests taking a meal on the veranda. The female guests are separate and elsewhere.*

5) *Young bloods dancing the Ambe around a fire in the dark.*

6) Left: A musician brought in with the traditional instrument, the chara ka.

7) Below: A young grand daughter of Azim Khan, a brother of the chief.

8) *The bride travelled for two days to her new home in Rode Jogezai beneath the hand painted sheet. She is here crossing a low pass on horseback as the camel was considered unreliable on the narrow, precipitous path.*

9) *A shooting competition held the morning after our arrival in Rode Jogezai.*

10) *Ahmad Yar Khan in 1971, aged about forty-four, eventually becoming more of a brother to me.*

11) *Sibbia, a daughter of Asraf Khan, in the little Tarawal school. She could cheek the boys because she could outrun any of then and escape vengeance.*

12) *An elderly man playing the rebab at the house of the new chief, Temur Shah. This is the traditional instrument of the Afghans and Pashtuns.*

from the windows of necessity, and passengers at the rear sometimes have to exit through a window, while pick-ups and gaudy trucks ferry local produce such as tomatoes or melons or apples to Quetta, while larger trucks cut through the valley to or from Karachi.

The following day a party of us went in cars to Adwal mountain to hunt wild mountain sheep. In the small gorge at its southern end where another ridge starts, A.Y.K. showed me a bullet mark on a rock where Sher Gul, the amorous Turraki from Kandahar, had fired at one of his pursuers. He, one of his brothers and I then headed along the foot of the hog-backed mountain to its northern end, while the other party were to climb up the near end. In the large patches of snow we saw tracks of wolf, leopard, mountain sheep and of course jackal. The last were plentiful and every evening after sundown an exultant chorus of their howls would sound across the great plain for a minute or two to signal that their hour had arrived. Only A.Y.K. and I made the climb and it was tricky at times, in one place we had to cross a steeply slanting slab of rock hanging by our hands, with me holding my pistol and holster in my mouth. We saw two sheep during our traverse of the entire ridge, too distant for a shot, for which I was not sorry, and deep snow drifts in shaded areas demanded care. Wearing only cheap plimsolls and without socks I found it cold going through the drifts. The descent was far less tricky.

The view to the south and east was magnificent, with jagged ridge after ridge as far as the eye could see, while to the north west the great plain of Zhob seemed endless, guarded on the far side by the Spin Ghar range that rises majestically in a series of spectacular, sheer cliffs cut here and there by deep gorges. Upon rejoining the others at the foot of the mountain two or three hours later, we learnt that they had seen no less than seventeen mountain sheep but had not managed to hit one although we had heard several shots. Near the foot of the mountain the servant with us had made a small fire and grilled gobbets of meat and baked some 'pasti', the oversized version of the Indian chapatti. I was ravenous: it was almost nightfall and 'breakfast' had been only 'poi chai' with some dried apricots and 'chilghoza' pine nuts: Pashtuns and Afghans rarely over-ate in those days and the habit has changed little since then. Once the sun set, the temperature plummeted so I ran to the tiny village where the cars had been left in order to warm up and was promptly invited into a house to take tea until the others arrived.

The next day saw my first tribal wedding when I went with Mohammad Hassan to Temur Shah's house to join the bride's male relatives. Anticipating how things would be, I carried plenty of ammunition. The bridegroom was one Jabar Khan, son of Salaam Gul, but his place in the clan I simply cannot fathom from the records I have. We of the bride's party waited at the gate for the groom's male relatives to alight from a motley of vehicles and advance on foot, both groups firing rifles, pistols or revolvers into the air. The groom's female relatives alighted discreetly some way off to the right and entered by a side entrance, holding up their 'takrai' or shawls to hide their faces. Once inside the walled garden, we men all sat on rugs and kilims along the extensive veranda where I was honoured by being placed next to the District Magistrate who in turn was next to the chief. In those halcyon days I had a formidable appetite and the feast that followed was magnificent. There was:

'shorwa', the equivalent of our soup course, made from small pieces of 'pasti' soaked in the juice from boiled landi', which I found and still find absolutely delicious, 'kreut', of crushed dried yoghurt and torn 'pasti' plus some crushed rock salt, moistened with boiling water, after which hot fat is poured into a hollow made in the centre.

This was eaten communally from large bowls. However, it varies greatly in quality, tasting too strongly sometimes, but it certainly packs out the corners,
stewed meat, with potato as a garnish (chillies, if used at all, were used sparingly),
stewed chicken, also delicious,
boiled 'landi', the dried meat and best when slightly high, my favourite,
intestine stuffed with lumps of fat and boiled – I opted out of that one,
intestine crisp fried and much nicer than it sounds,
fried cubes of meat,
cauliflower cooked in 'ghee'
plain boiled rice,
saffron coloured rice,
'pulao' of fried rice with small pieces of meat,
'pasti', as explained earlier,
salad of sliced onion, cucumber and tomato, un-garnished in any way,
yoghurt, prepared by the womenfolk from the household culture and the best I have ever eaten,
'shlombai' to drink, being yoghurt well shaken with water and therefore dubious at times,
'halva' made from wheat flour, sugar and 'ghee'; or jelly and custard as dessert then followed, when small spoons were used, all else being eaten with the fingers.
Finally there was sweet black tea and sweet green tea, in small bowls rather than cups.

Before we actually ate several young men of the household went to everyone in turn, with careful regard to hierarchy or status, carrying long-spouted copper jugs of hot water and copper wash basins with soap on their perforated lids for us to wash our hands. I love the name for the latter, which is 'larrsminzuni'.

Knives and forks were never used and still are not but spoons are creeping in, and each person had his own plate. As I sat next to the D.M., he put a choice titbit of meat on my plate from time to time, the person on my other side doing the same, both of them urging 'Da wokhra' or 'Eat that'. The 'larrsminzuni' were brought around again when the eating was over but before the tea. Using one's fingers, of the right hand please note, eating rice was not easy at first as the rice was fairly dry, while small torn pieces of 'pasti' are used to pick up pieces of meat. It was a moment of triumph when, months later, I eventually managed to eat rice without a grain lodging in my beard. Interestingly, my healthy appetite was quite a social asset as my various hosts were always and obviously pleased at the enthusiastic way I tackled whatever was put in front of me: somehow, it almost made me one of them in spite of any language barrier. Etiquette involved a hearty belch from time to time to show appreciation of the spread but there I compromised, raising my hand to my mouth in salute to a discreet or imaginary, silent belch.

After the feast, members of the bride's family and I were presented with a turban and sums of money by the groom's family. I received Rs.50, which was quite a sum in those days, and as might be expected I was immediately taught how to tie my turban in the style of the Sanjar Khel section of the tribe, which is by far the largest section and to which the Jogezai clan belongs. Other major sections of the Kakars are the Taraghara, Saraghara, Sanatia, Dumar (disputed) and Seenr; the last possibly having disappeared as a distinct section. This tying of my turban I managed tolerably well, to the great satisfaction of all, there being a long loose end and a long loop left hanging by tradition. It was about seven or eight yards long but in days gone by those who could afford it would have a turban as much as thirty yards in length. Somehow I missed the shooting but was eventually taken outside by Mohammad Hassan in time for a two-mile foot race across the stony waste. It was known by then that I had run for my university and as the Zhob champion was present there was much speculation as to the outcome. Indeed I got a distinct impression that my prestige rested to a considerable extent upon the result so I decided to run barefoot as the leather soles of my tribal shoes were so slippery that I would have no chance otherwise on the gravel and stones. I upheld Britain's honour convincingly but it was almost a Pyrrhic victory as I was pulling out dozens of tiny thistle spines for two or three weeks afterwards. It was a small price to pay and Nur Ahmad, one of the ten brothers, managed to come second so it was a bad day for the local champion.

Later we transferred to the family home of Mohammad Usman Khan three or four miles away, though I do not know why if the groom's father was Salaam Khan, and after dark a large circle of sixty or so men danced around a great log fire in the deep frost. With the 'Ambe', three men in the centre sang the verses, right hand cupping the ear, their voices high pitched. At intervals all the others would join in with a deep, growling choral chant of 'ambe', crouching, swaying and revolving as they slowly circled the fire and from time to time someone would move inside the circle to fire his rifle or pistol or revolver into the air. It was the most sinister and threatening thing I have ever heard but A.Y.K. assured me that it was a dance of happiness. Two other dances were the 'Uttan' and the 'Driss', the latter involving a hissing chorus and waving a handkerchief in the air as the men gyrated in a circle. It was stirring stuff and well worth a five-thousand-mile cycle ride. My friends and I retired at around two in the morning to sleep in Usman Khan's house that night, leaving the young bloods still at it.

Early morning is not my best time of day so I declined joining in the wrestling when invited before we left the next day although I always had a flair for it. Back in Tarwal, A.Y.K. and several of the Jogezai lads rode my cycle before I set off on foot with Mohammad Hassan three or four miles out across the great plain to Badderwal Karez. I had been invited to lunch with Sardar Azim Khan, a brother of the Nawab. He turned out to be a spry, wiry little man, aged about seventy I guess, about whom tales abounded, particularly concerning his pipe, which was filled with hashish at times, if not frequently. He was the antithesis of his older brother but, above all he had led a Kakar 'lashkar' or tribal army over a period of twenty-five years against the Sulaiman Khels, when the latter periodically raided across the border for camels, horses and sheep or anything else worth stealing. Finally, having got wind that a big sortie was in the offing, he laid a devastating ambush in one of the several gorges through which they were to pass in the rugged Spin Ghar range bordering the plain. Stationing his men among the rocks at each end of the gorge and blocking the end furthest from their approach with a wall of boulders, his men hidden at the other end rolled down large boulders that had been carefully positioned beforehand as soon as the raiders had passed so the Kakars managed to trap those on horseback and slow those on foot, killing as many as two hundred of the raiders it is claimed. At all events the severity of the blow led to a treaty being made between the two tribes which held thenceforth.

Azim Khan had a passion for guns but I was told that he often claimed that the manufacturers didn't always know their job and was reputed to file down the sights and make other 'improvements', often with less than happy results. He had four sons, about one of which there is an amusing tale later. One of his young grand-daughters was brought out for me to see and photograph. She wore a fine tribal dress and had blue eyes but she had not seen a European before and liked cameras still less so that it took an hour before we could calm her and take a photograph. Dear old Azim Khan took a fancy to my .22 pistol and I rather liked his chunky Colt .45: with its greater knock-down ability, were a leopard or hyaena to approach should I bivouac alone in the hills or desert. So a few days later we agreed upon a swap, after each had tried the other's pistol. However, a couple of days after that the D.M. got wind of the deal and that was the end of it for the .45 calibre was a completely prohibited bore outside the tribal areas, being a military calibre, – not that many tribesmen obeyed the rule when they visited Quetta, Dera, Ghazi Khan, Dera Ismail Khan, Bannu, or Peshawar.

One evening A.Y.K. took me to a nomad's tent a few miles away where another wedding had just been celebrated. As we sat under the stars drinking small bowls of 'shin chai' or sweet green tea, a sputnik, as they were called in those days, glided silently and steadily overhead and discussion focused upon it. The nomad was a fine, intelligent fellow but he could not understand how such a device could descend down into the earth to the east and then rise out of the ground in the west later on. It took some time to explain, with A.Y.K. interpreting, that the earth was spherical and that the satellite merely circled it every ninety minutes or so. My 'partook' were waiting on my wooden 'charpai' with its criss-cross strips of plaited dwarf palm frond upon our return to Tarwal and my difficulty in threading the five-foot 'wagga' through the thirteen-feet waist tube caused much amusement among those who thronged into my room. Mine used only seven yards of cloth whereas in the old days those of a wealthy man might contain as many as twenty-five, occasionally forty, yards of cloth.

In those days the Afghans made extremely handsome 'pusteens' of goat skin, worn with the hair inside. Sadly, army surplus greatcoats have gradually taken their place since then. The pale tan leather outside, dyed an attractive yellowish-brown with pomegranate skins, was embroidered either with red or yellow woollen yarn, the latter always being better done and more detailed. The sleeves were far longer than any arm and were very narrow at the cuff, being largely decorative though it was just possible to use them as sleeves. All in all, they were magnificent creations and I was anxious to get one, A.Y.K. driving me into Kila Saifulla in the morning to look for one but there were none, not surprisingly as the bazaar was and still is relatively small. We then visited Malik Launi, some twenty miles away in the Fort Sandeman direction. When I had ridden into Kila Saifulla during the blizzard some days previously in tribal dress someone had seen me from a distance, noted my reddish beard and so started a rumour that Malik Launi had bought a motorcycle, the elderly 'malik' dying his grey beard orange with henna. Similarly, at the wedding someone had asked if I was a member of the Azmatt family who lived not far away, that family being noted locally for the number of its members with blue eyes.

Back in Kila Saifulla that afternoon, there chanced to be a bus to Loralai, forty-six miles away, over the hills, so I boarded it as the bazaar there is far more extensive. There would be better 'pusteens' available the following morning I was told upon making enquiries after my arrival. Eating a simple meal, I was approached by a pleasant young Hazara who spoke good English. The Hazaras are of Mongolian origin and reputed to be descendants of Ghenghis Khan's soldiers, the name literally meaning 'thousands'. Most of them are settled in the central mountains of Afghanistan, to the west of Kabul, some with pure Chinese features, others with a blend. He insisted on paying for my meal and also arranged for me to sleep overnight in the shop next door, though the legions of mice that emerged after dark made sleep there a fitful business. In the morning a golden 'pusteen' was located but the asking price was Rs.200, a bit beyond my means even after selling my overland tent to Jehandar Shah, A.Y.K.'s older brother, who wanted it for hunting in the hills. However, Temur Shah appeared unexpectedly and bargained the price down to Rs.160. I was now better equipped to face the cold, especially if sleeping under the stars. I still lacked that essential of all modern tribesmen, a waistcoat, but a year later my tribal wardrobe was completed by the addition of a 'Kandahari sadri', instantly recognized by decoration of the upper pockets and special smocking of the lower ones. Without warning A.Y.K. appeared, a common pattern of unpredictability and impulse that I was to see many times, and I returned to Tarwal with him. On our way back we saw two mountain sheep perched on a pinnacle of rock high on a mountain near the road.

That evening we were entertained at the house of Abdur Rahman where, for the first time, I was introduced to a woman, his widowed mother. She was a large, handsome, bold and intelligent looking woman; a sister of Nawab Sahib. She wore a finely embroidered tribal dress and after a while I asked if I might take a photograph, but no. Only later did I learn that forty years earlier some levies under the British had gone to arrest her husband for something to do with the Pashtunistan issue. As the Third Afghan War was in progress there was probably a connection. Baz Khan had run for his rifle, firing his revolver as he went, but was shot dead before reaching it. As Sir Olaf Caroe tellingly says in his book, *The Pathans*, "many of them live all their lives on the brink of eternity". When looking at Mir Shams' genealogy of the Kakar tribe years later I noticed that Baz Khan was of the 'Nawab kahole' so that his marriage to chief's sister, who was of the 'Ishak kahole', was probably a 'political' one to link the two Jogezai 'kaholes' and prevent further deadly feuding.

Conversation included 'pusteens', taxes, hunting, other countries and their customs – or alleged customs as their ideas of our morals in the West were often very wide of the mark, certainly in those days if not today. It was firmly believed that Europeans in general hopped into bed with anyone whom they fancied and they found it hard to grasp that we did have our rules, even if not everyone followed them. Our eating of pork and our drinking of wine was impossible for them to accept, yet the smoking of hashish was regarded as only slightly reprehensible. To our credit, we Christians had a 'religious book', the bible, whereas the Hindus did not have quite the same and that was a severe deficiency it seems. Furthermore, Mohammad regarded Christ as a true prophet. I was of course pressed as to my own beliefs, especially as it was by now known that I was a biologist. To this I replied by pointing out that praying, even five times a day, was relatively easy but practising tended to be far more difficult. The point was taken. We broke off at midnight, returning to Tarwal in a deep, silent frost with brilliant stars above us. The only sound was the occasional, faint bark of a distant dog, possibly to warn of a prowling wolf.

Three days after that there was an informal village Olympics outside the gloomy, windowless little shop in Tarwal. I managed to win one of the three events and so was not disgraced. Later I set off for the tiny village of Nishpa a few miles away over the endless sharp ridges to the south-east, having been invited there by its part-time priest, Mullah Muzamir, but I got lost and ended up in a village called Barrg. However, I was well received by one, Sher Amir Khan, and tea soon provided. For the first time two girls in their teens were present, both very good looking, with rows of coins in addition to the usual embroidery on the cuffs. The family was clearly poor but a gigantic meal was then set before me: however, I was unsure whether the others had eaten so I ate sparingly. My doubts were confirmed when, with obvious hunger, they ate the huge amount that I had left. Such is the importance placed upon hospitality by Afghans and Pashtuns alike. While I had come to grips with basic Urdu / Hindustani fairly easily, and of course had learnt Farsi in Iran while stranded there, Pashtu was a quite different language and my hosts understood nothing else so conversation was difficult but they were very patient as I wrote down new words to extend my vocabulary. I had long since learnt that while being able to speak a foreign language is a huge advantage, just trying to speak it, however poorly, counts for a great deal when travelling. Somehow it shows a certain respect for the local culture and it breaks the ice rapidly.

The house I was in was half-built into the stony hillside, its walls made of large rounded stones and boulders held together by dried mud, plastered with mud inside and even decorated with a little whitewash here and there. Its roof consisted of the usual largish un-worked tree limbs topped with small branches crosswise on which was laid reed-like grass, crosswise again, topped with perhaps nine inches of soil. In such an arid climate, with perhaps only five to ten inches of rain and snow per year, the last is sufficient protection against the occasional storm provided the layer is thick enough to soak up all the water before any actually seeps through. The only rainfall records for the area seem to have been made in the early part of the twentieth century, when an average of five inches was noted over four or five years but it was a drought period and not typical. There was a barely separated area at one end of the dwelling where two or three little cows and a larger number of sheep were brought in for the night.

Having the livestock indoors at night in those days not only protected the animals from the large predators that were still quite plentiful but also provided warmth for the family when night temperatures might drop many degrees below freezing point. Though dried mud is a far better insulator than baked brick or concrete or stone, with so few trees in the area for fuel this heat from the animals is very welcome in winter, while in summer the mud walls of the houses minimised the summer heat which, even at five thousand feet at Tarwal, may reach 40° C. There is limited soil in such little valleys and even less water to irrigate even small plots so that the people in them are very poor: it is subsistence agriculture and everyone is lean, including the old. The entire furnishings of the house where I slept comprised an iron baking tray, a triangular iron griddle, a copper water jug with a long spout, an aluminium kettle, an aluminium drinking pot with spout, a few small china bowls for tea, two small tin boxes, four cushions and a heavy home-made felt rug with bright patterns. In addition of course there were padded cotton quilts and cushions but nothing else. Four other men slept there that night and the next morning a quite refined-looking and very handsome young woman came to make food. I asked if I could photograph her while she cooked at the crude fire grate cut into the earthen floor. Three of them agreed but the fourth, a rough-looking fellow, was obviously reluctant and became silent and sullen. As I prepared to take a photograph he abruptly flew into a rage, threatening his brother's face with a flaming brand from the fire should they let me continue. He did not threaten me, almost certainly because I was the chief's guest but I took the hint.

After returning briefly to Tarwal for something or other I headed for Nishpa once more, yet again nearly ending up back in Barrg until put on the right track by a man met on the way. I crossed several more minor ridges, some so sharp that one had to straddle them, and arrived just before dark. It is a pretty place, almost a tiny oasis nestling between several minor, arid but impressively sharp peaks. The Mullah was away but as usual I was well received. Marginally larger than Barrg, Nishpa is shown on several maps although it boasted no more than a dozen houses but it was clearly more prosperous, with some apricot and almond trees growing around its tiny plots: a more accurate description would be to say that it was less poor. A few potatoes, onions, tomatoes, cucumbers, chillies, tobacco and ladies' fingers or okra were grown, the last a strange vegetable not often seen in the U.K. Much of these crops were for use by its families but some would be sold in Kila Saifulla, the fleece from very small flocks of sheep providing most of the money for buying essential wheat, clothing and other things. The greater prosperity of the village revealed itself in the little mud house where I stayed, by having a flat-weave 'kilim' from Kandahar in addition to the home-made felt rugs. Dysentery disturbed my sleep and the fairly typical morning dash was necessary. Around mid-morning Mullah Muzamir returned and a village elder who spoke some Urdu acted as interpreter. I left at midday, after declining lunch, discovered that there is a lower Nishpa a mile or so away, and chewed some 'gurr', rough brown lumps of solidified molasses, on my way back to Tarwal.

Back in Tarwal the following evening, after a meal I was introduced to two traditional games. The first was Gutki, a simple game between two groups sitting opposite one another. One side provides a finger ring and offers a choice of it or five points to the opposing group to start play. All members of the starting group hide their hands beneath a turban or shawl and one of them takes the ring in his fist. When ready all the group hold out their clenched fists for inspection by the other group. One of the opponents, agreed by the rest of his team, will point to a fist which he thinks is empty and say 'pooch'. If right his team gets a point and so on. Alternatively, if one of the opponents is convinced that he knows which fist holds the ring, if his group let him he will point to the fist and say 'wrack', meaning 'give it'. If right his team gets a point and possession of the ring; if wrong the other team gets a point and continues to hide the ring. However, as the game warms up, all sorts of bluff are tried, fists are squeezed hard by the opponents on the basis that the ring may cause pain or there are attempts to prise apart the fingers of the person suspected of having the ring to feel if it is there. It gets quite boisterous and the group first to reach thirty points is the winner.

The second game, which we often played until far into the night was 'Wazir Badshah', meaning Minister and King. From four to twenty persons play sit in a circle and a sheep's knuckle bone is thrown by each player in turn. The two narrow sides of the bone represent the 'Badshah' and 'Wazir' respectively, the two broader faces represent a thief and a sheep, there being distinct differences between all faces of the bone. First, however, limits on punishment are agreed by all, a wise precaution as the game tends to become rougher as it progresses. Each man throws in turn and the first person's throw with the 'Badshah' side uppermost becomes the king but can do nothing until another's throw makes that person the minister. After that, if anyone throws for 'mayzh' or sheep nothing happens to them but when someone throws for 'ghal' or thief, the minister reports to the king that there has been a theft at the treasury and asks how the thief should be punished. The punishment may be twenty press-ups or knees-bend, to howl like a jackal, bark like a dog or bray like a donkey. Surprisingly, some players were quite embarrassed by the last three; but just as often the punishment is a number of slaps with two fingers to the underside of the wrist, decided by the 'Badshah' and administered by the Wazir.

When someone else throws king or minister at his turn then the previous office holder stands down. On extremely rare occasions the bone may come to rest on one end, when the first person to grab it and kiss it becomes the king or minister, as he chooses, for seven turns and is allowed to choose a friend for the other prime role. After two or three hundred such slaps during the course of an evening I have seen wrists inflamed and swollen to twice their normal size by the following morning; but to plead for mercy invited withering scorn. As might be expected, the game tends to polarise and become quite fierce, with threats as to what will happen 'when I become the king'. Friends may be pardoned by the king or a trivial punishment given. Rivals on the other hand get an extra dose and take revenge when the opportunity arises. All in all it's a robust game, to put it mildly, the sort of game one would expect from such rugged people as the Afghans and Pashtuns. Fortunately for me I had sinewy wrists, had done my share of hard manual work and so suffered relatively little as a consequence when my throws landed as thief.

Arm wrestling was another activity to pass the time and my fifteen months on a farm in Surrey before university no doubt helped me in this. The younger brothers were a lively bunch and we had a tremendous amount of fun. Of course they were as curious about life in England as I was about life in Zhob and most of them had a good smattering of English learned at college in Quetta. Among other things I taught them that beautiful but sad Persian song, 'Mara Beboos', meaning Kiss Me, that I had learned from the scouts in the Manzarieh camp while marooned in Tehran. This was very popular for, although they did not speak Farsi as such, unlike many of their kith and kin over the border to the west where Darri is the official language and is virtually the same, they had learned a little just as many of us learned French at school. It also had a certain prestige, having been the court language in Delhi in times past. Perhaps the languages of most organised societies develop tongue twisters for amusement and, rather surprisingly, as I never managed to reasonably master the language, I could recite some of those better than the young Jogezais.

In addition to the above there are three games using pebbles or whatever on different, special boards or simply on fields that can be scratched in the hard earth. 'Katal' has eighteen pieces to each of the two players and has similarities with draughts in that pieces are taken by hopping over one or more of the opponent's pieces and the game ends when one player has lost all his pieces, or when one player has managed to align three of his pieces across the rear of a triangular box at his opponents end. There is a precise system of points and the first player to total thirty six points is the winner of the game. In 'Roghmat', which is simpler, each of the two players has nine men that are moved one at a time in turn around a precise field scratched in the dirt to manoeuvre one's pieces to form a row of three whenever possible, taking off an opponent's piece at each success until he has none left. Both games involve considerable skill but the third game, 'Kholband' is very simple and more suitable for children, each player trying to bottle up his opponent's two pieces so that he cannot move them.

The Zhob Valley is vast, being about one hundred and twenty miles long and between ten and thirty miles wide. Its upper end at Hindubagh, since then renamed Muslimbagh, is almost five and a half thousand feet in altitude, while Kila Saifulla is roughly five thousand feet and Fort Sandeman (recently renamed Zhob by some silly bureaucrat even though the original village nearby is called Apozai and the entire district was called Zhob) is at approximately four and a half thousand feet. The Zhob River, or more precisely its course its, rises above Hindubagh but does not become perennial until it nears the tiny bazaar of Nissai, a little above which the fine Fakirzai River flows in from the north west. The name Zhob is derived from the word 'zhoo' meaning to ooze and 'obah' meaning water. Below that point the river cuts increasingly deep channels in the fine, pale soil, thirty or more feet deep in places, often with sheer sides and sometimes creating a subsidiary valley of its own three or four hundred yards wide, making it virtually useless for irrigation. A small cluster of trees in the barren wastes usually marked the course of a 'karez' and tamarisks often grow along the edges of the sunken Zhob River.

The magnificent range opposite Kila Saifulla and Tarwal along the north west flank is the Spin Gharr or White Mountain, which rises in series of awesome crags, one behind the other, to about eight and a half thousand feet, cut here and there by deep ravines. Higher up the valley and behind Hindubagh this range reaches almost ten thousand feet in one place and juniper trees grow. Lower down the valley in the direction of Fort Sandeman the range is called Shin Gharr, meaning Green Mountain and is less impressive. The hills bordering the south-east edge of the Zhob Valley consist of line after line of rugged but relatively low ridges. I found the Spin Gharr both inspiring and irresistible, especially in the setting sun when shadows reveal its features clearly. A.Y.K. and presumably Nawab Sahib, agreed to let me go to there, fifteen or so miles away across the valley floor and perhaps continue to the village of Sharan Jogezai, also called Rode Jogezai by locals, some twenty five or thirty miles beyond, in the great Khaisor Valley. The D.M. in Kila Saifulla showed unease when someone mentioned my plan to visit the Spin Gharr on the far side of the valley and possibly Sharan Jogezai beyond as well and tried to dissuade me from going: 'There is nothing to see there, there is no water to drink' and so on. I kept quiet but felt sure that he guessed my determination to go there.

Therefore, upon returning to Tarwal, I hurriedly made ready as I suspected that he might come along and ban me outright from going. A.Y.K. lent me a .32 long revolver, as it had a bit more power than my .22 pistol, and feeling that A.Y.K. was slightly concerned for my safety I drew up and signed a blood chit absolving him from all blame were anyone unkind enough to kidnap me or shoot me or whatever. I packed a few lumps of 'gurr', some flour and some leaf tea and hurried off, heading straight across the plain for the river. I had heard that there were some dangerous quick-sands in places, where camels were reputed to have sunk from sight, and when I descended the high bank to the sandy river margins dark shadows suddenly appeared around my feet as I approached the water. Thus warned I dropped my rucsac, remounted the high bank and collected a good bundle of longish twigs from the scattered woody herbs. From then on it was a case of trial and error, cautiously trying out the river bed with a foot and marking each firm spot with a twig until I reached the far side, after which I had to return to collect the rucsac. The water was shallow and only fifty or so feet wide but the operation took half an hour or more to plot an erratic but safe passage.

Up on the level plain beyond once more, I could see a distant cluster of trees slightly to my left and so headed for them, expecting that they marked the outlet of a 'karez' and a village. When I reached them at dusk, however, I was disappointed and although an unattended group of camels was grazing close by there was no water to make tea or food. Seeing a small group of gazelle gave some consolation but not much. Having seen what appeared to be wolf or hyaena prints in the sandy soil I made a rough shelter of large rocks and a few dead branches against a tree, rather more concerned that a hyaena or jackal might chew my precious 'pusteen' as I slept within its warmth than anything else. The night was intensely cold but with a sleeping bag and the 'pusteen' I was beautifully warm. In the far distance, at the foot of the mountains I could hear a dog barking. The only other sound was an almost continuous rumbling from the camels and I was soon oblivious of all.

In the morning I climbed one of the few and widely scattered sand dunes that happened to be nearby and, looking in the direction of last night's barking, I could see a wisp of smoke at the foot of the great range and headed for it. After an hour or so I entered a tiny hamlet nestling in a little side valley and was promptly set upon by three dogs but managed to keep them at bay with the small stones available until a man came out to meet me. I soon learned that the hamlet was Ghrolam Rassul. After a welcome drink of water in one of the small houses, tea was brought and food followed that. Another dwelling in the tiny hamlet was rather interesting as it was for winter occupation only, the nomad family passing the summer far away in Kakar Khorrasan along the Afghan border, returning to the hamlet each winter. It consisted of a low wall perhaps three feet high made of large stones and a few boulders, topped by a black goats hair nomad tent, a 'kuzhdei', to provide the roof. As the site was well sheltered from cold north-west winds sweeping down from the Hindu Kush, it saved the family from having to migrate across Zhob and on to the Loralai or Duki Districts whose altitudes were considerably lower so that they were milder in winter. After a chat it was suggested that I take an ancient .303 rifle belonging to one of the men and go hunting with one of their number in the mountains above. As was to happen so often afterwards, the wiry little chap, who was a few years older than I, gradually increased his pace up the steep track to try me out and I responded suitably, thanks partly to three years of training over the hills around Aberystwyth. From the top the view ahead and below us was like a lunar landscape, with ridge after ridge of steeply dipping, multi-hued rock strata many of which were shale, some greenish, blue, purple, pink and red. I was told that oil oozed from the ground in the valley ahead of and below us. However, there was no game of any kind to be seen, for which I was not sorry as I don't enjoy hunting.

In the village that evening several young men came to see me, having no doubt heard that the 'ferangai' staying at Tarwal had arrived. At first they were a bit silly, a frequent trait among young Muslim men I found, possibly because they were not allowed to meet girls alone I suspect and because as yet they lacked enough money for 'wulwer' in order to marry, but after a while they sang local songs and I really enjoyed most of these, even though I could not follow the story at all. The soloist would close his eyes and cup his right hand to his ear and those assembled would take up the chorus between verses. Most of the songs were distinctly plaintive, echoing the wild loneliness of the surrounding mountains and largely barren valleys between ranges. One was about Sher Jan, a Jogezai from across the mountains in Khaisor who, I was to learn later, had in 1940 shot the Political Agent, Major Barnes, in Fort Sandeman. He also killed Barnes's unfortunate 'peon' or messenger who happened to be present and who was to be pensioned that very day. Ironically, the luckless 'peon' had been asked to remain a while longer in order to receive a retirement present from the P.A. that was being brought from the bazaar. Most of their songs seem to be about violent deeds or love, like so many of our own folk songs. Later, back in Tarwal, Ahmad Yar Khan told me the story. Sher Jan had been made redundant from the Zhob Levy Corps, the militia which he lived for, but no one really seems to know why he shot the Major when another officer, Parsons, had made the decision in any case. Perhaps it was because Barnes, having explained the position to Sher Jan several times previously it was said, finally lost patience and threw the file at him, calling him a fool. Sher Jan had no hope of escaping from the fort and in due course was tried, then hanged in Mach gaol. Upon his arrest or execution – I'm not sure which – his six brothers took to the hills just over the Afghan border to show their displeasure until eventually pardoned nine years later.

Two years after this brief trip to the Spin Ghar I was to stay with three of them, Nasserullah Jan, Sher Ali Khan and Musa Khan, in their tiny village, shown as Sharan Jogezai on some maps, Rode Jogezai on others. They were a hardy bunch and raided for about nine years, stopping buses, looting lorries and so on. As per custom in such enterprises they collaborated with an equal number of Sulaiman Khels, their boldest exploit being the kidnap of a Hindu divisional road officer, one Chaman Lal. However, the alarm was raised more quickly than they expected and pursuit by the British authorities was swiftly organised. The outlaws were soon located by a spotter aircraft and as a result they only managed to reach the relative security of an isolated peak called Wakhlin Ghar in the Zhob Valley. This was promptly surrounded by a thousand militia men brought in by trucks. Nawab Sahib went there to try to avoid bloodshed but the kidnappers decided to shoot it out. Before darkness fell one militia man and one of the outlaws was killed. Early the following morning the spotter plane was sent over the peak again but there was no sign of the gang for, during the night, with their hostage they had managed to slip through the tight cordon. It was a remarkable feat. The government having failed to rescue her husband, the poor man's desperate wife approached the local road contractor, Khudaidad, for help as he was a personal friend of Chaman Lal. Four thousand rupees were forthcoming and Mohammad Usman Khan, a Jogezai whose hospitality I enjoyed many times, travelled to the outlaws' hideout, handed over the ransom and brought back the unfortunate man, unharmed but scared to death. After Independence and Partition in 1947, the new Pakistan government fared no better than the British in such wild terrain and failed to capture the band but it was more pragmatic and a couple of years later offered the brothers an amnesty and Rs.400 per month, to be shared, if they would resettle in their village. Thus they were in effect pensioned outlaws, no doubt saving the government a lot of money.

A woman joined us during the singing and I asked if I could take a photograph that included her, even though she was no oil painting. When the flash went off she screamed and threw herself backwards, to the delight of everyone once they too had recovered from their shock. Years later people were still laughing about the incident, such small, isolated communities in those days lacking radios and having limited outside contact so that anything out of the ordinary became memorable. Long after the event I learned that years earlier her new-born baby had been taken by a jackal while she was absent for a few minutes and that the loss had deranged her slightly. The next morning food was brought to me in the wooden bowl that had been used to feed the small cow the previous night: I just hoped that the cow didn't mind. A handsome girl joined us, with tattoos on her cheeks and forehead but as she was of marriageable age and more or less in 'purdah' I did not ask to take a 'photo, mindful of the previous incident in Barrg village. I had planned to take a shot of the interior of the hybrid tent-house nearby but discovered that the men were away so that it would tactless: I was learning.

By now the weather was on the change, with heavy cloud building up. I decided not to go on to Sharan Jogezai in case snow fell in the mountains, possibly trapping me there for days or even weeks, bearing in mind that I had to return to Dehra Dun within a week or so. As I left the hamlet it began to rain instead and in case the river rose I felt it wise to return via the regular ford on the path to Kila Saifulla rather than directly back the way I had come, where I might not find my crossing or the twigs might be washed away. It meant an extra twelve or so miles but, if desperate, I could get food in the bazaar before continuing to Tarwal. Arriving in Kila Saifulla, I had a long chat with Rehmat Tan, a refined, gentle shop-keeper and part-time mullah who spoke a little English, during which the local 'Tahsildar' came along to say how worried he had been at my going off alone to the Spin Gharr. Rightly or wrongly I was convinced that I could out-run and out-walk any tribesman, I was a competent shot and in those days people carried .303s so that provided their first shot missed one could be a hundred yards further away by the time they had reloaded and taken aim again. Therefore I just humoured him. I had three offers of shelter for the night but continued to Tarwal, arriving in a cold drizzle well after dark, having covered around thirty miles. I slipped quietly into my room but somehow A.Y.K. learnt that I was back and soon appeared with welcome tea and food and lit a fire. As we chatted, bit by bit I began to piece together the different tribes living in or passing through the area and some of the sections and clans of the Kakars. Having remained at Tarwal, unlike his three older brothers, Ahmad Yar Khan was in constant touch with local events and had a remarkable knowledge of tribal relationships and traditions. In short, he was an anthropologist's dream.

A notable inhabitant in Tarwal was Fukhruddin Khodadzai, a tough-looking, wiry, little chap in those days. As with Sheikh Rahmat, one of his uncles had been shot many years earlier, though in this case by some distant relative who alleged adultery. Now had Baitul, the allegedly wronged husband, managed to shoot the couple 'in flagrante delicto' all would have been well under tribal law and no feud follow. However, either he had muffed it in allowing the alleged culprit to escape or else he was lying and merely using the allegation as an excuse to get rid of his wife without repaying the 'wulwer' to her family. Whatever the truth, Fukhruddin's uncle fled to the Afghan border but returned about a year later, no doubt hoping or believing that tempers had cooled. He was promptly shot. Fukhruddin denied his uncle's guilt and, as his family's honour was at stake, took it upon himself to avenge him. He in turn slipped away to the border to await a suitable opportunity to shoot his enemy. After nearly two years Baitul decided to send word that, when she came of age, he would give his young twelve-year-old daughter in marriage without 'wulwer' if Fukhruddin would agree that his uncle was 'torr', literally meaning black but in that context meaning guilty, and drop the feud. For such a poor man, the opportunity to marry relatively young by simply agreeing that his dead uncle was guilty of adultery was too good to miss.

However, as the girl approached sixteen Baitul regretted his contract and secretly made plans for her to marry someone else. Not surprisingly, word of this filtered back to Fukhruddin who tried to settle the matter peacefully but Baitul was a determined man and had more close relatives to support him than had Fukhruddin. In short, Baitul felt that he could out-gun Fukhruddin and his family if it came to the crunch. So it was off once more to the border for Fukhruddin, on this occasion for a further three years, during which time he lived largely by outlawry and about which he was always very reticent. Dark rumour ascribes several other shootings to him but who knows. When ready, from an ambush at the place where the man watered his sheep in the wide Khaisor Valley, Fukhruddin shot him in the chest. Mortally wounded, Baitul took up his rifle but was too weak to do anything and Fukhruddin retreated to the border for a third time, on this occasion joining forces with Sheikh Rahmat for some six years until the early part of the Second World War when, as mentioned already, Nawab Sahib and Major Barnes toured Kakar Khorrasan along the border as was customary each summer but now with added urgency to settle any unrest there. A relative of Fukhruddin, Shinko by name, then generously gave a daughter in marriage without 'wulwer' to the son of Baitul together with two or three thousand rupees to settle the dispute. Not withstanding that settlement, made in front of a mullah, it was perhaps wise for Fukhruddin, like Sheikh Rahmat, to move to Tarwal.

As with Sheikh, this sacrifice of a dowry was a severe loss to the family and it was not until he was around fifty years of age that Fukhruddin had saved enough to gain a bride, a sixteen-year old one at that. When I was there in 1971, with Bob Chambers his happiness over his first-born son, then aged about three, knew no bounds. Twelve years later, in 1983, Newman our second son, who was then about thirteen years of age, and I took morning tea with Fukhruddin, having declined a meal as he could ill afford that sort of thing. While he was out of the tiny room something moved beneath an old, stained and crumpled jute sack on the earthen floor: I looked underneath it and was astonished to see a baby. One of his daughters, perhaps aged eleven or twelve soon joined us. She was quite handsome and, half jokingly, Fukhruddin said that Newman could have her hand without 'wulwer' when she reached sixteen. Newman failed to see the generosity of that offer, even when I pointed out that, given a good scrub and with her hair combed, genetically she had to be a winner to have survived such an impoverished environment. In 1990, I was there with my wife and Helga, a German friend of ours. Fukhruddin, then around eighty, came across to Ahmad Yar Khan's to invite us to a meal. Knowing all too well his financial state, although his four sons are good to him (one was a vaccinator, two were levies men and one a 'mirab' regulating irrigation water) and I always discreetly tuck away a few rupees in a corner, I said that just tea would be fine but upon wandering across the next morning we found a lavish breakfast of fresh 'paratas', a dozen boiled eggs ready peeled, pistachios and biscuits as well as the tea all laid out on a spotless cloth. His wife is a sturdy and wonderfully cheerful woman, with no qualms about 'purdah' and has born him twenty-one, or possibly twenty-two children, as no one seems quite sure.

But my 1958-59 holiday had to end and had been wonderful beyond words: my mind full of a whole kaleidoscope of new customs, people larger than life, almost overwhelming hospitality and awe-inspiring mountains spiced with wolves, leopards and even hyaenas. Elated and with considerable reluctance I retraced my route. As I descended the great gorge below Fort Munro towards Dera Ghazi Khan, locally referred to as 'Dijjikay', I came upon a line of camels that became so panic-stricken at the buzz of my little motor as I approached that I was obliged to cut it lest they plunge over the edge. It was not the first time that these beasts became so alarmed at that little motor yet they almost ignore trucks. From Multan, where vultures were crowding the wall of a reeking slaughter house, I made a day-night-day run as far as Ludhiana in India to make up time. There it began to rain and as I already had a severe cold I caved in and took a train to Dehra Dun via Saharanpur. I had no inkling that I would be drawn back again and again to Zhob over the years to follow and that Ahmad Yar Khan would become the next best thing to a brother, and possible better than many brothers. The three Achakzai 'maliks could have no idea what they had set in motion with their invitation. Further, with my interest thoroughly aroused, back in England six years later I would be able to buy books on Afghanistan and its borderlands and visit the India Office Library in London to find out more.

Chapter Three

An Early History of Zhob & Related Areas to 1890

The great Iranian Plateau stretches virtually from Ankara to the great ranges just west of the Indus River, a distance of around two and a half thousand miles, and at an average altitude of something like five thousand feet. The Sulaiman Range marks the eastern edge, rising to over eleven thousand feet at its northern end, and follows the Indus for almost three hundred miles before curving round westwards towards Quetta. In most places the mountains rise abruptly and dramatically from the Indus Valley, other ranges behind continuing until the main Toba-Kakar Range is met along the Afghan border, the eastern ranges having been thrust up by the Indian tectonic plate as it nudges up against the Asian plate. It is this encroachment that caused the devastating earthquake that levelled Quetta in 1935 and killed over thirty thousand people in a few minutes, lesser shakes occurring at long intervals. The bulk of Baluchistan Province lies to the south-west of Quetta and has a very sparse population of Baluch and Brahvi tribes but very few Afghans or Pashtuns. It is desert or semi-desert all the way to Iran. From Chaman border, northern Baluchistan extends vaguely nor-nor-east to the Gomal River bordering Waziristan, and south-east through Quetta, along the north side of the Bolan Pass and east to Sui then northwards along the eastern skirts of the great Sulaiman range.

Its western and central areas are populated by the Achakzais, Kakars, Tarins, Lunis and Mando Khels, all Afghan tribes ethnically, plus a few Sulaiman Khels of the Ghalzai confederation in the extreme north-west. To the east, in the northern section are the Sheranis and Musa Khels, also Afghan ethnically. South and east of them is semicircle of powerful Baluch tribes such as the Marris, Bugtis, Dombkis, Rinds, Khetrans and Gurrchanis abutting the Bolan Pass, the Sinde and the Derajat as one travels north,

The middle stretch of the Zhob Valley is approximately halfway between the eastern edge of the Sulaiman range and the Toba-Kakar range along Afghan border with lesser ranges in between. Needless to say, the people living behind such natural defences have enjoyed considerable independence over the millennia and, although the arid land was generally only suitable for flocks, at least life was generally undisturbed by the ravaging armies of the Persians, Alexander, Ghenghis Khan and the Mughals. Being semi-desert and relatively unproductive it had the advantage of being less easily negotiated by hungry armies with their hordes of followers and transport animals and it was less attractive to covetous eyes. At an average altitude of five thousand feet its summers are quite acceptable. The British moved in mainly because they feared the designs of Tsarist Russia towards India and wanted to push 'their border' as far to the west of the vulnerable plains as possible so that they could at least watch, if not actually enrol, the fiercely independent tribes of the area. In particular Zhob gave the British easy access to the Gomal River without the Waziris and Mahsuds to the north watching and waiting along their right flank, and the Gomal was a traditional migration route which the Russians might have been tempted to use in their Czarist expansion rather than the formidable Khyber and its Afridi guardians.

As the Zhob inhabitants were widely scattered over semi-desert they were less of a threat the British so that the great valley offered a less hazardous approach to the Gomal River from where any Russian advance from either Kabul or Kandahar could be intercepted. Further north, however, the real Pashtuns and Pakhtuns – the Waziris, Mahsuds, Orakzai, Bangash, Afridi and others – were less scattered, inhabited equally tough hills but with watered fertile valleys in between and were far more truculent. They could afford to be and were never really brought to heel by anyone. Also of course, a number of those tribes and the Baluchis had an uncomfortable habit of raiding the towns on the plains of what is known as the Derajat, along the right or west bank of the Indus. Further south the Baluchis raided the vast plain known as Kachi that touches the mouth of the Bolan Pass, and even the Sinde whenever funds ran short or life became boring. Naturally enough these forays irked the British administration, which had the finance, the arms and the organization to do something about it, though at a considerable cost both in money and men sometimes.

The one hundred-and-twenty-mile-long Zhob Valley is so large that its middle and lower reaches have the appearance of a plain rather than a valley. With a rainfall that probably averages less than ten inches per annum, at best it is semi-desert in spite of the Zhob River, which becomes perennial a short distance above Nissai bazaar, below which the Fakirzai River flows in from the north-west. Above that point only the occasional flash flood creates and maintains its course but until its lower reaches are met it is generally set too deep in the fine alluvial soil to be used for irrigation. Ahmad Yar Khan says that the name of the Valley derives from the place a little above Nissai where the river becomes perennial from the Pashtu words 'zhoo' and 'obah'. The Valley's upper end to the south-west has easy access to and from the Shal Valley and Quetta over a wide and fairly gentle pass, but its lower, north-eastern end is less accessible from Dera Ismail Khan and along the Gomal River, made more difficult in the past by the turbulent Sherani tribe of the Sulaiman

Mountains to the west of that town and the Wazir and Mahsuds lurking in the rugged highlands of Waziristan to the north of the river.

However, a more direct and centuries' old route between the Delhi and Kandahar than the Kachi Plain and the Bolan Pass, skirted to the east and south-east of Zhob. It was the Thal-Chotiali route which two villages are near Duki. So far, I have been able to discover very little about this route except that it seems to have passed through Kingri and Mekhtar to the east and Sanjari to the west. I presume therefore that it commenced at Dera Ghazi Khan and probably crossed the Sulaiman range near present-day Fort Munro, as does the road now. West of Sanjari I guess that the route probably went via a village called Shahrig then on to the Shal Valley. Ziarat is, or used to be before global warming, snow-bound for weeks in winter and therefore an unlikely route. At all events the route avoided Zhob, where food, forage and water supplies were extremely limited and so generally protected its inhabitants from armies invading India. There is now an alternative route from the northern reaches of the Valley through the fantastic cleft of the Chuhar Khel Dhana that slices through the Sulaiman range, just south of the Kaisar Ghar and Takht-i-Sulaiman peaks and leading via Mughal Kot and Daraban to Dera Ismail Khan.

It was reputed by local people to be a major nomad and commercial route for centuries until blocked by a rock fall some generations ago, according to Captain Crawford McFall in his book *With the Zhob Field Force*. The blockage was said to have led to the Gomal River further north, into which the Zhob river flows, becoming a major route in its stead. However, his personal account of that military expedition in 1890, when four days of tremendous effort and the liberal use of gunpowder were required to force the gorge, tends to refute the claim. Moreover, he mentions that the upper reaches had several waterfalls, eight to ten feet high but he fails to mention whether they are in the bedrock or formed from fallen or carried debris. If they are of the former type even unburdened pack animals, least of all camels, could not possibly have negotiated such obstacles. In theory such animals could have been lowered down them by ropes but unloading and reloading them each time would be a tiresome undertaking to say the least and not without serious hazard. Moreover the Sheranis of the area might be tempted by such vulnerability. By means of temporary sand bag bridges and blasting narrow ledges in the bare rock in places, the 1890 campaign managed to get camels through, again tending to refute local tradition Yet another hazard would be the risk of flash floods from the infrequent but violent storms that hit the area at intervals. To the north of the Chuhar Khel Dhana is the Kiddarzai Dhana, apparently a viable route. McFall mentions it in his book but I have no idea where it lies in relation to the three gorges named below.

Beginning in 1895 but not completing it until 1905, the British blasted a remarkable road in the sheer rock along the north side of the Chuhar Khel Dhana, well above the river bed of this tremendous cut through the mountain and I travelled by bus along it just once from Drazinda to Fort Sandeman. It is truly awesome, its almost vertical walls rising some fifteen hundred feet yet at the bottom it is said to be only ten feet wide in one place. Not surprisingly this road in the side of the gorge seems prone to blockage by storms that wash down debris from the soft, earthy conglomerate above, as a friend and I discovered in 1971. Further to the north, the spectacular Gat Tang has deep pools and is almost blocked by an immense boulder, passable only by people and then with difficulty. The Zao Tangi, the northernmost of the three defiles that cut through the Sulaiman range, can be traversed by 'lightly loaded' camels as it narrows to only six feet in one place and is generally very difficult. Both are around two thousand feet deep. I have visited neither but would dearly love to.

To the south-east of the Zhob Valley the next major valley is that of Loralai, also with deep, fine soil but blessed with a small river that is easily used for irrigation. Beyond that lies the District of Duki, much of which is less than three thousand feet and so considerably milder in winter, hence its annual influx of Shinwari, Kharoti, Dotani and other nomads from Afghanistan and a few Kakars from Kakar Khorrasan, Other members of these tribes plus Nassers and Sulaiman Khels still continue to the Derajat, in the region of D. I. Khan and D. G. Khan and some no doubt cross the Indus into the Panjab where labouring work may be found and their animals hired out for transport. Dera Fateh Khan, founded by the third brother, was destroyed by the Indus long ago. D. I. Khan can be reached fairly easily via Khajuri Kach village, where the Zhob River joins the Gomal River, and thence down the Gomal but such journeys were often under the hungry and ever watchful eyes of the Waziris and Mahsuds hovering in the hills overlooking the river, for which reason the British provided armed escorts for nomads travelling through. Of all the migrating nomads using the Gomal possibly only the Sulaiman Khels – numerous, well armed and tough – can do so with some confidence, provided they remain wary.

Volume 1 of the Baluchistan Gazetteer Series of 1907 covering the Zhob District lists seven ancient mounds in the valley, four of which I managed to locate, as described in a later chapter, but the authors were apparently unaware of another ancient mound tucked away in the low hills of the Bharat Khel clan to the south-east of the Zhob Valley. Also, in the Duki District ninety miles to the east of Zhob there are two similar mounds, one of which is truly gigantic. Presumably they are the remains of small mud-built towns and or forts inhabited over millennia and the sheer volume and quality of the often fine pottery shards scattered over such sites suggests a fairly prosperous civilization, while such concentrations of people suggests a kinder climate in the past. Unfortunately these mounds in northern Baluchistan have never been excavated professionally so that there are few direct clues as to their age but in Waziristan a mound called Sheri Khan Tarakai, not many miles from Bannu, has been systematically excavated until recently, when security halted the dig. That site pre-dates the Harappan or Indus Valley civilisation by more that fifteen hundred years and its lowest level dates from the last quarter of the fifth millennium B.C., making it around six and a quarter thousand years old and immediately following the Neolithic Age. The various pottery shards from two of the Baluchistan sites show strong similarities with those found to the north and so may date from the same period. The Gazetteer also mentioned 'rock carvings' near the village of Andrebiezh, which now at least is named Anderbez, and lies tucked away in the hills to the north-west of Hindubagh. However, they turned out to be petroglyphs, and as human figures are depicted they are pre-Muslim in age but no one seems to suggest date for them.

In 559 B.C. Cyrus the Great of Persia pushed his empire eastwards to the Indus and Darius extended it to include the Panjab, meaning 'the five waters', which vast plain gets its name from the five main rivers that both bless and curse it: the Jhelum, Chenab, Ravi, Beas and Sutlej, all flowing into the Indus. Both rulers would almost certainly have arrived via what is now Kandahar but Darius sent an explorer, Scylax, whose efforts are recorded by Heredotus, down the Indus from the Kabul River that flows into it. He is said to have forced the Khyber Pass, which rules out use of the Bolan Pass or the Thal-Chotiali route for his invasion of the Panjab.

Alexander the Great, in 327 B.C. or thereabouts, invaded the Peshawar area via Bajaur and Swat to the north of the Khyber Pass but two of his generals braved the Khyber and its Afridi guardians. Marriage to the daughter of a local chieftain probably helped Alexander, or Sikander as he is known locally, in gaining a safe passage. When sailing down the Indus to the sea, from the Jhelum it seems, and getting himself badly wounded whilst storming Multan, he would have merely fringed Baluchistan and would not have been anywhere near Zhob or Duki but a group under Krateros left the main army to travel westwards down the Helmand River and are thought to have traversed the Shal Valley, wherein Quetta lies. A Greek statue is said to have been found in the valley. If so they may well have had brushes with the Kakars on the way. Upon reaching the sea, another part of his army sailed westwards along the coast but Alexander himself is said to have crossed the Makran Desert near the coast instead and it is recorded that the group suffered terrible losses from heat and thirst on their way back to Persia. Having personally seen the gigantic sand dunes just south of the Quetta-Noh Kundl road in places, some perhaps five hundred feet high, if they extend to the coast their suffering and losses are not at all surprising. Tradition has it that earlier some of his men had settled in the north-east of Afghanistan, in Badakhshan, giving rise to the so-called Kaffirs, or the Nuristanis as they are now called. They were ruthlessly subjugated by the Kabul government in 1895, their spears and bows being no match for rifles and cannons. The evidence for this tradition seems partly to lie in their custom of using chairs, unknown elsewhere in the region until recent times but the Graeco-Bactrian coins that surface from time to time seem to confirm the tradition.

Around 200 B.C. the Graeco-Bactrians, the descendents of the Macedonians through Seleucos Nikator and others, possibly ruled Zhob nominally at least as their coins are sometimes found in the area. I have two such Indo-Greek silver coins, given me by a Kakar acquaintance many years ago. They were identified for me and date from around 100 B.C. The square one by Appollodotus has a zebu ox one side and possibly an elephant on the other, the round one by Strato has what appears to be a helmeted Alexander on one face and a figure bearing a basket of fruit on the other. I was careless in not writing down their origin at the time and my memory is doubtful but I have a strong feeling that both came from a low ancient mound near Manzai near Duki known locally as Dilera.

During the first century B.C. the Saka hordes, with their armoured cavalry, invaded the area and may have given the Afghan, Ghalzai and Pashtun tribes their basic language, Pashtu and Pakhtu, the southern and northern dialects respectively. Their relatives were the Parthians, whose archers on horseback put paid to a Roman march towards India, which ambition was not resumed, and gave the English language an expression, 'the Parthian shot'. In the third to fifth century A.D. the Sassanians of Persia again prevailed in the area at intervals but the Arabs under Qasim follow two centuries later, bringing Islam. The earliest known use of the name Afghan is by the Indian astronomer Varaha Mihira in the sixth century. Two centuries later the Chinese pilgrim Hiuen Tsiang actually visited Zhob and described the people there and one needs to remember that it was a recognized part of Afghanistan until the British wrested it from the Afghans by the treaty of Gandamak in 1879, of which more anon. It was probably too early for Islam to have been adopted there, the Arab forces taking Ghazni in A.D.644 and Kabul a year later.

In A.D.711 or 712 an Arab force invaded up the Indus in retaliation against a ruler in the Sinde who had seized an Arab ship. In another account it is claimed that some Baluchis of the Dombki tribe were responsible for the seizure. It was their first such incursion into what is now Pakistan, taking Sibi and penetrating as far as Multan, probably bringing Islam to the area. They had already invaded southern Afghanistan and Kabul roughly fifty years earlier.

In the eleventh century Al Biruni describes the Afghans as tribes inhabiting the mountains bordering India to the west as far down as the start of Sinde, where the Baluch and Brahvi tribes predominate. In the next century Mahmud of Ghazni ruled the area as a part of Persia, which he had conquered. Following that, in the thirteenth century Zhob and other parts of Baluchistan possibly came within the area raided by Ghenghis Khan, when the Persian warrior prince Jalal-u-Din was defeated and swam the Indus to escape. That was the only occasion ever when Ghenghis Khan showed mercy, forbidding his archers to shoot in recognition of the prince's valour. The river may also have saved India from the Mongol cataclysm but some authorities believe that the humid heat of the monsoon may have deterred them. Tradition has it that Ghenghis sacked Kalat to the south of Quetta from which the Brahvi chiefs ruled. I use the word Brahvi instead of Brahui, as used in all the books that I have read, as a Kakar friend's daughter is married to one. He calls himself a Brahvi, and he should know the correct name of his own tribal confederation, while Afghans and Pashtuns generally refer to them as Brahvi. I therefore suspect that originally there was an error in transliteration where someone read a V as U and that it has been copied without question ever since.

Next, in the fourteenth century, Timurlane probably ruled Zhob and Loralai; while his grandson, Pir Mohammad, led an expedition from Kandahar against the 'unruly' Afghans of the Sulaiman mountains. The troublesome Afghan tribe in question would almost certainly be the Sherani, who tend to call themselves Marani, some of whom later incurred the displeasure of the British for the same reason, though the fairly docile Tarins were also there until they later migrated to Chotiali, Harnai and Pishin. The most likely route followed would be through present day Loralai, where the thinly spread Kakars, Lunis and others would not pose a serious threat and water plus fodder were available, rather than from Ghazni via the Gumal River where an army would almost certainly attract the attention of the more concentrated, numerous and aggressive Wazir and Mahsuds. The Thal-Chotiali route, often referred to in Mughal and early British accounts and already discussed, seems to be long favoured and its southern stretches would almost certainly have been followed.

We now jump to the sixteenth century, when the army of the Mughal emperor Babur halted at Thal-Chotiali, where he had a garrison, as it returned from India. This almost certainly means that it would also have passed through what is now Duki whose original village was called Raha but renamed after Surgeon Major O. T. Duke when the garrison was set up there; or through Loralai, whose original name was Bori, which name is still used today by older people. Maps suggest a less mountainous route south-west towards Sibi but I have never been there and the Bugti and Marri Baluch tribes in the area would certainly have been a thorn in the flesh for any army straggled out in the passes there. Equally, Sibi can be an oven in summer while the Bolan Pass is ideal for tribal harassment, as the British learned when they embarked upon the First Afghan War. Later that century Babur's son and successor, Humayun, placed a Mir Sayyid Ali in charge of Raha / Duki as part of the Province of Kandahar. It would seem highly improbable that Bori / Loralai and possibly Zhob were not included as part of the Province. Raha / Duki, in addition to being more fertile, lay on the easiest and most direct route between Delhi and Kandahar. Later the Persians regain control of Kandahar, then the Afghan capital, and Quetta from the Mughals in Delhi but towards the end of the century the Emperor Akbar retook both, stationing a garrison of five hundred cavalry and a thousand infantry at Raha / Duki. Again both Bori / Loralai and Zhob were surely under his control, even though the latter's revenue would be very small. However, the Persians soon managed to re-assert their authority yet again.

In the same century, the first Englishmen to enter the region, Steel and Crowther, pass through Pishin on their way from Ajmer in the Indian Province of Rajastan to Isfahan in Persia, complaining that the tribesmen were robbers and slavers. It seems that they passed through Sanjari on the way and therefore followed the traditional Thal-Chotiali route. In the early part of the seventeenth century Sher Khan, a Tarin, became too independent and was brought to heel by the Governor of Kandahar, Ali Mardan. For a short time the Uzbeks from north of the Oxus River, under Imam Kuli, ruled Kandahar after the Persian governor fled at their approach to join the Mughals at Delhi, until the Uzbeks were driven out in 1634 by the Mughal, Shah Jehan. It was the Uzbeks first and last visit to the area and, nominally at least, Zhob might have been under them though that would have brought the Uzbeks perilously and intolerably close to the power of the Mughals. Five years later, in 1639, from Delhi Shah Jehan sent armies via Thal-Chotiali and the Bolan in an attempt to retake Kandahar from the Persians, whom he had reinstated, presumably as governors. Whether they were becoming too independent or his personal finances had improved or needed improving I do not know. He tried again in 1653 and is reported as having been opposed by the Kakars then.

In the first half of the eighteenth century a Persian brigand, Nadir Kuli Khan, gradually made himself the ruler of Persia and in 1738 or thereabouts took Kandahar, Ghazni and Kabul before raiding as far as Delhi in India, whereby he gained the Peacock Throne and the Koh-i-Nur diamond, the latter now gracing one of Britain's crowns. Kandahar was still the Afghan capital and Zhob would have been under his rule if only nominally. However, Nadir Shah, as he was later titled, was murdered by his Qizilbashi bodyguard and Ahmad Khan Abdali, an Afghan and head of another section of his personal bodyguard bravely but unsuccessfully tried to save him, then reflected that every cloud could have a silver lining and promptly stepped into the vacancy. Although Ahmad Khan's people were from the west of the country, near Herat, he looked east and north rather than west towards Persia, where he might bite off more than he could chew, and so founded the Durrani dynasty that was to create Afghanistan as a nation in its own right and hold it together for two centuries.

The later change in name from Ahmad Shah Abdali to Ahmad Shah Durrani is said to originate from his wearing a pearl ear-ring, because of which he titled himself Dur-i-Durrani or Pearl of Pearls. Keene puts forward an alternative theory that 'dauran', meaning cycle or age though in what tongue I do not know, was adopted by the tribe out of pride. In 1747 or 1748 Ahmad Shah invaded Zhob to punish some Spin Tarins (there are Tor Tarins elsewhere) in Raha / Duki who had murdered his governor. As he then conferred titles and official status upon two of the leading Kakars, Lalu Kakar and Baika Nika ('nika' means grandfather in Pashtu) of the Jogezai clan, one may guess that they had aided him in his campaign. Baika Nika, a great grandson of Joge himself, was given a gold ornament as a symbol of his authority and made 'Badshah' or king of Zhob. This appointment is important as his only son, Mukam, in turn fathered two sons, Ishak and Nawab, Ishak being the first-born. Their respective descendants today are the Ishak Kahole and Nawab Kahole sections of the Jogezai clan, between whom there has been fierce rivalry and some bloodshed, more of which later.

In 1802 Shuja ul Mulk, fleeing from Peshawar, passed through Zhob on his way to the Shall valley, where Quetta was merely a small village. Ousted from the Kabul throne for a second time, in 1813 the ever-hopeful Shah Shuja fled to his British supporters in Delhi but lost the Koh-i-Nur to the Sikhs on the way. In 1827 the remarkable but decidedly obscure Charles Masson on his way from Kandahar to Quetta, which was under Brahvi control, mentions that the Kakars raided the area at intervals. During that particular journey Masson was literally stripped of all his clothing, nearly died of cold as a result, and was only just saved from being sold as a slave by a mullah. He names his captors as being Nurzai, a tribe related to the Achakzai, but also the impressive Genealogical Tree of the Kakar Tribe drawn up by Assistant Commissioner Mir Shams Shah in 1901 lists such a clan in the Sanjar Khel section of the tribe, but frequently one finds a section or clan name shared by two or three other, distinct and independent tribes or clans. Therefore they could just as well have been Achakzais in that area, a list of whose sections and clans I do not have, and even Waziri raiders have journeyed that far south on occasion. He mentions in volume 2 of his work, *Journeys in Balochistan, Afghanistan and the Panjab etc* that in 1830 Dost Mohammad Khan, the Kabul ruler, had a Taj Mohammad Khan Kakar in his service.

Masson himself was a prodigious and enigmatic traveller for many years and made no claim to official status. He amassed vast amounts of detail, clearly was an excellent linguist and seems to have got on remarkably well with local people and their chiefs, apart from the Nurzais, as he flitted here and there between Kabul and Kalat but he makes no mention of his motives or his finances to permit such prolonged travelling. For many years I was puzzled by this until George Pottinger, in his fairly recent biography of his brave and talented forebear Eldred Pottinger, *The Afghan Connection*, states that Masson's real name was James Lewis, that he was a deserter from the East India Company's service though later pardoned, and that he was a secret agent, as was Eldred himself initially. George Pottinger casts doubt upon Masson's reliability, unlike Sir Olaf Caroe, but the remarkable man seems to have kept a thorough record of all those whom he met in Afghanistan and Baluchistan. Sylvia Mattheson in her book, *The Tigers of Baluchistan*, states that Masson was an American explorer interested in archaeology, and George Pottinger partly backs this by implying that archaeology was Masson's cover. You must make your own choice.

Having many years earlier established himself as the supreme ruler of the Sikhs in the Panjab, Ranjit Singh had grown steadily from strength to strength, capturing the Afghan dependencies of Multan in 1818, followed by Dera Ismail Khan and Kashmir three years later. He also built a fort on the west bank of the Indus at Attock as a foothold for future use. Then in 1823 he crossed the Indus, aided by Gurkha mercenaries, to defeat the combined Khattaks and Yusufzai at Nowshera, when general Mohammad Azim Khan poised on the far bank of the Kabul River refused to use his army and its cannons in support of his fellow Afghans before returning to Kabul. It was a disastrous error and Peshawar was temporarily taken. Some suggest that gold induced the Afghan general to stand aloof. Although Ranjit Singh's army soon withdrew, leaving behind a nominal Afghan governor, it was the beginning of the end for the Afghans for Peshawar, their winter capital, was finally retaken and occupied by Ranjit Singh 1834, to be held by his successors until they attacked the British, thereby provoking intervention and virtually bringing about their downfall.

Also in 1834 the exiled Shuja-ul-Mulk marched with an army through the Bolan Pass and Quetta in an attempt to retake the Kabul throne but was defeated at Kandahar by Dost Mohammad. Having bought the support of the Sikhs by ceding to them Kashmir and the Vale of Peshawar, not that either was his to cede, and presenting the Koh-i-Nur diamond to his protectors, he would have been unlikely to get much support from the Kakars or Achakzai on the way at another attempt to reinstate himself. Moreover he had been out of the country for twenty-four years so that the local population was unlikely to be ecstatic at his return but he was ever an optimist.

In 1837 the talented Lt. Eldred Pottinger mentioned above, who was only twenty six at the time, after a hazardous journey in various disguises, organised the Afghan defence of Herat and thereby saved the city from fifty thousand besieging Persians under Mohammad Shah who were being aided by General Berowski and other Russian officers with a few Russian troops. That general was killed in the fighting, a Count Simonich also joined the Russian contingent in the Persian camp, while a third Russian, Goute, almost pulled the rug from under Pottinger's feet with a last minute offer to the corrupt and venal Afghan

Wazir, Yar Mohammad. At the end of the terrible ten-month siege, during which Pottinger had to deal with the weak and debauched Shah Kamran and his devious, slave-dealing Wazir, three quarters of the population had either fled or were dead. When at last the Persians made their potentially victorious breach of the great walls, Eldred bullied the Wazir into rallying the dispirited defenders and thus saved the day. The Persians had had enough and were further encouraged to withdraw by exaggerated rumours of a British sea-borne feint on an island in the Persian Gulf. Pottinger was shortly transferred by Macnaghten who quite failed to appreciate his splendid efforts. A couple of years later Pottinger was in Kabul, where he soon found himself in another desperate situation but made an almost miraculous escape from the doomed British garrison at Charikar to that in Kabul, saving a seriously wounded colleague in the process, only to be captured during the disastrous retreat from that city and held hostage for many months.

1838-1842: in the course of the unprovoked and ill-advised First Afghan War, designed to re-seat the more compliant Shah Shuja-ul-Mulk on the Kabul throne in place of Dost Mohammad, who was by all accounts a far better man in spite of his faults, the ill-fated but grandiosely titled 'Army of the Indus' invaded Afghanistan by way of Sibi and Quetta, taking the ill-starred Shah Shuja and his six thousand Indian and Afghan levies with them. He was not a good bet for he had been deposed by his half-brother in 1809 and his attempt to retake the throne in 1834, after buying the support of the Sikhs, had failed badly. The force consisted of three armies with General Sir Henry Fane, who was i/c British government troops in India, in over-all command of the enterprise. Generals Cotton and Nott, to be met later, were 'Company men' and as such tended to look down upon British government officers such as Generals Fane and Keane, leading to friction at times which was unlikely to help matters. To bolster Shah Shuja's modest force of six thousand, there was the Bengal Army of the British East India Company, some nine and a half thousand strong and under General Sir Willoughby Cotton. Their two armies assembled at Ferozepur on the Sutlej River and marched down the river to Rohri on the Indus. The route was over a thousand miles longer than the direct route through the Khyber but the British did not wish to offend or embarrass their supposed allies, the Sikhs. The third force was the British government's Bombay Army of some five thousand, six hundred British soldiers under General Sir John Keane which landed at Karachi and marched up the Sinde, taking the opportunity to cow the somewhat defiant Sindi Amirs while passing through. However, it needs to be said that the two Sinde Amirs, who had a treaty with the British, were quite justified in their grievances against the Raj, which supported the Sikhs against them. One and a half million rupees tribute was demanded of them by the Panjab ruler, Ranjit Sing; and one million rupees were to be paid to Shah Shuja, even though the Amirs produced two deeds of release issued by the latter but which were ignored by the British. In addition to threats by Keane of enforcing payment if necessary, Sir Willowby Cotton proposed taking Hyderabad on his journey southwards, a considerable diversion, but he was over-ruled by Macnaghten and the city was saved from looting by his soldiers and camp followers. Whether the poorly treated Amirs were aware of that proposal is unclear.

The march from Ferozepur had set out with something of the air of a picnic but after crossing the Indus, the barren, dreary waste of the Kachi plain to Dadar at the entrance of the Bolan soon dispelled any such notions. Flat as a pancake and even today taking four or five hours to cross the one hundred and fifty miles or so by train, water was scarce and the British troops were issued a smaller loaf daily while the sepoys were put onto half-rations so that they all suffered dreadful thirst during the day and hunger at night. It is reputed to be one of the hottest places in Asia in summer, with temperatures sometimes soaring to 125° F or 52° C in the shade – and there was no shade. The Bolan Pass provided ample water but the troops and camp-followers numbered nearly forty thousand and the baggage was carried by no less than thirty thousand camels with the result that such a mob struggling to get through the sixty hemmed-in miles of the pass provided an irresistible opportunity for the tribes of the area who could easily disappear among their rocks when it became too hot for them militarily. The force was now severely harassed by the Baluch Bugti and Dombki tribes, as their territory abuts the Pass, but the Marri tribe seem to have done their share against the common enemy and some Brahvi joined in.

These marauders were replaced by the Afghan Kakars and Achakzais as the force continued westwards, sustaining considerable losses of supplies and animals and not a few men. It was not wise to lag behind. Amongst other things the British now discovered that the long-barrelled 'jezail' of the tribes easily out-ranged their Brown Bess muskets. Fortuitously Kandahar surrendered without a fight and such had been the general suffering that the armies halted there for two months, partly in order to recuperate and partly to wait for the local harvest to be brought in. When one reads that one particular brigadier needed no less than sixty camels for his personal baggage and that even subalterns were allowed up to forty personal servants while on campaign, one wonders how the British in India ever won a battle let alone a war in those days. But morale improved on the way to Kabul when the Ghazni citadel, defended by Dost Mohammad's able son, Haiddr Khan, and thought to be impregnable by the Afghans, was taken by storm in heroic style in just two hours to their astonishment and temporary demoralisation.

That feat was accomplished in spite of the force having complacently left its heavy siege guns at Kandahar. The mining party under Lt. Henry Durand blew up the gate with three hundred or nine hundred pounds of gunpowder (depending upon which account one reads) in spite of devastating fire from the defenders and the 'forlorn hope' led by Captain John Sturt suffered astonishingly light losses. Major General Sir Robert Sale followed with the main column and, after fearful hand-to-hand combat, the British losses totalled just seventeen dead and one hundred and sixty five wounded. Some fifty suicidal 'ghazis' were killed or captured and other Afghan dead numbered around twelve hundred, most of those defending the great gate no doubt killed by the tremendous blast, and a further three hundred wounded. Thanks for this welcome boost to morale seems mainly due to the efforts of an Indian 'munshi', a secretary or interpreter, Mohan Lal, whom we shall meet again. He bribed a disaffected nephew of the Dost to reveal that the Kabul Gate had not been fully walled up inside with mud and rocks against the expected siege, all the other gates having been rendered virtually impregnable in that way. An even greater bonus lay in the vast stores captured, just when the army's own were becoming low.

The end part of this foolish and tragic enterprise does not really concern us, though rumbles in Kabul were always heard in Zhob, but while Shah Shuja occupied the strong Bala Hissar fort in the city, the cantonment constructed outside the city for the occupying troops, possibly by General Cotton, was virtually indefensible. To almost ensure tragedy after General Keane had gone south, General Elphinstone was appointed to command the Kabul garrison when Cotton left in 1841. He was indecisive, ageing and gout-ridden and, after quarter of a century without active service, he was chosen because of his connections over the head of the blunt but competent General Nott who was actually his senior but at odds with Keane. Elphinstone, in fatal turn, was advised by the arrogant and politically ambitious Sir William Macnaghten whose role was Envoy to the Court of Shah Shuja. Sir William was a man apparently blind to events around him and totally deaf to the dire warnings of able men such as Rawlinson, the aforementioned Pottinger and others who had their ear to the ground. Lt. John Sturt was warned by the Afghans working for him of the impending uprising but Macnaghten simply ignored it. It was to cost him his life. General Keane warned Mortimer Durand of a 'signal catastrophe' in the offing.

In fairness to them, both Macnaghten and Elphinstone were seriously concerned at the obvious vulnerability of the cantonment and Elphinstone actually offered to buy surrounding land with his own money to better secure the camp but the Calcutta government under Auckland refused this generous offer yet would not provide extra money to build a strong fort on the site. Surrounded by orchards and several forts to accommodate enemy snipers and defended only by a ditch so shallow that even ponies could cross, it was a disaster waiting to happen. Almost unbelievably the stores were housed outside the actual cantonment, for which there could be no excuse. To cap it all the moody Brigadier Shelton, the second in command and formidable in battle despite having only one arm, seems to have been sloppy and disinterested to the point of insubordination at official meetings, to the disgust and demoralization of fellow officers. One source states that initially the army occupied the Bala Hissar but had to move out upon the arrival of Shah Shuja's considerable harem but that seems doubtful to me. Part of the Bengal Army, now regarded as superfluous, was sent back to India.

But there was cricket, pony racing, pukka gymkhanas, even ice skating on a frozen lake in the winter. Wines were enjoyed though not plentiful, there were complaints about the shortage of scent and soap, and the ladies held their soirées. It is a sad tale of complacency, arrogance, monumental incompetence and repeated treachery, mitigated now and then by almost suicidal acts of individual bravery. Alexander Burnes earned a reputation for enjoying the company of local ladies, allegedly lonely because their husbands had a liking for boys but nonetheless a dangerous pastime in a country where pride is so great. Whether the cuckolded husbands were enraged by this is unclear but the alcohol, the riotous parties and the liaisons were no secret and were anathema to orthodox tribesmen. The fuse was lit. Burnes and all his mission were murdered in the city, except his secretary and companion, the ever-enterprising and extraordinary Mohan Lal who somehow escaped the massacre. His vulnerable Residency had only a small bodyguard and he foolishly chose to ignore the sombre warnings of both Mohan Lal and Shah Shuja's Wazir. Then Macnaghten was treacherously murdered at a meeting with the Afghans and while one can sympathise with Akbar Khan, another son of the Dost, for the humiliation his family and the country had suffered, it was a sordid act. However, it may have been that Macnaghten was double-dealing and Akbar Khan was aware of it. Shah Shuja was to follow in due course.

The invaluable and all-hearing Mohal Lal warned of treachery at the Afghans' offer of a safe conduct yet in spite of Macnaghten's murder and that warning, and the knowledge that General Sale's brigade had to fight their way through to Gandamak when despatched towards India some ten weeks earlier (glossed over by Macnaghten as he wished to take up his appointment as Governor General), four and a half thousand troops and eleven thousand camp-followers straggled out from Kabul in January 1842 in the fullness of an Afghan winter. They had hardly any supplies of food and little ammunition. Hampered by panic-stricken camp-followers after the first devastating ambush in the Khurd Kabul pass, some disabled by snow-blindness and their muskets out-ranged by the Afghan 'jezails', the troops had little chance. The last remnant of the army made its final stand near Gandamak and died virtually to a man. Only the wounded but valiant Surgeon William Brydon, his horse also wounded and exhausted, his pistol gone and his sword shattered by a bullet, survived attack after attack as he fled from the final debacle and against all odds struggled into the British garrison at Jelalabad. Those waiting there for the retreating army were stunned.

Having earlier halved the allowances to the predatory Ghalzai tribes living astride the passes in return for their good behaviour, Macnaghten had thereby finally sealed the fate of the retreating army. Bar a handful of officers and wives and children, given or taken as hostages, a few Indian troops who filtered into Jelalabad during the next few days and four hundred Native Cavalry who deserted, the rest perished from the bullet, the sword or knife, hunger and bitter cold; or they were taken as slaves. It makes harrowing reading as recorded by the redoubtable Lady Sale in her diary, *The First Afghan War*. Whilst visiting Kabul in 1971 I saw quite a number of genuine British army and other pistols, percussion and flintlock, on sale in curio shops and most if not all dated from that time, being sold by their Afghan owners in response to demand by increasing numbers of visiting foreigners. Also more modern weapons were available from Pakistan's tribal gun factories in Durra Adam Khel and Razmak. Unfortunately I lacked the funds to collect any of these fine pieces. On the other hand, while wandering through some tiny back alley one day I came upon a man carrying a bundle of white, freshly made 'jezail stocks' and enquiries revealed that someone in Tehran had opened an old store room, found hundreds of unused flintlock actions and sold them to an enterprising Afghan. Those, fitted to the stocks I had seen and bits of iron pipe, all suitably stained or aged, would no doubt be snapped up by unsuspecting travellers.

The treacherous Akbar Khan treated his captives as best he could, no doubt encouraged by the fact that some of his own family were in British hands. His father, Dost Mohammad, had eluded his pursuers by fleeing northwards from Kabul into the protection of Amir Nasserullah Khan of Bokhara. The Uzbek

Amir was not a reliable protector, having murdered his own father, his elder brother and three younger ones. The Dost soon fell out of favour with his gruesome, bloodthirsty and slightly deranged host and, reputably disguised as a woman, only just escaped a fate similar to that of the British officer Stoddart held there. Left with little alternative he had come in to surrender. Elphinstone, after capture by the Afghans and having resigned his position without there being any replacement to hand, was completely broken in spirit as well as body and soon died from the rigours of being constantly moved from pillar to post. A severe earthquake did little to calm the remaining hostages.

Perhaps the most alarming thing for the British hostages was a chilling threat that they might be transferred to the care of, or sold to, the fearsome Amir of Bokhara to the north, bearing in mind that they almost certainly knew of the grisly imprisonment of Col. Charles Stoddart since 1839. He had been sent there to negotiate the release of some Russian prisoners and was joined later by his would-be rescuer, Captain Arthur Conolly, in the verminous pit at Bokhara and both were beheaded in 1842. On the less gloomy side, four bonny babies were born to those in captivity and one of the women, Mrs. Wade the wife of a sergeant, even had an affair with an Afghan chief. Meanwhile Pottinger, still suffering from his own wounds sustained during his breath-taking escape from the doomed garrison at Charikar before the final carnage, during which escape he had managed to bring out Lt. Houghton who had recently lost a hand and was wounded in the neck and back, negotiated skilfully and firmly on behalf of those held with him. Such were his principles that he even refused the offer of a ransom by the Calcutta government to secure their release on the grounds that it would set a bad precedent. Later, however, as the tide was turning, he did negotiate a private deal with their chief guard; a deal apparently thought up by the resourceful Mohan Lal who somehow managed to get messages through from Kabul. The deal led to their rescue near Bamian by some seven hundred friendly Qizilbashis led by Sir Richmond Shakespear. It seems to have been just in time. The hostages had been captive for eight months.

Well before that final rescue, Sale, having already disobeyed orders by remaining at Jelalabad and aided by several able officers, had reinforced its defences and defeated a determined attack by Akbar Khan's men. Equally important, in view of his scant food supplies, a sudden sortie from the fort managed to net five hundred sheep. He further risked his career by telling General Nott at Kandahar to ignore orders and remain there, instead of returning to India, prevaricating while those in Calcutta tried to make up their befuddled minds. Finally General Pollock was chosen to redeem British honour and, adopting advice given him by the Political Agent in Peshawar, Frederick Mackeson, he beat the Afridis at their own game by 'crowning the heights'; meaning the placement of troops on overlooking hilltops, thereby forcing a relatively bloodless passage through the Khyber to relieve those at Jelalabad before moving on to Kabul. At the same time Nott moved up from Kandahar. Having re-taken Kabul and 'shown the flag', wisdom prevailed and the armies soon left. Pottinger was rewarded for his decisive efforts at Herat, his rescue of a fellow officer and his crucial negotiations whilst a captive of the Afghans by a courts martial: fortunately he was exonerated. Clearly he disliked the taste of boot polish.

Returning to 1838, a temporary garrison was set up in the Shal Valley at the village of Quetta, with the agreement of the Khan of Kalat, a Brahvi of the tribal confederation of tribes unrelated to the Afghan or Baluch tribes. Also a Lieutenant Loveday was stationed in Kalat, to the south of Quetta, but his brutal and arrogant behaviour, that included setting his dogs on to people, which was also an affront to the Muslim faith, caused the Brahvis to revolt in 1840. A group of them from Mastung were to combine with Kakars and take the Quetta garrison which the British had foolishly left in a weak state. However, the Kakars believed that there was great wealth stored there and attacked early in the hope of grabbing it all for themselves but they failed. The Brahvis then invested the garrison but prompt reinforcements sent by Lt. Leech from Kandahar under a Lt. Travers, aided by some six hundred hired Achakzais on horse, saved the day. The Roman adage of 'Divide et impera' often worked like a charm and many if not most tribes were only too pleased for an opportunity to settle old scores against an offending or rival neighbour. Whether the opportunity or the payment was the greater incentive is not always easy to judge.

Dissent among the Brahvis and the defection of one of their largest contingents as a consequence then led to retreat from Quetta. The threat receded and the southern line of communication remained open. Ironically Captain Bean, who was in charge of the Quetta garrison at that time, had been planning to instigate the Kakars against their neighbours, the Marris, who had been so troublesome in the Bolan Pass. It is perhaps worth noting that while Sir Olaf Caroe speaks of Pishin tribesmen allying themselves with the Kakars against the Quetta garrison, which would suggest Tor Tarins, Masson says that it was the Brahvis from Kalat and Mastung: and he was there at the time. Incidentally, the unlovable Loveday failed to escape the uprising, was first imprisoned and then paid the ultimate price for his violent and rash behaviour. Clearly Masson had little sympathy for the man but George Pottinger's verdict is kinder. Almost needless to say, the news of the British disaster during the 1842 retreat from Kabul led to an uprising of tribes in the general area of Quetta and a small British force was routed by Kakars at Haiderzai (Gwal Haiderzai I presume) though this was soon reversed.

In 1839 a Captain Broadfoot travelled with nomads from Ghazni in Afghanistan to India, presumably along the Gomal River. In the same year, their attentions in the Bolan Pass being remembered, Dera Bugti, the main stronghold of the Bugti tribe was razed, their chief Bibrak exiled to the Sinde for three years and the Marris' main town, Kahan, was occupied by the British. However, a returning column of one hundred and sixty rifles and fifty sabres sent to get supplies somehow allowed to lag behind, or possibly left behind, eighty riflemen. Those were wiped out to a man by a Marri attack. The rest of the column was then attacked and on the Sartaf Pass their ammunition ran out and only twelve of the eighty rifles but all fifty cavalry men managed to escape to the fort at Kahan. The Marris are thought to have lost three hundred men in the engagements. The survivors of the column rejoined the one hundred and forty rifles holding the fort, supported by one field gun. The siege lasted for three months, poor water and inadequate food causing dreadful ulcers among the troops. Probably due to pressing needs for men elsewhere, unless someone seriously underestimated tribal strength, courage and ability, the relief column sent to their aid consisted of only four hundred and sixty-four rifles and thirty-four gunners with three twelve-pounders. Plagued by heat and thirst and heavily outnumbered, it was beaten back to Phuleji, losing seven officers and one hundred and seventy nine other ranks in the retreat, in addition to ninety-two wounded. Because of this the Kahan garrison was forced to surrender under a safe conduct which, unlike the Kabul one to follow, was honoured by the Marris who then left the Sinde in peace for the next ten years, until 1849, probably a measure of their own losses in these fierce encounters.

In 1840 the British stormed Kalat and the ruler, Mehrab Khan, was killed in the fighting. Shah Nawaz Khan was placed there but Mehrab Khan's son retook it next year, to be soon ousted by General Nott. However, this act seems to have been as unjust and ill-chosen as the Kabul one if Charles Masson is to be credited in his fourth volume, *Narrative of a Journey to Kalat etc.* published in 1843. The allegations against Mehrab Khan were several.

According to Masson, Alexander Burnes was deputed to arrange supplies for the Army of the Indus when it arrived in upper Sinde and a minor misunderstanding on account of the Khan's somewhat rascally brother over some grain in Kachi was misconstrued as being obstruction by the Khan. Secondly, after Burnes and the Khan had signed a treaty which, amongst other things, confirmed the Khan in his position, the small caravan carrying this document to Quetta was waylaid in the desert and the Khan was blamed; whereas it seems that one of his advisers, Mullah Hassan, was double-dealing and hatched this plot to discredit his chief. Another person accused here, said to have actually employed the robbers, was Sayyid Sherif who accompanied Burnes and wished to ingratiate himself.

Thirdly, the unfortunate Khan was accused of instigating serious raids on the columns as they negotiated the Bolan in 1838. Again, the evidence gained by Masson was that these attacks were the work of two brothers, Ghulam Khan and Khan Mohammad, wishing to avenge the execution of their brother and representing to the British that the attacks were promoted by the Khan. Lastly, the Khan did horde grain at Kalat as accused but this appears to have been on the advice of his Hindu agent, Diwan Bacha, who expected to profit from such a monopoly but in any case the accumulation of grain was begun three years earlier. To ensure the Khan's 'guilt' he had got on badly with Lt. Leech who had visited him. After the storming of the Kalat fort, letters were found in Mullah Hassan's quarters revealing his duplicity and he was arrested but the damage was done and public acknowledgement of the Khan's innocence was hardly to be expected, even if proven beyond any doubt, such was and is the nature of politics.

In 1843 the Sinde was annexed without much pretext and, although Quetta had been abandoned by the British, the veil is slowly being lifted from Zhob. At this point the dashing John Jacob, in whose honour Jacobabad is named, gallops in with a small but elite and highly mobile band of men. Personally brave, fair dealing and energetic, he chastised the Marri and Bugti tribes who were in the habit of raiding the Sinde Province from the security of their wild hills west of the Indus and north of the Bolan. He even chased their raiding parties into the hills but at the same time he won over their chiefs by his tough, straight personality and his courage. He was a sort of Sir Francis Drake on horseback. Although outside our area, it is perhaps worth remembering that in the north the Sikh Kingdom in the Panjab, reaching down to Multan and across to Bannu, with pretensions to include Sinde, was still independent although the astute and able Ranjit Singh had died in 1839, but their sun was setting as a result of internal conflicts and their second attack on the British in 1848 saw their kingdom annexed.

In 1842, upon the return of Bibrak Bugti from three years' exile in the Sinde, the tribe resumed raiding the lowlands so that in 1845 General Simpson with 7,000 troops, duly aided by some Dombkis and others, marched into their hills where their traditional enemies, the Marris, blocked their retreat so that they were severely mauled before surrendering at Tarakai Marav. The British then withdrew and the Bugtis recommenced raiding but in 1847 a 'lashkar' numbering 700 was cornered by Lt. W. Mereweather with 130 Sinde Horse near the Zamani river. Too brave for their own good, they refused offers to surrender until around 600 of their number had been killed. Unable to sustain such loss they held their peace for some years after that.

We must now jump to 1869 when, after his defeat at the hands of Sher Ali whilst trying to defend the Kabul throne of his father, Afzal, Abdur Rahman passed through Zhob on his way to Seistan on the Persian border. He had with him some three hundred followers. About two thousand Kakars barred his way at a place near Dihbring to levy a 'tax' but backed off when he made ready to fight. Later some of his horses were stolen by the followers of a man claiming to be a saint. Shah Jehan Jogezai, poorly dressed and on a worn-out horse, next appeared and led the party off course for some unknown reason but was forced to lead them to safety at night after Dost Mohammad Khan Jogezai, not the Kabul Amir but the great grandfather of Ahmad Yar Khan and his brothers, with around two thousand men tried to rob them. This about-turn was because Dost Mohammad was his mortal enemy and Shah Jehan feared for his own life. Twelve years later Abdur Rahman became the Amir of Kabul.

In 1871 a new policy in tribal relations by Sir Robert Sandeman as Agent to the Governor General resulted in good relations with the Marris and Bugtis which lasted until the Second Afghan War in 1878. Five years later, in 1876, Sandeman with a small escort took Quetta and signed a treaty with the Khan of Kalat to garrison troops there permanently. A year earlier Sandeman had saved the Khan from an attack so that the latter was under some obligation. This forward move was prompted by the Russians taking the hitherto independent kingdoms of Khiva and Bokhara north of the Oxus River and arriving almost at the gates of Herat as well. To the British rulers in Calcutta it seemed but a matter of time before Kabul went the same way. To await the Russians on the banks of the Indus was not sound strategy so the British began to edge westwards. However, this forward move greatly alarmed Sher Ali, the ruler in Kabul.

In 1878, in response to the Quetta move, Sher Ali received a Russian mission led by Colonel Stolieteff but refused a British one under Major Cavagnari, firmly stopping it halfway up the Khyber Pass. Some opinions hold that the Russian mission was thrust upon a reluctant Amir who felt unable to resist the Russian bear's diplomatic advances after the British had refused to promise aid should the Russians invade. It was the start of the Second Afghan War, the lessons of the first one having been fairly well learned by the British, though they were subsequently ignored by the Russians a century later. A three-pronged invasion of Afghanistan was mounted across the mountainous border by way of Khyber, Kurrum and Khost; while Kandahar was occupied a little later. The Afghans fought bravely but the Russians failed to support them and they were heavily out-gunned. At Gandamak, some thirty miles west of Jelalabad and where the last fighting handful of the Army of the Indus had been cut to pieces in 1842, the fighting stopped. That same year the Deputy Commissioner of Dera Ismail Khan, Major Macaulay, set out to survey the Gomal River and penetrated the passes for some thirty miles before a raid by Mahsuds on the town of Tank necessitated a hurried withdrawal. Ten years later, in 1888, a similar expedition under another District Commissioner of D. I. Khan, Mr. Ogilvie, with various officers made as they thought, financial arrangements with the tribes of the area for a safe passage up the Gomal starting from Tank but it was only a matter of days before a retreat became necessary, about which there is more anon

1879 the unfortunate Sher Ali died, to be succeeded by his son Yaqub Khan who signed the capitulation and was forced by the one-sided Treaty of Gandamak into ceding various districts in the north and west: Bajaur, Khyber, Tirah, Kurrum and most of Waziristan; and to the south: Zhob, Bori and Raha (now Loralai and Duki) plus Quetta, Sibi on the Kachi plain to the east of the highlands note and presumably the Makran desert tract as far as the Persian border. Its repercussions echoed on until recently in the Pashtunistan movement but both the Russians and the tribes now living to the east of the Durand Line, as the border is often marked on maps, must have reason to be glad of it upon reflection. Cavagnari was then received and a Residency set up in Kabul but a mutiny over lack of pay and other things by ill-disciplined Afghan soldiers back from Herat wiped it out to a man and Yaqub Khan soon abdicated. Next Ayub Khan, a brother of the ex-Amir, marched from Herat towards Kandahar with a large force at which a small British force was sent out to locate and possibly oppose it. The British were caught by surprise at Maiwand and badly battered but managed to extract their field guns. General Roberts marched from Kabul to relieve the siege of Kandahar that ensued and the British finally withdrew two years later. Thus ended another Afghan fiasco, though it was not nearly so costly as the first.

Encouraged by the Maiwand disaster of the previous year, Shah Jehan Jogezai of Zhob, a man of strong character and locally regarded by some as a saint and miracle worker, his lot much improved since his encounter with Abdur Rahman ten years earlier, with about four and a half thousand men opposed part of the British force withdrawing from Kandahar via Thal-Chotiali, which route the British planned to revive. This was at Baghao near Sanjari, south of the Zhob Valley and the Kakars were heavily defeated. Thal and Chotiali were occupied and a station promptly set up. When Cavagnari was murdered in Kabul that same year, in spite of warnings that trouble was brewing, there was renewed unrest among the Kakars.

A year later, in 1880, when Yaqub Khan abdicated his Kabul throne, a Captain Showers with an escort of Baluch Guides was murdered by members of the Kakar Panezai clan on the Uzhdapasha Pass between Hanna and Khost (not the Khost in Afghanistan), and a British post at Kach was attacked. Shah Jehan, was considered to be the instigator of these various flare-ups. He was of the Nawab Kahole and de facto head of the tribe as a whole but Dost Mohammad Khan of the rival Ishak Kahole was pressing for leadership, backed by a hereditary claim of seniority. The neighbouring Marris also joined in the fray, attacking a convey returning from Afghanistan near Kuchali on its way to Sibi, killing forty-five troops and looting a large amount of 'treasure', meaning silver and other coinage I would guess. As a result of this General MacGregor marched through their hills to teach them better manners, met little stiff resistance this time and Kahan, the Marri 'capital', was occupied once more though briefly. While there was both a political and religious element in all these flare-ups, one which gave them a touch of respectability locally, it is undoubtedly fair to say that it provided a bit of excitement for the young bloods with little else to do and provided the chance of some loot if all went well: no small incentive in such an impoverished land and perhaps enough to gain a bride. In fact it was their centuries' old practice, often adopted by sturdy hill people who have little to lose in the material sense and who are more robust physically than those living on the plains nearby.

In 1881 Sandeman settled a war between the Spin Tarins of Raha / Duki and the Utman Khel and Dumar clans of Kakars around Sanjari, thereby embarking upon his so-called Forward Policy of infiltrating step by step into the hitherto closed tribal areas. This gradual encroachment was followed up in 1883 by a local and singularly brave man in government service, Yusuf Sharif, who started from Dera Ismail Khan to survey the Gomal River secretly up as far its junction with the Zhob River. Zhob was felt to be a safer, back-door entrance to Waziristan and commanded the traditional migration route. Control of this important route by the British would allow them to thrust into Afghanistan rapidly to cut the road between Kabul and Kandahar in the event of an invasion by the Russians, either from the west and south or from the north.

In the following year, 1884, further attacks by Shah Jehan and his followers resulted in the deaths of seven coolies near Raha / Duki who were building the Dera Ghazi Khan – Pishin road. A punitive expedition was sanctioned by Calcutta and marched later that year from Thal-Chotiali against the Kakars in nearby Bori / Loralai. The force consisted of four thousand two hundred and twenty bayonets, five hundred and sixty one sabres and ten field guns commanded by Brigadier General Sir O. V. Tanner. The Bori chiefs submitted but Dost Mohammad Khan and Shah Jehan of Zhob, both Jogezais but of rival 'kaholes' or sections, refused as did the Kibzai clan and the Musa Khels, an isolated clan of the Panri tribe. The force continued over the hills to Zhob, razing Shah Jehan's fort and the village of Akhtarzai where it was situated, some ten miles north-east of Kila Saifulla. It also seized his flocks and crops, inflicting heavy losses on four to five hundred of his followers who opposed them The force went on to blow up the towers of Saifulla Khan, whose owner fled but whose name lives on as the Valley's central bazaar, and the village of Dost Mohammad Khan.

The hereditary chief of the Kakars was Shahbaz Khan of the Ishak Kahole, a cousin of Dost Mohammad Khan and a second cousin of Shah Jehan of the Nawab Kahole, but he was weak and under the latter's thumb, and had in practice relinquished the leadership to him. Heading south-west, the force clashed with the Khodadzai clan near Hindubagh, blowing up the fort of Bisharat Khan, a son-in-law of Shah Jehan, and the villages of Bisharat and Chikala before returning a hundred miles north-east to Mina Bazaar where the Kibzai clan then submitted. Leaving Zhob, the force headed west over two considerable ranges to the Musa Khel's main village where the rest of the Kibzai clan submitted. The expedition ended at Nalai near Mekhtar. Fines were imposed where resistance was met and the various tribal leaders were forced to permit the permanent stationing of troops in Zhob and Bori / Loralai, if and when the British wished. Also hostages were taken to ensure good conduct, a practice far less heinous than it may sound. Also in 1884 a military mission was sent to survey the Sherani territory at the northern extremity of the great Sulaiman range and reached the summit of the 11,300' Kaisar Ghar peak but did not attempt the lower but far more difficult Takht-i-Sulaiman adjoining it. Presumably this expedition set out from Dera Ismail Khan. In any case the veil is being lifted. The following year, 1885, Shahbaz Khan was confirmed by the British as overall chief of the tribe although Shah Jehan was clearly the leading light.

In 1886 the road from Pishin to Dera Ghazi Khan was extended. The army cantonment at Raha / Duki was transferred to Bori which was then named Loralai, presumably after the small river there as 'lora' means river in Pashtu, while posts were established at Sanjari, Mekhtar and Kingri to protect the road being constructed. This mounting pressure, coupled with an eruption of the violent feud between the two Jogezai 'kaholes', when Bungal Khan killed Shamal Khan, prompted Shah Jehan and his son Shingul Khan to surrender, the former doing so at Sibi and Shingul Khan at Quetta. This fierce feud within the Jogezai clan of the Kakar tribe is discussed in detail in Chapter Six. In the same year a Political Agent was installed at Loralai, An important feature of this is that tribal law was accepted by the British authorities, the P.A. keeping an eye on things and virtually rubber-stamping decisions and judgments reached by tribal 'jirga'. Their judgements and decisions were backed up by armed levies, recruited locally and funded by the government. Unfortunately to my mind, this system no longer obtains, officially at least. For all its possible shortcomings it was swift, it was cheap and financial bribery was virtually out of the question. It gave the poor man a chance to obtain justice, an opinion borne out by the experience of a friend Jehandar Shah as mentioned later on.

In 1887 Dost Mohammad Khan, allied with Sultan Mohammad of Mina Bazaar, carried out raids around the lower, north-eastern part of Zhob to the extent that the neighbouring Mando Khel tribe appealed to the influential Malik Urmar Khan of the Kakar Abdullazai clan to curtail their activities. He therefore gathered a force and compelled the Mina Bazaar people turn out Dost Mohammad, the latter rejoining his son Bungal Khan in the rugged mountains on the far side of the Zhob Valley. Sultan Mohammad, however, continued his attacks on road builders and others but was captured by the local 'maliks' and turned over to the British when he ventured into Murgha Kibzai village.

I do not know his fate but it was probably deportation to the Andaman Islands. The unrest continued into 1888 and Sandeman used the newly constructed road to make another tour de force in the Musa Khel area with a military escort and a picked troop of Baluch, Brahvi and Pashtun horsemen. Using recruits from other tribes of course avoided any conflict of loyalty should a skirmish occur. Faced with such a threat, all the petty chiefs submitted except Urmar Khan, but he with his family was captured after what the official report rather nicely describes as 'a spirited chase'.

At this point the 'sardar' of the Mando Khel tribe, Khanam Khan and his leading 'maliks' invited Sandeman to visit Apozai, their main village. This he did and accepted their petition to be taken under British protection. The Mando Khels would pay the revenues set but they would also be given tribal allowances to keep them happy. The reason that they asked for such protection, apart from its financial advantages to the tribal leaders, was that they were probably under pressure from their powerful neighbours to the east, the Sherani, and they had been unable to contain Dost Mohammad and his Kakar allies to the south-west. In addition it may well have been that the enclave of Sulaiman Khels in Baluchistan to their west was also difficult to handle. The Sulaiman Khels living in Afghanistan had plagued the Kakars frequently until Azim Khan Jogezai pulled off his devastating ambush of one of their raiding parties in the early 1900s and, while visiting Fort Sandeman in 1996, I was told by a Mando Khel that his tribe was currently in conflict with that pocket of Sulaiman Khels, though what was the cause I forget. As Sandeman returned from Apozai, at the village of Gwal Haiderzai, Shah Jehan asked that Zhob too be taken under British protection in return for revenues to be collected though why he and not Shahbaz Khan should negotiate is rather odd. In particular Sandeman's foray stressed the importance of Zhob as an easy, back-door to the belligerent tribe of the Takht-i-

Sulaiman, the Sherani, as well as the Gomal route that hitherto had been closed to all except tribals because of the Waziris and Mahsuds along its north bank. Further, lower Zhob commanded the several passes through the Sulaiman range to the Panjab, as yet unexplored by the British.

Earlier in 1888, In Tank arrangements were made with twelve influential 'maliks' to accompany a surveying party up the Gomal River and route as far as Khajuri Kach, where the Zhob River joins the Gomal. From there 'maliks' of the Waziri Zilli Khel clan, together with Dotani, Sulaiman Khel and Nasser clans of the Ghalzai confederation were to guarantee a safe passage for the party as far as the junction of the Kundar River and the Kundil River (called the Gomal in some maps) from Afghanistan, where they form the Gomal, the lower stretches of the Kundar today still forms a section of the Afghan / Pakistan border. All were to be paid for their services. The expedition under the D.C. of Dera Ismail Khan, Mr. Ogilvie, with Captain W. A. Wahab, Captain A. H. Mason and Lt. J. W. C. Hutchinson set out from D. I. Khan with an escort of one hundred and fifty foot soldiers. When the expedition arrived at Tank between two and three thousand hostile and armed Waziris were found to be gathered there, having heard of the arrangement, and a murder was committed by a Mahsud during the second night there. In spite of that ominous start, ten days later the party set out and reached the Gomal River that evening.

During the first night there night shots were fired into the camp, one bullet passing through the Deputy Commissioner's tent, two others through police tents. Other Mahsuds, who now appeared upon the scene, brought their number to around eight hundred and stole some of the expedition's supplies during the next day, becoming increasingly violent. Finally, despite of the presence of their 'maliks', at Nilai Kach some Mahsuds picked a fight with the Waziris accompanying the expedition, mainly no doubt because they feared that their Waziri neighbours as well as their own 'maliks' were allowing the 'ferangai' too close a look at their highland stronghold, thus betraying their long cherished 'purdah'. About a dozen men were seriously wounded in the skirmish. The expedition now recognized that discretion was the better part of valour in view of its limited strength and the belligerent mood of the tribesmen. Ordered back across the Gomal, the Mahsuds obeyed but only after a menacing pause and the party was very fortunate to enjoy a bloodless retreat.

I should mention here that, in contrast to their neighbours to the south, who strictly speaking are Afghan tribes and who have imbibed from their Baluch and Brahvi neighbours considerable regard for hereditary leadership, among the Waziris and Mahsuds traditional 'sardars' do not exist and 'maliks' hold authority in proportion to their personal courage coupled with wisdom. Among those two tribes, not to mention others further north, it is strength of character that counts, and even then it may need backing with sufficient family firepower. A slightly puzzling feature of these arrangements is the involvement of both the Sulaiman Khel and Nasser tribes, between whom a violent enmity existed and no doubt still exists today, though to a lesser degree. The extent of this traditional conflict was such that around 1900 many of the Nassers migrating along the Gomal rather than through central Zhob gave up keeping flocks because grazing in semi-desert made the dispersal of their family and village groups essential during the annual migrations and this in turn made such small groups vulnerable to attack by the powerful and predatory Sulaiman Khels, who were also better armed.

In 1889 there was a flare-up between the Mirza and Khodadzai clans which was settled by the British who then decided that the Zhob Valley had to be occupied permanently if peace were to be maintained. Therefore a force of five hundred rifles of the Bengal Infantry and four hundred and seventy sabres of the Bengal Cavalry under a Colonel Jennings, with a mountain battery from Peshawar, went down the valley to Apozai. The force, accompanied by Robert Sandeman and the D.C. for D. I. Khan, R. I. Bruce, was to deal with the Waziris across the Gomal and with the Sheranis of the Largha section that dwell in the Sulaiman range facing the Indus as they were being troublesome: raiding their neighbours and giving refuge to several outlaws. These fiercer hill tribes, together with the Mahsuds, were still in the habit of raiding the nearby lowland towns to the west of the Indus, then retreating to the security of their inaccessible hills before things became too dangerous for them.

At Apozai the Zilli Khel Waziris, Mahsuds, Dotanis and most clans of the Sherani tribe sent in representatives to the 'jirga' but the Kiddarzai clan of the Largha section of Sheranis, who occupy the north-eastern extremity of the Sulaiman range, refused and a group of them under Rani Gul fired upon Jennings near Kapip. The Mando Khels were given Rs. 25,000 for their services, a lot of money in those days but a good investment. In passing it should be mentioned that the Zhob Agency, as it was then called, in addition to the Zhob Valley covered a huge area that included Loralai, the Murgha Kibzai and Musa Khel areas to the north-east of Loralai and even Barkhan well to the south-east, which is in Khetran territory but near Baluchi lands. Finally, the force with its six hundred and forty three camels and four hundred mules continued to Khajuri Kach on the Gomal, and thence down it to Nalai Kach, completing their tour at Tank. For once the Mahsuds were on their best behaviour, in recognition of which a tax on their goods imported into British-controlled territory that had been imposed as a fine for their violent behaviour the previous year was suspended. It was the carrot following the stick. Apozai was garrisoned, the new fort and bazaar named Fort Sandeman, and Captain MacIvor, supported by a bodyguard of three hundred and fifty troops, was appointed as the first Political Agent of the newly expanded Zhob Agency that now extended all the way up the great valley to Hindubagh. Presuming that it extended from the Gomal River, the Agency spanned around one hundred and fifty miles in a straight line. The veil had now been lifted and the Zhob Levy Corps under Captain A. D. O'Mealey was created the following year, recruiting local men.

1) *Pretty young servant girl who brought lunch to Bob and me every day in Tarawal. She has a new dress for Eid.*

2) *Fukhruddin (Khodadzai) with his dearly beloved first-born son. He was aged then in his early fifties and his good wife (married at sixteen) had borne him twenty-one or twenty-two children, of whom eleven survived. A feud prevented him from marrying at a normal age.*

3) *Two Turraki well diggers from Kandahar work a windlass on Nowi Kashmir Karez. This Iranian (?) system of horizontal wells is now largely replaced by bore holes powered by electric pumps in Zhob since electricity has been led down the valley.*

4) *The young boy of the group working below ground in Nowi Kashmir Karez.*

5)   *Sheikh Rahmat (Akhterzai) in 1971, a one-time right-hand man to the chief. Although always joking outrageously, he was pragmatic and astute. He too married late because of a feud and had four sons.*

6) A British-built strong-point atop a mountain ridge approaching South Waziristan, seen when Bob and I were mistakenly allowed through Sambaza fort.

7) *A stark, fortified Mahsud home built on a bare hill in South Waziristan.*

8) Bob chatting with two schoolboys in the Hindu Kush, on the way to Mazar-i-Sharif. They became quite aggressive a while later, demanding money.

Chapter Four

An Outline History of Zhob and Related Areas after 1890

Early in 1890 there was a report that Dost Mohammad (Jogezai) and Bungal Khan his son had raised a Kakar 'lashkar', including some 'badmash' to quote official reports, meaning villains, to attack Fort Sandeman but the two hundred and fifty or so turned back at Chukan. Then there was a rumour that eight thousand Sulaiman Khels and Waziris had been instigated by Kabul to attack Fort Sandeman. However, some Waziris did attack Kajuri Kach but lost fourteen men to the defending militia composed of Mahsuds. Finally, members of the Kiddarzai clan killed Sahoo, a government servant and Sherani malik of the western Bargha section. Maliks of the Largha Sheranis, apart from the Kiddarzais, as a result of the 1889 expedition had undertaken to bring in the Kiddarzai ringleaders within six months and this they more or less managed but Murtaza Khan, the main outlaw, still held aloof and carried out further killings and robberies. These repeated pin-pricks prompted Sandeman to make a second request for an expedition to expel the two Jogezais, to curtail the Kiddarzai clan in particular and the Largha section in general, and to explore the upper reaches of Kundar River. It was granted and in 1890-91 a second and two-pronged expedition into the Sherani heartland was launched after traversing Zhob and exploring the hills to the north-west of the Valley. Titled the Zhob Field Force,

115

while its main intention was to cow the defiant Kiddarzai Sheranis, in addition Dost Mohammad and his son Bungal Khan were still raising the dust at intervals, while the Khaisor Valley situated to the north-west of the Zhob Valley was as yet unexplored by Sandeman and inviting enough to anyone with blood in their veins.

The Zhob Field Force consisted of two thousand six hundred and fifty-six troops in all under the command of General Sir George White. For anyone interested in the details of those involved and routes covered, see the appendix at the end of the book. As the country was so barren the force had to carry virtually all its food supplies and much of its fodder using government mules and camels plus hired animals, almost certainly with their handlers. The mules carried one hundred and forty pounds, the camels four hundred pounds. An intriguing detail here is that the mules are described as 'being first class and second class', the latter being given a slightly smaller grain and fodder ration even though they are not reported as carrying lighter loads. For what it's worth, my guess is that the first class ones were born of mares and therefore larger, while the others were born of female donkeys. As there had been a drought that year local supplies of maize, wheat, millet and fodder were even scarcer than usual but the army must have been aware of that beforehand. Also most of the flocks, the mainstay of the area in those days, had been sent to the more fertile areas in Musa Khel territory over the hills to the south-east of Zhob.

It is now apparent that at least some of the harsh lessons of the First Afghan War, when the baggage of General Cotton and his personal servants alone required a staggering two hundred and sixty camels and even a brigadier might use sixty, had been learnt for Captain Crawford McFall in his book on the campaign, describes his baggage allowance as being an eighty-pound tent, seventy pounds of personal effects and a meagre ten pounds for his servant's things, making a total of one hundred and sixty pounds – just over a mule load. McFall also details the men's equipment, their daily rations, ammunition and so on. British troops slept ten men to a tent while locally recruited men bivouaced in the open. With luck they may have been armed with the new Martini-Henry rifles, introduced that year, rather that the old Brown Bess muskets.

The whole operation was meticulously planned and the entire area, including the northern end of the Sulaiman range, was quartered by various columns or groups. It was so thorough that one must surmise that a great deal of information had been gathered in advance from local tribesmen from the various areas. Of course in such a barren region the population was so small and so widely scattered that, although the terrain away from the major valleys is often ideal for guerrilla warfare, the risk of serious opposition or ambush was almost nil. Further, the splendid mountain ranges of northern Baluchistan are generally separated by broad open valleys where cavalry could operate devastatingly against men on foot. Were an expedition of this nature and on the same scale to be attempted in Waziristan or the Tirah further north, it would have been risky in the extreme. An interesting political detail was that the Amir in Afghanistan was advised of the campaign lest he became alarmed at the possibility of the British grabbing yet more of his territory. Kakar Khorrasan, west of the southern arm of the Kundar River was still regarded as Afghan territory and was not traversed during the campaign even though it meant breaking off a pursuit of the two leading Jogezais.

Except for the 3rd. Baluch regiment brought up from the Sinde by train to Khanai, the last station west from Quetta at that time, the main body split into two columns to facilitate camping and to better cope with the limited water along the way. They marched from Quetta to Hindubagh in five stages and even in those days Hindubagh was an established bazaar.

McFall makes the puzzling observation that at Shina Khwar, one march beyond Hindubagh, the Royal Engineers took careful observations in order to correct their 'Quetta time' to 'local time', quote, a difference of roughly one hour he says but why local time should be different as he says I cannot fathom. Perhaps needless to say, the operation took place in October to avoid the heat.

A small group of twenty-four Baluch rifles under Captains Mason and Mackenzie was sent off from Shina Khwar northwards into the hills through the Dahna Tangi ('tangi' means gorge) to Babu China on the Fakirzai River. Its purpose was to survey the land and, if possible, cut off the two Jogezais and their followers – who would be called freedom fighters today but in those days they were simply outlaws – to the east-nor-east of the group retreating from their stronghold on Tanishpa peak in the Torr Gharr range situated north-west of the Spin Gharr range and Zhob. On the way this intercept group climbed Sakir, a peak of 10,125 feet, from where the southern and upper reaches of the Kundar River were plotted. Thence they followed down the Khaisor River to the village of China (also referred to as Jogezai Kach in the book and so it probably refers to Sharan Jogezai of today, aka Rode Jogezai. They then headed north to Tanishpa to join up with the No. 2 column under Colonel Nicholson. The H.Q. staff were also there but not their troops of No. 1 column, who had been left some twenty miles back at a place called Kuriawasta for the time being. A Kuriawasta is shown on the U.S. Army Map Service 1:1,000,000 series (sheet NI42) but is sixty miles away to the north-east so perhaps there are two such places.

From Shina Khwar the main force continued down the Zhob Valley along its left flank, where the water supply was better, with Nicholson's No.2 column a day behind the H.Q. column for a short distance until it left No. 1 column to turn north into the hills before reaching Kazha, passing Maidan Kach and other

118

villages en route to the Khaisor Valley, then down its river to 'China', for which read Sharan Jogezai. Sir Robert Sandeman and Lt. Southey of Intelligence accompanied Nicholson. The two reunited groups then advanced upon Tanishpa some eighteen miles away hoping to engage the Jogezais and their followers but found that the forty or so Kakars had fled the night before their arrival, leaving behind an old and valuable Koran that had been stolen and a few other incidentals. The stronghold was near the summit of Tanishpa peak, whose altitude is 8,800 feet, and from the front huge boulders made it safe even from artillery. Immediately a pursuit party under Lt. K. Chesney, accompanied by Lt. C. Archer and Captain I. McIvor, was sent after the fugitives. That party covered some fifty to sixty miles in fifteen hours and one horse died from exhaustion but the rebels escaped across the Kundar River, then regarded as the de facto frontier between Afghanistan and India of the Raj along its upper reaches, and the chase had to be abandoned. Further north, as explained previously, the Kundar is still the border between Afghanistan and Pakistan. In the meantime, the Tanishpa stronghold was blown up by the Sappers and nearby a mule driver named Mazulla was kidnapped by some Kakars, stripped of his warm clothing and tied to a tree overnight but as they failed to take his foraging knife he managed to escape and was found exhausted near 'China', almost certainly meaning Sharan Jogezai,.

At the same time that Mason's small party set off into the hills from Shina Khwar, the General with his H.Q. column set out on a long, dry march down the Zhob Valley to their first halt at Kazha. On the way hundreds of local tribesmen, described as being 'spread right across the valley and all armed to the teeth', galloped in to pay their respects to Sandeman who was with the column. Such a display by local tribesmen speaks well of Sandeman's personality and his dealings with them and he was said to know all the major 'maliks' by name. In four marches

No. 1 column reached the Toi River where it enters the Zhob River from the north, having diverted briefly to Ali Khan Zhaba village tucked away in a side valley for better camping and water at one halt. At the Toi the column were joined by the 18th Bengal Lancers and the 2nd Baluchis who had marched over the hills from the Loralai garrison and across the Valley. With their numbers thus swelled, the H.Q. column itself was forced to split into two groups to ease the water situation on their way up the Toi River to Sharan Kach, aka Sharan Jogezai today, and on to Kuriawasta in the wide Khaisor valley. Leaving the troops at Kuriawasta, the General and his Staff immediately went on to China where Nicholson's column had already arrived by their shorter route, as related earlier.

After remaining at Kuriawasta for five days, the H.Q. column set off on the 15th for Tanishpa, and was issued with nine days' rations and seven days' forage for the next stage; while Nicholson's lot were issued with eight days' rations and seven days' forage for theirs. Having done this, Lt. Col. Morgan with a considerable number of men was sent back down the Toi to the Zhob River and down it to Fort Sandeman with spare stores for the Takht-i-Sulaiman expedition that was to follow. Yet another but much smaller group of twenty-five Baluchi Rifles under Sub-Surveyor Asqar Ali was sent north-east via Shaighalu to Fort Sandeman to survey that route. From Tanishpa No. 2 column marched out on the 16th down the Kundar to Nigange, where the river becomes perennial, but below there the column forked right, away from the river and over to the Chukan River to eventually rejoin the H.Q. column at Gustoi War. Their last march was seventeen miles and so difficult that some camels took sixteen hours to arrive. On the way Lt. Southey and twelve sepoys left the column to explore a place called Uzhda Wazha while another small group went ahead to make a track where necessary for the camels, whose soft feet find stony or rocky going painful. The H.Q. column left Tanishpa on the 17th but followed the

Kundar most of the way to Gustoi War to meet No. 2 column. The two columns continued to Hussain Nika Ziarat, a famous shrine to be detailed elsewhere, where they received supplies from Fort Sandeman and camped two miles apart. Nearby, a grass cutter was attacked but his assailants managed to escape a group of cavalry sent after them.

Beyond this point the two columns again separated, H.Q. column continuing down the Kundar to Domandi, where it joins the Kundil to form the Gomal, at which place shots were fired at the Zhob Levies escort from Fort Sandeman which had joined the column at Hussain Nika Ziarat but no one was hit. Also at Domandi a Major Scott, who was surveying a proposed Zhob railway, joined the column with his own small escort. At Gul Kach, down the Gomal, H.Q. column with its two additional groups headed south to Fort Sandeman, diverting on the way to visit the post at Mir Ali Khel. In the meantime, from Hussain Nika Ziarat No. 2 column under Nicholson headed more or less directly for Fort Sandeman, where the entire force assembled at the station established the previous year by the village of Apozai and a bit of a show was put on to mark the end of the second phase of the expedition.

The objective of the third phase was to quell the truculent Sherani Khiddarzais. Members of the clan, led by Murtaza Khan, were shielding four alleged murderers and also had carried out raids into Zhob and on Dera Ismail Khan. Their most remote strongholds such as Namur Kalan, naively thought by their occupants to be virtually impregnable, were reached without any real fighting and the three main columns communicated by means of heliograph. This ability to co-ordinate widely separated groups of troops by such means greatly impressed and helped to overawe the Sherani maliks who had submitted and were watching events closely. The tremendous five and a half mile long Chuhar Khel Dhana gorge proved to be a difficult task and the men doing the work were allowed sixteen sheep per day to help sustain them as they sometimes worked waist-deep in icy water. McFall mentions several hot springs along its length and oil oozing from the ground that 'had a colour like that of the best Irish whisky' and burnt readily. Commenced four years later, a road was eventually blasted into the sheer rock face well above the torrent, the route taking ten years to complete.

A third force, under Colonel A. G. Ross and totalling one thousand one hundred and sixty-one troops, set out from D. I. Khan, via Daraban and Drazinda (Draban and Drazanda in McFall's account, in which several other places have different spellings or different names) and approached Mughal Kot near the lower mouth of the stupendous gorge, to meet the expedition coming down it. The party experienced sniping at intervals and lost one man, a Sikh, but there was no concerted attack, Sikhs and Gurkhas always being priority targets for tribal snipers. Their task was to bring pressure to bear on the Largha Sheranis in general along the eastern slopes of the twin peaks, Kaisar Ghar and Takht-i-Sulaiman (Soloman's Throne), outflanking and hemming them in if necessary. Murtaza Khan and his followers fled from Namur Kalan, a series of hamlets tucked away in a high valley guarded on three sides by tremendous peaks. The Khiddarzais believed that, if even an enemy managed to find and enter the easy route, they could always escape up and over the precipitous flanks of Mura Muzh behind and that the British could not tackle such a difficult obstacle to follow them. Therefore General White decided to take the place via this 'impassible' route, having already reconnoitred it the day before. It was to be an impressive performance. One hundred and thirty men of the King's Own Yorkshire Light Infantry and one hundred and seventy men of the 2nd Battalion of Baluchis set off at six in the morning, each fully equipped with rifle and forty rounds of ammunition plus greatcoat and personal bedding and three days' rations. The climb up was seventeen hundred feet and the descent three and a half thousand feet. Both were very difficult, the rear guard not reaching Namur Kalan until almost eleven o'clock at night yet the distance covered was estimated at being a mere seven miles. The Khiddarzais got the message.

When everything else had been achieved, even the Takht itself, which has an important 'ziarat' or shrine perched on a tiny ledge twenty feet down a horrendous cliff, which only the very bravest actually manage touch, was climbed up the difficult east face almost to the top. To be precise, the Manzalara Kotal at 11,000 feet was reached by six officers with fifty men of the King's Own and fifty men of the 2nd Baluchis, all fully equipped, to show the Sheranis just what the force could do. They did not attempt to scale the final summit as there was little time and the main climb took three days, whilst bivouacing in deep frost added to the strain. However, the following year Major I. MacIvor, P.A. of Zhob, and Captain A. H. McMahon not only reached and climbed down to the daunting shrine but, after a freezing bivouac on bare rock among snow patches, went on to climb all three reputably unscaleable peaks of the Takht itself. They were the first Europeans to do so, two stalwart members of Mountstuart Elphinstone's mission to Kabul in 1809, Messieurs Fraser and Harris, having tried but failed. This sort of feat not only indicates the calibre of that elite band of British officers and officials chosen to work among the turbulent tribes along the frontier but it also shows how they generally gained the respect, and often the regard as well, of their adversaries. There was no room for namby pamby administrators or bureaucrats along the N.W. Frontier. McMahon followed MacIvor as P.A. and his relationship with the leading Jogezais was excellent, so much so that A.Y.K. asked me to trace his descendants in order to make contact. However, Sir Arthur Henry McMahon, as he became, left two daughters and no son so that searches in the Kew registry, followed by letters to two possibles failed.

Finally, the Uba Khel, Hassan Khel and Chuhar Khel clans of the Large section were fined for offences committed in Zhob and Dera Ismail Khan and some 'maliks' of the Bargha section along the western flanks were rewarded for their co-operation. Having shown their capabilities and imposed a good measure of control, the expedition's regiments went their different ways, some back up the fantastic gorge, the Dera Ismail Khan force back to that town, others southwards via Vihowa to Dera Ghazi Khan and thence to Quetta, and so on.

Two years later, in 1892, the P.A. of Zhob went to the Afghan border at which the Dost Mohammad and Bungal Khan fled once more over the Kundar River into Kakar Khorrasan. Later, however, Dost Mohammad surrendered, with his two younger sons, but Bungal Khan remained in Afghanistan. Also in that year Shah Jehan died of natural causes and Dinak Khan killed Shingul Khan, at which the latter's eldest son, Mohammad Akbar, was made acting chief of the Kakars by the British mainly because Bungal Khan, who had a better claim, was still a fugitive and a tiresome one at that. One can anticipate the family conflict ahead but more on that later. Another notable event of the year was the capture of a notorious outlaw Gola, with four of his gang, to be hanged by the British for a series of murders. In the far north of the Zhob Valley that same year there was a bit of excitement when the governors of Katawaz and Mukur in Afghanistan suddenly arrived at Gul Kach with one hundred and fifty of their 'sowars' or soldiers, visiting Girdao and Sri Toi before setting up a small outpost at Gul Kach on the north bank of the Gomal River before returning to Kabul with several Waziri, Sherani and Sulaiman Khel 'maliks'. Some six months later another Afghan party under Sardar Gul Mohammad appeared at Gustoi, which was within the Zhob District, but Major MacIvor hurried to the spot with a small force of troops and levies and the Afghans withdrew, persuading a number of 'maliks' and others to accompany them to Kabul. The British promptly set up their own outpost at Gul Kach but on the south or right bank of the Gomal. At this point, the Amir of Afghanistan told Bungal Khan that he should either come to Kabul or quit Afghan territory, probably concerned that the British might eventually lose patience, cross the border in pursuit of him and then think of yet another 'forward' move.

While the above was going on Amir Abdur Rahman in Kabul had watched with growing concern the railway extension from Sukkur on the Indus through Jacobabad, Sibi and Quetta to Chaman and right on his border. Constructing the Khojak Tunnel proved to be difficult so materials for the railway were transported by road over the Khojak Pass. Although he was possibly unaware of it, during the Second Afghan War of 1878 the British had carried out a survey of four possible railway routes from Chaman to Kandahar but in any case the sheer bulk of the materials accumulated at Chaman would have given a hint of what was in mind and ring alarm bells. The first such plans were mostly lost but later on other plans, which also proposed extending the Khyber line to Dakka and Jelalabad in Afghanistan, were drawn up by the N.W. Railway in 1925 and published in 1927 as a highly detailed and technical document labelled 'secret' which I came across in the Oriental and India Office Collection, now a branch of the British Library. Whether these plans were to be presented to the Afghan government for agreement, if felt desirable, I have no idea and to this day Afghanistan lacks a railway. Amir Abdur Rahman therefore suggested that the border between Afghanistan and India, as it was, be agreed upon and properly demarcated. At the same time he renounced all claim to the territories ceded under the Treaty of Gandamak, even though they had been given up under duress. It must have been an agonising and bitter move on his part, suggesting a touch of panic and desperation but no doubt he felt powerless against the British colonial juggernaut.

In 1893 Sir Mortimer Durand met the Amir in Kabul, at which

the joint commission agreed upon the boundary between 'British India' and Afghanistan. During the 1890 campaign by the Zhob Field Force you may recall that when the two Jogezais fled across the Kundar pursuit was dropped. However, by the agreement that section of the 'Indian' border was pushed north-west to incorporate the whole of that barren, rolling plateau known as Kakar Khorrasan so that the Amir did lose yet more land. The British group worked during the next two years erecting cairns of stones at intervals to mark the border, which meant working in previously closed tribal territory, much to the resentment of the tribes, which led to frequent and fierce fighting in Waziristan where a system of forts linked by roads had to be set up in to restrain the Waziris and Mahsuds so far as possible. One of the main leaders of this resistance was the Mullah Powinda, called the 'Mad Mullah' by the British, who travelled up and down that northern border preaching 'jehad' or holy war, but that is another story and outside our area though no doubt the ripples were felt in Zhob. Also in 1893, given the earlier ultimatum by the Kabul Amir and probably influenced by the capture of Gola, which showed that the sanctuary of the wild hills could no longer be relied upon, Bungal Khan recognised the hopelessness of his struggle, surrendered and was pardoned.

He was officially recognised and made a 'sardar' or a leader of the Kakars, though not the chief of the tribe. He promised not to seek the chieftainship and kept his word until his murder fourteen years later, during which period he rendered good service to the British. Official reports on him are full of praise. That he was clearly recognised as the de facto leader of the Kakars, even by the Taimani clan living far to the west in the Siahband mountains near Herat when he was with the Commission, also does him credit. He was then useful in helping the Boundary Commission marking the border, the so-called Durand Line. As a very effective form of diplomacy, he was taken on a tour in India, where he saw buildings, communications and power beyond his wildest dreams. It was a far cry from his tangled hills and arid plains, however beautiful they might be, and he was suitably impressed. I know nothing of the background to this tour but it shows that the British respected his ability, saw that he enjoyed widespread local support and thought it worthwhile to win him over. In short, they regarded him as a troublesome foe and a useful ally.

The next decade was one of almost unremitting turmoil. Between 1892 and 1898 there were raids each year into Zhob by the Waziris, almost certainly involving Mahsuds as well, with as many as thirty-seven attacks in 1893 alone. North of the Gomal, a dawn attack by three thousand Mahsud swordsmen almost over-ran the Wana camp in 1894. In 1895 Lt. Home, the officer i/c building the Chuhel Dhana Khel road, his servant, three Zhob Levies and four coolies were murdered at their Mani Khwar camp by some Sheranis. The gang went on to murder five people in the Chuhel Dhana Sar bungalow, including a girl, before escaping into Sulaiman Khel territory and moving on to Kandahar. As seemed to happen not infrequently, an inter-clan or inter-tribal dispute entirely unconnected with the later victims was the flash point or excuse. In that case it was the abduction of a Bargha Sherani woman of the Chuhar Khel clan by some Kiddarzais of the Largha section. As much as anything else perhaps it was provoked by the delay on the part of the authorities in dealing with the dispute: in other words, it was a violent grumble that escalated. The delay, however, was due largely to an impractical administrative arrangement whereby the Bargha section of the tribe in the western part of the Sulaiman range came under Zhob jurisdiction, whereas the Largha section in the eastern part was under Dera Ismail Khan in the Derajat.

Adding to those problems, many of the Ghalzai nomads travelling along the Gomal River to and from the Derajat and Panjab were being molested. In addition, the Derajat itself along the west bank of Indus was suffering tribal incursions and the situation demanded action. Accordingly, from December 1900 to March 1902 a blockade of the two troublesome tribes, the Mahsuds and Waziris, was mounted, extending from Gustoi on the Kundar River to Domandi, where the Gomal begins, then down the Gomal, over the Zhob River and cross-country to the Zao Dhana. All trade across this line was stopped, on the simple maxim that the easiest way to many a conscience is through the pocket. At the same time, in addition to setting up strong points at strategic intervals, migrating nomads were escorted from the Afghan border by Zhob Levies to a large, guarded camping ground at Gul Kach, then on to Kajuri Kach and Tor Khulla where the South Waziristan Militia took over. Their caravans on other migration routes in north-eastern Zhob were similarly guarded and roads greatly improved to a width of nine feet in places. The official report mentions that the Zhob Levies suffered severely from scurvy, pneumonia, fever and diarrhoea.

When the blockade ended, it seems that the Mahsuds managed to control their predatory impulses for a while but the Sheranis did not, with Ahmad Khan killing Arbab Farid Khan, the Extra Assistant Commissioner to the Largha section; while a gang of thirteen shot a trader and burnt his shop in Dhana Sar at the head of the pass but they were too slow in escaping and were wiped out to a man. Although the 1900-02 blockade was successful to a large extent in settling the area, in the following year a gang of fifteen Mahsuds and Sheranis attacked the Khuni Burj Levy Post, killing two levies and making off with thirteen greatly coveted rifles. Also in 1903 the Thal-Chotiali Agency was dissolved to become part of the Sibi District. A new Loralai District that included Sanjari, Duki, Musa Khel (previously part of the Zhob District) and Barkhan was created.

1906 brings us almost to a surviving generation for Sher Ali Khan, a brother of Nawab Mohammad Khan and last surviving son of Bungal Khan, died a year or two after my wife, a German friend of ours and I had dinner with him at his 'kila' in 1990.

At the 1906 'jirga' held in Kila Saifulla, the 'Acting Sardar' of the tribe, Mohammad Akbar Khan of the Nawab Kahole publicly insulted the Ishak Kahole. He was promptly shot and wounded by Zarif Khan whose his father, Bungal Khan, was killed in the ensuing fracas, the full details of which are in the next chapter. In 1907 Zarif Khan was made chief of the Kakars but died shortly of natural causes. Ahmad Yar Khan told me that it was probably a brain tumour, whereas Jehandar Shah believed that T.B. was the cause but at least it was natural. He was succeeded by his brother, Mohammad Khan, who was next in line and who remained chief until 1978. Mohammad Khan also had a strong personality, was physically strong, energetic and industrious, and politically astute. Begetting in the fullness of time ten surviving sons, and seven daughters I believe, most or many of whose marriages would ensure outside support (although there is a family tendency to marry first cousins) put the chief's immediate family in an even more powerful and secure position and one which it still enjoys. Also in 1907 Britain and Russia agreed in St. Petersburg that Afghanistan should be a buffer state between them and, while Britain was to remain in control of Afghan foreign policy, it undertook not to annexe the country

Linking with the broad gauge line at Khanai, the narrow gauge railway to the chromite mines near Hindubagh was laid in 1910/1911 and subsequently extended northwards down the valley, finally reaching Fort Sandeman in 1927. The Great War of 1914-1918: resulted in some of the older, experienced British officers being transferred to the fronts in Europe and the border tribes, ever watching for the slightest sign or hint of weakness, began to feel that the time was ripe for a few raids. For the Waziris and Mahsuds of course it had always been a case of "business as usual", so far as it was possible of course, but the tribes to the south of Waziristan – the Sherani, Mando Khel, Kakar, Musa Khel, Luni, Tarins plus the Marri, Bugti and other Baluch tribes – had been fairly quiet for some time. However, as the struggle in Europe progressed year by year, the tribes began to think that the hitherto almost invincible British might not be so invincible after all and things began to change. Sawan of the Musa Khel, his son and brothers clan carried out a series of raids between Fort Sandeman and Murgha Kibzai until they were captured and hanged in Loralai.

Next, in 1916 the Bijrani clan of the Marris, well to the south of Zhob, moved north to loot sheep and camels from nomads wintering near Loralai. Even in 1971, when I was at the Ghabar Ghar nomad wintering ground some thirty miles east of Loralai, two days earlier a party of Baluchis had rustled a flock of sheep belonging to Shinwaris camped a few miles away. In response to the 1916 raid by Marris, the P.A. of Sibi headed for Gumbooz but the pass over to Kohlu was blocked by three thousand unspecified Baluchis who then attacked the Gumbooz fort. The fort was manned by only fifty sabres, reinforced by a few police, but they just managed to hold out and the Marris among the besiegers lost a thousand men in the desperate battle. The 'tehsil' or administrative centre in Kohlu was torched in 1918 and then a 'remount' train was attacked on the Harnai line. At Fort Munro the Post Office was burnt to the ground and the 'thana' or police post was attacked. This time the Baluchis were aided by Khetrans who decided to join in and as Fort Munro is either in or very near Gurchani clan territory that Baluch clan may have been the main culprit. For good measure the Barkhan 'tehsil' was plundered, telegraph lines were cut and military pickets on the Harnai-Loralai road were attacked. In response to all these events a punitive expedition was launched against the Khetrans, who claim to belong to the Baluch confederation but who are probably a mixture of genuine Baluchis, Jats from the plains and Afghans. They soon capitulated but the Marris responded by derailing a goods train above Babar Kach, killing several staff, though whether their deaths were accidental or from shooting is not made clear in the official report. Things finally came to a head that year when a large Marri 'lashkar' was routed near Mamand, following which their chief 'sardar' submitted four days later.

In 1919 the brief Third Afghan War took place, instigated this time by the Afghans. It was a serious misjudgement on their part, leading to further losses of tribal territory to what was then British India and which now forms part of Pakistan. Habibullah, the Kabul Amir, was murdered because of his progressive reforms and Western ways and his third son, Amanullah Khan, seized the throne. To what extent, if any, a subversive team of Germans and Turks under Oskar von Niedermayer was involved in this affair seems unknown. Suffice to say that, in order to enter Afghanistan and foment a 'jehad' or holy war against the British in India, the team had cleverly managed to outwit a Russo-British cordon in Iran. Be that as it may, Amanullah Khan felt that the time was opportune to attack the British, pinning his hopes on the disturbances throughout India at that time, and laid claim to a small patch of land in the Khyber as a provocation but informers warned the British of his plans to attack via the Khyber, Kurrum and Quetta. No doubt he also reasoned that the British were both war-weary and weakened from their efforts in Europe and many experienced British officers were retiring from service. Such an adventure would strengthen his new position at home, he might even regain some of the territory ceded at Gandamak in 1879, and the border tribes would surely rally to his cause. However, the tribes failed to come to his aid and the British now had warplanes, though the impact of these was probably far more psychological than physical. After a month the Afghans sued for peace but the repercussions were felt in Waziristan and Zhob and were quite serious for the British. However, the bitter pill of defeat was sugared by control of foreign affairs being handed back to the Afghans after forty years of that humiliation.

The year 1919 was to be a frantic one for the British. The more northerly tribal areas of Waziristan, the Tirah, Khyber and Bajaur, in what was still India and hugging the border, were always tinderboxes just waiting for a chance spark to ignite one or other. In this case the spark was an Afghan Brigadier, Shah Daula, who entered Waziristan and suggested that the British were about to withdraw from that Province. Then a rumour that four Afghan battalions were somewhere to the north of Kajuri Kach created alarm among the British who responded by moving two hundred Gurkhas, always hated by the tribes and tortured horribly if captured, from Harnai to Fort Sandeman; while a machine gun company was sent to Loralai. They were deeply concerned at the possibility of a determined invasion via Kammaruddin Karez in Kakar Khorrasan or via Gul Kach on the Gomal. However, while the Afghans did invade, it was Waziristan instead of Baluchistan, though how many were involved I do not know, and they penetrated as far as far as Nilai Kach and Sarwekai. Faced with the unrest and mounting hostility among the local tribes, Major Russell was ordered to evacuate the key post of Wana and six hundred Waziri and Afridi militiamen mutinied, so that they and the exultant attacking Waziris managed to lay their hands on the post's Treasury, twelve hundred modern rifles, possibly Lee-Metfords that were introduced in 1907, and seven hundred thousand rounds. To the tribesmen it was the stuff that dreams are made of for it levelled the playing field considerably. Also the posts along the Gomal were evacuated and, for once, few if any Mahsuds were involved. However, five days later the Mahsuds, assisted by Waziris, attacked Jandola. The subsequent army relief column suffered two thousand casualties, which included forty-three officers killed.

For the Major, his six officers and three hundred loyal militia men from the Wana post it was the beginning of a nightmare. After a desperate day-long running fight over forty-two miles of difficult terrain, they managed to reach Mughal Kot in lower Zhob, the one west of the Sulaiman range, not that below the eastern mouth of the Chuhar Khel Dhana. There they were joined by the Zhob Militia and rested for two nights. One can picture the exultant tribesmen streaming along ridges on either side, stopping now and again to fire with their newly acquired modern weapons upon the fleeing group then sprinting on to new positions. To make matters worse the retreating party would be slowed by taking the wounded with them, for to abandon them would be to sentence them to frightful torture by the Waziris or Mahsuds before death, a vital factor in maintaining morale under such intense and continuous attack. I should add that such a practice was not the custom of the Kakars, Mando Khels, Sheranis and others in Baluchistan. Only good training and firm discipline saved the group from total annihilation.

After their arrival at Mughal Kot, the post was soon invested by a large force of Waziris and the retreating group should have pressed on the next fifty miles to Fort Sandeman the following morning but they were too exhausted from their recent ordeal. This allowed Waziri reinforcements to arrive and the situation became critical, for the survivors had only one day's rations left and the water supply was situated outside the fort and exposed to enemy fire. To cap it all the expected relief force from Fort Sandeman (presumably summoned by heliograph) failed to arrive on the second morning as requested. The bleak decision was taken to cut their way out through the ring of tribesmen, who rarely lack sound strategy or good aim. Having set fire to the post to deny it to their pursuers, under constant and heavy fire with men dropping frequently, the retreat became a rout. The main group pressed on south towards Fort Sandeman, some small groups retreated towards the Derajat, and others just laid down their arms and fled as best they could, simply deserting. However, after four or five miles the desperate remnants met the Zhob Militia coming to their aid and those survivors reached Fort Sandeman. Even so, five of the officers were killed, the remaining two wounded and forty other ranks either killed or wounded.

In the meantime, believing that Fort Sandeman would also

be abandoned, many Sheranis and Mando Khels joined the fray while numerous Kakars of the Zhob Militia deserted. On the other hand there were examples of almost astonishing loyalty, as in the case of Subadar Major Ghulam Khan who marched a small force of men sixty miles in pursuit of Subadar Haji Mir and ten fellow deserters. When Ghulam Khan and his men finally caught up with the deserters in a village they shot every one. Lt. Col. Paul i/c the Zhob Militia now saw that the uprising was both serious and widespread and wisely pulled in the regular Gurkhas from their barracks outside the perimeter camp covering the fort proper at Fort Sandeman. He also ordered in the posts along the road to Mani Khwar but fortunately rescinded that order after further consideration. The Adozai garrison retired to Lakaband but returned to their post that same evening. A serious turn was when the Mani Khwar post fell to a mere two hundred and fifty Sheranis. The militia there consisted of Ghalzais from Afghanistan, according to the official account, which I find difficult to understand. Be that as it may, they surrendered tamely to the attackers, duly encouraged by the exhortations of a mullah. Their three Indian officers who fled to Fort Sandeman claimed that a 'charm' had been put upon their rifles. This loss was followed by a report that Kapip had also fallen. It was only a rumour but the both the Babar and Gwal garrisons were withdrawn to the Lakaband post as a precaution.

At this juncture two British officers with two hundred Gurkhas arrived at Zarozai, presumably from Loralai, accompanied by forty-five mounted Zhob Militia. They continued to Fort Sandeman, avoiding Kapip, where the rumoured victorious tribals would have captured modern weapons and thus be far more dangerous. After passing Adozai and Arangzai, fifteen miles south of Fort Sandeman, the men were becoming exhausted from lack of food and little water: it was now June and hot. When only six miles from relative safety they were attacked from two hillocks, one on either side of the dirt road. One hillock was taken but the tribesmen held the other until fifty mounted infantry and fifty Gurkhas from Fort Sandeman appeared and captured it, earlier heliograph communication to request help having been impossible, probably due to intervening high ground rather than because of cloud.

'Local tribesmen', presumably Mando Khels and Sheranis but possibly including Kakars, looted and burnt the bazaar at Fort Sandeman and there was continuous sniping at the camp until seventy Zhob Militia men, covered by long-range machine gun fire, drove off the hostiles from nearby hills killing ten for the loss of one of their own men. This action was followed up by the dispatch of two hundred rifles to relieve the post at Kakip, earlier rumoured to have fallen. The Kakip garrison was sent back to Fort Sandeman and was attacked by some two hundred hostiles but those were easily driven off, losing nine of their number. Upon learning of all these disturbances Quetta sent reinforcements to Manikhwar under Brig. Gen. H. de C. O'Grady, from where it was to have moved on to Fort Sandeman but in view of the limited water supply there it went only as far as Kapip. A search of the area revealed that the Waziris and Sheranis had gone home. The traditional weakness of all tribal 'lashkars' is the total lack of an organised commissariat, each man carrying his own dry rations for four or five days tied in a corner of his shawl so that unless he can loot food within that period he is simply forced to head for home. The force then retired to Loralai via the Zhob Valley, destroying hostile villages and confiscating their stores.

Still in 1919, July saw an ambush on a convoy near Kakip by a body of Sheranis, during which the attackers lost no fewer that thirty of their number. Later that month a 'lashkar' of around seven hundred Kakars of the Abdullazai clan and Waziris attacked the temporary camp at Lakaband. This was followed by an attack involving an estimated eight to nine hundred Waziris on a convoy just beyond Babar travelling from Lakaband to

Drewal. The convoy retreated to the ruins of Babar fort and there split, leaving eighty men with two Lewis machine guns while a small group under Captain Godden tried again to reach Dewal. The officer was killed just two miles short of the post, the men gave up and the mules stampeded. The officer at Drewal, Lt. Daws, saw the mules gallop past hotly pursued by eager tribesmen and, having only forty rifles at his disposal, promptly retired to Lakaband virtually unmolested while the Waziris were busy capturing the animals before pausing to loot the tented camp which the group had just abandoned. While this was going on the eighty men under two Indian officers remaining at Babar managed to hold off five to six hundred hostiles surrounding the fort – or what was left of it – for seven hours until relieved by a body from Fort Sandeman. The Waziris and others left thirty dead. It had been a close-run affair and the entire force headed north along the road for Fort Sandeman. Near Kapip three men dressed as Gurkhas were seen but upon being approached by one of the officers they shot and fatally wounded him. The enemy then appeared on both sides of the gorge and in spite of artillery support three officers were soon killed (Captain Copeland, Lt. Dobbin and Lt. French); Lt. Gilbert being the only British officer remaining. At dusk the Waziris and Sheranis, with some Sulaiman Khels from Afghanistan, rushed the small force but the two field guns were put out of action before the convoy was taken, at which the surviving officer beat a retreat with fifteen men that he had collected. Other ranks killed in this costly engagement numbered forty-nine while sixty-nine were wounded.

Things were coming to a boil and in late July seven hundred tribesmen again attacked Fort Sandeman, their number increasing to around four thousand during the next few days. Mainly they would have been Waziris and Mahsuds but members of local tribes probably joined the fray. Non-belligerents outside the camp and fort would know the precise identity of the besiegers and other details rather than those holed up in the fort and fighting for their very lives. On this occasion a plane from Quetta bombed the 'lashkars' encampment then landed by the town to refuel before returning to Quetta. Fortunately for the British, inter-tribal rivalry and jealousy coupled with mutual mistrust, prevented a co-ordinated mass attack on the perimeter and fort: otherwise the outcome might have been very different. As it was, the situation at one stage became desperate and this was the occasion when, according to Ahmad Yar Khan, one of the officers had the inspiration to open all the stables and chase the animals out into the countryside as a lure to distract the besiegers. Few tribesmen could resist fine horseflesh simply asking to be caught. It worked perfectly and the crisis passed. The official report, however, blandly states that 'eighty-five horses and twelve mules were lost' but A.Y.K. is very reliable and I will settle for his account. A mobile column coming in from Mani Khwar to aid Fort Sandeman was unopposed and it was the last major flare-up.

While Zhobis in the lower or north-eastern part of the Valley were apparently involved in some of the battles, hence the razing of several villages in the Valley as mentioned above, Loralai District was relatively calm throughout this turbulent period though minor skirmishes took place at intervals. When one reads that between Peshawar and Dera Ismail Khan the 1919-1920 period saw no less than six hundred raids involving three hundred murders, four hundred victims wounded and four hundred and sixty-three kidnaps it gives some idea of the unrest that also took place along the more northerly part of the tribal belt. Many English politicians of a left-wing nature and liberals today tend to castigate British actions in what was India as aggressive and brutal but those at the receiving end of such raids by tribesmen – meaning unarmed farmers, traders, shopkeepers and local officials – almost certainly held a very different view.

In 1920 a party of U.S. oil prospectors under a Mr. Howell was fired upon by Baluchis near Ruckni, killing him and a clerk, while the following year saw several incidents. In one of these, around three hundred Kharoti and Sulaiman Khel cross-border nomads led by Sher Jan Kharoti carried out a raid near Mekhtar, ambushing a military patrol and killing two, but they were over-ambitious, attacked Mekhtar itself and were driven off with the loss of ten men. Some Ghorezais raided the outskirts of Loralai bazaar but lost one dead, one wounded and five captured so that it was not their day either. Perhaps unwilling to be regarded as faint-hearted some 'Zhobis', therefore Kakars, raided Smallan bazaar near Sanjari but seem to have fared rather better than the two previous groups. At Rizgai, between Harnai and Loralai, a gang of between thirty and forty men held up traffic until driven off by a military patrol; while Captain Bright, a veterinary officer, was killed by a group of Mardanzai Kakars and Machezais (whom I cannot trace) on the Dilkhuna Pass, most of whom were soon shot or captured. All in all there was hardly a dull moment for the authorities, whether civilian or military.

The year 1922 witnessed a raid near Zirra by Sulaiman Khels but nearby Malik Ghunduk Khan of Loralai and a party of Khodadzai Kakars (Fukhruddin's clan) drove off a group of raiders, killing one and retrieving twenty-three donkeys that had been stolen. The Dilkhuna Pass was again the scene of an ambush in which Captain Baker Jones was killed and the P.A. of Zhob, Major Finnis, was ambushed and fatally wounded on his way to a 'jirga' to be held at Mani Khwar. Two years later Amanullah invited the Russians to send advisers to set up a Royal Afghan Air Force but in 1928 he was deposed as his reforms also were too progressive and proved unpopular, especially his emancipation of women, at which a Tajik soldier of fortune or brigand, Habibullah Kakkani, who became known as Bacha-i-Saqao, seized Kabul. There followed a nine-month reign of terror at his hands and at those of his followers until General Nadar Khan, a distant cousin of the lawful Habibullah, returned from Europe to set things right. Although his attempts to enlist the aid of the Afridis and Orakzais east of the Durand Line to secure his position in Kabul were thwarted by the British so far as possible, the Mahsuds and Wazir rallied, drove out the frightful Bacha-i-Saqao the following year and seated Nadar Khan on the throne. After only four years Nadar Khan was assassinated in 1933 and his son, Mohammad Zahir, took over.

To the north, in 1923, Ajab Khan, his brother and two or three other Afridis kidnapped a young girl, Mollie Ellis, from Kohat after killing her doctor father and cutting her mother's throat because the son of one of his men had converted to Christianity after being treated in Peshawar's missionary hospital. The gang and their hostage fled to Khani Bazaar in the Tirah. To avoid a major campaign, Lilian Starr, a missionary nurse volunteered to accompany a group of about forty 'Tirahwals' under political officer Moghul Baz Khan, an Afridi of the powerful Kuki Khel clan, to negotiate her release, Lilian's role being to comfort the terrified girl. The negotiations were difficult but successful and the girl brought back unharmed though orphaned.

In 1935 a devastating earthquake struck Quetta, almost destroying the town and killing upward of thirty thousand people. Roughly a year later a Hindu girl was kidnapped from an unspecified 'settled area', perhaps Kohat, Bannu or D. I. Khan, and spirited away to Waziristan where she was converted into Islam, no doubt to be married to a local Mahsud who either lacked 'wulwer' to do things in the usual way or simply wanted to save money. A court hearing pronounced this illegal and, quite rightly but optimistically, demanded her return. Almost needless to say that did not happen and a virtually unknown Waziri mullah, 'Haji' Mirza Ali Khan of the Tori Khel clan in the tiny tribal town of Ipi in the hills, began to stir up demonstrations and then attacks on strategic installations. He is said to have been encouraged by the Nazis but demanded too much money. In turn Mirza Ali Khan soon became a thorn in the flesh for the British authorities, becoming known as the Fakir of Ipi. He gathered a strong following among his fellow Waziris so that military operations were mounted to try to catch him. This time the British made extensive use of aircraft to bomb his headquarters' cave near Arsal Kot village in the mountains and destroy other villages regarded as being involved. Warning leaflets were dropped before such attacks on villages but most Mahsuds and Wazir were illiterate so that many women and children are reported to have been killed. It caused considerable bitterness among the tribes people and also was considered by them as being against the usual rules and rather unsporting. The man died of natural causes in 1960 according to Victoria Schofield in her book.

In 1940 the Political Agent for Zhob, Major Barnes, was shot dead in Fort Sandeman by Sher Jan, one of the Jogezai clan but from Sharan Jogezai in Khaisor, not Zhob. Escape was impossible and Sher Jan was duly tried and hanged, at which his six brothers, including Nasserullah Jan, Sher Ali (not the Zhob one) and Musa Khan with all whom I stayed in 1960, took to the hills for nine years. As might be expected Sher Jan became a local hero and passes in the folklore of the area with a song in his memory. Independence took place in 1947, swiftly followed by Partition into India, West Pakistan and East Pakistan, at which Baluchistan opted to be part of the latter, though the Achakzai 'sardars' were in favour of remaining with India while the Brahvi leader was for complete independence. Nawab Mohammad Khan was a prime mover in this opting to become part of Pakistan. Two years after that, Afghanistan began demanding an independent Pashtunistan state for Pashtu and Pakhtu speakers, a move leading to many repercussions. However it seems unlikely that their own Pashtun and Pakhtun areas, about which the Afghan leaders maintained a deafening silence, would be included in any such new state. The new Pakistani authorities fared no better than their British predecessors in capturing the shadowy Jogezai brothers as they flitted here and there in the wild hills and after two years they were not only granted an amnesty but a monthly pension, to be shared, in return for good behaviour. I find the idea of their being 'pensioned outlaws' rather novel.

In 1951 Liaquat Ali, the President of Pakistan, was assassinated and Mirza succeeded him, standing down after seven years when, prompted by widespread corruption and a gradual breakdown of government, Martial Law was declared in 1958 by General Ayub Khan, a Tor Tarin, and I happened to reach Pakistan just as these events were taking place. In response to the Pashtunistan Movement emanating largely from Afghanistan, the border with that country was soon closed and the huge nomad migrations dating back centuries, if not millennia, were stifled though not completely stopped by any means, as such a long, isolated and often mountainous border cannot be fully closed. Three years later Pakistan severed diplomatic relations with Afghanistan over the issue, in 1962 Martial Law ended and Basic Democracy was established. Elections in 1965 confirmed Ayub Khan as President for a further five years while irregular forces crossed from Pakistan into Kashmir whose Hindu ruler, Hari Singh, had opted to join India at Independence in 1947 although eighty per cent or so of his subjects were Muslim. However, in 1968 the limitations of the franchise under Basic Democracy lead to riots by students and members of the intelligentsia, Ayub Khan resigned and Yaqub Khan his successor immediately re-imposed Martial Law.

The 1971 elections in East Pakistan on the far side of India were held invalid by the authorities in West Pakistan, who sent in troops. Amid appalling bloodshed, ten million refugees fled into India, which then intervened and an independent Bangladesh state was created as a result. Yahiya Khan resigned and Ali Bhutto took over, only to be executed in 1979 and followed by General Zia ul Haq. The general died in a mysterious plane crash but the popular explanation in Quetta and Zhob at the time was that a member of his party boarded the plane bearing a box of mangoes, then promptly decided to transfer to another plane but left behind his box of mangoes.

Over the border, in Afghanistan, in 1963 Mohammad Daud Khan, Prime Minister of Afghanistan and cousin of the king Zahir Shah, resigned and diplomatic relations with Pakistan were restored. Ten years later Zahir Shah, whilst in Europe and in keeping with the Afghan and Pashtun 'tarboor' tradition whereby your fraternal cousin is often your worst enemy, was replaced by his cousin Daud and remained in Italy in exile. After more than two centuries he was the last of the Durrani line, but Daud in turn would rule only for five years until 1978 when, in the singularly bloody massacre of himself and most of his family including young children, he in turn was overthrown by Tarraki. A couple of months later, being out of touch with news after driving overland from England to Mazar-i-Sharif in the north of Afghanistan with two senior boys and two senior girls from my school plus our young son James, as we returned to Kabul on our way home we were unaware of further tensions caused by the attempted return of one of Tarraki's men sent abroad to be out of the way. The troops were very edgy but, being able to speak Farsi at three road blocks leading into the city, in spite of levelled Kalashnikovs, we experienced no trouble. The rather surprising thing was that no one in Mazar – in our hotal or when changing travellers' cheques in the bank or when buying rugs – mentioned the new unease. Perhaps they were simply disinterested, having seen it all before?

Only a year later Hafizullah Amin, hitherto Tarraki's right-hand man, skilfully shot his way out of an ambush by Tarraki that wiped out his bodyguard and managed to turn the tables on his boss, who was then strangled or suffocated with Russian connivance. However, the Afghan army suffered mass desertions and was unable to quell the popular uprisings throughout the country, while Hafizullah Amin turned out to be too independent for the liking of his Russian sponsors. Therefore during the very last days of 1979 the Russians invaded and hatched a plot to drug and remove him quietly. This was bungled and Amin escaped briefly but after a stiff gunfight he was killed, to be replaced by Babrak Karmal brought back from Russia. Karmal, having also aroused the hostility of his fellow countrymen, became regarded by the Russians as a liability and was removed by them in 1986, bloodlessly by way of a change, and Najibullah was installed in his stead. Uneasy has lain every head that wore the crown in Kabul for centuries but one is forced to admire the sublime optimism of these recent ones who have grabbed the big chair in the capital one way or another. The 1988 withdrawal of the Russians did not witness the collapse of the Afghan government and army, to the surprise of most, but Najibullah did not try too hard to hold on in Kabul. For those interested, George Arney's book *Afghanistan* details minutely the above convolutions in Kabul.

I hoped that better fortune would attend Ahmad Shah Mahsud once the Russians left but warlords in different parts of the country selfishly vied for power and let in the Taliban. The assassination of Mahsud removed the one strong bulwark against those outsiders and their local allies. He was educated, courageous, a good war strategist, an able organiser and untainted by corruption but he was a Tajik and as such it was unlikely that he would have been accepted by the Pashtuns. Years ago, while the 'mujahuddin' were still fighting the Russians, when I extolled what I considered to be his virtues to intelligent, rational and tolerant Kakar friends they agreed with all the points I made then pointed out to me, with well-meant regret, "But he is a Tajik."

The 1979-88 Russian occupation of Afghanistan devastated the country and almost a quarter of the population fled, roughly one million refugees westwards into Iran and around three million eastwards into Pakistan. Of these Zhob had its share, with a huge camp sprawling out from a barren side valley onto the Zhob plain a few miles east of Hindubagh – since renamed Muslimbagh by some bigoted bureaucrat and in any case A.Y.K.

insists that its original name was Hindobagh. At first there were only tents there but gradually houses replaced them and the place had almost a permanent air when I last saw it in 1999 although many had returned home but the water supply is very limited, both for agricultural and domestic purposes, so it is not a viable township. A smaller camp lay over the hills near Loralai close by the road to Kila Saifulla while Pishin, which is a little outside our area, also had thousands of these destitute people. Also there was an unofficial camp near Kuchlagh on the Quetta-Chaman road, while a steep mountain side on the eastern edge of Quetta has or had a heavily armed colony known locally as 'Pashtunistan', which was said to be virtually a no-go area to the authorities.

Water being often a strictly limited commodity in any case, this influx created a huge burden in spite of U.N. help, both on local resources such as firewood and water and on Pakistan as a whole, but the country coped remarkably well with this immense problem, perhaps better than its own problems. Many 'muajjar', as they are called locally, have now returned to Afghanistan but conditions in that country are not encouraging and of course quite a few may feel that there are better prospects for themselves in Pakistan, where many have set up businesses. Others who were not really refugees managed to put their fingers into the 'Aid' honeypot by pretending to be 'muajjar', and I have seen Sulaiman Khel families carrying out their traditional migration across Zhob with their worldly possessions piled on top of modern trailers towed by smart tractors, all donated. What happens when the things eventually break down or wear out is anybody's guess but I'll put my money on those who have retained their camels or donkeys when that day comes. Needless to say a few 'bad eggs' have arrived with the genuine refugees and at least one gang caused considerable problems for local people and truck drivers passing through Zhob and Loralai as related elsewhere.

Chapter Five

Further Glimpses, Frustrations and Tigers.

In 1959, was eager to return to Zhob as soon as possible but my expedition equipment was still being held in Bombay, and even rescinded threats by the chaotic and dubious Customs to auction it made it wise to travel down there as soon as the school term ended in early June. Helped behind the scenes by influential parents, the demurrage was finally waived by the Bombay Port Trust, who were just as much victims as I of the Customs' intransigence, to put it nicely. The demurrage had by then risen to the equivalent of eight months' salary. In theory I could have paid both duty and demurrage at the very beginning to secure the release of my things and then sought to reclaim what was due. However, I had been told by a friend in Delhi about one Customs' rebate that took eight years to finalise and I had little reason to believe that I might be more fortunate in my negotiations. Further, a Sikh friend in Delhi struggled for seven years to get a tax rebate, and I suspect, from what he let slip, that even then a 'consideration' was necessary to get justice. In Bombay I was fortunate to be the guest of a delightful Parsi family, the Pochkhanawalas, whose young son was at the 'Doon'. The head of the family, Noshir, ran a canning factory and their already excellent cuisine was enhanced daily by delicious chilled Alfonso mangoes, probably the finest of all of India's four hundred or so varieties, even surpassing the Saharanpuri ones up north. My baggage was forwarded to the Customs in Delhi for final collection and I returned thence. It was finally freed on the 27th July and I had no real complaint about the duty charged on my guns and medicines.

Anticipating that the process would be slow and tortuous, I had been fortunate to arrange temporary work in the British Council library. As it would be unfair to pay me other than a local salary, which was abysmally low by British standards, Croom-Johnson i/c generously invited me to stay with him. He was a dynamic man and treated his servants with a courtesy that they would be unlikely to experience from their fellow Indian employers, men or women, who often seemed to be curt with servants and demand attendance from early morning until late at night. Bihari Lal was in charge of the library: intelligent, gentle and with a good sense of humour, it was a pleasure to work with him. An entertaining story he told me concerned his brother. The latter had been unwell with dysentery and was on his way to the hospital by bus to deliver a stool sample. This less-than-jolly item was carefully imprisoned in a tobacco tin in his pocket. As usual the bus was crammed full of passengers and he had to stand. As he entered the hospital he discovered that, whilst on the bus, someone had picked his pocket, stealing the tobacco tin with its unpleasant contents. It was poetic justice.

Sitting in a small park one lunch time, I got into conversation with a terribly sad and tense English woman sitting nearby. I forget her name and it might be insensitive to mention it in any case. Her story, which came out gradually in response to my prompting, revealed that she and her Danish husband were both secret agents of the British during the Second World War and operated in mainland Europe. Both were arrested towards its end and he was sent to Belsen while she was sent to Auschwitz. The Nazis were not sure whether the couple were agents and so did not execute them, in case they could glean information. In her camp was a young and beautiful S.S. woman doctor but appearances were very misleading for the doctor's personal

146

'entertainment' was to bind the arms and legs of any pregnant inmate that went into labour and watch her agony until the prisoner died. When the concentration camps were liberated in 1945 the Allies immediately sought out their known agents that may have survived. They found her husband in Belsen and flew him to her. Upon his arrival she carried him from the plane in her arms: he had sunk to eighty-four pounds in weight and survived only another two weeks. Talking to her I had the sad impression that the mental scars were so great that any future happiness for her was out of the question. I never saw her again.

So in August 1959 with two weeks to spare before the start of the new term, after taking my two released trunks up to Dehra Dun, I hot-footed it across to Peshawar for a first look at that ancient city as Zhob was too far to make another visit worthwhile in the time available. This time I surrendered my pistol (licensed in India only) to the Pakistani Customs at Wagga, having recently read of a German traveller that had been imprisoned for trying to smuggle a revolver through. The Customs officials there were in a gleeful mood, having just intercepted a South American diplomat who had been smuggling gold from Kabul and were telling everyone willing to listen, proudly they showing me the car. A sharp-eyed official had noticed a tiny 'rust hole' in the big American car's frame below a rear door, then registered that the vehicle was new. Curious, he pushed a pin through the hole, at which there was a click and the top lifted off to reveal a row of gold ingots. Taking a quick meal in Lahore, someone in the restaurant told me another story though it could be apocryphal. A man came through from India pushing a bicycle with a sack of sand on the crossbar. He was ignored the first time but after a couple more such journeys suspicion grew and the sand was tipped onto the road. A search revealed nothing other than sand and the same thing happened half a dozen times then stopped. Shortly afterwards, an off-duty Customs official came across the man in a cafe in Lahore and asked him what was special about the bag of sand. The man said that it was simply sand but the bicycle was a new one each time, India manufacturing them but not Pakistan.

In full summer Peshawar is not the best place to be, with temperatures up to 121° F / 50°C at times, but Afridi and other 'hajis' just back from Mecca were met by relatives and friends at the station amid wild rejoicing and to my Western eyes their exhilaration was quite extraordinary. I then went with one group in a lorry to their village where I was allowed to take some cine film of the homecomings. After that I went down to Bannu for a couple of days, a truly tribal town although situated on the plains of the Derajat between the hills and the Indus. It was swarming with Waziris and Mahsuds down from their hills, and not a few Khattaks in addition to the local Bannuchis. Some of hillmen were huge fellows, often armed with both a rifle and a revolver or pistol, and all with long hair jutting from beneath Chitrali caps or turbans wrapped around conical 'kullas' embroidered with silver thread. I was six feet-two inches in height, wiry and very strong for my lean twelve stones but some of these tribesmen were quite awesome. The town had a certain air of wildness about it and whetted my already considerable appetite to see and learn more of the Pathans – as I was still calling them. Chatting to a local man in a largish 'hotal', I remarked on a sullen, brooding hulk of a man restlessly pacing up and down and was told that a few months earlier he had killed his own brother. He looked liable to go berserk at any minute and I suspect that most of us present were careful to avoid eye contact. There I saw the Area Commissioner and back in Kohat I asked the Deputy Commissioner about the possibility of making a film on the tribes but they both referred me to H.Q. in Peshawar. On my way back to Peshawar in Kohat an army officer and his wife kindly put me up for the night.

Back in that largely traditional and fascinating city, I was given a room in Edwardes College by the Australian Principal but forget how I came to meet him. Although well away from the heat-trap of the narrow bazaars, the narrowest of which at only ten feet wide were severe fire hazards, even out-of-doors I found it impossible to sleep before one in the morning. Wearing only a pair of underpants, I would lie on a sheet on my 'charpai' with its criss-crossed ropes of woven palm leaves and beads of sweat would trickle down between my ribs. The place was an oven and everyone suffered. It was easy to see how so many of the Red Shirt followers who attacked Peshawar in 1930 died of thirst or heat stroke when pursued by the army as they fled back to the hills following their inevitable defeat.

The Assistant Commissioner for Tribal Affairs in Peshawar turned out to be something of a religious fanatic and he enhanced that with a touch of paranoia. He was convinced that I must have some ulterior motive in wishing to film everyday life in a tribal area. Our meeting was fruitless and less than happy: we had a barely restrained quarrel. My strong impression was that most officials had little or no sympathy for the hillmen and it was a foretaste of future dealings with officialdom when tribal areas were involved. The tribesmen, by way of contrast and with hardly an exception, I found to be refreshingly uncomplicated and responded instantly to a straight approach but most government officials were a different species, unless they happened to originate from a tribal area and so were not truly urbanised. In those days many, if not most, government officials and police officers tended to be Panjabi and not infrequently made little attempt to hide their distrust and dislike of the tribals. Of course they would hotly deny this but as a newcomer upon the scene and one who had not been conditioned in any way, rightly or wrongly that was my clear impression. Worst of all, even if not in search of a bribe, those officials down the chain of authority had little or no power to use their own discretion and make decisions themselves.

As a result of this, the system was top heavy and deadeningly slow, as much as anything because the man at the top, even if keen and conscientious, was overburdened with work, much of which could and should have been delegated. Challenged about this, the invariable response was that this stultifying bureaucracy was inherited from the British, which was probably true. However, at that time twelve years had already passed since Independence and Partition and little seemed to have changed: officials wouldn't say yes and they wouldn't say no. And more than twenty years after independence, during the expedition with Bob Chambers of Tehran days, it was much the same but made even worse by the outbreak of another war with India. On the train back to Lahore, the crowds trying to get aboard were so unyielding that those wanting to get out had to do so through windows. Arriving at Wagga at seven in the morning, the 'go-down' or store was locked and normally did not open until noon but the poor man with the key was sent for so that I was able to collect my pistol by nine-thirty and continue my journey to Dehra Dun. It was another and brighter side of the coin.

A teacher friend, whom I had met in the U.K. shortly before I set out from Britain, had gone to work in what was then Southern Rhodesia but after a year there felt dissatisfied and I had arranged for her to teach in Welham Girls' School under the remarkable and redoubtable Miss Oliphant. Naomi arrived in mid-September 1959. She had an elderly uncle living at Bhim Thal and we arranged to spend Christmas there. Out of the blue, as he was not in Hyderabad House to which I was attached, there came an invitation from one of the boys in Kashmir House to join his family and their friends over Christmas on a tiger shoot. It was to be in the Bijrani hunting block which lay next to the Jim Corbet National Park in Kumaon, the nearest town being Ramnagar. Although not keen on hunting, it was too good to miss and, having already arranged to spend Christmas elsewhere, it was agreed that I would join the shooting party two days later.

Naomi's uncle had few remaining close relatives in the U.K. and after both retirement and Independence decided to stay on in the country. Many such people had very limited means and some were even in desperately straitened circumstances, which was why the U.K. Citizens' Association was founded. Some found it difficult to integrate with educated Indians on account of their racial conditioning while others simply lacked the funds to enjoy prosperous, educated Indian society on equal terms. Either way, such socially marooned souls tended to live rather isolated and inward-looking lives, and while many educated Indians recognised Christmas to a limited extent one could hardly expect them to have quite the same feeling for it. In the absence of a family gathering, such occasions had an element of sadness for those lingering English people.

Much of the time at Bhim Thal was spent boating and fishing on the beautiful lake, nestling among lush wooded hills. Leaving Naomi with her uncle and his English lady neighbour on Boxing Day, I went to Bijrani via the tiny hill town of Rani Khet, meaning Queen's Field. From there the view was spectacular and one could see perhaps a hundred and fifty mile stretch of the Himalayan snows: Trisul, Nanda Devi and Badrinath being among the giants clearly visible. Luck was with me and I was soon on a little bus heading for Ramnagar. To my surprise and considerable relief the good driver knew the entrance to the Bijrani shooting block, which was some miles before the town was reached, and kindly put me down there. I set off on foot down the track through the jungle, hoping that I would not meet a tiger or a bear but planning how to react were such a situation to arrive. After a mere mile or so I was relieved to come across one of the shooting parties. Raj Srivastava my hostess, though I had not met her previously, guessed who I was but I introduced myself in any case as her young son Vijay who had extended the invitation was not with the group. Within a minute or two we were in several cars heading back to the camp for lunch, saving me a two or three mile walk. Humans without a weapon of any sort are rather pathetic physically if confronted by a sizeable wild predator and I always feel naked if completely unarmed, even a spear being a potent weapon and a heavy stick instilling considerable confidence.

In the camp compound I met Sonni Srivastava, Vijay's father and host to quite a crowd of people there. Owning four textile mills, he was nonetheless a very modest man, refined without being stuffy and as handsome as his wife Raj. It was what I later learned about him, from others of course, that most impressed me. He had laid on such tiger shoots for many years for in those days there was no shortage of the magnificent beasts. Indeed, at intervals the *Hindustan Times* and the *Statesman* newspapers would report the activities of some man-eater here or there and even run a government advertisement for a hunter to track down a particularly elusive and troublesome one. Anyway, over the years Sonni's guests had wounded but lost three tigers. If left at that, suffering some more or less serious injury, such beasts were liable to turn man-eater if the handicap made game too difficult for them to catch. Simply to forget them was extremely unfair on the local villagers and so Sonni had on all three occasions taken it upon himself to track down the wounded animals on foot, an extremely dangerous and nerve-wracking task. For me, this set him apart from most men and I often quoted his courage to my Kakar friends when, during the course of some discussion, they tended to look down upon all Hindus as being soft. Of course the 'banian' or Hindu shopkeepers whom they had come across in the local bazaars and the big towns before Partition may have been a timid lot, but my Kakar friends tended to forget the formidable Rajputs who would calmly don a yellow robe when embarking upon a 'forelorn hope' from which they did not expect to return. There were the Marattas as well, and one should not forget that militant offshoot of Hinduism, the Sikhs.

One of the guests on the shoot was the Polish Commercial Attaché, Jan Drobot. Like me he simply wished to enjoy the jungle and its wildlife so we would often go off together on a couple of elephants, sometimes wandering into the adjoining Jim Corbett National Park. He was excellent company, surprisingly open for the representative of what then was an Eastern Block country, and with a fine sense of humour. Further, his son Adam went to school in Simla rather than one back in Poland, though not to an Indian government school, for which he can easily be forgiven. Among other things, he confided to me how surprised he had been upon finding that most Indians liked the British, just as I had been surprised by elderly tribesmen on my way through Baluchistan. Going up a particularly steep ridge, he would turn around and say to me that his elephant had just changed gear but that the clutch seemed to be slipping a bit, and so on. He was ever restless, taking charge of the camp fire in the evenings and having his leg pulled as a result. I had an open invitation to visit them in Delhi and regret that I did not take it as they were such a nice family.

Another guest was the Yugoslav Ambassador, who had been a remarkably young general and had fought the Germans throughout the occupation of his country. However, I found him hard and overly ambitious, so that it was no surprise when I heard that he defected to the West later on. He was obsessed with hunting and quite desperate to bag a leopard, in spite of which he reluctantly allowed me to accompany him at a goat bait, provided that I didn't move a hair or breathe. It turned out to be a fruitless wait and for two hours I balanced motionless on the limb of a nearby tree, there being only one 'machan' or shooting platform. While we waited tensely as the sun went down, a little party of small village women carrying bundles of grass on their heads passed in single file along the little path beneath me, quite unaware of my presence. However, earlier during the shoot he rather blackened his copybook one night by shooting a deer from a pick-up, using a powerful spotlight. It was completely unsporting and akin to murder, though everyone was too polite to make a real fuss, while its antlers were in velvet and therefore useless as a trophy. However, as the animal was unloaded, one of Sonni's three sisters, Shakuntala I believe, said in a clear and deliberate voice, "Oh, what a shame and it's in velvet." There was a pregnant silence for a few moments at that. Sonni had three sisters, all present at the shoot and all artistically talented. Sarala was a classical dancer, Shakuntala was an accomplished artist and Sushila was a classical singer with a beautiful voice and a repertoire of Yugoslav songs learnt when her husband was ambassador to that country. Shakuntala's husband was Rajeshwar Dayal who had an endless fund of diplomatic incidents and faux pas with which to entertain us around the huge log fire in the evenings. He had been sent by the U.N. to the Nigerian civil war among other things and was currently Ambassador to Pakistan. I found him as unprepossessing as his wife was handsome but he had a first-class intellect coupled with a robust sense of humour and was a fascinating raconteur. All good things must end: the Yugoslav Ambassador dropped me in Meerut on his way back to Delhi, where I met Naomi from Bhim Tal as arranged and we hurried off by train and bus to Peshawar.

Somehow or other we were invited to a big official dinner in honour of a large American trade mission there but I in particular lacked the formal dress necessary for such an event. This was a blow as we might have made useful contacts and I promptly ordered a dinner suit from the best tailor in Dehra Dun when we returned later. Tactfully we had earlier had an outfit resembling local dress made for Naomi, including a long brown cloak complete with a hood. We then travelled down to Tank by bus, hoping to get into Waziristan as I had been told during my first visit that the Political Agent there could grant such permission. The P.A. was Izzat Awan, a massively built, urbane and impressive man, as one might expect for such a sensitive and tough post, but he soon made it clear that only the Peshawar H.Q. could issue such a permit. That 'shuttlecock tactic' by officials was to be met many times. We were his guests for two days and then accepted his offer of a lift back to Peshawar. Naomi's great grandmother had been an Afghan lady of some standing and Naomi showed these genes in her fine figure and handsome features. There was little doubt in my mind that the consideration we enjoyed was because of that inheritance rather than my enthusiasm, as had been the dinner invitation perhaps.

After four days of official prevarication in Peshawar we gave up as time was short and headed south by buses. On the way we met a middle-aged Yorkshire couple near Bannu, the husband having been invited from the U.K. to re-organise four textile mills in the area that were steadily losing money. We spent a very pleasant evening with them and stayed the night. After two days we reached Drazinda, a barren village with an enormous graveyard near the outliers of the Takht-i-Sulaiman with its sprinkling of snow. There we spent the night as guests of the officer in charge of the Frontier Constabulary, a Marwat Pashtun, and I was also allowed to meet his wife. Early the next morning we were aboard the small single deck bus bound for Fort Sandeman. The inside of the bus was crammed full and we were installed on the roof directly above the driver's cab, blessed with warm sun, bracing air and an unimpeded view. Sitting next to Naomi were two teenage tribal girls who plied us with roast lentils, both is finely embroidered tribal dress and one strikingly good looking. Had an emergency stop been made, all four of us would have catapulted forwards onto the road but I doubt if the brakes would have been equal to such a demand.

We swayed and jolted for ten hours until nightfall, picking up or dropping off people in the most outlandish places, seemingly miles from any habitation. The road through the awe-inspiring Chuhar Khel Dhana gorge is cut into sheer rock in places, high above the tiny stream which created it, and all of us on the roof had to dismount and walk a couple of hundred yards while the little bus edged its way along the half-tunnel. Further on several men lost their turbans to thorn trees as we passed and at one torrent all the men on top had to dismount to help the bus through when it got stuck in the gravel, getting soaked in the process. At a later stop five young Sheranis, all armed with rifles, boarded the bus but refused to pay when approached by the driver's assistant. The driver refused to continue and there was a tense stand-off, so much so that I discreetly checked to make sure that my pistol was ready just in case things really turned nasty. Fortunately the 'conductor' was as tactful as he was persistent and after about fifteen or twenty minutes of haranguing and argument, out came the little notes and coins, grudgingly perhaps but out all the same. In the end we on top numbered twenty-four, many sitting on top of baggage, but just before entering Fort Sandeman we all had to dismount and walk past the check point, as riding on a bus roof is illegal. It was a farce but allowed the check post to turn a blind eye to the obvious and no doubt a few notes changed hands as well.

In the bazaar we chanced to meet a young lad (I was an 'ancient' twenty-nine year old then) whom I had met previously in Loralai and we were hosted for the night. The father was an Anglo-Pakistani and the family was Christian. Sadly they were virulently anti-Muslim and regarded the local people as savages, thus isolating themselves completely and no doubt making life far more lonely and difficult than necessary. As a nominal Christian who had been marvellously befriended and helped by the very people they so disliked and despised, I found it very embarrassing and so self-defeating. Interestingly, while non-tribal people in the towns and on the plains were also often very hospitable, when thanked they would invariably say, "It is my duty", meaning their duty as a Muslim, whereas tribesmen seemed to be more motivated by humanitarianism and by their tribal code of 'melmastia' or hospitality than by religion: certainly they never said that it was their duty. The difference was subtle but very real and I found that it mattered to me.

At Tarwal the chief welcomed us warmly, honouring me with an embrace rather than just a double handshake: I was therefore accepted. It is fair to say that Naomi was treated as an "honorary man", as were my wife Sheila and our German friend Helga thirty years later, everyone shaking hands with her unhesitatingly and talking freely, something they would not do with an unrelated tribal woman of any standing. His young twin sons, Anwar and Selim aged ten or twelve and by a later younger wife, were bubbling with excitement at our arrival as I had previously taken them up Seerzha peak 'looking for wolves and leopards' but Ahmad Yar Khan was away. I presented the chief with a new copy of Sir Olaf Caroe's book, *The Pathans, 550 B.C. – A.D. 1957*, sent out specially from the U.K. He would be unable to read it but A.Y.K. could just about cope and in any case it was a small token of my regard while books were something of a status symbol anyway. In the evening we were taken into house itself, having been installed in the separate guest house, and shown family heirlooms that included a 'chopan' or robe of silk and gold thread from his grandfather, Dost Mohammad Khan, and several antique weapons inlaid with silver and gold. Naomi but not I met various wives and daughters in the 'purdah' quarters: all were good-looking and one was absolutely beautiful, their dresses finely embroidered with silk and silver thread across the breast and around the cuffs. One donned her wedding dress and jewellery for Naomi: the latter including a golden crown and a heavy silver bracelet studded with seed pearls and rubies that had five rings attached to it by five fine chains. Some of the dresses had so many silver rupees and other coins sewn onto the neck and cuffs that they probably weighed as much as eight pounds, Naomi thought.

Time was short and the next morning we headed for India,

otherwise they might have allowed Naomi to photograph them. Taking the Lorala – Mekhtar – Fort Monro route, we spent one night in the first town with Sardar Hashim Khan, head of the Luni tribe and linked by marriage with the Kakar chief. Few towns or cities in Pakistan could boast of public toilets in those days and, as we were about to leave Loralai, Naomi had urgent need of one, it being that time of the month. Going to a nearby barber's shop in some desperation, the good man pushed his five or six customers into the street, two with lather around their faces, and we were saved. The unfortunate customers were wonderfully understanding. A day later we were waiting for a bus at Rackni when Naomi was forced to fall back upon natural cover, with me strategically sitting guard pistol in hand in case a warning shot into the air should prove necessary to catch the attention of any Baluchi inclined to wander too near. It was not an easy situation. Back on the plains once more, the difference in attitude and self-esteem became apparent when one of a group three young men in the bus sitting just in front of us sneakily flicked cigarette ash over his shoulder so that it landed on Naomi. It was done so quickly yet carefully that it took me a second or two to be sure that it had been deliberate. I waited for him to repeat the act, hoping that he would, but he didn't. The Pashtuns have an expression to describe that sort of person: 'bazaar lowg' literally meaning 'bazaar people', the second word being Urdu, but it has a far deeper and derogatory connotation.

Sporadic but fierce fighting was continuing across the Tibetan (Indo-Chinese) border and I had become resigned to the fact that my proposed high-altitude trek along the Himalayas was virtually out of the question under such circumstances. Delhi friends with access to people in high places made it quite clear that the essential Inner Line Permits were not being granted to anyone. With an ever-deepening interest in the border tribes this was far less depressing than it would have been otherwise and the idea of making a film about the tribes grew ever more appealing. I had no experience of filming but I did get on well with the tribal people. In any event, there was little point in staying on at the Doon School, while the School itself deserved a more precise arrangement, though no one said so and I arranged to leave at the end of my second year, in June 1960. Naomi did the same at Welham and we hoped to get permission to film, forming a partnership with friend Bob Chambers back in his local bank in Australia. However, the powers that be in Islamabad were not in a helpful mood and after four or five days we continued to Peshawar. There we chanced to meet one, Terry Tovey, a young warrant officer attached to the British Embassy at Kabul. One of his duties was to drive the Embassy light truck to Peshawar and back once a week to deliver and collect the diplomatic mail. He was about to return to Kabul and we gladly accepted his offer of a lift.

A few miles beyond Jelalabad one was reminded of the First Afghan War, when in 1842 an entire British army were annihilated almost to a man, the last remnant falling at Gandamak, when only the redoubtable Surgeon William Brydon reached the Jelalabad garrison under Sale. Along one stretch, the road followed the swift Kabul River and our benefactor told us that a series of hydro-electric power stations had been built by the Germans but that the highest one could only operate for two months of the year, in spring when the snows melted, as there was insufficient flow at other times. In other words it could never pay for itself and the aid was largely wasted. As we approached Kabul our new-found friend asked where we intended staying and, as this was the first visit for both of us, we had no idea which of the several cheap hotels to choose. However, it did not matter as he then proposed that we share his flat in the Embassy Compound and we accepted his generous offer. He was not married and was not the type of person to fit in happily with the hierarchical and somewhat snobbish Embassy staff so that our company made an agreeable change for him.

In addition he took us up to a swimming pool at Pagman in the nearby hills and, if my memory serves me correctly, we there met Daud Khan, the Prime Minister at that time. He was a tall, imposing and cultured man who spoke good English and was very friendly, being altogether an impressive figure. We also accompanied our host to a cocktail party given one afternoon by the American Assistant Army Attaché. When my friendship with the Kakars and others over the border was mentioned someone quietly hinted that information about attitudes there towards the Pashtunistan issue would be welcome. I suddenly clicked that it was an attempt to recruit me but I was not interested in anything that might even remotely jeopardise any of my tribal friends or possibly give government officials a genuine reason for suspicion and acted as if I had not registered. In any case the very fact that I had taught in India almost certainly made the Pakistani authorities very suspicious of my movements and motives. Altruistic interest seemingly did not exist in the view of Pakistani officials, for whom there had to be a political or financial reason behind my wanderings.

Kabul itself was remarkably tidy, partly at least because consumer goods and wrapping were limited, but there were police everywhere and some tended to throw their weight around, one slapping a pedestrian who was slow in crossing a road. Russian technicians also seemed to be everywhere, in groups of twos and threes and on foot, quite unlike most Western embassy staff who were driven around the bazaars and left their cars only briefly to hurry into some nearby sophisticated shop that displayed European goods and tolerable English was spoken. Others did not even do that but sent in their drivers. Moreover, many of the Russians spoke Farsi and I frequently heard them speaking Darri with local shopkeepers and others. Although some five thousand feet up, Kabul was quite hot but it was a dry heat and quite different from that in Peshawar. Another aspect that intrigued me as a newcomer was the number of people of

Mongolian origin to be seen, but whether they were Hazaras or Tajiks or Uzbeks I did not know, but some looked as if they were pure Chinese.

The Kabul River within the city was no more than a series of unconnected stagnant pools in summer, green with algae and reeking, yet everywhere men were washing themselves and women soaping clothes in the filthy water. No wonder the Afghans are such a sturdy lot, for only the genetically lucky ones survived beyond childhood. Zahir Shah, the king, was progressive and discouraged the wearing of the 'chadur' by women, many of whom in Kabul were clearly glad to abandon it but this displeased the conservative tribes people in the countryside. School girls in particular invariably went unveiled and were often quite flirtatious towards young foreigners such as myself. Kandahar on the other hand was extremely conservative and not a woman's face was to be seen in the streets.

It became clear that one might make a little money by carefully changing sterling into 'afghanis' and the 'afghanis' into Indian rupees. Naturally neither of us carried much ready money but we heard that it was possible in one of the bazaars to get cash in exchange for a cheque drawn on bank accounts in Britain and I negotiated £120, no small sum in those days. Many if not most embassy and consular staff met their local expenses this way as did a host of other expatriates and we were introduced to a helpful trader. At that time no British person had betrayed that remarkable trust, though one German and one American had done so we were told. Such cheques sometimes took six months to surface in Britain, being passed from hand to hand at face value, sometimes carried by traders and perhaps nomads across China or Russia in the process. About four months after my deal a rather frantic letter from my bank manager in Wells, Somerset, caught up with me asking what to do with a cheque bearing my signature that had been presented by a Mr. Zarahov. I explained the situation. His reply reprimanded me for breaking the prevailing currency regulations concerning countries outside the sterling area but he honoured the cheque and I behaved myself thereafter.

Such a trusting state of affairs was destined to vanish within a decade. The European and American hippies and back-packers who flooded in at the end of the 1960s were of a different ilk. Not a few wasted little time in devising ways to cheat the initially trusting Afghans who, in spite of having fought the British fiercely, came to trust our word and were accustomed to a completely different ethic. This new, mongrel breed would hand over travellers' cheques for goods or in return for cash then promptly telephone the issuing bank or travel agent at home to claim that the cheque or cheques had been stolen and would the bank please not honour them; and that they did in a poor, third world country. Another disgusting ploy was to stay in a hotel for several days, then leave before dawn one morning without paying. My Kakar friends in Quetta told of hippy girls selling themselves for a few smokes of hashish, or their boyfriends hiring them out. Needless to say, my friends were deeply shocked and simply could not understand this new type of Briton. What had happened to the British they asked repeatedly. I personally saw one bare-footed European begging on Lahore railway station, to the considerable embarrassment of the Pakistanis he approached. As might be expected, that behaviour changed the attitude of the Afghans in turn so that when I returned in a minibus in 1971 I soon learnt to check the petrol pumps carefully when filling the vehicle, some of whose meters had clearly been tampered with. The locals responded in other ways too, such as throwing plastic bags of animal blood at the front of tourist cars or vans as they sped along some road. There were toll barriers at long intervals and police posts where the blood throwers had accomplices. When the blood-spattered vehicle arrived the occupants would be accused of having had an accident and injuring a villager, the 'evidence' of which was plainly visible. The choice was to pay 'compensation' on the spot or elect to go to trial, and the latter course meant remaining in the country for several or many weeks, if not months.

Back in England some years later, when I mentioned this cheque experience to an elderly ex-army friend, he related how five officers escaped from the Turks after the disastrous British surrender at Kut-el-Amara in Iraq during the First World War, and virtually walked across Iran to India. They had no money but simply issued IOUs on scraps of paper for all they required; giving name, number, rank and regiment; and of course all were honoured when presented to the army authorities. During the Second World War this same friend, Tony Chadburn, was on leave in Bombay when an urgent order came to return to his battalion in Kohat on the Frontier. There was an early train but the banks were not yet open. However, the informal chits which he issued were accepted for the rail ticket, for restaurants and taxis during the journey. Very few officers betrayed this privileged system and any who did were disgraced. How times have changed.

Upon calling upon Izzat Awan a second time, in 1960, he had to go to Peshawar again so we availed ourselves of the opportunity to go with him once more. In Peshawar, further approaches to officials for permission to film met with an unequivocal no but at least we now knew where we stood so far as Pakistan was concerned. When we travelled third class on the Bolan Mail down to Quetta I measured 109°F in the shade. After dark for some unknown reason the train stopped for a while near Sibi. It was sweltering, without any moving air and even an ancient, withered tribesman opposite me had runnels of sweat down his face. Upon reaching Quetta rather late at night, we went to the Dak Bungalow rather than trouble friends. During the journey Naomi had found the heat distressing and I had been less than patient with her. With just a hint of chivalry and to make amends, I gave her what I thought to be the better bed, the one with nice, smooth strips of canvas instead of the

163

other one with its rough twisted palm ropes. During the second night she woke me to complain of being bitten by something but switching on the light revealed nothing and I harboured uncharitable thoughts. Two or three hours later she again woke me and I began to realise that something really was amiss. A quick search immediately the light went on revealed a large bed bug. The thorough search that then followed produced a final tally of fifty of the hungry beasts, mostly in the loose joints and beneath the canvas strips where they touched the wood. A further fifteen were located in the bright morning sun when the bed was taken outside. Her dozens of bites swelled and itched for four or five days.

A couple of days later we pressed on to Kandahar, roughly one hundred and twenty miles away across the desert, travelling by bus. When Bob Chambers had visited the town in 1950 it had been surrounded by a great mud rampart with towers at intervals but in the interests of modernity the ancient wall had since been razed to the ground. It was essentially a country town, though it had been the capital of the country for a period, even supporting a stable of seven hundred elephants during Mughal times I later read. Its sole claim to fame during our visit was its delicious grapes and 'hookah' or water pipe stems beautifully decorated with beadwork – now a thing of the past. It lacked, so far as we could see, any sophisticated shops and in those days the streets were dirt. Down one side of the main one ran a rivulet, a recipient for melon peel, grape stems and other rubbish yet one often saw men drinking from it. If a local person drank alcohol, other than in diplomatic circles, it meant a prison sentence and Afghan prisons had a reputation for being less than cosy, yet we were given some quite passable local brandy, albeit discreetly. The town had a restful atmosphere and the bazaars were strictly specialised: there was one for copper smiths, another for ironworkers, an area for vegetables, a section for rugs, felts and kilims and so on. A small, swift stream ran through the centre of the town and a small mosque was set astride it, offering quiet and rest as well as a place for prayer. Unlike Peshawar and Quetta, women thronged the bazaar but were completely shrouded by their 'chadur', even the face masked by an embroidered visor.

After five days there, during which time I acquired a fine woven kilim and two felt rugs by dint of hard bargaining, we returned to Quetta. A day or two later Ayub Khan, now promoted from General to Field Marshall and head of the country as Martial Law Administrator attended a 'jirga' at Pishin where, in a ceremony called 'dastur bandi', he had a turban tied and was proclaimed 'Sardar' of the Tor Tarins. As one of the Jogezais was married to a Tor Tarin, Nawab Sahib with two of his sons was present and we managed to get an invitation. The President, as he was soon re-titled, although a Tor Tarin himself, addressed the gathering in Urdu which puzzled me somewhat. However, it was the content of his speech that raised many eyebrows, especially among the non-Tarins present who regard that tribe as the weakest and most degenerate of all the Afghans and Pashtuns. Indeed, I was told that much of their land had been given to neighbouring Achakzais and Kakars over the years for 'protection', in reality meaning non-molestation. He claimed that the Tor Tarins had valiantly resisted the Mughals, then the Sikhs (who had never been anywhere near the area) and finally the British. This last certainly held a measure of truth because a British Tommy at a well had been hit over the head with a clay pitcher and killed by a Tor Tarin woman, no doubt because he was being offensive or too familiar.

The Kakars may not equate themselves with the Wazir or Mahsuds or Afridi for tribal valour but when a foray was brewing in the old days they used to exhort their young bloods "not to kill or hurt women and children, old men, Hindus or Tarins'. Unfortunately, in some cafe a few days later a group of young Jogezais were laughing about the speech and encouraged me to join in. Foolishly I did so, for we were overheard and reported it would seem, and I was officially blacklisted though unaware of it until later. In addition the Jogezais were a powerful clan and too independent for the likes of many officials, many of whom were Panjabis who packed government posts with their own group as often as possible and were overtly hostile towards Afghans and Pashtuns in any case. At that time even the President of Baluchistan Province was, I believe, a Panjabi and this irked the locals considerably. Clipping my wings would be an oblique way of getting at the Jogezais without provoking too strong a reaction but I was yet to discover this.

As filming in Pakistan was definitely out of the question we split up, Naomi boarding the Khyber Mail northwards to visit Kashmir before returning to the U.K. via Japan and Russia. I managed to store my tin trunk with some Jogezais living in Quetta and, although it was late afternoon, took a bus to Kuchlagh, where the road to Zhob turns off. Travelling with only one tin trunk when baggage wheels were unavailable was a tiresome enough business and upon arriving at a place I would usually secure it to a station bench or a street telegraph pole with a length of chain and padlock. That left me free to explore the town, take a meal, or visit some official unburdened and I never lost one. From Kuchlagh, carrying just a rucsac, I set out on foot for Zhob as there was no bus. Passing a Sulaiman Khel encampment as the sun went down I was invited to spend the night in one of their black tents but declined, partly as I wished to press on as far as the village of Bostan and partly as I was mindful of their reputation as robbers. A few miles further on some distant relatives of Ahmad Yar Khan recognised me in the dark, stopped and gave me a lift. They were on their way to Loralai via Ziarat so, not having previously visited Ziarat, I got out there while they continued. At eight thousand feet it was a true hill station but being so high it was also snow-bound and deserted, except for a solitary watchman, for several months in winter and enjoys the distinction of having the largest juniper forest in the world after Canada.

During a visit to Tarwal many years later, one evening A.Y.K. related a rather sad tale about a British army captain around the end of the First World War who went hunting in the mountains around Ziarat: as they comfortably top 11,000 feet so he was probably after 'markhor' rather than wild sheep. One day he came upon a beautiful Kakar shepherd girl of the Sarangzai clan tending the family flock and was so taken by her that he went to her father to ask for her hand in marriage. The father said that he could not allow his daughter to marry a non-Muslim but otherwise he had no objection. So the captain became a Muslim, they were married, had two sons and a house was built for her in Ziarat. Possibly he anticipated that in the normal course of events he would die before her, perhaps being considerably older, and that as a widow she might wish to return to the hills. Perhaps it was so that they could visit her family from time to time but in relative comfort: who knows. The captain seems to have died of natural causes and in the Second World War both sons were killed. Presumably her parents-in-law were dead by then and, especially if her husband had no brother or sister, the distraught woman had lost virtually everything. In any event she returned to Baluchistan, where her own parents would almost certainly have been dead. Any brother or sister there would almost be a relative stranger, leaving the poor woman desperately lonely and vulnerable in such a country. An elderly man whom A.Y.K. had met many years previously said that he had seen her in Quetta in the office of the Assistant Governor General and that she was somewhat deranged. For some reason or other it appears that the government had confiscated her house so that the poor woman was probably forced to buy a home or have one built for herself, not the easiest undertaking for a woman in those parts let alone one who has become unbalanced. A.Y.K. did not know the final outcome.

The following morning, after climbing the main peak nearby, a bus caught up with me as I walked and picked me up. In Loralai I was given shelter by a complete stranger, a pleasant young Hazara, as I made for the Dak Bungalow. The next day was a Sunday, there was no bus for Kila Saifulla and I was anxious to return to Tarwal. I knew that there was an old camel track across the mountains and I hankered to explore it in any case. I discovered roughly where it commenced but I was also solemnly warned about the distance – around thirty-five miles, whereas the road was fifty-three – a lack of water, the possibility of robbers, a jumping snake that was 'deadly and so on. Visiting Loralai years later I must confess to being puzzled how I managed to find even the start of that faintest of tracks winding its way through the tangle of mountains. The blazing sun took its toll and by eleven o'clock my two pints of water were finished. It was full summer and an hour later I came upon a deep well in a shallow valley but was without a length of string to reach the water with a bottle. Late in the afternoon I saw a black nomad tent to the left of my path and made for it. Gulping down their water, I heard a young man who arrived moments after me ask my benefactor who I was. The latter had apparently recognised me from two or so years earlier and explained that I was the 'bicycle wallah'. I was then pressed to take tea but time was short so I hurried on. Further on, to my great surprise I met some Baluchis who pointed me back to the correct trail that I had somehow missed so that I just managed to descend the last, steep, tricky section of camel trail down into the Zhob Valley before it was quite dark. An hour or so later I reached Tarwal, having covered some forty miles due to my inadvertent detour. I drained my blisters, downed several glasses of water, had my first food of the day and chatted contentedly with Ahmad Yar Khan, somehow feeling that I had reached home again.

There was a lot of scurrying to and fro the next day, an air of tension and secrecy prevailed. Obviously something was up, but for the moment no one would tell me what it was. In the evening all was made clear. A local woman had been shot and killed by her husband, who alleged that she had been committing adultery, which would have justified the killing if proven. However, there was no proof as the husband had failed to get the lover, if there was one, alleging that he had managed to escape. The Jogezais and other locals wanted to deal with the case themselves rather than submit it to the magistrate, and they were doubtful about the truth of the husband's claim. They suspected that he simply wished to be rid of his wife without returning the 'wulwer' to her family, perhaps having a new wife already in mind but lacking any justifiable reason for a divorce that might allow him to retain it. Unfortunately I forget their eventual judgement but it would have been honest.

The 'jirga' system had much to recommend it and the British were happy to 'rubber stamp' decisions reached by 'jirgas'. Disputes and crimes were dealt with by an assembly of locals of some standing, meaning 'sardars', 'maliks', mullahs and possibly one or two others. This is not to say that it was always a perfect system but those petitioning or defending were invariably well known to the members of the 'jirga' so that embarrassing or inconvenient evidence was not easily hidden. Secondly, no fees were paid to the 'jirga', other than perhaps tea or a meal provided by the accuser during the case, so that a poor man in conflict with a rich man would not be disadvantaged by the latter hiring a clever, expensive lawyer to plead his case, or able to bribe the judge or magistrate. In other words, so far as possible it provided a level playing field whereas the standard legal system that has replaced the 'jirga' system in north Baluchistan, though not in Waziristan, the Tirah and one or two other strongly tribal territories is, I was constantly told, wide open to malpractice. In short, one's chance of a favourable judgement these days all too often depends upon one's wallet, as can be the case with us in Britain though for different a reason. In addition, the old system provided almost immediate redress and on the spot as well, whereas its replacement may involve months of waiting and, if serious, be adjudged far away to the considerable disadvantage of a poor man. And, when considering these points, one must remember that most of the tribal population is poor. This is not to imply that they are depressed or demoralised by their poverty: far from it, as both Fukhruddin and Sheikh Rahmat showed. Simply they generally lack material possessions.

One modification imposed by the British on the 'jirga' system of justice was that a feud killing must receive a prison sentence, usually of seven years or so in the 'sixties if not today, which remission usually reduced to four years. I do not know the reason for this but possibly it was to allow for a cooling of tempers. If that was the reason then it did not always work, as my experience at Ruckni had shown for Afghans and Pashtuns have long memories. In addition compensation must be paid to the victim's family or a young woman given in marriage without the usual 'wulwer'. Needless to say, there is sometimes another side to this coin. Munir Khan is one of the four sons of dear old Azim Khan, a brother of the old chief Nawab Mohammad Khan. He is a rugged, quiet and totally honest man. In 1967 he sold some tobacco to a Mahsud from Kanigurum in Waziristan and, as Munir had done satisfactory business with the man a few years previously, he was content to deposit the leaf in the warehouse of Kadder, an Urmar man there whom he also knew, upon the promise of payment after one month. However, the Rs.10,000 was not forthcoming as promised so Munir went to Kanigurum once more and was again fobbed off with a promise to pay after one more month. The month passed and no money arrived and another visit to the north was decided upon. However, his brothers felt it unwise for him to go there under the circumstances and persuaded him to take our resourceful Sheikh Rahmat as a companion, just in case things became difficult...

As the pair passed through Fort Sandeman on their way north, the ever pragmatic Sheikh suggested that they impound one of the several Mahsud trucks parked in the bazaar, drive it down to the security of Kila Saifulla and there hold it hostage until the debt was paid. The reasoning behind this was that the unfortunate owner would be forced to bring pressure to bear upon his fellow tribesman to pay up. However, Munir felt this to be unfair and the idea was dropped. Upon their arrival in Kanigurum the debtor, Mashuk, claimed that Munir was breaking their contract and called up a 'jirga' to decide the case. To the surprise of no one I'm sure, the 'jirga' found in favour of their fellow tribesman, Munir was found guilty and fined Rs.500. Of this sum, Mashuk was awarded Rs.200, Rs.100 was allotted for food and refreshment to the 'jirga' (that had been so obliging) and Rs.200 were returned to Munir out of hospitality or 'melmastia' as he was a guest in their country. A nice touch that last: Pashtuns often have a wry sense of humour. The debt? Munir returned to Zhob with a modest sum of money, an old Ford car, a rifle and some other oddments in payment.

Chapter Six

True Afghans, Pashtuns & Ghalzais; the Kakars and the Chieftainship

For a country of its size, Afghanistan has a remarkable racial mix that includes both Caucasian and Mongolian people plus admixtures. Being the crossroads of Asia this should not be so surprising. Its original tribes seem to be confederations of the so-called true Afghans, the Pashtuns or Pakhtuns and the Ghalzais or Ghiljis who share a common language. In the centre and to the north, as a result of later invasions or immigrations to these must be added the Hazaras, Tajiks, Turkmen, Uzbeks and Chahar Aimaq confederations plus a few Kirghiz. In the south of the country is the Baluch confederation which spills over the border into Pakistan and Iran. These seem to be relative newcomers to the area, probably from Iran but they are also reputed to be from what is now Iraq. The Brahvi confederation, found in the extreme south of Afghanistan and over that border in south and south-west Baluchistan, is apparently of Indian origin and speaks a Dravidian language. To the east on both sides of the border are mainly Pashtun tribes along the northern reaches, with a number of 'true' Afghan tribes along the southern stretch of that border, again on both sides. Further east, along the Sulaiman range bordering the Panjab and Sinde, are more Baluchis. Finally there is the tradition that some of Alexander's Macedonians and Greeks settled in the extreme north-east of the country, their descendants being the people known formerly

172

as Kaffirs but is now more respectfully called Nuristanis. Plenty of their Graeco-Bactrian coins, spanning two hundred years, surface from time to time and traditionally the Nuristanis use chairs, unlike all other Afghans, which lends weight to this claim. My concern is with the first three confederations: the true Afghans, the Ghalzai or Ghiljis and the Pashtuns. The name or term Ghalzai is the one my Afghan friends use, as does J. A. Robinson in his book detailing their tribes, whereas the scholarly Sir Olaf Caroe insists upon Ghilji. I am used to the first name and will stick with it.

To the newcomer the tribal chart is utterly bewildering, and it took me many years to begin to sort it out: to complete it seems unlikely. The difference between the so-called true Afghans, the Pashtuns and Pakhtuns, and the Ghalzai is both subtle and confusing, the redrawing of political boundaries in the last hundred and twenty years further confusing the issue in the case of the so-called true Afghan tribes such as the Kakars and others that live in what is now Pakistan. All three groups speak the same language in one or other of its two variants, Pashtu to the south and Pukhtu in the north, which language I find very difficult. The differences between them may seem to be academic to outsiders and their different putative origins mythological but to the people involved they are enormously important, especially in inter-tribal dealings and alliances. Unfortunately the shadowy traditions as to their origins are backed by no written evidence and little archaeological evidence. Khushal Khan Khattak, their one writer of note, was a poet not a historian and such written 'evidence' as exists is by outsiders and of course is not contemporary. Worse still, it is often contradictory. Great mounds in the lower part of the Zhob Valley and elsewhere mark the sites of cities that probably date back more than five thousand years, based on C14 dating, as outlined earlier but precisely who those people were and what happened to them seems to be unknown.

The earliest written account is by Herodotus in the fifth century B.C., when he describes the people living to the west of the Indus as being the most warlike, which suggests that the Afghan and Pashtun tribes were already in place and Alexander seems to confirm that. The traveller Al Biruni, writing around 1000 A.D., comments on the rebellious Afghan tribes west of the Indus. Much later, Neamatullah, a scribe at the Delhi court of the Mughal emperor, Jehangir, in the seventeenth century wrote on the origin of these tribes saying that they are from the banished and lost tribes of Israel, which hypothesis is un-substantiated but apparently still favoured by some Pakhtuns in the north. British commentators such as Raverty, Elphinstone, and Burnes in the nineteenth century; then Robinson and Caroe in the twentieth century, who spent many years on the Frontier and in Afghanistan have tried to unravel it and all have made their contribution but they often disagree with one another. It is a daunting if not impossible task. The one thing which seems generally agreed is that the true Afghan and related tribes as they are today probably originated somewhere west of the Sulaiman range bordering the Derajat; possibly in the region of what is now known as Kakar Khorrasan – to distinguish it from the Iranian province of Khorrasan over four hundred and fifty miles away to the west.

I have no preferences of my own and will therefore outline the fabled account quoted by Sir Olaf, which he debunks completely but which seems to be generally accepted by those actually concerned. Their progenitor is said to be one Qais, alias Abdur Rashid. Over the centuries people must have had astonishing memories for this worthy man is said to have been descended in the thirty-seventh generation from King Saul, known to Afghans and Pashtuns as Malik Talut. As the period spans some one thousand, seven hundred years, each generation must have married rather late in life, at an average age of forty-six to be precise. That appears to disprove the tradition from the very start, but to continue: Qais was called from Ghor, which we now call Afghanistan, to meet the Prophet at Mecca and learn of the new faith. Having done Him good service, Qais came to the notice of the Prophet who saw that Qais was a Hebrew name and therefore re-named him Abdur Rashid. Now Qais is said to have returned to the west of the Sulaiman range, and had three sons. The eldest of these, Sarbanr or Saraban, is said in turn to have had two sons, Sharkhbun or Sharkbun. The elder of the two is reputed to have given rise to the so-called western (true) Afghan tribes, meaning the Abdali (later also known as Durrani) from whom arose the Achakzai, Mohammadzai, Saddozai, the Sherani, both Tarins, the Urmar and others. From the younger son of Saraban, Kharshbun, are said to be descended the so-called eastern Afghans who include the Ketran, Mohmand, Shinwari, Tarklanri, Yusufzai and others.

Qais' second son was Bitun or Bait, and his legitimate descendants in the male line are the Bittani tribe alone. But he also had a daughter, Bibi Matu or Bibi Mato, who married a complete outsider, Shah Hussain, but only after a bit of illicit romance, of which more below. Her first son will be dealt with later. Her second and legitimate son, Ibrahim Lodi, gave rise to the Dotani, Lodi (who sat the Delhi throne for a while), Marwat, Niazi, Surr and other tribes.

The third son of Qais, Ghurghust, is said to have had three sons. Dani or Danay, Babi or Babay and Mando. The first, Dani, gave rise to the Gadun, Kakar, Musa Khel, Panri and Safi tribes. The second son, Babi, founded the Babi tribe only. The third son, Mando, is also the progenitor of a single tribe, the Mando Khel.

So what of the true Pashtun or Pukhtoon tribes such as both Waziris, the Mahsuds, Zhadrans, Orakzai, Bangash, Khattak, Afridi, and others, many of whom feature so prominently in the history of the North West Frontier Province, as it is known today? Their origin is even more shrouded in the mists of time. Briefly, it is related that two brothers of the Urmar tribe came upon an abandoned child in a field where an army had just decamped and one of them adopted it, being childless at the time. Later a daughter was born to the man's wife and in the fullness of time the adopted foundling, named Karlanri, was married to his step-sister and their two sons are said to have given rise to the two groups of Pashtuns and Pakhtuns.

We are now left with the distinct and powerful Ghalzai confederation of tribes: the Sulaiman Khel, Tarraki, Nasser, Kharot, Aka Khel, Ali Khel, Hotak, Sohak, Tokhi and others. For these we must return to the beautiful, so it was said, Bibi Matu. The story goes that a refugee named Shah Hussain came from the west and was taken in by her father. In spite of his reputed saintliness, a romance between Bibi Matu and the newcomer progressed a little too far and the couple were married, just in time. This son, conceived though not born on the wrong side of the blanket, was named Ghalzai, 'ghal' meaning thief and 'zai' meaning' born of', in effect 'son born of a thief', not the most delicate choice of name given the circumstances. So from this union, via Shah Hussain's first son, the Sulaiman Khel, Hotak, Tarakai and others are said to have descended. The Nasser and Kharot are commonly included among the Ghalzai but Captain Robinson disputes this in his book, *The Nomad Tribes of Eastern Afghanistan*. He also mentions a suggestion that the Ghalzai originated from a Turkish tribe called Ghilji who moved into eastern Afghanistan some time after the eleventh century. The suggestion is based solely upon the name similarity. Be all that as it may, they managed to rule at Delhi for a short period during the thirteenth to fourteenth century. Of the Ghalzai, the Sulaiman Khel is by far the dominant and most numerous tribe and until recent times some of their clans were a byword for robbery and murder. Perhaps a little unkindly they have been summed up by one writer as being 'robbers by birth, instinct and inclination'. The Shamal Khel is the largest of their four main sections but the Jabbar Khel of the Ahmadzai section is recognised as the 'sardar khel' or leading section, one of their leaders being executed during the eighteenth century by the Kabul Amir, Abdur Rahman, for becoming too influential. The Amir also removed thousands of them to north Afghanistan, probably both as a bulwark against any expansion southwards by the feared Uzbeks north of the River Oxus, who had previously invaded much of the country for a brief period, and to disperse the potentially threatening power of the Ghalzai.

Returning to the Kakars, strictly speaking they are a 'true' Afghan tribe ethnically and, for what it is worth, by tradition are closely related to their neighbours to the north and east, the Mando Khels and Musa Khels. Like most of the Afghan and Pashtun tribes they are Sunni Muslims, the Turis well to the north being an exception that comes to mind. Their population is considerable but they are distributed over a huge area. They were in fact under Kabul rule, nominal though it might have been, until the British grabbed their territory from Yaqub Khan by the Treaty of Gandamak in 1879 as a sequel of the Second Afghan War. Today it would be incorrect to call them Afghans as that would make them nationally or politically Afghan when clearly they are in Pakistan. To emphasise the point, note that Sandeman's officers in their reports referred to them as Afghans when they first moved into the area. Further, some years later when pursuing Dost Mohammad Jogezai and his son Bungal Khan, the British felt obliged to let the pair escape across the south-west stretch of Kundar River into Kakar Khorrasan because they regarded the country beyond the river as being in Afghanistan, the border not having been formally demarcated as yet in spite of the Gandamak Treaty. So when Ahmad Yar Khan introduced himself as a 'Pathan' at the road-rail bridge near Muzaffagar it was simply a way of distinguishing himself from the Panjabis, Sindhis, Brahvis and others, whom he will consider inferior. However, I am sure that he would not regard the Baluchis as being inferior, though I have never asked him.

Continuing with Afghan and Pashtun tradition, Ghurghust, the first son of Qais, fathered Dani who in turn fathered Kakar and four other sons according to the *Genealogical Tree of the Kakar Tribe* by Mir Shams Shah, a Settlement Assistant Commissioner, published in 1901. Sir Olaf Caroe, however, apportions only three sons to Dani. We are now getting onto home ground as Kakar is said to have had six sons: Taraghara, Saraghara, Dumar, Sughruk, Jadram and Seenr in the order drawn up by Mir Shams Shah, presumably in birth order and not in their order of importance based upon the number of their descendants today. Of these Sughruk posthumously had a son Sanjar or Sanzer by a Saeed wife named Lazgi. Bearing in mind how spartan and uncertain life was in those distant days, Sanjar astonishingly fathered twelve surviving sons and these gave rise to all the clans of the dominant Sanjar Khel section of the Kakar tribe who, at the turn of the century, outnumbered the next section, the Sanatia, by eight to one. A tomb and shrine attributed to him is at Kot, about twenty-seven miles from Fort Sandeman towards Murgha Kibzai and a mile off the dirt main road, so now we seem to have more concrete evidence. In 1996 Humayun Jogezai, the second of Jehandar Shah's four sons, with an escort of several men, obligingly took me to this shrine, and it was quite a moving experience.

The next of Kakar's sons in importance was Jadram, whose son Hussain fathered Sanatia mentioned above, which grandson gave rise to that second largest section of the tribe and its numerous clans. Taraghara gave rise to three clans, and a few Saragharas were recorded then, but the descendants of Dumar were very thin on the ground and held in low esteem according to the Zhob Gazetteer of 1907. This was due to a local tradition holding that they are descended from a female slave or musician of Sanjar. I find this difficult to understand as Mir Sham's

1) *The main entrance to the magnificent Mosque of Ali in Mazar-i-Sharif.*

2) The great, ruined walls of Balkh, where sometimes human bones of the original workmen, who had displeased their overseers in some way, are sometimes washed out during rare but heavy storms.

3) The old ruined castle in Tashkurgan / Khulm in Afghanistan. It was the only place we were not offered hashish.

4) To show our military escort out of Waziristan on our journey south. The officer in the army's post of Mir Ali where we were entertained overnight seemed rather keen that we should leave Waziristan, providing us with an escort.

5) *A Zahdran villege on the move whom we chanced to meet shortly after being escorted out of Waziristan to Bannu in 1971.*

6) *The author briefly resting on the last range of the Torr Ghar before Kakar Khorrasan and the Afghan border. He covered around fifty-five to sixty miles in nineteen and a half hours.*

7) *Mair Jan, a Mahsud refugee from Waziristan because of a feud with a larger family, working on Hashim Khan's (Luni not Jogezai) at Manzai, eighty miles east of Tarawal.*

8) *Wali Jan (Shinwari) and two relatives, from Chagchalan in Afghanistan, camped for the winter at Ghabar Ghar. They are narrating the events of the previous day when Baluchis, thought to be Marris, ran off 200 sheep. The Shinwaris lost one man but the Baluchis lost two in pursuit and so were satisfied.*

genealogies record Dumar as a son of Sanjar so possibly Dumar's wife or concubine was a slave or musician. Descendants of Seenr are even thinner on the ground, perhaps having disappeared altogether in the male line for Ahmad Yar Khan, in discussing these main tribal divisions, made no mention of them at all. The above is all very complicated and the 'tribal charts' make it much clearer.

Divisions within a tribe are as complicated as those between tribes. Very roughly speaking any group with 'khel' or 'zai' in its name may in general be regarded as a section or a clan within a tribe but no one seems to be precise about it and one immediately asks what about the Sulaiman Khel, the Mando Khel, the Achakzai and the Yusufzai tribes? In turn some sections and their sub-sections often have one or other of the two suffixes, and so it goes on. The only precise division appears to be the 'kahole', which is a distinct, closely related group within the Jogezai clan that shares some relatively recent ancestor. To make errors even more likely to the outside observer, two or three tribes may have a section or clan of the same name: for example the Kakar, Tokhi and Sulaiman Khel tribes each have a Jalalzai section; while both the Kharot and the Sulaiman Khel tribes have a Ya Khel or Yahiya Khel sub-division. There are many others besides these quoted here.

The dominant Sanjar Khel section comprises twelve main sub-sections, each descended from one of the twelve sons of Sanjar Nika, meaning 'Grandfather Sanjar', as a token of respect. As already implied, to have fathered a dozen surviving sons in those days indicates a particularly good set of genes in both parents and he seems to have cut a dashing figure, for tradition has it that he became enamoured of the only daughter of Miro Khan Mughal, the Governor of the district, but her father disapproved of the match. Beyond this point the story varies somewhat: one version is that Miro Khan voiced his disapproval a little too strongly while the other is that he plotted to kill Sanjar. Whatever

AFGHAN, PASHTUN AND GHILZAI TRIBES & TRADITIONAL GENEALOGIES

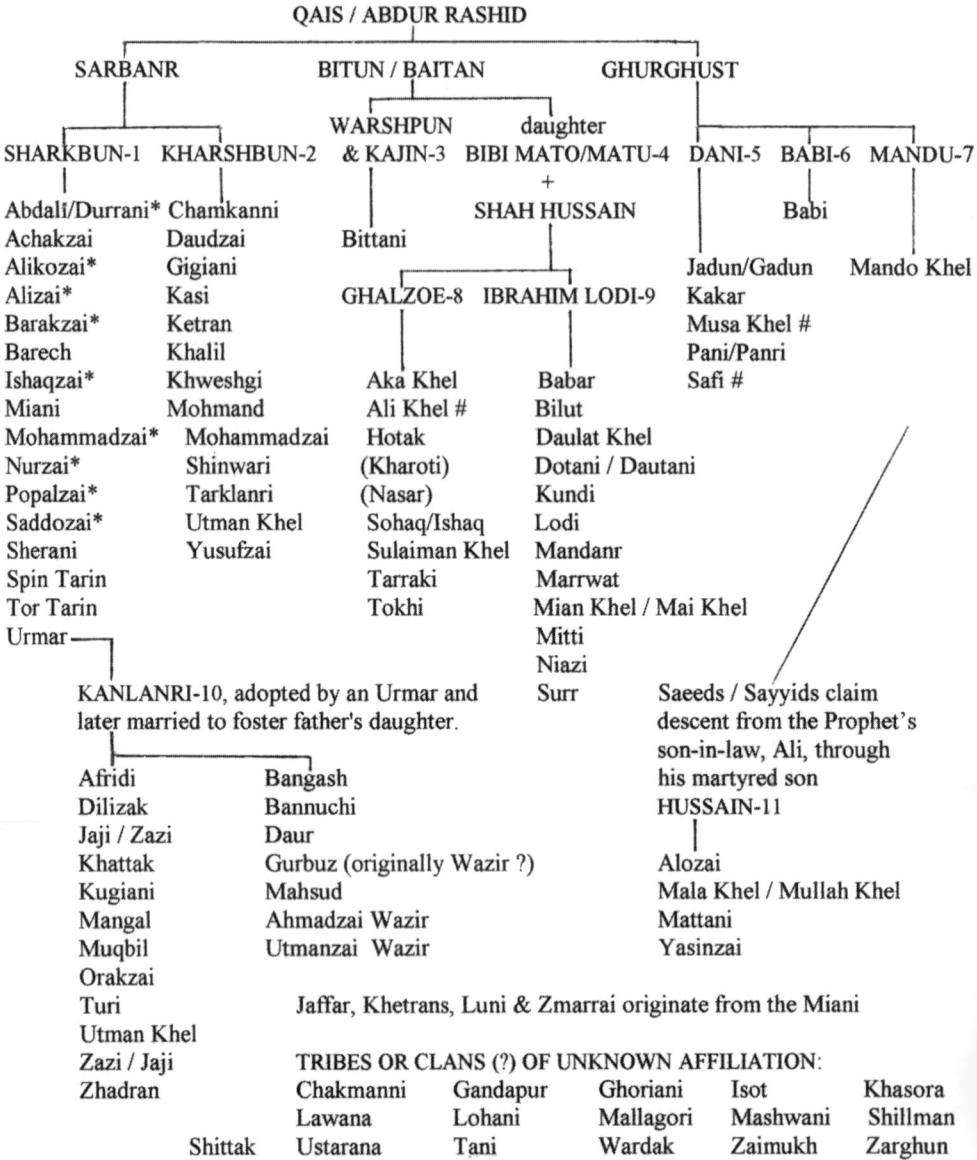

QAIS / ABDUR RASHID

SARBANR   BITUN / BAITAN   GHURGHUST

WARSHPUN   daughter

SHARKBUN-1	KHARSHBUN-2	& KAJIN-3	BIBI MATO/MATU-4	DANI-5	BABI-6	MANDU-7

SHAH HUSSAIN

Babi

Abdali/Durrani*	Chamkanni				
Achakzai	Daudzai	Bittani			
Alikozai*	Gigiani			Jadun/Gadun	Mando Khel
Alizai*	Kasi	GHALZOE-8	IBRAHIM LODI-9	Kakar	
Barakzai*	Ketran			Musa Khel #	
Barech	Khalil			Pani/Panri	
Ishaqzai*	Khweshgi	Aka Khel	Babar	Safi #	
Miani	Mohmand	Ali Khel #	Bilut		
Mohammadzai*	Mohammadzai	Hotak	Daulat Khel		
Nurzai*	Shinwari	(Kharoti)	Dotani / Dautani		
Popalzai*	Tarklanri	(Nasar)	Kundi		
Saddozai*	Utman Khel	Sohaq/Ishaq	Lodi		
Sherani	Yusufzai	Sulaiman Khel	Mandanr		
Spin Tarin		Tarraki	Marrwat		
Tor Tarin		Tokhi	Mian Khel / Mai Khel		
Urmar			Mitti		
			Niazi		

KANLANRI-10, adopted by an Urmar and
later married to foster father's daughter.

Surr   Saeeds / Sayyids claim
descent from the Prophet's
son-in-law, Ali, through
his martyred son
HUSSAIN-11

Afridi	Bangash
Dilizak	Bannuchi
Jaji / Zazi	Daur
Khattak	Gurbuz (originally Wazir ?)
Kugiani	Mahsud
Mangal	Ahmadzai Wazir
Muqbil	Utmanzai Wazir
Orakzai	
Turi	
Utman Khel	
Zazi / Jaji	
Zhadran	

Alozai
Mala Khel / Mullah Khel
Mattani
Yasinzai

Jaffar, Khetrans, Luni & Zmarrai originate from the Miani

TRIBES OR CLANS (?) OF UNKNOWN AFFILIATION:

	Chakmanni	Gandapur	Ghoriani	Isot	Khasora
	Lawana	Lohani	Mallagori	Mashwani	Shillman
Shittak	Ustarana	Tani	Wardak	Zaimukh	Zarghun

NOTE. Names in capital letters are the putative founding ancestors of the tribes listed below them.
Those tribes with an asterisk * belong to the Abdali / Durrani confederation; those marked
with # have status as full tribe disputed by some authorities; confederation membership of the two
tribes bracketed is disputed. Numbers 1-7 = Afghan tribes, 8 = Ghilzai tribes, 9 = Lodi tribes,
10= Pashtun tribes, 11 = Saeed tribes. The above chart is based upon 'The Pathans' by Sir O.Caroe
and 'The Nomad Tribes of Eastern Afghanistan' by Capt. J.A.Robinson.

the case, Sanjar burnt down the Mughal's fort, the remains of which are called Khani locally and are said to be near Shina Khwar some sixteen miles from Hindubagh, abducted his bride, who seems to have been quite willing if not actually conniving, and fled on horseback.

The twelve sections descended from their sons are the Alizai, Abdullazai, Kibzai, Harmzai, Utman Khel, Barat Khel, Nas Khel, Arab Khel, Paraizun, Taimani, Nissai and Hindu Sanjar Khel. All except the last one are named after the sons, that last group being descended from a son who emigrated down into the Sinde and took up the Hindu religion. My friends' place in this tribal maze comes down from the first section of the Sanjar Khel, the Alizai, and on via Shado, Shmo, Jalal and six further generations before Joge or Jogi himself, whence come the Jogezais. The meaning of 'zai' has already been explained, so that it is much like our Johnsons or Williamsons, whose distant ancestors were literally the son of a John or a William. Joge's tomb and shrine is at a place called Khushnob on the north side of the Zhob Valley almost opposite Kila Saifulla but I have not visited the site. The next main section of the tribe is the Sanatia, very much smaller and divided into two main divisions, the Harun Khel or Harum Khel and the Isa Khel, then numerous clans or sub-divisions. The Saraghara section is smaller still, although it is divided into three divisions, the Sam Khel, the Mandazai and the Harunzai according to A.Y.K. (the genealogical table of 1901 omitting this detail); while the Taraghara seem to consist of three small groups or clans, the Ahmed Khel, Barakzai and Sulaiman Khel – the last two not to be confused with the Durrani and Ghalzai tribes.

There are also at least three anomalous small sections in addition to the above groupings according to the Zhob Gazetteer. A branch of the Akhtarzai, Sheikh Rahmat of Tarwal's own clan, known as the Sibzai is said to have been a section or clan of the Ghalzai Hotak tribe originally. If correct, one may surmise that the Sibzai were driven out from their homeland and were given land and protection by the Akhtarzai, the local term for such adopted refugee groups being 'wasli' or 'hamsaya'. Then there is the Adozai section or clan, said to be descended from an unknown widow's son who was abducted by a merchant from Kandahar named Sulaiman and returned later to settle at Gosa, south-east of Zhob. However, it does not mention if the widow was also abducted. This Adozai section is associated with, and I quote, 'the Sulaimanzai Kibzai': which I would interpret as meaning a section descended from the Kibzai, or if one prefers a distinct section of the Kibzai. Finally, for good measure, we have the Yasinzai, said to originate from a foundling and claiming alliance with the Abdullazai. However, there is also a Yasinzai section among the Sanatia and one wonders if there was some confusion.

I do not wish to derogate the impressive work of Mir Shams Shah but he frequently uses the term 'tribe' quite indiscriminately, when in fact he is referring to a section or sub-section or clan within the Kakar tribe. To his credit, so much might have been forgotten by now had the tribal genealogy not been drawn up then, when traditions were still carefully committed to memory and passed on by word of mouth. Virtually every book on the tribes focuses on disputes between tribes or clans within a tribe as being due to 'zar, zan, zamin', meaning over gold, women or land, almost as if it is a tribal doctrine, but two or those at least can apply to almost every powerful country in the world or its people throughout history. The Pashtun code of life is called 'Pashtunwali' or 'Pakhtunwali' and has three tenets: 'nanawatai, badal, melmastia', in order meaning giving sanctuary when asked, avenging a wrong or an insult, and providing hospitality to anyone who comes to the house or tent – even sworn enemies – for three days before asking their business.

But back to my personal friends: Joge's great-grandson was

Bekar Khan or Baikar Khan, clearly a recognized and accepted leader for Ahmad Shah Abdali in Kandahar, later Ahmad Shah Durrani, founder of Afghanistan and the dynasty of that name, pronounced him 'Badshah' of Zhob and presented him with a gold ornament as a symbol of authority. Legend has it that, being slow in collecting taxes, Bekar was summoned to Kandahar and put into a cauldron of boiling water to encourage a bit more enthusiasm in the collection of revenues, but he emerged unscathed. Now Bekar Khan had five sons and his first-born, Mukam, fathered two sons, Ishak and Nawab. This is important as the two brothers gave rise to the Ishak Kahole and Nawab Kahole of today, between whom there was not a little bloodshed in the past. Ishak was the first born, whence his descendants, the Ishak Kahole, claim the leadership and provides the 'sardars' or leaders. The Jogezai clan is the predominant one among the Kakars. The name 'Nawab Kahole' can be rather confusing as it has nothing to do with the honorary title 'Nawab', later conferred upon Mohammad Khan Jogezai by the British in 1928.

Shah Jehan was one of the seven sons of Nawab and the most influential man in the tribe in his day, being regarded by many as a saint and a miracle worker. Also he had resisted and harassed the British fairly persistently, if not very successfully, between 1879 and 1884. His nephew, Shahbaz Khan, the elder son of Rashid who was Ishak's first-born, was by seniority the tribal 'Sardar' but he was weak and under Shah Jehan's thumb to the extent of tacitly relinquishing the leadership. However, Dost Mohammad Khan, described by one British report as being a violent and dissipated man, was vying for power although his father, Murghai, was the second-born son of Ishak. In 1870 Dost Mohammad had shot Jallandar Khan, one of the eight sons of Shah Jehan but I do not know on what pretext or for what reason. In retaliation, and I do not know precisely when but probably in 1871, another of Shah Jehan's sons, Fateh Khan, shot Fazal Khan, one of Dost Mohammad's two brothers. Following that, in 1885 Bungal Khan killed Shamal Khan with a sword, and in 1893 Dinak Khan killed Shingul Khan by the same means.

In May 1906 a 'jirga' of the Kakar leaders and elders was held at the Rest House in Kila Saifulla. Mohammad Akbar, Shah Jehan's grandson, was acknowledged by the British as 'Acting Sardar' of the tribe, as had been his father Shingul Khan, simply because at the time of his appointment Shahbaz Khab was considered unsuitable and Dost Mohammad and his son Bungal Khan were still outlaws, Stupidly, as he had been provocative on numerous occasions previously and thus generated a lot of ill-feeling, Mohammad Akbar made some taunting remark regarding the Ishak Kahole in the hearing of Bungal Khan's eldest son, Zarif Khan. Tempers were already near breaking point because Mohammad Akbar had persuaded Zarghun Khan, the son of Shahbaz Khan and first in line for the chieftainship, to drop his friendship with Bungal Khan and support the Nawab faction. This public insult was the last straw and Zarif Khan immediately drew his revolver and wounded the offender in three places though not seriously. Zarif Khan then left the veranda and his father Bungal Khan followed to remonstrate with him, asking him to give up his gun. As he did this Mohammad Akbar's cousin, Baran Khan, reported as being insane, fired three fatal shots into Bungal Khan from behind and at such close range that his clothes caught fire. The weapon he used belonged to Mohammad Akbar but it was unclear whether he had snatched the weapon from his cousin as the latter was dragged inside to examine his injuries or whether Mohammad Akbar gave it to him on purpose. At this, Baran Khan was in turn attacked by Bungal Khan's brother, Uma Khan, and Shamal Khan's other son, Luni (brother of Dinak Khan then tucked away in the Andeman Islands), receiving a sword cut and two bullet wounds before he managed to escape. All four directly involved were arrested.

In September 1906, a Mr. Tucker convened a special 'jirga' in Quetta of leading men from neighbouring tribes to ensure impartiality in the eyes of all to 'enquire into and report on the facts of the case'. Its President was Diwan Gunpat Rai and its members were: Shahbaz Khan Bugti and Khair Baksh Khan Marri from their tribal areas, Bahram Khan Mazari and Jalab Khan Gurchan from Dera Ghazi Khan, Azim Khan Kundil and Captain Moyuddin Khan from Dera Ismail Khan. The 'jirga' awarded Rs.5,000 to the Ishak Kahole as 'blood money' and Rs.2,500 to the Nawab Kahole for Mohammad Akbar's injuries but decided that the latter should not be allowed to return to Zhob. In addition to the 'blood money', the Nawab Kahole had to give four girls in marriage without 'wulwer' to the bereaved Ishak Kahole, the award stipulating 'two born and two unborn girls': a nice touch, presumably not to put too much strain on the finances of Mohammad Akbar Khan's family. The four arrested were to remain in custody but Uma Khan was released for health reason and died immediately after his release.

The constant feuding between the two leading groups of the tribe was liable to create instability and unrest, hence the banishments, initially to Kuchlagh near Quetta but later some at least were allowed to move to Loralai. Wisely the British did not interfere in the choice of the next chief. Initiating a third 'jirga' to settle everything was delayed until July 1907 to allow tempers to cool. Also held in Quetta and under the same President it consisted of: Bahram Khan Mazari, Jalab Khan Gurchani, Mir Shams Shah, Mehrab Khan Bugti and Mustapha Khan Barozai. Mohammad Akbar was generally unpopular for his partiality when dealing with tribal disputes and for his avarice. He was now blamed for this killing of a very popular, rugged and able man. The 'jirga' decided that Mohammad Akbar could no longer be 'Acting Sardar' of the tribe (his appointment followed the murder of his father, Shingul Khan) and that the 'Sardari' should revert to the Ishak Kahole by right of their seniority. Zarghun Khan was rightfully the heir but lacked a strong character and, in siding with the Nawab Kahole, had lost popular support. Although Zarif Khan had fired the first shot he had been greatly provoked and hitherto had led a blameless life and possessed a sufficiently strong and stable character and the family enjoyed widespread sympathy and support. It was also felt that his sixteen months of imprisonment would have matured him. Therefore, although only aged eighteen, he should become the chief.

Mohammad Akbar should not be allowed to return to Zhob, partly as he was responsible for what had happened, partly because of his attempt to blame Zarif Khan for killing his own father, and partly as he would no longer be safe: 'his life would not be worth a moment's purchase' ran the official report. Other members of the 'Nawab Kahole' also banished from Zhob were his brother Ayub Khan and sons, Kalla Khan nephew Rahin Khan and Narai and sons. The deportation of two others Nawab Kahole members, Saeed Khan and Lajwar, was suspended provided that they remain in the Zhob Levy Corps and did not enter Kila Saifulla. Another man to be banished from Zhob was Khanai, a close associate of and advisor to Mohammad Akbar, described in the official report as being a 'very mischievous fellow'. He was a Bostanzai Jogezai but I cannot trace him in Mir Shams' genealogy of the tribe. In view of this considerable penalty upon various members of the Nawab Kahole, the compensation award of money and girls in marriage was annulled The various allowances of 'muafis', cash and grain were awarded or re-apportioned to both 'kaholes, and lands 'mortgaged' to ensure good behaviour. As to the 'muafis', as 'muaf' is an Urdu word meaning 'exempt' I guess that a 'muafi' is an area of cultivated land granted freedom from government taxation. The final draft was signed by fifty-one leading and influential Kakars. These days all seems well between the two 'kaholes', possibly cemented by appropriate marriages.

The new chief, Zarif Khan, died of natural causes only a year later as already mentioned, and his half-brother, Mohammad

Khan, succeeded him in 1907 at the age of twenty-two. We are almost into the present for Nawab Bahadur Mohammad Khan Jogezai, to give him his full title, died in 1978 aged ninety-three years. His last surviving brother, dear old Sher Ali Khan, and his last surviving wife, Ahmad Yar Khan's mother, both died about fifteen years ago. The Nawab's eldest son, Temur Shah, succeeded him but when he died in 1988 his eldest son, Asadullah Khan was not confirmed as chief, the position going to his grandson Ayaz Khan. For a long time my enquiries as to why Asadullah Khan had not been adopted as chief were met with a vague reply that 'he was not suitable' and I began to suspect some dark secret. However, when I was his guest briefly during my migration with the Shahizai family I found him to be a very quiet, rather diffident man and the question was answered. His very retiring nature, the result of an unhappy childhood I was told, appears to be the sole reason. I suspect that he has not lost much sleep at being left to live in his own tranquil way and in any case he has the satisfaction of seeing his son, a sturdy and very presentable young man, take on the burden.

Mohammad Khan Jogezai had a total of four wives, eleven sons and possibly eight daughters. Genes will out and it was fairly easy to allocate the sons to their different mothers simply on appearance. The chief's first wife, of the Arab Khel clan, was the mother of Temur Shah, Jehangir Shah and Jehandar Shah the eldest three of the brothers and in order of birth. Wife number two, Taj Bibi, was from the Luni tribe and mother of Ahmad Yar Khan, Mohabat Khan, Mohammad Hassan, Ashraf Khan, Nur Ahmad Khan and the twins Salim Khan and Anwar Jan (who died before his teens). She ended her days in A.Y.K.'s house and my wife met her in 1990, remembering her with considerable affection. His third wife was a Jogezai but was childless. Wife number four was also a Jogezai and bore Nurullah Khan who happens to be older than Mohammad Hassan and those that followed. Apart from the expected differences due to large age gaps, all the brothers seemed to get on remarkably well but I discerned an extra bond between those from the same mother, as might well be expected. I hope to have correctly sorted out conflicting information proffered at different times. As to the Nawab Kahole, the relationship between some of them whom I knew and the Ishak Kahole appeared to be friendly and normal.

When I first met him, Temur Shah had recently retired from the army in which he had been a major and is best described as being very 'pukka', almost an English gentleman one could say. Years later, when he in turn was chief, his wives and /or daughters made a beautiful and colourful traditional dress for Sheila, hand-embroidered with silk and silver thread, without having seen her at the time and it fitted. The next brother, Jehangir Shah, lived in the Panjab and was a senator later in life. I saw little of him but remember him as a very big, ebullient man. Only one of his sons I knew well, Safdar Khan, physically strong, very intense and brave as the two Afghans who stole one of his uncle's camels discovered to their cost. However, I understand that he has been shot but have no details.

Jehandar Shah, who was a District Commissioner in Las Bela for some years, was quiet and extremely shrewd or 'canny' as a Scot would say, growing quite rich by astute but honest dealing on the side. For this reason I was somewhat wary of him in the early days and of course he was several years older than me. His last appointment was as Commissioner in Quetta to investigate corruption. He stuck it for a year before resigning from sheer frustration as many of those he unmasked greased the palms of justice to escape it. As he bluntly put it, he achieved very little but made enemies in the process. Living in Quetta, even before his retirement, fellow tribesmen with a difficulty would come to him for advice and sometimes for help. Certainly it was paternalism, like the help given by his brother Ahmad Yar Khan in Tarwal but it helped many fellow tribesmen who were unable or unlikely to find help elsewhere. His first wife died after Nadar Shah was born then his second one, a Tor Tarin, produced three handsome, sturdy sons and at least one beautiful daughter. Stopping over in England while on his way to America for a heart check-up with a relative many years ago, I met him and his wife at Heathrow, after which we went to the flat in Knightsbridge of a Baluchi 'sardar' related by marriage. For his wife it was the first time out of 'purdah' and facial exposure was an ordeal for a day or two. Moreover, on a day-visit to our home in the country, she could not bring herself to take food at the table with us. However, we 'did' London, saw the Koh-i-Nur diamond and a host of other things but it was small repayment for his repeated hospitality in Quetta.

It was Ahmad Yar Khan who introduced me to the Jogezai clan and the Kakars in general, for which I am eternally grateful, and gradually we became as brothers. Apart from his integrity, and lively sense of humour and curiosity about the world in general, in his more mature years he also took to helping those in need and a fairly steady stream of them found their way to Tarwal. During the Russian Afghan debacle he somehow came upon Wazir, an Afghan refugee boy aged about twelve years whose father had been killed in the fighting and whose mother and sister eked out a poor existence in the huge, sprawling refugee camp near Hindubagh. A.Y.K. employed him as a servant simply to help the bereaved family although there was no real need for domestic help. Wazir was extremely bright, eager to help, quick to comprehend and in Britain would likely as not end up in a good university. He later went to Quetta to work for Farouk and must be a young man now. A similar beneficiary was Kabir and his wife detailed elsewhere. Sheila grew very fond of his wife, Taj Bibi, during our visit in 1990 and, secretly, both of us would have been happy for our James or Newman to marry his daughter Naida, strikingly handsome and full of vitality, but she had been engaged to a cousin years earlier when only seven years of age. A.Y.K. has five surviving sons, the fifth being added

JOGEZAI ISHAQ KAHOLE, KAKAR TRIBE.

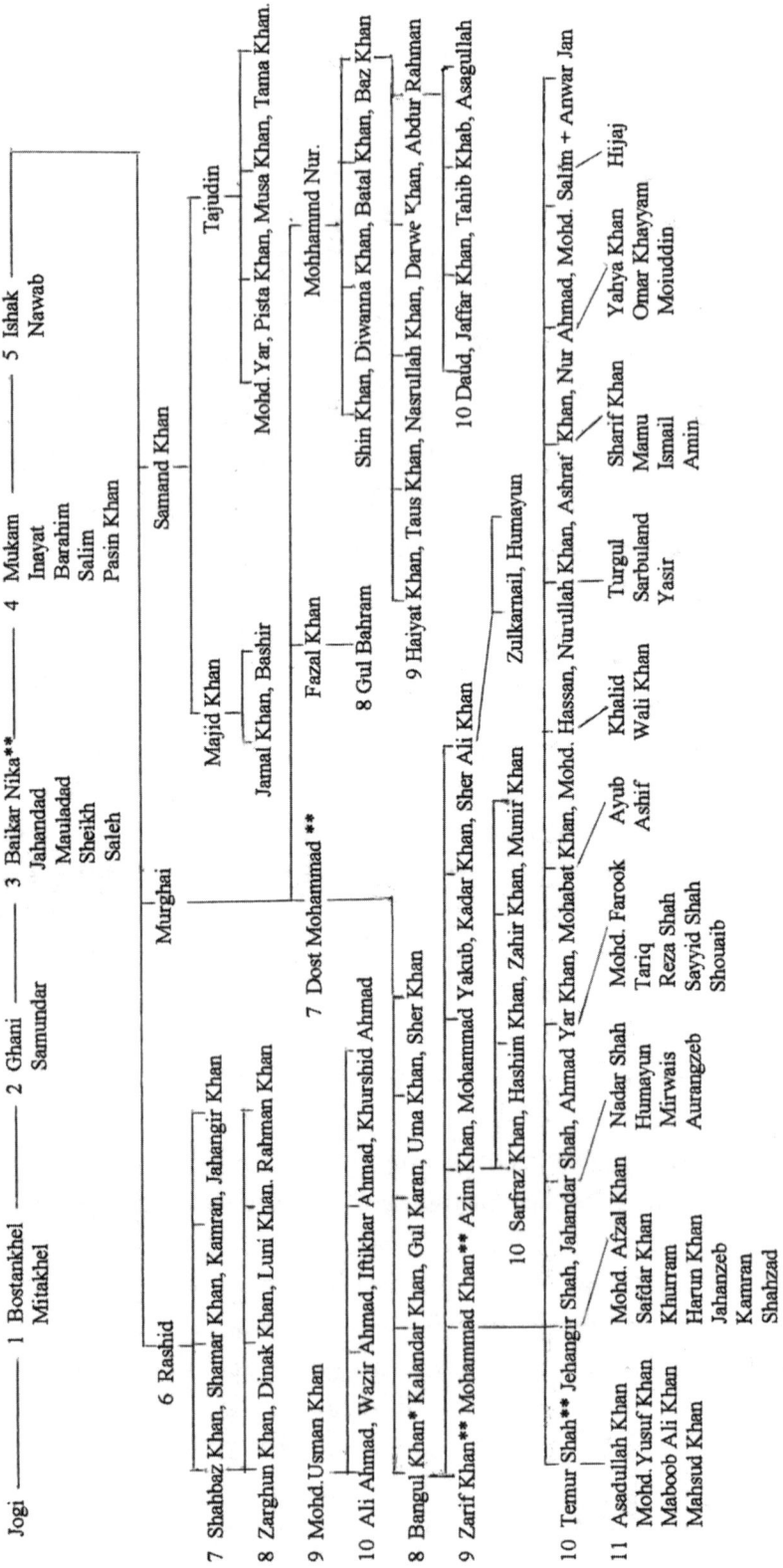

Jogi — 1 Bostankhel — 2 Ghani — 3 Baikar Nika** — 4 Mukam — 5 Ishak

1 Bostankhel
Mitakhel

2 Ghani
Samundar

3 Baikar Nika**
Jahandad
Mauladad
Sheikh
Saleh

4 Mukam
Inayat
Barahim
Salim
Pasin Khan

5 Ishak
Nawab

6 Rashid

Murghai

Samand Khan

Tajudin

Mohd. Yar, Pista Khan, Musa Khan, Tama Khan.

Mohammd Nur.

Shin Khan, Diwanna Khan, Batal Khan, Baz Khan

9 Haiyat Khan, Taus Khan, Nasrullah Khan, Darwe Khan, Abdur Rahman

10 Daud, Jaffar Khan, Tahib Khab, Asagullah

Majid Khan

Jamal Khan, Bashir

Fazal Khan

8 Gul Bahram

Zulkarnail, Humayun

7 Shahbaz Khan, Shamar Khan, Kamran, Jahangir Khan

8 Zarghun Khan, Dinak Khan, Luni Khan. Rahman Khan

9 Mohd. Usman Khan

10 Ali Ahmad, Wazir Ahmad, Iftikhar Ahmad, Khurshid Ahmad

8 Bangul Khan* Kalandar Khan, Gul Karan, Uma Khan, Sher Khan

9 Zarif Khan** Mohammad Khan** Azim Khan, Mohammad Yakub, Kadar Khan, Sher Ali Khan

7 Dost Mohammad **

10 Sarfraz Khan, Hashim Khan, Zahir Khan, Munir Khan

10 Temur Shah** Jehangir Shah, Jahandar Shah, Ahmad Yar Khan, Mohabat Khan, Mohd. Hassan, Nurullah Khan, Ashraf Khan, Nur Ahmad, Mohd. Salim + Anwar Jan

Khalid
Wali Khan

Ayub
Ashif

Mohd. Farook
Tariq
Reza Shah
Sayyid Shah
Shouaib

Nadar Shah
Humayun
Mirwais
Aurangzeb

Turgul
Sarbuland
Yasir

Sharif Khan
Mamu
Ismail
Amin.

Yahya Khan
Omar Khayyam
Moiuddin

Hijaj

11 Asadullah Khan
Mohd.Yusuf Khan
Maboob Ali Khan
Mahsud Khan

Mohd. Afzal Khan
Safdar Khan
Khurram
Harun Khan
Jahanzeb
Kamran
Shahzad

Ayaz Khan **, son of Asadullah Khan & grandson of Temur Shah, is chief of the Kakars now (2008). Previous chiefs, recognised by Afghan, British then Pakistan authorities have a double asterisk. De factor or acting chiefs have a single asterisk. Of necessity the genealogy drawn up by Mir Shams in 1901 descends only to the 9th generation from Jogi. Note that Mohd. Salim's twin brother, Anwar Jan, died in his early teens of natural causes. Daughters are not shown.   AFMB   2008

JOGEZAI NAWAB KAHOLE, KAKAR TRIBE

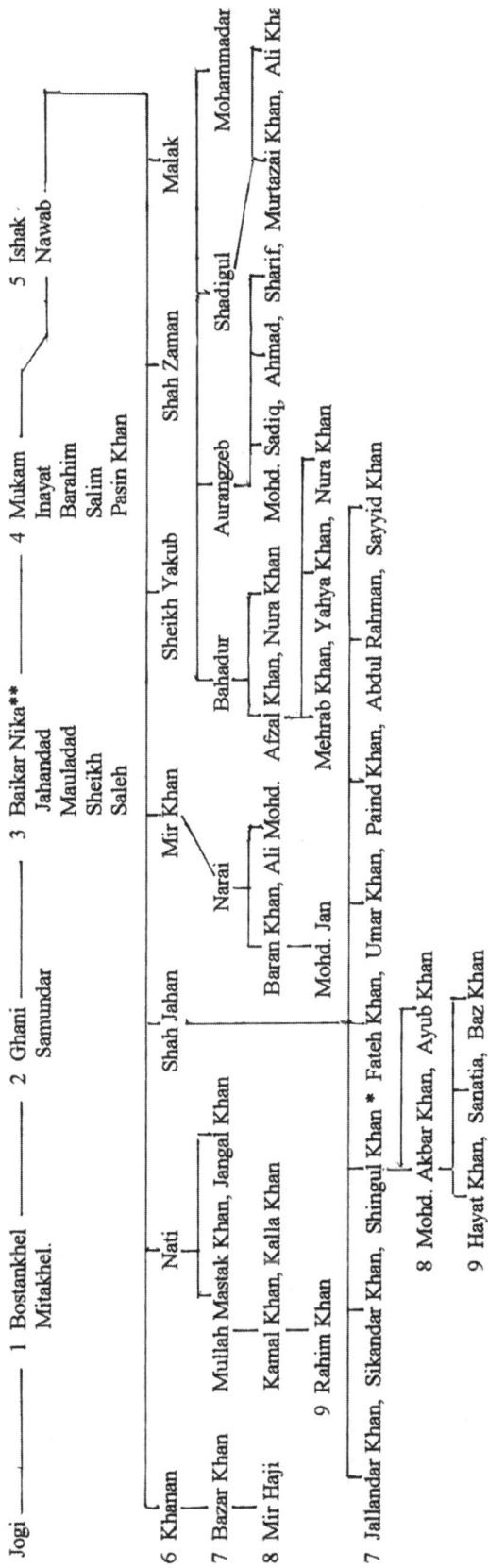

Jogi
— 1 Bostankhel
   Mitakhel.
— 2 Ghani
   Samundar
— 3 Baikar Nika**
   Jahandad
   Mauladad
   Sheikh
   Saleh
— 4 Mukam
   Inayat
   Barahim
   Salim
   Pasin Khan
— 5 Ishak
   Nawab

6 Khanan
7 Bazar Khan
8 Mir Haji
9 Rahim Khan

Nati — Mullah Mastak Khan, Jangal Khan
Kamal Khan, Kalla Khan

Shah Jahan — Mir Khan — Narai — Baran Khan, Ali Mohd.
Mohd. Jan
Mehrab Khan, Yahya Khan, Nura Khan

Sheikh Yakub — Bahadur — Afzal Khan, Nura Khan
Aurangzeb — Mohd. Sadiq, Ahmad, Sharif, Murtazai Khan, Ali Kha

Shah Zaman — Shadigul — Mohammadar

Malak

7 Jallandar Khan, Sikandar Khan, Shingul Khan * Fateh Khan, Umar Khan, Paind Khan, Abdul Rahman, Sayyid Khan
8 Mohd. Akbar Khan, Ayub Khan
9 Hayat Khan, Sanatia, Baz Khan

VICTIMS OF THE KAHOLE FEUDING TO 1906 none since then)

1/ Jallander Khan, 1st son of Shah Jehan (Nawab Kahole) —————— shot & killed by Dost Mohammad (Ishak Kahole) in 1870

2/ Fazal Khan, brother of Dost Moammad. (I.K.) —————— shot & killed by Fateh Khan, 4th son of Shah Jehan (N.K.) in 1870 or 1871

3/ Shamar Khan, 2nd son of Rashid (I.K) —————— killed (sword) by Bangul Khan, 1st son of Dost Mohammad, (I.K.) in 1885

4/ Shingul Khan, 3rd son of Shah Jehan (N.K.) —————— killed (sword) by Dinak Khan, 1st son of Shamar Khan (I.K.) in 1892

5/ Mohd. Akbar Khan, 1st son of Shingul Khan (N.K.) —————— shot & wounded by Zarif Khan 1st son of Bangul Khan (I.K.) in Kila Saifulla meeting of 1906

6/ Bangul Khan (I.K.) —————— shot & killed by Baran Khan, 1st son of Narai (N.K) at the same meeting with the Political Agent in 1906

7/ Baran Khan (N.K) —————— shot by Luni Khan (I.K.) and sword cut by Uma Khan (I.K.), brother of Bahgul Khan, at same meeting but not killed.

Note that an attempt by Bangul Khan upon Shahbaz Khan, 1st son of Rashid, was foiled by a warning from Khan Bahadur Hak Nawaz Khan, the Duki Native Assistant. Since 1906 there has been no more feuding and relations between the two kaholes appears to be good. The apparent absence of male offspring in many cases, by Mir Shams Shah, does not mean that there were none: simply space was limited. Daughters are not included.

since this manuscript was begun. His walled garden used to be very attractive but it is no longer practical to deepen the huge well every two years as the water table drops threateningly and so his pistacchio and his pomegranate trees are withered.

I hardly knew Mohabat Khan, in spite of briefly meeting him several times, as he lives and works elsewhere but he is very quiet and reserved, far more so than any of his full brothers. Next comes Nurullah Khan, a 'zamindari' like his three other brothers in Tarwal. Like Mohabat Khan he is rather serious, quiet and retiring but less reserved, the sort of person one can rely upon. Being a half-brother to the others may account for that to some extent. Mohammda Hassan very much resembles A.Y.K., but while remaining in the village after college in Quetta, he joined the civil service as already noted and has built himself a house in Tarwal, graced by a huge satellite dish to enjoy television, the B.B.C. Overseas Service and 'Discovery' programmes being very popular. One of his two sons worked in the Hindubagh refugee camp and took me there one day, where a cheeky little Afghan boy slapped me through the open car window and fled before I could grab him. When in Tarwal with Sheila and Helga I was allowed to meet his daughters who, as might be expected, were nice-looking, quiet and refined.

Ashraf Khan is the super-industrious one of the brothers, planting vast apple and other orchards fed by three gushing boreholes but, sadly, eager to shoot almost anything that runs or flies. That second activity he shares with Saudi princes who also like to draw their sights on Houbari bustards and gazelle during the crisp winter months. During one of their visits they presented him with a fine rifle whose stock was inlaid with a kilo of engraved gold. I was told that one year their obsession with falconry was gratified by a rare, cream coloured bird near Peshawar that cost them three and a half million rupees and was collected by a specially chartered jet. Afghans, their land and climate generally being what it is, seem to regard the garden rose as the epitome of civilization, prosperity and presence of water: Ashraf Khan exemplifies this and has an extensive lawn of grass surrounded on all four sides by rose beds adjoining one of his estates although he still lives in Tarwal some miles away.

Nearing the end of the list is Nur Ahmad. He too remains in Tarwal although, like Ahmad Yar Khan, he is lured by the bright lights of Quetta at intervals and is a 'zamindari', growing tobacco, chillies and melons amongst other things. Short and stocky, in the nicest possible way he is the Peter Pan of the family, often greeting me by hoisting me off the ground, one of the disadvantages of being tall. While in Quetta towards the end of a visit in 1996, he and a friend took me to the extraordinary village of Vesh in the desert two or three miles into Afghanistan. Passing through a hilly stretch known as Gulistan on the way to Chaman, several Achakzai villages were pointed out where the Ghabai and Hamidzai clans had been engaged in an unusually fierce and bloody feud for several years. The police had tried but were unable to control the perpetual fighting and estimates put the number of dead at between two and three hundred.

What really intrigued me was that we entered Vesh driving on the left, as in Pakistan, but upon passing under the high arch made of steel halfway along we had to change to the right hand side of the street. There were a number of rather flashy youths from Karachi and elsewhere in their Pujaros, clearly in the buying mode, and the whole thing was rather surreal for the place was obviously no secret to anyone, least of all Pakistani Customs officials and government ministers. As it is Achakzai territory I guess it is their enterprise though I cannot imagine the Taliban failing to demand a generous percentage of the income when they held power. The strange settlement has shops on either side of the street that are large, steel shipping containers in various sizes and various colours, set sideways or end-on to the road, with doors crudely cut in them where wished.

They offer National & Duckhams motor oils, tyres in yellow or red or blue wrappers and almost anything else to do with cars, pick-ups and small trucks. Behind this array of goods to be smuggled into Pakistan are extensive mud-walled compounds filled with thousands of vehicles awaiting customers from Pakistan. A figure of forty-five thousand vehicles was quoted, probably too high but indicative of the scale of it all. These all had white U.A.E. export plates with Arabic numbers and lettering in blue, including the port of origin such as S.H.J. for Sharjha, A.J. and U.A.Q. The customs pay in cash, documents are forged and the sellers obligingly have the goods driven across a quiet section of the unmarked border further north. Told that duty on officially imported vehicles was two hundred and fifty per cent, I can understand the temptations of the Vesh vehicle bazaar. After a couple of hours nothing suitable had been seen and we returned innocently to Quetta. However, government officials must know about the place.

Salim Khan, the surviving twin and youngest of the brothers is ever restless, has hawk-like features and is quite dark. Some years ago he was accused of armed robbery against a bus and several of his brothers rushed to Quetta in some alarm to support him. When recently I decided to ask about the final outcome, I was told that he was imprisoned for a week and so apparently was judged guilty but clearly that was a token sentence, partly in deference to the family's position and status but also, I suspect, that his brothers stood surety for his future good behaviour. I was advised not to raise the matter with him as he becomes angry. Suffice to say he has led a blameless life ever since. The old chief's family had a tradition whereby anyone marrying one of his daughters had to shoot an earthen pot placed in a tree from so many paces but one young groom was unable to pass this test, whereupon young Salim at the tender age of twelve successfully stood in for him. His twin brother, Mohammad Anwar died in his early teens. There is a strong tendency among the leading Jogezais to marry cousins and genetically that is not a wise practice.

Having taken so long to complete this work, Jehandar Shah has since died and so has missed the satisfaction of seeing recognition of his considerable help in print; so has Abdur Rahman the 'gentleman of Zhob' whose company was such a pleasure, and Fukhruddin the old outlaw likewise is no longer though his cheerful and remarkable widow will be given a copy to share with their four sons. There are of course one or two Kakar clans just over the border in Afghanistan, cut off by the Durand Line, but the isolated Taimani clan who live some three hundred and fifty miles to the west of Zhob, in the Siah Band mountains to the east of Shindand are something of a mystery. There, according to his knowledgeable book on Afghan rugs, R. D. Parsons states that they are one of four tribal groups that make up a confederation known as the Chahar Aimaq, 'chahar' meaning four in Farsi while 'aimaq' is a Mongolian word for nomad, suggesting that at least one of the other three is of Mongolian extraction. Moreover, from their neighbours the Taimani have learned to knot rugs, one of which I picked up some years ago in a London auction. As Parsons travelled widely in Afghanistan as a buyer over a period of seven years his opinion carries weight. Taimani himself and his eleven brothers, not to mention unknown sisters, is twenty-one generations before Ahmad Yar Khan and his brothers according to the Genealogical Tree of the Kakar Tribe drawn up by Mir Shams Shah in 1901, so they probably became separated about four hundred years ago; yet, although isolated and far to the west, they have not lost their tribal identity.

Mir Shams Shah visited Herat in 1893 and met some Taimani there who introduced themselves as Sanjari Kakars, meaning people descended from one of Sanjar's or Sanjar's twelve sons, as indeed they are according to the genealogy. No Zhob Kakars know how, when or why the Taimani clan came to settle there.

Recently A.Y.K. told me, and he is usually correct, that the Kakars as a tribe came from the region and that the tomb of Nika Kakar, the reputed progenitor of the whole tribe through his six sons, is at the great mosque in Herat. That city having been devastated by the Russian war planes, his tomb may no longer exist of course. Therefore it seems fairly certain that Nika Kakar died at Herat but whether his six sons were there at the time or had already migrated east to the present day tribal area seems unknown. However, the tomb of his grandson Sanjar through his fourth son Sughruk is at Kot, south of Fort Sandeman and which I have visited. The graves or tombs of Nika Kakar's six sons seem to have been forgotten or lost. So did Sanjar and his eleven other sons, not to mention daughters, emigrate from Herat and leave Taimani, his twelfth son, behind for some reason, such as marrying into another tribe, or did Taimani return there after the rest of the family had settled in the Zhob area? And what of Sughruk and Nika Kakar's other five sons, tens of thousands of whose descendants are very much alive today in Zhob? Did they also emigrate eastwards or could it be that they were all born in or near Zhob and their father Nika Kakar, perhaps accompanied by his grandson Taimani, happened to die in Herat while undertaking a pilgrimage to Mashed or Qum. Whatever the case, Kakar tradition in Baluchistan says that their ancestors threw out the resident Mughals when they moved into the area and evidence for this is a ruin or mound near Hindubagh, called Mughalo Kila, the Mughal's Fort. Then there is the village of Mughal Kot far down the Zhob valley.

As to why they emigrated, it is of course just possible that all Nika Kakar's sons and grandchildren except the Taimani were moved by some Persian ruler, as did Shah Abbas later in the seventeenth century when he transported Kurds from their homeland in western Persia to Khorrasan in the north-east of the country as a bulwark against incursions by Uzbeks. Later, in the eighteenth century, Nadar Shah transported many Ghalzais from Kandahar to Nishapur in eastern Persia as a punishment for their resistance. But one would then expect to find written records of such an event if instigated by a Persian ruler. Otherwise tribal migrations seem generally to be in response to pressure from or attack by a more powerful neighbour, whose own land-hunger may be caused by an increasing population or perhaps by a prolonged drought. At all events it is hardly undertaken lightly as it may involve having to fight to gain the new area. Several small groups from elsewhere, and the important word is 'small', have been allowed to settle in Zhob and Loralai by the Kakars and others. Such 'hamsayas' or refugees are more or less protected by the established tribe. The feud between the Akhtarzai and Batozai clans in Zhob, detailed elsewhere and possibly romanticised, was precisely for such a reason. Typically, quarrels and feuds among Afghans, Pashtuns and Ghalzais, whether between tribes, between clans or between families involve land. Mair Jan Mahsud's difficulties, related elsewhere, and the Ruckni quarrel illustrate the point.

Another probable tribal movement apparently lost in the mists of time is a tradition among the Yusufzai of Dir and Swat to the north-east of Peshawar that they migrated from a place called Ghwara Murgha in Kakar Khorrasan. This becomes the more plausible when one hears that the Kakars in that area, unacquainted with the Yusufzais over three hundred miles away to the north, have a folklore that tells of a tribe emigrating to the north. Further, when Henry McMahon was encamped at Gustoi on the Kundar river early in the twentieth century he came across traces of a large, ancient walled encampment called Ghwara Murgha. Enquiries among people of the area, who knew nothing of the tribe in Swat, revealed that their tradition held that a tribe called the Yusufzai had lived there. In turn it seems that the Yusufzai hold a tradition that they had migrated from the south to their present territory. Other sources suggest that the Tarklanri and Utman Khel tribes far to the north also came from the same area.

Purely for the sake of the record and in large measure for the benefit of future generations of Kakars and others of the area, who are unlikely to have access to many old books regarding their history as they are increasingly hard to find, I list the troops involved and the recorded routes of General Tanner's punitive Zhob expedition of 1884, of Sandeman's small scale expedition in 1889, and of the extensive 1990 military expedition through Zhob and neighbouring areas by the Zhob Field Force leading to permanent occupation of the area in an Appendix at the end of the book.

Chapter Seven

A Longer Stay and Closer Look

By the summer of 1960 it became clear that the continuing intermittent incursions by the Chinese from Tibet across India's border and the heavy fighting involved meant that any hope of realising my original ambition of traversing the Himalaya from west to east was out of the question. No Inner Line permits were being issued to anyone and therefore I resigned from the Doon School and soon found myself back in Tarwal with no precise time limit and I was becoming more and more interested in the area and particularly its people: my only limitation really was cash, or a lack of it. Equally important, Ahmad Yar Khan's patience was standing up well to my constant questioning about life there and about the language. While I had picked up everyday Farsi fairly quickly, things were very different with regard to Pashtu. There were three reasons for this: firstly, my visual memory is far better than my aural one, I could find no logically written book on the language, while those that had been written dealt with the northern variant of the language, Pakhtu, to further complicate things. Secondly, nouns are declined and plurals vary a great deal. Thirdly, verbs seemed to be very irregular and, lastly, the pronunciation of not a few words is subtle to the ear and difficult to emulate. If that were not enough, as with almost every language, learning them is made more difficult by grammatically poor speech and strong dialects. Still I could just about cope with the basics.

Learning the language was tiresome for both A.Y.K. and me, but his tribal folklore was fascinating and seemingly endless. It was somewhat like King Arthur and the Knights of the Round Table in its blend of honour, violence and chivalry. An example of this was illustrated by the Batozais who are a Kakar clan dwelling about forty or forty-five miles north of Tarwal, in and near the Shin Ghar range, and the Akhtarzais, a neighbouring clan to their south-east (Sheikh's clan). About one hundred and fifty years ago a clan of the Hotak tribe came from the west into Kakar territory and asked Alaf Khan, the Akhtarzai chief, if they could settle on a certain piece of land. He agreed but later they noticed some better land nearby and asked Alaf if they could settle there instead. This was granted but the Batozai chief, Ghunduk, sent them away. Returning to Alaf they asked why he had given them land that was not his to give. Embarrassed, he sent word to Ghunduk stating that they were 'brothers' and that the land in question was shared between their two clans. However, the Batozai chief was adamant. No doubt realising that his men would be unenthusiastic about fighting on behalf of interlopers from another tribe, Alaf called a gathering and went to it without his 'partuk' or baggy trousers, a symbolic gesture to show that he was without aid. The men told him to put on his 'partuk' as they were his followers. He then explained the position and asked them to fight. The small battles and raids went on for a year, after which many of the Batozai, being up against a larger clan, refused to continue the struggle.

So Ghunduk went to Alaf's 'kuzhdei'. As was the custom, Alaf vacated it and his enemy was looked after for three days by the women folk without any questions being asked. Returning to his tent at the end of that time Alaf learnt about the other chief's difficulty. He suggested that Ghunduk should discreetly mark the camels and donkeys belonging to him and his loyal supporters and that they should cut their own hair short (from Waziristan southwards long hair was customary among men). Alaf and his men would then harry only the reluctant Batozais and so goad them into supporting their chief. This was done and the struggle continued at intervals for twenty years, when after losing eighteen men killed in the last battle Ghunduk gave up and the promise to the Hotaks was fulfilled. How much of this tale is fact and how much is fiction is difficult to say but A.Y.K. assures me that the Hotaks are still there.

One day A.Y.K. mentioned a cave in a mountain about fifty miles away by jeep track in Batozai 'surra' or territory. Rumour had it that there were walled-off passages, Mughal carvings of camels on the walls and deep vertical shafts. With such a reputation the young men of the locality dearly wanted to go in and find the treasure that was surely hidden there. However, they were afraid of the 'djins' or spirits that guarded it. In the end they persuaded a mullah to enter in order to drive out the 'djins' so that they could follow him but unfortunately a leopard had taken up residence in the cave. As the mullah entered the leopard rushed out, very upset, and the mullah didn't fancy angry leopards so the cave remained inviolate. Aware that I used to go caving in Somerset, Ahmad Yar Khan suggested that we take a look at it. I was as eager as he but one look at the old rope that he produced for the purpose, upon which our lives might depend, was sufficient to put me off the idea. A while later it occurred to me that it might be a good idea to take a brief look at the entrance so that I would at least know where it was. A.Y.K. was tinkering yet again with his old Chevrolet at the time but Fukhruddin had time on his hands so I asked him to show me the place. He was a hardy little chap and by walking directly across the desert, the distance then being thirty-five or forty miles, we could reach it in a single day. No, he couldn't take me there. Puzzled, as he had neither land nor a flock to attend, I persisted and he prevaricated for some time but eventually the reason came out: 'bahdi', meaning a feud. He had enemies in the area who might decide to settle old scores given such a chance.

The only rainfall records for Zhob that I have found covered five years early in the 1900s, during a drought period it seems, so the average annual record of five inches might be half or less than the norm. I do not know if anyone has kept such records since but a 'guesstimate' of ten inches might be a reasonable one. With so much grazing by flocks of sheep and goats, of locals and of passing nomads, the natural vegetation on the valley floors must be greatly modified. What is left seems to consist of widely scattered small woody herbs, coarse tufted grass here and there and, along torrent beds and rivers, tamarisk trees. In the higher hills wild olive and pistacchio grow but an ever-increasing population and their flocks have wiped out these from many areas and above seven thousand feet one finds gnarled junipers. In some of the small side-valleys is another robust but short tree that seems doomed to extinction because grazing apparently destroys all saplings even though the trees seem to bear fruit every year. When I asked its name of someone, I was told 'wana' and only later learned that this simply means tree, in the same way as the Sahara seems to have earned its name among Europeans. What helped this confusion was that most of the Jogezais tend to use 'drakht' instead, which is virtually the Persian word. They may have been the wild olive.

Until the early twentieth century a large proportion of the local population was nomadic or semi-nomadic and flocks were the mainstay of the immense Zhob Valley; some people migrated with their flocks for the summer months to the high plateau of Kakar Khorrasan which, at around seven thousand feet, is much cooler with slightly better grazing to be found. Others migrated to Maimana, Herat and the Siah Band mountains in western Afghanistan to spend three months of the summer collecting Asafoedita for sale as a component of cough medicine. The four-hundred-mile journey took around two months each way and mainly involved tribes such as the Babars, Haripals, Kibzais, Mando Khels and Sheranis. So how did the Jogezais and others live in such an arid climate, apart from a few springs and streams issuing from deep valleys here and there whereby meagre cropping is possible. On a smallish scale there were, and to a limited extent still are, two ways of growing fairly substantial crops. The first and simple way is to raise low earth dams or 'bunds', four to six feet high, across the lower reaches of small valleys in which the soil is good to trap the sudden rush of water from storms. The water held then soaks in and a crop such as wheat or millet can be grown. Such crop lands, limited in extent, are called 'khushk-aba', translated literally as 'drywater'.

The second system, now derelict in Zhob since the advent of electricity and pumps for boreholes but thriving until the early eighties, is the 'karez' well. However, when cutting through Afghanistan from Ghazluna to Loeband in 1992 I saw one apparently under construction. As mentioned earlier those in Zhob are reputedly Mughal in origin, such wells being called 'qanat' in Iran where they were very common. According to Robinson's book on nomads, the Kharoti tribe were skilled in their construction but small teams from other tribes such as the Tarraki and the Tokhi carried out the annual clearing of the 'karez' near Tarwal. In Zhob no one could tell me exactly how these wells were built in the first place and obviously it took skill and experience, in addition to a lot of money, but I am fairly sure that it must be something like this: it could hardly be any other way. Firstly, desert plains in the vicinity of mountain ranges have very gently sloping floors even though they appear to be flat and secondly, even if there is no water at the surface, there will be a steady flow underground from the mouths of valley systems opening onto the plain. The 'karez' digging team choose their valley and at anything from one to three miles from its mouth sinks a vertical shaft down to the water table. If it happens to be ten or so feet down good, if less then it's back to the drawing board and a short move towards the valley to try again. Assuming that all is fine, a trench down to the water table will be dug from there down along a shallow gradient but gradually rising above the water table and the spoil deposited further on to gradually create a low bank along the top of which the water can eventually flow. This will allow water to be led off by gravity to small plots surrounded by low banks just a foot or so high when the 'karez' is completed. Some water must be reserved for the house or hamlet nearby and will be led on to run along an ordinary ditch, the word 'nearby' meaning anything up to two or three miles away. How the diggers judge the gradient so precisely is anybody's guess. It may have been a matter of trial and error largely but clearly considerable skill is needed.

Next, a second shaft is dug down to the water table in the direction of the chosen side valley. One digger then digs a narrow passage horizontally from the trench towards the first shaft, the other man digging from the first shaft back towards what is to be the 'karez' exit until they meet, and creating a passage about two and a half feet wide and at least six feet high but as much as nine feet in places, as I discovered in Nowi Kashmir Karez that used to supply Tarwal, excavating perhaps nine inches down into water table The process is repeated again and again until the mouth of the side valley is reached, water seeping into the tunnel along its entire length to give a permanent flow. However, whereas the creation of the right gradient from the mouth of the 'karez' seems to be precise, the distances between the vertical shafts of any one 'karez' show considerable variation while the average distance between shafts of different 'karez' may be anything from fifteen to thirty-five yards. Some of the spoil from the shaft and tunnel will be banked around its mouth to prevent surface storm water from flooding down the shaft and eroding it, leaving a small gap in the downhill side. The problem is to tunnel directly towards the other man and sudden kinks here and there underground where the two diggers show that minor errors are made but even so the skill is impressive. They will have a primitive oil lamp and put the soil into a goatskin bag or into a bucket made from lorry tyres to be hauled to the surface on a crude winch by two more team members.

As the team progresses, the water table and shafts tend to get deeper up the gradual incline as the valley mouth is neared. Behind the diggers water seeps in from the sides increasingly as the tunnel lengthens so that a proper flow gradually develops, underground then along the trench which is eight to ten feet deep at first, gradually rising to ground level, thereafter along a shallow trench along a bank created from the shafts' and tunnel spoil. Needless to say, it was a prolonged and expensive enterprise, often beyond the pocket of even a relatively wealthy man so that several might contribute to the expense and share the water accordingly. Also the system must be annually maintained by 'karrigurrs' from over the border to dredge out accumulated silt: Tarrakis were employed near Tarwal in the autumn of 1971. The beauty of the system is that it does not lower the precious water table appreciably. The flow may diminish during a prolonged period of drought but will recover when the rainfall permits, sooner or later: an 'overdraft' is impossible unless a second 'karez' is dug too near. Modern boreholes with electric pumps on the other hand are causing water tables to drop by as much as a meter per year in not a few places and, in the absence of restraint, a time must come when they either cannot cope, as at sea level a vacuum pump can raise water only for about thirty-two feet – or they become uneconomical. Therefore the natural vegetation will then possibly or probably fail and the area become more desert than it was originally in the catchment areas of such boreholes. Opposite Tarwal in 1999 the Zhob River was bone dry for the first time in memory, admittedly during a drought yet there have been many droughts previously at intervals without that happening. Also during that visit Newman and I saw a young fruit orchard that had withered yet several boring rigs were at work.

Sharing such vital water is on the basis of the 'shab-ana-roz' unit, basically a Persian term, literally meaning 'a night and a day', whereby the water is allowed to flow onto an area of land chosen for twenty-four hours. The area soaked is then rationalised into small rectangular plots surrounded by low earth banks to retain the water. This is done sixteen times along the small banked canal so that, when complete, the sixteen 'shab-ana-roz' each receive a thorough soaking with water once every sixteen days in strict rotation. The size of the 'shab-ana-roz' depends entirely upon the flow and so varies from 'karez' to 'karez'. Together the sixteen constitute what is known as an 'awara'. One 'karez' at Manzai near Duki had such a good flow that it became practical to divide each 'shab-ana-roz' into two 'horr', each inundated for twelve hours only but on the same sixteen-day cycle. On favourable land it will be possible to create four or five 'awara' to be used in turn on a four or five year rotation to avoid exhausting the soil. Even so salination tends to become a problem eventually. Stealing such water is a serious and dangerous business and so a 'mirab', a 'water king', is employed to do the work and ensure fair distribution. In Iran, when returning from Babolsar on the Caspian, I was given a lift in an ambulance rushing to Tehran with an unfortunate policeman who had been shot four times while intervening in such a dispute. With water available more or less indefinitely on a sixteen-day cycle, fruit orchards of apple, almond, apricot or pomegranate may be established or crops such as tobacco, potatoes, chillies, melons, onions and tomatoes grown.

However, in the late 'eighties, electricity was brought down the Zhob Valley and all the ancient 'karez' were left to fall into ruin. Today pumps suck the water from boreholes at a prodigious rate, a five-inch tube drawing forty thousand gallons per hour. The orchards are huge and burdened with fruit to the extent that many branches break under the weight but as a result the water table is dropping at an alarming rate in such places. A.Y.K. had a wide well about twenty-five feet deep in his garden for household use and had to dig it deeper by around five feet every year or two but it is now beyond practical use. In the Shal Valley around Quetta, the water table is dropping at the rate of a metre per year I was told by a Scottish scientist in the Arid Zone Research Institute there. In addition to his enormous and magnificent orchard, one of the Tarwal brothers even has a quite lush garden in the middle of arid wastes. I pointed out to him that the water table was dropping seriously and he blandly agreed – then switched on one or other of his three pumps. Even worse, so I was told by A.Y.K., the electric company's inspectors were nervous of the tribesmen and reluctant to read meters in Zhob so that trivial bills were presented. As a result, for some years many pumps were running far longer than necessary as it cost so little but a while ago I heard from a Jogezai visitor that the army has recently been deputed to read the meters and cut off the supply of anyone who fails to pay up.

Up to and even in the 'sixties most tribesmen were extremely poor and unable to pay regular cash rents for irrigated land, nor were they paid wages to work as labourers: instead they became the tenant farmers of 'karez' owners, cultivating up to twenty 'jirub' or ten acres, and were paid in kind when the crop was harvested. It was a reversed tithe system in effect. Landlords such as Nawab Mohammad Khan therefore provided tools and seed, in addition to the land and water, while the tenant provided the animals and labour required. His eventual share of the crop depended upon the nature of the crop as some demanded more attention than others. With wheat, maize and millet the tenant received one third, though Nawab Jogezai gave his tenant cultivators half; but with crops such as potatoes, tobacco, onions, chillies, melons and vegetables the tenant received one half. That larger share was because those crops demand more labour in the form of planting and weeding. The 'karez' system was often limited in extent and affected by drought but it did not deplete the water table in the long term.

An important advantage of the system was that in the event of a poor crop, damaged by pest or heavy rain or hail or drought, the tenant did not become burdened with debt, though he would have less to eat and sell. Also he did not have to outlay money on seed and tools and the more successful he was the more he personally gained. The landlord alone paid government tax, at one sixth of his share until Marshall Law under Ayub Khan introduced an acreage tax. The landlord would also be expected to pay a tenth of his share 'to God', of which half would go to the local mullah and the other half to needy people such as the blind, cripples, orphans, and aged people without children to help support them. However, the above 'karez' system as a rule was only applicable to larger valleys such as the Shall Valley, Zhob, Loralai, Duki and others. Elsewhere, a small fertile valley might allow a 'bund' to be created to trap storm water while tiny springs in little valleys may support a household or two but over the arid wastes, high plateaux and mountains sheep and goats formed and still form the mainstay of many local people, wealthier ones perhaps owning a small cow. When spending several months in Zhob in 1960, to have a bath at intervals, I used to go to a secluded stretch of the 'karez' near its end below Tarwal when no one was about. However, unlike Delhi during the monsoon, where everyone was dripping with sweat so that they and their clothing smelt 'stale', the extremely dry air in most of Baluchistan means that even when the temperature is well over one 100°F or 38°C in the shade, sweat evaporates instantly and one is never clammy.

In the region of Hindubagh there are or were small chrome mines of long standing and in the early 'sixties one of the leading lights seems to have been a solitary Englishman. I never came across him but A.Y.K. used to pay him the compliment of describing him as a 'dairr takra serai', meaning 'a very energetic man'. Lumps of white material, small pieces often resembling python droppings, are still being dug out here and there as far down the valley as Nissai and a little beyond mainly by individuals but such efforts are hardly commercial. However, I cannot find out the nature or use of these tiny deposits today. The presence of chrome ore was the prime reason for building the narrow guage railway to Hindubagh in the first place, its extension to Fort Sandeman possibly to allow the rapid movement of troops if necessary to counter Russian expansion.

Shortly before I arrived on the scene in 1958 there had been an American couple living with the Baluch Murri tribe in their mountains flanking the Indus and well to the east of Zhob. They lived by means of a flock and the man was doing research for a Ph.D. degree. However, he fell victim to malaria at the same time as suffering from amoebiasis or Giardia, a deadly combination, and died within days. His heart-broken widow returned to the States and seemingly was not heard of again. Whether she published an account of their six years living as tribes people I do not know but if not then it is a great loss. The couple may have been a Bob Pearson and his wife. About that time I was offered land and water by one of the family, who suggested that instead of returning to the U.K. or going off to Africa to work I should settle down there in Zhob, and paid me the even greater compliment of further suggesting that I marry one of their girls. However, while it was very tempting, the lack of books, of photographic items and other things in the long term weighed against the generous offer. Also I realised that, while I loved the people, their desert and their mountains, there would be times when I would miss my blood relatives and yearn for the green of Sedgemoor in Somerset.

In such a harsh environment and where an almost medieval code of conduct persisted, one was bound to come across individuals that are larger than life, one way or the other. One such character near Adwal mountain, not far from Tarwal, was a man by the name of Mustuk Akhtarzai. I failed to meet him but have seen his photograph and he died naturally in or around

1968. It seems that many years earlier he was indulging in a secret relationship with the wife of one Nur Mohammad, when the husband's brother, Kashmir, and two friends came upon the couple. The woman escaped as Kashmir attacked the offender with a sword and literally cut him open, at which Mustuk collapsed unconscious and lay as if dead, possibly feigning. He came round some time later, after his attackers had gone, and was none too pleased to see that his intestines had literally spilled out though they had not been cut open. Nothing daunted, he propped himself against a rock and methodically picked off the bits of gravel sticking to his entrails, pushing them back in bit by bit. When all was done he took off his turban (at least seven yards of cloth), wound it around his waist to hold all in place and staggered off to the house of a relative. There, it is related, he took out the intestines once more and washed them in water before wrapping himself up in the turban again. He was then taken on horseback the eight or nine miles to Kila Saifulla where he was stitched up by a doctor or paramedic who was presumably attached to the Levies' post there. He went on to reach a respectable old age. I can guess what happened to the erring wife but presume that Mustuk's family provided a bride or brides without the usual 'wulwer' to avoid a blood feud that might continue down the generations.

'Purdah' in the countryside was and is a luxury largely for those who are well-off as they have servants to draw water, collect kindling and milk animals. So people there, both the young and the not-so-young do see members of the opposite sex, married and single, and often fall in love. Assuming that such feelings are reciprocated, in the event of a married person converting these feelings into secret actions the liaison may well have fatal consequences. In the case of unattached young people, however, all may be well, unless the parents have other plans – for reasons of land, status, political or clan alliance, feud, family relationship and so on. If the parents have not yet chosen a bride for their son, then as a token of respect he will get a third party to tell his mother of his choice and she will pass it on to his father. If necessary the mother or close female relative will then ascertain whether the girl is suitable and, if so, the father will then meet the girl's father and male relatives. All being well the 'wulwer', the equivalent of our now abandoned dowry system but in reverse, will be agreed and the boy's father, brother or other close relative will fire three shots at the girl's home to announce the engagement, the duration of which is usually a year but may be longer among poor families who may need time to raise money for the wedding dress and other things. The boy's father gives money for an engagement dress and presents are exchanged. The 'wulwer' may consist of both cash and kind.

Once engaged the girl must observe 'purdah' with regard to the boy's male relatives even if cousins, which means hiding the face with a shawl and generally keeping her distance. She must not call them by their normal names and after marriage must invent imaginative names not only for them but for her husband's female relatives also. However, her husband's father and mother are called just that and children of that family born after the engagement are called by their normal names. Once the 'wulwer' has been paid in full the girl's family will select the wedding date and arrange the wedding feast but the boy's family send out the invitations. On the day appointed the boy's male relatives approach the bride's house firing their guns, her waiting male relatives doing the same. Female relatives of the groom enter separately and discreetly through a side entrance if there is one. In the evening the bride is taken to the groom's house for a second feast. Following this a mullah separately asks each three times if they wish to marry the other, at which a shy girl may elect someone such as the groom's sister to reply for her.

Many years ago an audacious but extremely unwise mullah in Zhob was elected as spokesman for a singularly beautiful bride and, being alone with her, promptly married her to himself. Whether he lived long enough to consummate the outrageous marriage before the bridegroom got to him I forget. Suffice to say, thenceforth a spokesman in the form of a brother of the groom or bride is usually present, plus two or three witnesses, and no longer is the mullah admitted to the bride's room alone. When the groom's parents are poor and have a house with only one room or are nomads living in a 'kuzhdei', privacy for the couple to consummate the marriage is difficult so the parents will arrange to stay with friends or relatives for three or four days to allow what we would call a honeymoon.

If a young bachelor greatly fancied a girl but both her father and she were not sympathetic, he might throw a sheep's head or skull in front of the house or publicly fire a shot by her home or cut off a plait of her hair should the opportunity arise. This signified that she was to be his come what may and that anyone else who tried to marry her might be shot. The skull or head token disappeared around the 1930s but the others probably continue to a limited extent in more isolated villages A.Y.K. told me. It was 'throwing down the gauntlet', to use an old fashioned expression, and only a very bold, favoured or accepted admirer would continue his suit after such a threatening gesture by a rival. However, the girl's father would have been disgraced and so a higher 'wulwer' had to be given to soothe his hurt pride; or the preferred boy's family may give some dowry plus a sister or a cousin without dowry to compensate for the loss of face. On the other hand, if such an admirer is a especially rugged, aggressive and feared and has the patience to hold out for three or four years the father may capitulate – for he has to continue feeding an extra adult – and eventually give the daughter without 'wulwer'. Should our bold suitor later change his mind he became disgraced and no local girl would marry him afterwards. If the boy's own father is against the marriage the same action may be taken. If the father still refuses to support his son then he incurs considerable disgrace locally and the girl's father is humiliated by his daughter being regarded as unsuitable by the other father. Extra 'wulwer' may be given therefore to smooth things over and hard bargaining will take place. If on the other hand the girl is keen on the match but her father is against it, by mutual arrangement the boy will 'kidnap' the girl at night and leave her with some of his relatives while he goes off to the mountains. After three days or so he will return, with a mullah, and both will be asked three times if they wish to marry one another. Should the girl be too shy then she will let a female relative of the boy answer for her. After such a 'kidnap' other boys in the area would be reluctant to marry the girl even though she is still a virgin, so her male relatives are unlikely to intervene physically to prevent the marriage and as a result the 'wulwer' in such a 'tushta' marriage is lower that it would otherwise be. In a fundamentally poor society, raising 'wulwer' for a son may be slow and difficult. A way around such a difficulty is for two families to exchange daughters in marriage without any 'wulwer'. Ruziamat Shahizai, the Kakar nomad with whom I travelled to the Afghan border in 1992 was, and still is I guess, placed in an impossible position by having one daughter but six sons. He cannot possibly raise dowry for his other four or five sons.

The last basis of marriage is to compensate an aggrieved family for the murder of one of its members, the offending family giving one or perhaps two brides without 'wulwer'. Its prime purpose is to avoid starting or continuing a blood feud that could last for generations. When Bungal Khan was killed the initial settlement, you may recall, was four girls, two born and two unborn, but he enjoyed great personal prestige and considerable status. Fukhruddin's return to Zhob was similarly arranged by his relatives giving two girls in marriage to the dead man's family. Being so important in such a society there are special terms or expressions in Pashtu for all these marriage situations.

As might be expected in a society that lived a precarious existence until recent times and where the male is so predominant, family relationships are very important and relatives are named with a precision not met among European languages so far as I know. For example maternal and paternal aunts and uncles are precisely differentiated, there are three words for a sister-in-law depending upon whether she is via a brother or a husband or a wife, and the word for cousin depends upon the sex and so on. When some of my younger Kakar or Tajik friends write or e-mail me, out of courtesy they address me as 'Tony kaka', 'kaka' meaning a paternal uncle and slightly more prestigious than 'mama' which is a maternal uncle. Widows traditionally become the brother's wife or a dependant at least, depending upon circumstances such as whether he is already married, his financial status, her age and appearance and so on. Local custom often gave her no say in the matter but in 1892 a test case under the British decided that, as under Muslim Law or Sharia, a widow had the right to re-marry whoever she chose and no 'jirga' would be allowed to act otherwise. However, it was allowed that the new husband or protector would still have to pay 'wulwer' to the dead man's family, widows attracting roughly half the amount expected for a virgin. In the early 'sixties dowries averaged Rs.3,000 to Rs.4,000 and to put that into proper context a man hired as a 'khassadar' to guard a road against outlaws was then paid Rs.2 per day. Whilst travelling in Kakar Khorrasan with the Shahizai family in 1992, Ziauddin told me that the father of a very pretty girl in a tent a mile from ours was demanding a 'wulwer' of Rs.25,000 at a time when agricultural labourers in Zhob were earning Rs.50 per day. Even with some hard bargaining this is an enormous sum for most nomads, especially if the family has more than one son and is without daughters to bring in 'wulwer'.

Grounds for divorce might be on account of unattractiveness, bad temper or suspected immorality and the custom used to be to throw three stones or a clod of earth into the woman's lap, or that of her father or brother if she were absent, in front of two witnesses. Today the husband has to say, in front of witnesses, 'I divorce you', three times. For the first two reasons a part of the 'wulwer' must be repaid. Unless immorality was alleged then she can remarry within the tribe. If adultery is claimed then any man who marries the woman, presumably the one already involved, as no other is likely to seek her hand, must give compensation to the husband, but as already said if caught in the act then the shooting of both is quite possible, even likely. Conversely, a woman could divorce her husband if he proves to be impotent but she can only act through her parents who will approach a 'malik' or 'sardar' for adjudication. However, if her husband is unfaithful, and there is no wrathful cuckold or father to consider, there seems little that the woman can do. Needless to say, increasingly better and more available education is modifying such traditions and attitudes.

The case of Buk Nama was slightly different. She was married but eloped with one, Amir Jan, also of the Khodadzai clan, having wisely replaced the explosive in her husband's cartridges with dust beforehand. For some reason unknown to me, Amir Jan was given twelve years in Mach Gaol where he later died, in 1932 or 1933. For her own safety, following his arrest she had been lodged in the Nawab's house which was then at Manki instead of Tarwal. This was done officially and she became a servant there. Unfortunately I failed to record whether her family compensated the husband but presume that they did. A.Y.K. was then a small boy and broke the news of her lover's death in prison to her, at which she became greatly distressed. Wishing to see where he was buried, she stole a .38 revolver from the Nawab's house, complained of ear-ache and was sent to Kila Saifulla bazaar seven miles away under the escort of our dependable Sheikh Rahmat. He was completely unaware of the concealed gun and upon arrival in the bazaar she promptly shot a Hindu sweeper and a Hindu shopkeeper, probably not fatally though I do not know, so that she too would be sent to Mach. Grabbed before she could do any further mischief and taken to the British officer in the Levies post, she was seen to be trembling. He thought that it was from fear and said so to her. On the contrary she replied, she would shoot him also given half the chance 'as you are a great man and I would become famous'. Clearly the officer combined humour with sympathy as he bought her some new clothes in the bazaar to thank her for the compliment.

Usually, eloping couples fled over the Afghan border to Sulaiman Khel territory or to Waziristan where pursuit by the husband and his family would be a very risky business; and they probably still do this if unable or unwilling to earn a living in some distant town. The reason for this is the Pashtun code of honour whereby any person coming to you for sanctuary must be protected at all costs and no one would deliberately challenge such a protecting family of these two tribes lightly. If such a fugitive dies while under your protection you have first call on any of his property so the deal is not entirely one-sided. Should either or both of the runaways became tired of exile, the only real option is to return secretly to the village of the chief and stay there. The husband will bring a mullah and divorce the woman, whose family will compensate him, after which she may remain in the sheltering household as a servant for many years and is generally safe. The guilty man will either stay away or, if he returns, keep his head down and avoid the bazaar if he is wise. However, she is then not allowed to remarry anyone from her own clan or from that of her ex-husband's clan or her lover's clan if they happen to be different. Obviously there's a limit to the number of such outcasts that can be reasonably sheltered and the chief or 'sardar' may arrange a marriage to a poor man of a neighbouring clan or tribe who is unable to raise a 'wulwer'. If that is possible it's a case of every cloud having a silver lining.

Fortunately, love denied is not always so violent and impassioned as the above, as the case of Dewana Khan, a distant relative of A.Y.K. and long dead, shows. He was in love with a girl some distance away but her parents had already engaged her to another when she was very young and Dewana Khan was duly married to someone chosen by his family. For some years the girl, Khailoh Daulatzai, steadfastly refused to marry her fiancée and for nearly thirty years Dewana is said to have ridden on horseback twenty-five miles each way at night whenever possible to meet her secretly until, no doubt facing an uncertain old age, she consented to marry the original man. One must admire him for his steadfastness and patience. Dewana claimed that the only time there was any physical contact between them was one windy night when he had difficulty in lighting his pipe, at which she used her 'takrai' or shawl to shield him and their hands touched.

Some years before I arrived in Zhob a 'madam' from some distant town thought of all those healthy young men who were unable to arrange a 'wulwer for the next several years and, quite rightly expecting to enjoy a monopoly in the trade, set up a brothel in Loralai in order to brighten their frustrated lives. Of course she brought her own 'staff' with her, local recruits being quite out of the question even to her naive eyes. The local elders got together and tendered their solemn warning but it fell upon deaf ears. One night they moved in and before the local Levies could intervene one girl was shot dead and several wounded as they fled.

A thing I noticed early on at Tarwal was the egalitarianism that prevailed within age groups, age being much respected still. Nawab Sahib was a notable exception, even allowing for his seniority: he was held in near awe by all except his brothers and one or two others, and few argued with him. The men servants would bring a meal to a crowd of us sitting on a carpet and at the end they would clear away the plates, then bring in tea. After that they joined into the conversation as equals, helping themselves to tea if any were left and using anyone's cup that happened to be at hand and help themselves to the nearest packet of cigarettes without a word. In any case there is no word for please or for thank you in Pashtu. Also variation in skin colour is considerable and more swarthy men such as Fukhruddin were referred to as being 'torr', literally meaning black but in this context dark, quite casually and in front of the person if it were appropriate to the conversation; while paler ones whose noses tended to get red or sun-burnt in summer would be referred to as 'surkh', meaning red literally but pale in this context. Although extremely poor and, for want of a better expression, of lower social status, Sheikh Rahmat, Fukhruddin and others would wander across from their little mud houses nearby, come in through the big gates and join whoever was sitting on A.Y.K.'s. verandah. It is not done thoughtlessly, however, for should an important meeting clearly be in progress then they would discreetly turn around.

Greeting anyone is quite a long and ritualised ceremony. With intimate friends or in certain formal situations one embraces but with others a two-handed shake is the norm. The essential preliminary greeting is 'salaam oleikum' by the first person to speak, to which the reply is basically a reversal of that. The next thing is 'sturry masheh', used as the title of this book. It means 'be not tired' literally but implies may you not be tired: the reply to this is 'khaire yuseh' meaning 'may you be contented', varied as 'khwar masheh' up north in the Pakhtu dialect, meaning 'may you not be poor'. After that there is a series of wishes about the well being of the other person: that they are in good health, not cold (winter only) and so on. This ceremony is carried out with all members of the other party in turn, with careful regard to seniority and hierarchy, though it may be curtailed if there are many people present. Bearing in mind the lack of 'please' or 'thank you' in the language, this prolonged courtesy always seemed somewhat incongruous.

Faces changed quite frequently among the Tarwal entourage, those going once their problem had been solved to have their place taken by others in a day or two. Ahmad Yar Khan in particular seems to help all sorts of waifs and strays these days, now that he has his own house, some of whom come from far away, having heard of his good sense and kindness. His brother in Quetta, Jehandar Shah, was similarly importuned by various tribesmen with a difficulty, especially by the poorer, more vulnerable ones. It is almost feudal in a way but were they to approach the courts instead they might stand little chance of redress against a wealthy oppressor or opponent. For those with 'trendy' views or with a leaning to the left, such paternalism is regarded as almost unclean and humiliating but most in the West enjoy the luxury of an impartial law and financial independence and have no idea of the vulnerability of a poverty-stricken tribal man, especially if he cannot afford a rifle or pistol.

During my lengthy stay at Tarwal in 1960, a Mahsud was employed as a driver though there seemed no good reason for this as the chief and all his grown sons could drive. I suspect that he had fled from an unequal feud or even a killing in Waziristan. He was a big, raw-boned fellow, distinctly untamed, aggressive and menacing and there was something quite manic about him. A rumbling volcano might be a suitable simile to describe him. One evening a small crowd of us were chatting in my room when for some unknown reason he started picking on me. Why he should want to needle me I failed to see but, bit by bit, things escalated and I was not prepared to back off beyond a certain point. I felt that I was probably young, strong and fast enough even if a couple of stones lighter to hold my own if it came to the crunch but he was such a wild, unpredictable sort of chap that I feared he might draw a concealed gun or knife on impulse. I think the young Jogezais present were quite apprehensive at the tense situation and, sitting on my 'charpai', I remember quietly feeling under my pillow to check that my pistol was in the right position for a fast grab should the worst come to the worst. Fortunately for all of us he quietened down, realising that I was not going to be bullied and possibly sensing that I might not be a push-over: and the tension subsided. He left not long after and I have a suspicion that it was because he was 'a bit too hot to handle'.

Being summer, in spite of the height of the valley, the temperature topped 100° F / 38° C during the day but the air was extremely dry and it was even warm at night so that most slept outside. I too quit my room for the courtyard outside and one night was woken by the frantic growling and scuffling of three large, crop-eared, shaggy curs that raced into the courtyard in pursuit of a careless jackal that had strayed too close. They got him just three yards from my 'charpai' and repeatedly threw the dying bundle high into the air. No one had volunteered or been told to remove the corpse by noon the following day so, mindful of rabies, I carefully picked it up using newspaper and deposited it outside the compound. By evening its presence could be smelt and I felt compelled to remove it to a more distant place. In Peshawar I had seen a bloated donkey by the side of the road, while dead dogs were not uncommon, perhaps having chased a passing car or truck too closely.

As already said, the poor water supply from a distant' karez' with Entamoeba, Giardia and other spores blown in led to many child deaths but also there was less access to vaccination, fewer home comforts to help those who became sick, often a poor diet and limited availability of medicines in the early 'sixties. As a consequence, as many as sixty per cent of those born died within their first year or two. Today, the situation has changed and people can buy all sorts of drugs cheaply and without prescription, including antibiotics, as questionable advice or fancy takes them. However, even if properly advised, many forget the dosage and frequency and are unable to read the instructions included. Ruziamat Shahizai, with whom I travelled for four weeks thirty years later had quite a collection of tablets that he had saved over months or even years but had not the faintest idea which to take, while some were probably long out of date. When he asked me which he should take I knew only half of them and any printed instructions were long lost. Equally undesirable, when I gave him some of mine for a worse than usual bout of dysentery I was fairly sure that he did not take the heavy initial dose and subsequent ones in full, preferring to reserve some for a future occasion: argument was futile and my command of the language was insufficient to explain the problem posed by such actions.

To give an idea of the situation in those early days, A.Y.K. had four surviving sons and three daughters but two of each had died when young. More recently, as already mentioned, Fukhruddin lost eleven of his infants, leaving him with twelve survivors. It was very much a case of 'Darwin rules' and sometimes still is in more remote areas far from any dispensary. Apart from the widespread prevalence of protozoan infections such as those mentioned above, cirrhosis of the liver was quite common, poor diet being blamed by the medics. Tuberculosis is more common than one might expect, again aided by poor diet but abetted by crowded living conditions and indiscriminate sharing of drinking vessels and eating communally from a bowl, even the sturdy nomad being prone to it as I saw when visiting one of their tents in the Torr Ghar where the owner asked me to remove a plaster cast. Seemingly he had T.B. of the spine. The situation in Afghanistan was somewhat worse, which explains the sometimes astonishing efficacy of such modern drugs seen by Foreign Aid medics treating badly wounded 'mujahuddin' near Quetta. In 1982, when buying a few Turkoman rugs for our small, part-time business, a Swiss volunteer met on the train from Karachi told me of a 'mujahuddin' fighter who had been badly shot through the stomach and had then taken four days to reach the special hospital set up for such cases near the border. One would have expected him to have died from peritonitis yet all was well after a shot or two of penicillin after he had been sewn up.

Whilst buying rugs in 1983 I was invited to join a dozen 'mujahuddin' commanders, who had come over the border for a meeting, for dinner at Temur Shah's place in Zhob after he had succeeded to the chieftainship. Without thinking I accepted a large glass of 'shlombai', yoghurt well shaken with water from a distant 'karez'. For two days I paid a heavy price and have never touched it since. The 'mujahuddin' were without exception very big, bold, powerful men unused to soft living. The thing that struck me particularly was that they repeatedly said that they didn't want cash help, no doubt aware of its temptations and how much of it was vanishing in Peshawar. They wanted anti-aircraft missiles above all else. The jet bombers were too fast to be accurate while the guns of tanks could not elevate sufficiently to hit the higher hilltops so that neither bothered them unduly but they greatly feared the helicopter gunships. Those heavily armed Hinds could slip up some adjoining valley, unseen and unheard, then cross the intervening rocky ridge and be upon them without warning within a couple of minutes and there was no cover. This was shortly before the Americans supplied them with Stinger missiles that changed the course of the war and showed how well such men understood the military situation.

The Stinger ground-to-air missile marked the beginning of the end of the Russian occupation and the Russians should have read the old British accounts of the country before setting out. From the outset I had backed the Afghans in the long term, always provided the West supplied them with modern weaponry to level the playing field, and men like those at the dinner simply confirmed my belief. While their extreme anarchy is their greatest strength when invaded, that and self-interest happen to be their greatest weaknesses when it comes to self-government. In 1823

Kabul lost the fertile Peshawar Vale for ever because Azim Khan with his artillery failed to check the Sikh guns on the other bank of the Landi River or fire a single shot in support of the twenty thousand Yusufzai and Khattaks near Naukhar village who were facing Ranjit Singh's Sikhs and Gurkhas. Sadly, this became all too evident during the Russian occupation and the more so after their withdrawal, thereby allowing in the Taliban.

During the course of that evening Temur Shah quite suddenly asked me how tall was my wife. Rather taken aback and not really knowing, I made a guess, which turned out to be correct. Having forgotten the incident I was surprised five days later when an almost spherical package, tightly wrapped in brown paper and endless thin string, was delivered to me at Tarwal. Temur Shah had got his wife and daughters to make a superb tribal outfit for Sheila. Made of silk, it was beautifully embroidered in traditional style with silk and silver thread, plus some mirror work (adopted from the Baluchis), while the 'shalwar' or trousers were of brightly striped Multani silk. Even more surprising, when I returned home it was found to fit very well.

Returning to 1960, we were into September now and the nomads started coming through from Afghanistan, ragged Nassers with long lines of heavily laden camels carrying all their worldly possessions and a few trade goods such as dried fruit, ghi, almonds, 'chilghoza' pine nuts and goatskin 'pusteens'. None had flocks, possibly because it slowed them when migrating, but much later I read that to the north predation by the Sulaiman Khels along the Gomal route was the cause of those Nassers ridding themselves of flocks in the early 1900s because grazing over wide areas of semi-desert and away from competing flocks meant that family groups were widely separated and therefore vulnerable. They were not handsome as are so many Afghans and Pashtuns and as they carried few guns between them that made them vulnerable to raids by Marris, a Baluch tribe to the east of Zhob, and Sulaiman Khels to the north. Indeed, during the days of the Raj, groups migrating along the Gomal were given special protection and guarded camp sites because of the Waziris and Mahsuds along the left bank of the river. The 'kafilas' or caravans were all heading for the Derajat, fresh ones passing through Kila Saifulla day after day. It was a fascinating flood of humanity. Because of their long-standing feud with the Sulaiman Khels, some of the Nassers migrating further south avoided the Gomal route, instead passing through the Chuhar Khel Dhana along the road cut into a sheer face of that tremendous chasm.

The British instituted a system of taxes upon all such animals passing through and collected by local officials called 'Risaldars' and A.Y.K. had been one for a time. Thus the numerous nomads passing through Zhob were not regarded a burden by local people, whose land they grazed in passing but who benefited indirectly from the revenue. On the other hand a longer stay might not be so welcome when there are local though small flocks to consider. The Zhob Gazetteer of 1907 estimated that nearly ten thousand nomads passed through central Zhob twice each year; possibly a further four or five thousand through Fort Sandeman; while the route along the Gomal marking Zhob's northern boundary witnessed the passage of around fifty thousand such people. Today there is a mere trickle by comparison for a variety of reasons outlined later in the chapter on nomad migration. The majority of those crossing central Zhob would over-winter in camp sites in the Loralai & Duki Districts, those following the Gomal heading for the Derajat along the west bank of the Indus or the Panjab across the river but a few used to travel right across India to Calcutta and other parts of Bengal to act as money lenders to the unwary. The Ut Khel clan of the Nasser tribe was reputed to visit India solely to thieve.

At the end of September there was a big wedding at the fort of Haji Hayat Khan, a member of the Nawab Kahole, out across the plain. The daughter of his son, Asadullah, was being married to the son of Nasserullah Jan from Sharan Jogezai over the mountains in Khaisor. I was very excited as it had been arranged for me to accompany the bridal escort party to her new home when they returned there. At long last I was going to cross the Spin Ghar as I had so longed since first seeing the range. As the sun gained strength a crowd of us sat on large rugs in the open and were given the usual presents of turbans and cash. Prayers were said by the mullahs from both villages then the entire village saw us off, Sardar Azim Khan leading the crowd and firing a pistol. The bride was beneath a brightly decorated bridal sheet on one camel, four female relatives from her home-to-be were on two others and a fourth carried baggage including my rucsac. Half a dozen of the escort had ponies and in our party were Nasserullah Jan and his brother Sher Ali Khan, outlaws until pardoned in 1949 and brothers of the strange and impetuous Sher Jan. It was probably around 40° Celsius in the shade but the air was so dry that it didn't matter.

We crossed the river by a ford and found that the country beyond was quite sandy. I was offered a pony to ride but at first refused as I had a pistol, a camera and a small tripod hanging from my neck by various straps and was concerned lest I fall off and get sand into them. However, I saw that my refusal was suspected of being from timidity so I then accepted. It was wonderful fun, racing against the other horsemen across the desert. And as I was wearing tribal dress it seemed a good idea to get a photograph. Therefore after a while, I dismounted and 'parked' the pony. When all was ready and the delayed action going I went to remount but the little brute had other ideas and moved away each time I approached. After packing my things I tried to catch the beast and for perhaps fifteen minutes chased it across the arid plain until someone on a pony caught it for me and we returned it to the owner.

After three or four hours we reached a line of extremely low, gravely hills at the edge of the vast plain, well in front of the hills and great crags behind. To my astonishment a fine spring was there, its pool perhaps ten or twelve feet across. The only snag was that, while the water was clear, the bottom was littered with goat and sheep droppings. Upon learning that we had another two or three hours to the next water I joined the rest, face down. In the late afternoon we reached a camp of three 'kuzhdei'. The nomads had made a crude trough from slabs of rock on edge sealed with clay and filled it from a nearby spring: it was muddy but we gulped it down thankfully. They were obviously awaiting our arrival, 'poi chai' was soon ready and later we were sitting around steaming bowls of good 'kreut'. It was almost dark and breakfast had been little more that 'poi chai' and a couple of biscuits with nothing except water since then. I ate so ravenously that my hosts were quite impressed. I paid for that gastronomic enthusiasm during the next eight days in Sharan Jogezai when every invitation to dinner saw this served and little else, the word having gone around that 'kreut' was my favourite dish.

Some of our party slept in the tents, others including me under the stars beneath heavy cotton quilts. In the morning, after liberal pourings of 'poi chai' followed by a substantial breakfast of 'shorwa' and ample fried meat and 'pasti' as we sat on felt rugs in the early morning sun, we set off through the seemingly endless, multi-hued shale ridges and headed for the great limestone peaks and crags beyond. The scenery was spectacular. I was at the front of our straggled party of twenty or so with Sher Ali Khan, a hard and wiry chap, and suddenly I became aware that the pace was quickening: it was the usual test and as usual I responded suitably. Hours later we entered a narrow gorge where the four women keeping the bride company dismounted to walk ahead and suddenly we were faced with a solid rock wall about eight feet high which would be a waterfall in times of rare spate. It was easy enough to climb but I wished to take a photograph and suddenly it dawned upon me that the bride was not among the women and that she could not possibly come that way on her camel. Hurrying back, sure enough I saw that she had been transferred to a pony, camels being less sure-footed, and was on a tiny track high above us. Racing up the steep rocky slope, often jumping from boulder to boulder, I just managed to get there in time to take a couple of shots.

Miles further on in another gorge we came upon a group of young men waiting in the shade. They had come out from Sharan Jogezai to accompany us for the last few miles. Eventually we reached the edge of the great Khaisor Valley where our party halted to load both cartridges and guns. With some concern I watched a number of group as they knocked detonator caps into spent .303 cartridges using stones but none exploded and the powder was then added, followed by bullets. Half a mile before reaching the village we came upon a large group of young girls compactly huddled together to one side of the torrent bed, waiting to get a glimpse of the bride: it was quite touching. The sun was almost set as we arrived, to my great frustration as my camera had only an f3.5 lens and the colour film was slow in those days. Most of our party started firing into the air and even the mullah with us drew a pistol so that the air fairly crackled, those waiting for us firing in reply. At this and the general excitement the ponies kicked and bucked but no one fell off. A great square of carpets had been laid out and, as we exchanged greetings, the bride and four women disappeared into the old fort followed by the crowd of girls. We were then repeatedly plied with small bowls of sweet black tea, our first drink since morning and prayers followed. Later, a good meal was brought for the entire male assembly, following which the older ones chatted while the young men sang and danced around a great fire until the early hours, the women also dancing and singing but inside the fort. At six thousand feet or more it was cold once the sun went down.

The little village is cut into two by a wide torrent bed that had small, scattered pools in places and boasted a mosque decorated with the horns of markhor and mountain sheep. It also had a tiny school whose one teacher was a Panjabi. Secretly he both feared and disliked those around him, even trying to enlist my ear in order to whinge on about the 'savage Pathans'. The villagers sensed this and when the usual shooting competition took place the next day, the target being a large stone on the nearby hillside, he was extremely reluctant to compete but was mocked into taking part. To the unconcealed delight of all present he made a mess of it and I had no sympathy for him either. Levies from the small militia post nearby joined in and also did poorly, much to the satisfaction of the locals. I also missed the distant stone but my shot was near enough to 'save my face'.

I spent eight days in Nasserullah Jan's house and took food with all five of his brothers at various times, the only unfortunate thing being that I was supposed to adore 'kreut'. He, like the Nawab, had blue eyes and he had four surviving children, four having died. Musa Khan was another of his brothers, a gentle elderly man with a ready laugh who quit his house in the summer to live nearby in his 'kuzhdei' where I spent a number of afternoons and evenings chatting and drinking endless cups of tea while his daughters, the older of whom kept her veil up at all times, husked maize cobs or prepared food. He had six surviving children but ten had died. The life was pleasant in summer, even in the autumn, but winter was often harsh. In such an isolated community memories linger and traditions remain important so that the village still talked of a winter some seventy years earlier when the snow reached the tops of trees and then, within the space of a few days mysteriously turned pink. Decades later I saw a similar thing in the Canadian Rockies, the cause being the unicellular alga Chlamydomonas nivalis. The people were also rather proud of the leopards in a great mountain nearby, so big that they sometimes killed cows.

However, at the same time that would not deter them from blasting the daylights out of any such animal that was careless enough to show its face during the day.

Taking a meal with the village headman, Malik Juma, I was surprised at a remarkable pistol he produced, no doubt made up north in Durra Adam Khel, which took .303 cartridges so that its kick when fired must have been tremendous. One day an ancient old man by the name of Loghuni walked briskly into the village to Musa Khan's tent, having just come twelve miles from his camp on the edge of the Torr Ghar range along the far side of the Khaisor Valley. He claimed to be one hundred and thirteen years old and if his face was anything to go by I will not dispute it. When young he had once walked from Tanishpa in the Torr Ghar range, across Khaisor and the Spin Ghar, and on to Kila Saifulla in a day. In all the distance is about fifty-five miles. Among other things he was said to own six hundred sheep and goats plus ten camels which made him rich by local standards After a brief chat, a drink of water and a little business he went off back again at a fast pace. He really was remarkable. I believe it was he who later set up the 'trading post' of Badani on Afghan border for the purpose of smuggling. Since then it has become a quite large, thriving bazaar although it is not shown on any map but I visited it with Ruziamat Shahizai in 1992 and know that it exists.

I had heard many stories about the Torr Ghar mountains, where Dost Mohammad and his son Bungal Khan had a stronghold on Tanishpa peak when resisting the British, and about Kakar Khorrasan along the Afghan border and longed to visit them. The Torr Ghar was at least within reach, rising just twelve or so miles away on the far side of the wide Khaisor Valley. It was insisted that I take a guide or escort with me and a lad in his late teens or early twenties was chosen. For the walk a 'tikkuni' was baked for us. It is specially for travel, being a thick disc of unleavened bread containing honey and a little

229

fat. I also took some extra clothing in case it was necessary to sleep out. Setting off at eight o'clock in the morning, a brisk twelve or so mile walk across the desert brought us to the low foothills where we got some foul water from a tiny pool. A little further on we got clear water from a hole dug in a dry torrent bed and covered with a slab of rock near a nomad encampment where we took a brief meal. A young man in one of the 'kuzhdei' had what I am fairly sure was T.B. of the spine and asked me to remove the plaster so 'I gave him a reprimand and a pep talk' according to a diary entry. In another tent was a very sick baby about whom I was asked advice but the poor mite was obviously dying slowly, probably from some protozoan disease and for which I had nothing suitable. However, I was expected to do something so I gave some sulphathiazole tablets, with careful instructions, but was honest to the parents about the chance of these doing much good.

Not wanting to be outdone by Loghuni, I was determined to reach the far side of the great range but the sun was hot and my escort was flagging. He wanted a longer rest in the nomad camp so I told him to sit tight while I went on. Having no doubt been given strict instructions to stick with me come what may, he and someone from the camp followed me after I had gone two or three hundred yards. The track led over a number of deep undulations and each time I was in one I ran as fast as I could unseen for a couple of hundred yards before walking again and soon had put quite a distance between us. I did feel a little mean but could see no alternative if I were to reach the far side of the range and get a glimpse of fabulous Kakar Khorrasan. Finally I came to a very steep though small mountain to the right of the track and ran up it, guessing that my companions would not follow, but when out of sight beyond the crest I turned right, back towards Khaisor, instead of left as might be expected and descended. It worked and I lost them, then found a vague jeep track heading in the right direction and walked flat out

230

along it for most of the way. At one point an odd thing happened: a naked tribesman leapt up from some rocks and raced across the track for cover over a small ridge. No one else appeared to be about and sunbathing was not a local custom. It was late afternoon by the time I reached the last ridge and from there I looked down across the wilds of Kakar Khorrasan. For some strange reason it seemed like Eldorado to me after all the tales I had heard about it and I planned to return as soon as possible.

As I sat there enjoying the solitude and desolate hills a stone rattled on the far side of the small valley just below me. Instantly wary, I was thrilled to see a magnificent pair of dark markhor bounding effortlessly over the rocks of the hill and disappearing over its shoulder. Because of their size and fine spiral horns they had become rare and are now even rarer, being gone from many, if not most, of their former haunts. The sun was setting as I turned back and enjoyed another long drink at a spring by a deserted militia post half a mile away. To my surprise, thinking that the area was devoid of people, I met three shepherds with their small flock and they invited me to spend the night at their village of Tanishpa nearby but I declined. Further on I came upon two men accompanied by a woman on a horse. They also invited me to spend the night in Tanishpa and said I was mad to continue to Sharan Jogezai when I could have food and shelter and go on tomorrow but I wanted to equal Loghuni's walk. The moon was brilliant and I walked hour after hour through the silent peaks, arriving back in the village at three in the morning. The open backs of tribal 'sapplai' or chapplis expose the heels to the hot sand and the skin of one of mine had dried then cracked to create a deep fissure. It was extremely painful but I had covered at least fifty-five if not sixty miles in nineteen hours and was satisfied. Rubbing 'ghee' into the fissure worked wonders after a couple of days.

I planned to walk back to Kila Saifulla in single day, in case the fissure re-opened and made travel too painful and difficult, but Nasserullah Jan heard of a lorry that had come from Quetta via Fort Sandeman into the Khaisor Valley to buy wool from some encamped nomads. They were only seven miles down the valley from the village so we walked there along the main torrent bed then up a dry tributary. The area was quite extraordinary in having a number of sheer rock towers, perhaps two or more hundred feet high and flat-topped, very much like the mesas of Monument Valley in Arizona. The largest had scree slopes and I managed to climb up a short gully on to the top of it to look for signs of hyaena and leopard but was disappointed. The two trucks included an old Bedford and were almost loaded with bales of wool when we arrived. It was a pioneering enterprise by the owner-driver to buy wool out in the desert and he deserved to succeed for taking such a risk. Nearby there were two enormous 'kuzhdei', by far the largest I have seen and when measured proved to be thirty-two feet long, excluding the separate four-foot end panel, and sixteen feet wide, whereas the average ones are around twenty feet in length and twelve wide. As might be expected, such luxurious accommodation was not the home of one family but of two brothers with theirs, the older brother being blue-eyed and also calling himself Malik Juma by coincidence. We slept in their tents the night and enjoyed some excellent meat.

After setting off the next morning, the lorry we were in had to descend the torrent's abrupt gravel bank diagonally to avoid getting stuck amidships. The truck rolled alarmingly under its heavy load and I thought we were lost but the driver kept his nerve and all was well. On the way we passed the Shaighalu militia post in the middle of nowhere and in the late afternoon reached the boundary of Fort Sandeman. At the Levies checkpoint some way outside the town I was closely scrutinised and questioned for a long time, so long in fact that I told the driver not to wait but to go on into the bazaar.

Arriving on foot in the bazaar, I was greatly irritated by the delay as there were few buses in those days and there was to be a big wedding the following day, starting in Duki and ending near Tarwal. At the little bus station I learnt that I had missed the last bus by some twenty minutes. As I consoled myself with 'poi chai' in a small 'hotal', which we would call a café, I became aware that three young tribesmen at a nearby table were staring at me. I was wearing tribal dress but my unusual accent and the rucsac on the floor beside me made them curious. I was still angry about the long delay at the militia checkpoint that had made me miss the bus up the valley and their stare began to irritate me. I asked them what they wanted. They responded mildly and asked who was I and what was I doing so I told them. In turn they told me that they were Sulaiman Khels of the Shamal Khel section and Sultan Khel clan. The tribe as a whole has a less than enviable reputation but these three were bright-eyed and bushy-tailed so that I took to them immediately. I invited them over to my table and ordered more pots of tea for all of us.

They were returning to Afghanistan through Waziristan though it did not occur to me at the time that this was really in the opposite direction to what one would expect them to be travelling in September. More to the point they invited me to join them, upon hearing of my interest in the border tribes. This was a very tempting offer, especially as the last European to cross the border with nomads was a Lt. Broadfoot, who travelled with nomads from Ghazni to Rajastan in India in 1839. His route was most probably down the Gomal and extremely unlikely to have been through Waziristan unless his companions were Sulaiman Khels. I could easily send a message to those in Tarwal but a quick check showed that I had only nine exposures left in my camera and no spare roll of film as it was very hard to come by in those days. Equally important, word of my journey would eventually reach the Pakistani authorities who would become very alarmed and even more paranoid than usual. In all probability I would be banned from Zhob and my friends so, after careful thought, I said no and have regretted it ever since.

If I joined the trio such a journey would probably be the first ever by a European and even in Waziristan I would have been safe in their company though I would be forced to return to Zhob alone and that might be hazardous. Around that time a Belgian girl had travelled from Kabul down to Kandahar with a group of 'koochis', the northern term for 'powindas' or nomads, causing consternation among officials when they found out, fearful that she could have come to harm. Mine was the chance of a lifetime and I let it slip. Still angry as missing the last bus because of the interrogation, I waited just outside the town in case a truck should be passing south but gave up as darkness fell. Returning to the bazaar I was astonished to meet Asadullah Khan Jogezai, who had serious news. The bus I had missed had swerved to avoid a cow and rolled over, killing seven passengers. As I always travelled on the roof and invariably at the front to enjoy the fresh air and the view, it was probably my lucky day after all. A family whose son I had met a year earlier then gave me shelter for the night when I came upon them by chance.

I enjoyed the second part of the wedding, held near Tarwal, but a new type of gut infection was becoming increasingly unpleasant and was obviously a protozoan, for which I had no medicines and my sulphonamide drugs had no affect upon it whatsoever. So I hurried to Quetta, where I lodged with Mohammad Usman Khan, also a Jogezai but of another branch of the Ishak Kahole. A boy aged about twelve in the household had a nasty cluster of sores around his mouth and, as no one seemed to be very concerned about it, I treated him for several days and he was soon fine. I presumed that no one had noticed this bit doctoring but many years later, when I had completely forgotten, someone reminded me of it. As soon as possible I went to the Mission Hospital where I met Dr. Holland, the son of the remarkable Dr. Henry Holland who, in the course of his lifetime saved the sight of around one hundred thousand tribesmen along the frontier, often carrying out cataract and more serious operations under canvas. His autobiography makes fascinating reading. Things were so bad inside me by this time that I ate nothing for over two days, simply drinking endless cups of strong, sweet black tea. Attacks came roughly every half hour and there were no public toilets so, as the post office was twenty minutes there and back, I could just post my letters and return to his house but it was a little nerve-wracking. When the test results came the cause turned out to be Chilomastix mesnili, and chloroquine plus something or other cured it in a matter of three days.

One hundred per cent once more, I took a bus for Kila Saifulla but when we stopped in Hindubagh a Levies man asked me to step into their post. Puzzled, I asked why but he would not explain. Inside the post the o/c said that there was an order from the Political Agent banning me from Zhob. I was thunderstruck at first, then slowly angry and upset for it was like being banned from my own home. Ostensibly the reason was that I lacked a tribal area permit, a document about which I was unaware. In any case I had been coming and going frequently in the area for two years and it was no secret Thoroughly miserable I returned to Quetta, despising paranoid bureaucrats and politicians. I was still unsuspecting that it might be a way of having a dig at some of my friends and that my foolish comments about Ayub Khan in that 'hotal' may have played a part. What it is to be innocent. Anyhow, I needed to have a medical examination in Delhi for the renewal of my life insurance policy and wasted little time in setting off, though much earlier than planned, after A.Y.K. had sent down my things from Tarwal.

Back in India I heard from the West of India Automobile Association that, contrary to my express instructions on no account to pay up on the carnet for my bicycle's clip-on motor, which would deny any chance of a fair deal, the R.A.C. in the U.K. who had issued the document had paid the excessive duty demanded. Naively I thought that that was the end of the matter, apart from having to reimburse the R.A.C. but two months later the Indian Customs confiscated the cycle and motor, left in Dehra Dun – "as it had been imported illegally", quote. The Customs and I had been exchanging acrimonious letters in the *Statesman* newspaper for eighteen months but this was defeat. A week back at the Doon School saw me giving a general studies talk on the border tribes to the upper school, there was a row regarding two young teachers who had been spreading a rumour that I used to miss classes at intervals, and John Martyn suggested that I apply for the headship of a school being set up in Mussoorie for Tibetan refugees by the Dalai Lama and his entourage. However, I had already applied to work in the ill-starred Federation the Rhodesias and Nyasaland. It was good to see Shanti Swaroop and wife again but I was steadily heading for a 'cash flow' problem. To head off this I decided on a trip to Tehran, the idea being to buy Afghanis (the Afghan currency) there, change them into Indian rupees in Kabul and lodge those in my bank account in India. Whilst getting the two visas in Delhi I had also applied for a firearm permit at the Pakistan High Commission. I was legal in India but when entering or leaving Pakistan I had merely tucked my pistol under my belt and now felt that sooner or later my luck would run out. I was promised that it would be waiting for me in Lahore.

Arriving in Lahore three weeks after my application I found the official concerned and waited patiently for half an hour after explaining my business. His initial reply had been a trifle non-committal but fairly re-assuring. Each time I reminded him of my presence I was duly re-assured but after almost two hours I decided to pin him down. Blandly he told me that all was in order and if I would come back in twelve days time the permit would be ready. It was a clever ploy and often used: one is made to feel that all is well then, slap, all is not well. The effect is quite shattering. Like most people I get irritated when poorly treated but when I eventually realised what was happening in spite of the promises in Delhi it somehow touched a raw nerve and I could barely control my rage. I abused him in Urdu and threatened to go in person to the Martial Law authorities in Islamabad, all the time standing close to him in my pent-up rage. After some minutes of my tirade he capitulated. He would see the magistrate on duty immediately. As I began to calm down I realised that every door and window was completely filled with faces, some apparently enjoying the scene, having perhaps having suffered similarly themselves with little if any chance of redress.

The 'babu' returned after some time, saying that 'the magistrate was out on flood duty'. Menacingly I told him that I would check that for myself. It turned out to be true and I returned to the office. The permit 'would be signed and ready the next morning': and it was. In Kabul after a crowded bus ride I saw Terry Tovey and gave him a couple of summer shirts from India as a small thanks for earlier help. Returning to my freezing hotel fairly late at night a policeman across the road demanded where I had been and after twice being told in Darri to mind his business somewhat to my surprise he did so. The bus journey to Kandahar started at six a.m. and as it was December, wisely I sat inside for once since during the day it was warm but bitterly cold at night. We arrived well after dark and the men on the bus roof were so cold and stiff from the deep frost and rushing air that they descended the ladder at the back slowly, painfully and with considerable difficulty even though they were all young and hardy.

I had already been delayed for several days and was dismayed to learn that there was no lorry to Shindand or even Farah, let alone Herat, for several days at best, and buses did not ply that route. In the main, government hotel were a number of Russian technicians building the road across the south of the country and I did not envy them going out at five a.m. in the Afghan winter. Also in the hotel was a disgustingly amoral German traveller. He had spent several months enjoying the beautiful vale of Swat north of Peshawar, where the Wali, still the hereditary ruler, had kindly loaned him a house to live in free of charge. To 'repay' his host's generosity, the man had secretly bought a large number of emeralds smuggled from his host's mine by a foreman but towards the end the man became even greedier and refused to pay the thieving foreman the full sum agreed. Thoroughly angered, the foreman had informed the Wali in spite of the risk to himself and the German was arrested immediately after his grand farewell party. He even had the gall to ask for the money he had 'invested' to be returned to him before being deported from the state. What really appalled me was that even then he was scheming to return there and buy more gemstones stolen from his former, generous benefactor.

After seeking a lorry each morning, I wandered through the bazaars, among other things buying a number of felt rugs for Terry and his colleagues in the Embassy in Kabul as a small repayment for their help and hospitality. Many were very attractive and were very cheap, and the manager of the hotel agreed to store them for me until I returned from Iran, if transport materialised. Upon returning to the 'hotal' one evening, in the foyer I came upon a Russian talking to the manager and his assistant in quite good Farsi but rather volubly. He was not actually drunk but it was obvious that he had been drinking and was in an expansive mood. The two Afghans suspected this: did he drink, they asked him? He replied that in Shoravi, the Afghan name for the U.S.S.R., he drank but in Afghanistan...perish the evil thought he implied. In any case it was by then quite late but, like me, he suddenly sensed their suspicion so we departed, he and I along the same corridor.

Arriving at his room, he opened the door and said in a furtive whisper, "Bia inja," – come in. For a brief moment I had visions of another attempt to recruit me as an agent and became cautious but followed him into the room. Reaching under his bed, he withdrew a huge, two-litre bottle of genuine Scotch. However, he lacked any glasses but I had two in my room so, bottle concealed inside his jacket, we tiptoed down the corridor and enjoyed a few glasses. As said earlier, discovery meant prison. Anyway, he was a nice fellow so I gave him a new pair of Afghan knitted stockings from Kabul to make the bitter dawns more tolerable, there being none sold in Kandahar.

I had an invitation to a second Christmas tiger shoot in Kumaon and now had to make a choice: Kumaon, twelve hundred miles away, won and the hoped-for money transactions lost. On the bus back to Kabul an Armenian rug dealer from Tehran attached himself to me. He was a very small man and sniffing out the market potential for buyers in Afghanistan and Pakistan. I suspect that his attachment to me stemmed partly because he was a bit over-awed by the burly, rugged Afghans and, although perhaps double my age, he made me feel quite fatherly. He was interesting company and taught me a lot about rugs, among other things explaining how he had bought a new rug over a year previously for four thousand tomans and left it out in his garden over the winter to the mercies of sunlight, frost and snow. As a result of that seemingly risky treatment, the colours had mellowed and its value doubled. It was one-upmanship on merely laying rugs in the street for a week or two as I had seen when there. On the way there occurred the incident mentioned in my preface when a poor Afghan sitting next to me insisted upon sharing his small piece of bread. I delivered my felt rugs in Kabul, bought several embroidered sheepskin jackets and waistcoats plus a bottle of Scotch for helpful and generous friends in India, and a good Rolex watch as potential foreign exchange. This last was because Indian exchange control was so ponderous, if and when I went to work in Africa, that obtaining foreign currency would take far too long. My Armenian companion left me in Peshawar and I delivered the felt rugs. Three days and two nights later I reached Ramnagar.

After the shoot, I went to Rawalpindi for one last try for a permit to film and the refusal was clearly final. On the Bolan Mail down to Quetta sitting opposite me was a quite refined but very sad and frail-looking man, although he was not really old. Without warning he slumped to the floor, conscious but too weak to raise himself. He was literally starving and quite broken in spirit. The rest of us in the compartment were all deeply shocked and distressed by the incident. We lifted him up and I got him a meal. That evening another passenger and I separately bought him more food and he began to recover. As is so often the case, those most in need of help rarely ask for it. I hope never to witness anything like it again.

The Queen and Duke of Edinburgh came to Quetta on a state visit shortly after I returned to the city and Nawab Sahib presented a sheep to them as was customary in the old days. I was still barred from Zhob and became increasingly friendly with an Anglo-Pakistani police officer, Derek Middlecoat and his wife Lorna, living in Quetta. He loved photography but could afford very little and was fascinated by all technology. Above all, I admired him for his integrity when, just after joining the force, he had been offered the equivalent of three years gross salary simply to sit, duly uniformed, in a car going into the Karachi docks. It was obviously a criminal enterprise and he turned it down without a second thought. I often had meals with him and his wife, and soon felt that his honesty, religion and mixed race were unlikely to help his promotion. He felt the same and emigrated to England shortly afterwards before going to New Zealand some years later after their three children had all taken good degrees. One day we decided to climb Chiltarn, an eleven-thousand footer not far from Quetta to the south-east, one of three high peaks surrounding the town: Murdar, to the north and the nearest dominating it, while Takatu rose defiantly to the north-west. On his beloved Harley Davidson we drove across desert along a torrent bed to reach the main ridge but had to turn back because a deep gully barred our way. At our last attempt, we reached what we believed was our mountain and had climbed about halfway up when the bitter wind increased to a gale that threatened to tear us from the mountain. When a particularly nasty bluff checked us we called it a day. Later we discovered that by mistake we had attempted to climb another peak, Mir Gutt.

The month-long fast of Ramazan was then in progress and the front doors of the cafes in Jinnah Road were closed but 'Isai', meaning Christians, could enter by side doors to have food and tea: I was astonished at how many there seemed to be, complete with beards and turbans. Derek told me that when the fast coincided with the long, hot summer days, road accidents and murders doubled, because the strain of thirst and not smoking became too much for some. One day at Jehandar Shah's house lunch was pressed on me in spite of my protests so I took a few bites as they bravely watched and the compromise satisfied both parties. The Pashtunistan issue was hotting up again and it leaked out that fourteen men had been secretly arrested in that connection. The younger Jogezais from Tarwal were at college in Quetta and I joined them in the family bungalow in a small village on the edge of the town. There was a heavy snowfall and five of us took on twenty-five locals in a snow fight for hours: it was kids' stuff but fun. A part-time job with the British Council in Tehran was offered me but a full-time job in Nyasaland beckoned and I took it. My idea was to work there for a year to save enough money to buy the equipment needed to film in Afghanistan but in the event I stayed there for three years, returned to the U.K. and bought a pair of dilapidated cottages to store my ever-increasing personal things. That used all my money so that there was not the faintest hope of returning to Afghanistan and Baluchistan in the near future. A year later I became married and after a three-year residence in the U.K., Sheila, baby James and I returned to what had become Malawi for three more years.

I gave my treasured .22 pistol to Ahmad Yar Khan as a farewell gift when he came to Quetta briefly and just before I left for Karachi a permit to visit Zhob came through but by then it was too late. Earlier I had been told that two detectives were tailing me constantly and wondered whether one or other would have continued following had I gone to Tarwal. On the train down to Karachi there was an interesting Spanish Lt. Colonel who was distinctly cool on Franco and three Germans, one of whom was a middle-aged and shameless scrounger. We joined forces for baggage security and in Karachi, checked into a grubby hotel near Lea Market, a slum area, but it was so foul that we transferred to the Y.M.C.A. the next morning in spite of the extra expense. At the U.K. Consulate an official there told me the sad tale of an uneducated and rather unworldly English girl who, wooed by visions of the Arabian nights, had wed a Pakistani from the Sinde whose father was a 'village chief'. The couple had gone to the man's village in the middle of the desert, very dirty and even hotter, where she was kept in absolute 'purdah'. Quite unable to cope, and I would certainly never consider the Sinde for a possible home in any case, the girl had tried to escape, been caught and so badly beaten that one arm was broken. Her second attempt was successful and she somehow arrived at the Consulate desperate, destitute and on the point of collapse. They shipped the poor thing back to the U.K.

The good news for me was that there was a ship soon sailing to Beira in Mozambique but there was only deck accommodation available. That would suit me but the bad news later was that we delicate Europeans were not allowed to travel deck class.

1) A young Shinwari girl embroidering in the sunshine outside the family kuzhdai.

2) *Another village headman at Ghabar Ghar, Pir Mohamad, Wali Jan being the first.*

3) A Dautani woman repairing clothes outside the family kuzhdei. Although extremely poor, she was constantly smiling and contented.

4)   A rare and unusually small kuzhdei at Ghabar Ghar with only two roof seams instead of three.

5) *The owner of the kuzhdei, a Kakar from Kakar Khorrasan near the Afghan border.*

6) *Upon our return from Mazar to Zhob we were transferred two miles down the road to the Akhterzai Thana (a redundant police post) as a tactful move and photographed the southern half of Kulli Akhterzai, with the Spin Ghar on the far side of the great valley rising to 8,000 feet.*

7) *The Shahizai nomad family with whom the author travelled for almost five weeks in 1992: L-R: Ruziamat Shahizai,.Malanga fifth son, toddler Dwardi, Rahmatullah his fourth son, an unknown, and wife "Bibi" Ruzaimat.*

8) *Fording the River Zhob with lambs and kids, Wali to the right, Ziauddin first right. Notice the white cliffs to the right, which indicate the level of the valley floor.*

Hoping that Bombay might offer a better chance with a different company I took a deck passage thence and was quietly transferred to a vacant second-class cabin by a ship steward but in Bombay the hope of a deck passage proved to be false so it was a B.O.A.C. flight by Comet to Nairobi. I had ample funds in the Allahabad Bank in Kanpur but the airline office would take only cheques on local accounts. Noshir Pochkhanawala, the Doon School parent who had earlier helped me with my baggage saga, rescued me with cash and, unable to arrange foreign exchange in time, I managed to buy £7-10 shillings in notes in the bazaar: to get me from Nairobi to Salisbury, a matter of fifteen hundred or so miles, mainly by dirt roads, although I did not realise that it was that far at the time. Fortunately the plane did not suffer the fate of three later ones.

Chapter Eight

The Expedition With Bob Chambers

I had left Baluchistan and the Frontier in the early part of 1961 and nine years later left Africa for a second time. As my service had not been pensionable, a useful gratuity was given instead, some of which I used in advance to buy a Rollei SL66 camera. In 1970 I had hoped to do an M.Sc. in wildlife management in Edinburgh, with a view to new career in African game ranching that had struck me as having several ecological and biological advantages over cattle rearing but it seemed that at forty years of age one was a 'has been' and 'in a rut' and certainly not worthy of a grant to study. Bob Chambers, whom I had met in Tehran when travelling overland to India and currently back in the bank in Sydney, was contacted and we agreed to still my nagging regret at having turned down the offer of the three Sulaiman Khels in Fort Sandeman. Before leaving the U.K. for Pakistan, I bought a .32 calibre long-cartridge Webley & Scott revolver as a thank-you to the chief for his hospitality and trust, paying the Brighton dealer to send it to him in Zhob, as I considered it too risky to carry it with me in addition to my Colt .357 magnum. A Smith & Wesson would have been far better but the chief preferred the other make against all my persuasions. In the end the dealer failed to dispatch the gun for many months and eventually needed a firm nudge but it got there in the end.

Much needed to be done but in 1971 I drove overland in a

new V.W. Microbus to Wagga on the border with India while Bob flew to New Delhi and eventually travelled to our new rendezvous by train and bus. Money ever limited, I took an Indian family and an English woman with me at a modest charge per head. The wife and two children were as sensible and helpful as the man was petty and inept. In spite of precise instructions and sensible weight limitations (in view of some rough stretches of the route), in London he had arranged only two visas of the seven required and instead of two hundred pounds of baggage turned up at the very last minute with around four hundred so that I could not very well refuse. As we had a ferry booking it was a piece of blackmail. To this was added a large package delivered to the U.K. port to avoid purchase tax and money loaned to pay for that was only reluctantly returned ten days later when I refused to continue otherwise. After finding in Switzerland that the rear axle weight was exceeded, three cartons of books were despatched from Trieste. Three faulty new tyres, one exploding and the others blistering, did not help things. For me at least it was a traumatic journey and I was overjoyed when we reached Kandahar and they decided to get out and fly on to India from there.

It was only thirteen years since I had made the journey by bicycle but almost every town along the route in Yugoslavia and beyond had changed out of all recognition. Literally thousands of miles of dirt tracks had become tar or concrete roads. There were tourists everywhere plus motels to cater for them, and hordes of hippies. It was an astonishing transformation. As a result, attitudes in several countries had changed as well: stones were thrown at us four times in Mashed while some Afghan petrol pump meters had been tampered with, which led me to a fierce confrontation when re-fuelling in Kandahar. On a happier note I had one of the best cameras of the day and as much film as we could wish, saved from the oven heat of Afghanistan's southern desert by the simple expedient of draping a sodden towel over the cool box, thus lowering its temperature by 15°C. In addition I carried fairly extensive caving gear to explore the fabled cave lower down the Zhob Valley in Batozai Srra. My smaller goodies included an altimeter, prismatic compass, and a maximum & minimum thermometer set; while Bob was bringing an excellent tape recorder from Singapore on his way, a hygrometer, clinometer and so on.

Arriving in Quetta I found that it was being supplied with water by tankers as no useful rain or snow had fallen for three years. There Sardar Usman Khan dined me before I continued to Tarwal, carrying five tribesmen to Kila Saifulla after firmly refusing three more lest our equipment be damaged. I called briefly at Tarwal, arriving late at night and savoured the utter silence before sleeping in the vehicle. The next day, after meeting the chief but not A.Y.K., who was away, and storing much of our equipment there, I hurried north to meet Bob. Zhob also had not had rain for three years and was even more dun-coloured and stark than usual. I gave a family of three a lift from Kila Saifulla to Loralai and suspected that both mother and child had T.B. Just beyond Loralai I picked up three Kharotis from Ghazni on their way to D.G. Khan where they hoped to find work.

The severe drought in south-east Afghanistan had caused great suffering among tribes people such as these and many were crossing the border is desperation although it was supposedly closed on account of the Pashtunistan issue. Some pastoral nomads had lost three-quarters of their flocks I was told. We arrived at Mekhtar after four in the afternoon to find a barrier across the road because of bandit activity further on so we had to spend the night there and I bought us all four of us a supper. I was fairly certain that they were destitute but I could ill afford to give them money also as the three tyre failures had already severely depleted my limited finances. On from there, due to tremendous damage to the gravel road caused by storms and because of the worrying state of my surviving tyres, it took three hours to cover one stretch of forty-three miles. As we approached Multan my Kharoti companions, who felt that they had a better chance of work there, returned my help when the vehicle's body became stuck on an earth ridge along an appalling section of dirt road. I soon had another passenger, a young businessman going to his home to Lahore where I enjoyed the luxury of a hot bath in his house.

Yet another war with India seemed imminent and because of that I had advised Bob by five telegrams and six letters to come on from Delhi to Lahore, for if I were to cross the border we might find ourselves stranded in India if the threat materialised. Concerned in case he was waiting for me, beyond D.I. Khan I drove from six-thirty in the morning. until three the following morning, setting off again at five. In Lahore my third tyre simply collapsed, which left me with no spare. Equally bad, in reply to two formal requests sent in early May and July I found a brief letter from the Baluchistan government barring us from Zhob. Interestingly, it was not sent to my home address in the U.K. and it was dated the day after I actually passed through Zhob. To cap it all, the starter motor had to be stripped and cleaned of the dust that got in when stuck near Multan. In the face of all this my Entamoeba or Giardia trouble since Tehran, which fortunately only attacked morning or evening, was trivial. Suddenly the omens were not good.

I waited in Lahore for four days, driving into the countryside each night to sleep, accompanied by a young English traveller who was down on his luck and without shelter though I forget the cause. The U.K.H.C. helped greatly by storing one or two valuable items so that security was less of a worry but the stress of waiting blind was too much so I then went to Wagga itself, the one and only crossing point. Waiting near the Customs I noted grimly that every overland vehicle from Europe that passed had been more or less extensively damaged. One had hit an unlit bullock cart in the dark and was ripped open as if by a giant can-opener, others had been incautious enough to cross traffic lights at the green without carefully looking right and left to make sure that it was safe, and so on. To the intense relief of both of us, Bob appeared two days later. He had received one of my five telegrams, and that had taken eight days to reach him.

We decided to make some enquiries at Islamabad and there camped discreetly near a green of its golf course. The next morning the manager of the club panicked upon finding us as some high rankers were due to play an early round so we moved on. Brief enquiries at the Home Affairs Ministry referred us to Quetta: it was not their business they said. We were unaware that we were about to become human shuttlecocks. In Peshawar University we chanced to meet a lecturer in Geology, Safdar Khan, who not only turned out to be a Kakar, though he had never visited the tribal territory, but had taken his doctorate at my own university college at Aberystwyth in Wales. On our way south we spent a full day in the Durra Adam Khel tribal gun factories getting photographs of the various manufacturing stages. As the government had recently allowed in supplies of high grade steel, most of the weapons were quite good though their .303 rifles still commanded only a tenth the price of a genuine Lee Enfield. Most of the weapons were copies, whether rifle, pistol or revolver but the .25 calibre pen pistols were of local design and hardly expensive at £2 a time. All day long gunfire was heard at intervals as potential customers tried out weapons that appealed to them and the nearby hill must have collected tons of lead over the years.

We saw one twelve-year-old boy turning a rifle barrel on a lathe and the furnaces to heat the metal were surprisingly small. We heard that the Pakistan army sent some of their mortars and light field guns here for repair. Since then, due to the Russian intervention, both Afghanistan and Pakistan have been flooded with modern weapons by the Americans, Chinese and others. The old trade has slumped and the town is said to be more concerned with heroine, reputedly Pakistan's largest foreign exchange earner at one time. Two American Narcotics Agency men had gone there to investigate the new trade and were promptly kidnapped we were told, at which the army acted swiftly, ringing the place with tanks and artillery. That determined move secured the men's release, intact. Even in '71 there was a hashish store in Durra with an honest sign above the door proclaiming its commodity

Continuing south, we gave two Waziris a lift. They were a shifty looking pair and their keen interest in our mass of equipment prompted me to check the Colt under my seat as I drove but there were no problems. After dropping them off we picked up another pair of Waziris who looked totally honest but upon being diverted into a large police checkpoint they were unceremoniously ordered out of the vehicle in spite of our protests. The Panjabis there said that they were probably bandits. It was a singularly stupid thing to suggest and one which Bob and I found very offensive. In the end, in spite of our continuing protests, we had little choice but to leave them there. Beyond Bannu the weather looked black: the rains had come with a vengeance and we found the Drazinda road blocked. After crossing one difficult stream in spate, a flood ahead barred us but when we tried to return our retreat was cut off for an hour or two until the flood level dropped to about eighteen inches. Back on the main road we learned that the D.I. Khan and D.G. Khan road to the south were cut off so we tried the Chasma Barrage but the approach to that was also impassable. The only alternative now was to head back north to Kalabagh.

The Nawab there had a smallish but fine wildlife reserve and we hoped to meet him. Asking the way at the police station, three men who sauntered in behind us offered to show us his house. We presumed that they had friends among the police.

Just before reaching the Nawab's place, they asked to get out where it happened to be dark. Suddenly, as they walked away towards a solitary distant light, Bob noticed two books on the ground but they had not been carrying any books when boarding the Minibus. The books had to be ours. He then registered that one of the men had slipped behind the Microbus before rejoining the other two heading towards the lit area. Suspicious, Bob checked the back seat and was startled to discover that the precious tape recorder was missing. Searching the far side of the road he found it but the men were gone by then. The Nawab was away and, as we returned the way we had come, in our headlights we saw the three thieves walking on the embankment leading to the road-rail bridge over the Indus. Thinking to drag one of them to the police station, I left Bob in the vehicle, doors locked, and chased after them. It was very dark and it seemed quite probable that if they heard me following them they might lay in wait for me behind a girder of the bridge, perhaps knife me and dump my body into the river so I had my Colt in hand ready cocked. Perhaps it was just as well that they had gone to the far side. Upon mentioning the incident the following morning to a local man, his opinion was that the three were probably off-duty policemen.

The next morning we went south through Mianwali, its main bazaar being so narrow that there was no more that a foot's clearance on either side, making it impossible to open the two front doors of the microbus. It was quite claustrophobic and very unpleasant. After skirting the Thal Desert for mile after mile, we re-crossed the Indus over the Taunsa Barrage as a great storm struck, sped through D.G. Khan, reached Fort Munro in the dark and camped two miles further on. From Ruckni the road to Mekhtar had been severely damaged and it took six hours but, after enjoying the luxury of Loralai 'paratas', as we had been banned we took advantage of the dark to slip through Kila Saifulla and Hindubagh, camping near Khan Metarzai, at 6,800 feet the highest railway station in Asia and certainly chilly. On the way, having stopped to photograph a hedgehog I discovered that my almost new Rollei flashgun and the most advanced at that time, was completely out of action.

In Quetta we had an interview with the Home Secretary to the Baluchistan Government. He blandly told us that his provincial government had no objection to our researches and that his letter had merely passed on the decision of the Central Government. We needed to return to Islamabad. Usman Khan's hospitality soothed our feelings a little that night. The following evening we returned to Kila Saifulla after dark and slept discreetly behind the Post Office in order to collect mail immediately it opened in the morning. Avoiding the main bazaar with its ears and eyes, we went through Loralai without stopping and on via Murgha Kibzai to Manikhwar. We hoped to go through the fantastic Chuhar Khel Dhana gorge, which route avoided Fort Sandeman and its checkpoints. Unsigned roads and a faulty map led us ten miles north into Sherani country lying due west of the Takht-i-Sulaiman instead of east through the gorge and we gave up at a tiny village, until people from another one just a mile along the road advised us that their neighbours were thieves. True or otherwise we moved to their village and had a peaceful night.

The Sherani on the western side of the range belong to the Bargha section of the tribe and there is a little story as to how they got there from the eastern slopes. About three hundred years ago the tribe had been at intermittent war with the Bittani tribe nearby until the Sherani chief came upon a Kuresh orphan boy. Somehow this boy miraculously enabled the Sherani to overcome their traditional enemy, the Bittani. The boy was named Dare Khan and when he grew up he was married to a Sherani girl. On the other side of the range, to the west, there was a vacant area known as Bargha that had been vacated earlier by a group of Hazaras and had since lain waste from fear of the

Waziri tribe to the north. Having been so useful against the Bittanis it was thought that Dare Khan might be able to handle the Wazir equally well so the leaders of the tribe sent him off with a number of followers and their families to settle on the Bargha lands. They settled and prospered and now form the Bargha section of the tribe. It does seem that orphans and refugees have thrived along the Frontier over the centuries when one considers the traditional origin of the Kharoti and others

Returning to the main road in the morning, with several passengers as usual, too late we saw a road by-passing the militia checkpoint near Manikhwar so that to turn back would be even more suspicious. The officer i/c had to 'phone the Political Agent's office in Fort Sandeman to see if we could go on to Drazinda and Draban and we were then given tea and a meal. Three hours later permission came through but ten miles into the hills we met a lorry that we had seen earlier returning from the gorge which was totally blocked by massive landslides from the soft conglomerate above the hard limestone. It was more than just a long shot but we returned to the militia post, rather than to the P.A.'s office which would certainly say no, explained that the gorge was blocked and asked if we might go through Waziristan to Tank. Now Waziristan has always been closed to foreigners and not without good reason, yet to our utter astonishment permission was granted. Before other opinions might prevail we tanked up with fuel nearby and hurried off, scarcely believing our good fortune.

Sambaza Fort sits astride the road and the barrier made sure that we could not slip through as we would have preferred. Convinced that we would be turned back, after all sorts of palavers we were invited into the fort by the young officer i/c, a Bengali. His three fellow officers were away but certainly we could drive through to Tank. It then dawned on us that the warlike situation had led to older and experienced officers along the volatile Frontier being called to the Indian border, younger and less experienced ones being transferred to such vacated posts. We had a cold but wonderful bath, followed by an excellent meal. Chatting with us after that, the officer related how a couple of years earlier a visiting general had insulted some Sulaiman Khels settled in a small pocket in north-west Baluchistan. It was extremely foolish thing to do and the man could not have been a Pashtun or he would have known better. Anyhow, about a year previously the Sulaiman Khels were tipped off that he would pass along the road that lay ahead of us. They were waiting and neither he nor his escort of forty men in trucks survived. However, it cost the Sulaiman Khels dearly, for the army retaliated and as many as two hundred tribesmen may have been killed. Our host's enthusiasm for that response severely jarred both of us.

Arriving at Gul Kach the next morning, the Gomal River was deeper that I would have wished, the water covering the front bumper but, with Bob wading in front to guide me, the VW made it. We were now in Waziristan and feeling quite excited. Beyond the forbidding concrete fort at Gul Kach there were wonderful strong points at intervals, perched atop jagged ridges overlooking the road where an ambush might otherwise be launched, and we saw them signalling to one another by heliograph. We dropped a Waziri passenger with us at the Mahsud village of Shaeer and were promptly approached by a pleasant local teacher who spoke good English. It was in a prosperous highland valley with irrigated fields of lush maize but we learned that there was often shooting so it had much to tell. Minutes after leaving him we came to a large and quite extraordinary house by the road. Its lower walls were of mud, like all the other houses in the village, but the entire upper story was consisted of massive steel plates welded together at various angles and with loopholes cut here and there. Fantastic really is the only word to describe such a fortified house and it must have cost a fortune, its construction a tribute to skill and ingenuity. I dearly wished to take a photograph but no owner or occupant could be seen and without express permission it would have been foolhardy to do so. Clearly the family had serious neighbour problems and might have been inclined to shoot first and ask questions afterwards.

A little unwisely we stopped at Jandola for a modest meal. It was not long before an official-looking person among the crowd at the 'hotal' began to ask us searching questions but fortunately I was able to create a diversion over our water bottles that were being filled by yet another Waziri passenger. That man was of a remarkably hopeful disposition for when we dropped him off in D.I. Khan instead of Tank, as he had asked initially, he demanded Rs.10 to pay for a return fare by jeep. We had to disappoint him. The sign-posted turnoff to the Chasma Barrage was under two feet of water but two local boys showed us a raised alternative track and also the house of the watchman who was needed to unlock the approach gate. We had been travelling for nineteen hours over difficult roads before stopping at three in the morning, thirty miles short of Rawalpindi.

Our first official in Islamabad was the head of the States & Frontier Regions section in the Ministry for Home Affairs. He surprised us by stating that his department had no objection to our plans, which had by now been converted from plans to hopes and faint ones at that. From what he said it appeared that Quetta had not contacted him. We were then shunted on to a Mr. Mahmood-i-Ilahi, who was a / the protocol officer in the Ministry of Foreign Affairs. He likewise claimed not to have been contacted by Quetta. Everyone was very polite, bland and obviously playing safe. There is little point in further detailing the protracted saga that followed, other than mentioning that we also visited the U.K. High Commission, who simply wanted us to go home, and the Australian one which was far more positive but, in fairness, the U.K. bunch did gradually warm to our project and had earlier supported my application for a firearm permit.

After three nights by the golf course, which we called the

Islamabad Club 'Annexe' to prop up our flagging morale, we were told of a beautiful little river only five miles out in the countryside, the Kurang, where we could camp in peace and swim in the rocky pools of its mini gorge. Only a mile or so to the north of our new base rose a sudden line of lush green hills that gave some solace at the end of each frustrating day. Every day we laid siege to this or that person, and always tomorrow would be the day of our deliverance. In the bazaar Bob's rather wild beard attracted snide comments in Urdu from various twenty-year olds until one day I had had enough, grabbed the offender by his shirt front and waved a fist under his jaw whilst deciding whether to beat him or not. His two friends looked on but wisely kept their distance. Finally, the possibility of violent action filtering back to government officials with whom we were negotiating granted the lout a reprieve. However, the word must have spread through the bazaar for we had not even a meaningful glance from then on. As my Kakar friends would say: "Bazaar lowg di," – they were bazaar people, which explained it all.

I had been in Pakistan for a month but had driven a further 3,630 miles since arriving and we had nothing to show for it. Worse still, letters from my wife revealed financial difficulties at home when I was already living off Bob because of the tyre disasters. Luckily I managed to sell my watch a day later and set that right. After a month of all this frustrating nonsense between Quetta and the capital, we decided to go off to Afghanistan to soothe our raw nerves. Kabul was full of hippies, often barefoot and some in 'koochi' or nomad dress, but its 'tikka kebabs' were not to be missed. They have a flavour not to be matched anywhere else in the world. A sign of the times was the sale of local brandy at ten Afghanis a glass in cafes, while the British Embassy listed three girls reported as missing by their families and a worried father had come out to search for his son. With so many European weirdoes around we decided to move on and visit Mazar-i-Sharif.

As we mounted the Hindu Kush we stopped to photograph a particularly beautiful valley. While so engaged a couple of school boys aged around fifteen years came along and stopped. After a few minutes of conversation with Bob they asked for money, which was refused. At this they became more and more insistent, emboldened by our wish to be tolerant, and became quite predatory. When we made ready to leave the older one stood in the way of my driver's door and ignored firm demands to move aside. Psychologically and socially it was quite intriguing but I had had enough: I pushed him hard in the chest and sent him sprawling against the earth bank, saying in Pashtu 'do you understand now', and he obviously did. We wondered if they had previously encountered wimpish Europeans who readily caved in to such blatant attempts at extortion.

The new road over the Salang Pass in the Hindu Kush was built by the Russians and rises to 10,600 feet, the top section being a tunnel with a roofed extension at each end to deflect avalanches. Descending from the pass the brakes behaved normally but seven years later, when accompanied by four pupils and our eldest son James, apparently due to the altitude, they behaved alarmingly. Arriving in Mazar in the early morning we had a snack by the VW and as we did so two boys in their early teens approached, kicking stones along the road and showing a certain 'evil intent'. Sure enough, after they were well past us they turned and a stone struck one of the vehicle's wheel trims. Often travellers put up with that sort of thing, possibly from timidity or because they cannot speak a word of the language should officials become involved or because they cannot run fast enough to deliver retribution. As a result such behaviour proliferates and escalates but I was after them like a shot. Seeing that I was rapidly gaining on them they screamed in terror – rather satisfyingly – ran into a park and clung to a group of men for protection while I circled vengefully but with no chance of getting my hands on them.

The Balkh Nights hotel was both passable and very cheap but we slept in our vehicle inside the compound. Trustingly I used the urinal after a shower and my bare feet were suddenly sprayed with warm liquid: the down-pipe simply ended a few inches above the floor. Among the crowd of foreigners was one thin, pale, distraught and fearful looking European girl who spoke to no one. We wondered if she would ever get back home but she did not ask for help so what could we do? The Masjid-e-Ali is remarkably beautiful and attracts many pilgrims though whether the shrine really contains the body of martyred Hazrat Ali, the prophet's son-in-law, is in some doubt. The mosque is also unusual in hosting the only beggars in the country so far as I was aware but they were quiet, dignified and undemanding as they sat in the lofty entrance with their boat-shaped, copper begging bowls. After that we visited the vast but ruined surrounding walls of Balkh, established around 2,500 B.C., and eventually well and truly sacked by nobody's friend, Ghenghis Khan. Heavy but rare storms erode the high mud walls that surrounded the ancient city so that from time to time human skulls and bones fall out, witness to the victims buried alive during its construction for laziness or causing some other offence to the wrong person. We were offered countless, very attractive fine triangular bronze arrow heads for a few afghanis but refused on principle, tempted though we were.

When returning to Kabul we visited the covered, traditional bazaar at Khulm, or Tashkurgan as it is also called. It was quite unspoilt, free from hippies and, by way of a change, we were not offered hashish. Its adjoining ruined mud fort was overshadowed by immense slabs of steep, bare rock reaching to the top of a high mountain. Unable to change travellers' cheques in Mazar just before leaving as it was Friday – something we had overlooked – after the first or second toll along the road we discovered that we lacked sufficient cash to pay. This was quite worrying and, without much hope I explained out position.

To our astonishment and considerable gratitude the guard then let us through without a ticket and we were both impressed by such a trusting and understanding attitude.

We returned to Islamabad after eleven days to be met with a firm refusal, which was laid at the door of the Baluchistan government. No one had objected in Islamabad we were assured but somebody was being very economical with the truth. Apart from filling in spare time by lusting after fine Turkoman rugs, we decided to return to Baluchistan via Peshawar in order to visit its Seraffo Bazaar to look at gemstones as the extreme north of the country produces quite a variety in addition to its emeralds and Bob had a diploma in that field. In the narrow bazaar, while buying a couple of warm 'naans' for us I felt a slight movement at my side trouser pocket and quietly looked down. Although the pocket was deep and therefore secure, or so I had thought, my wallet with all my money was delicately being withdrawn by someone's hand. It was so unexpected that I took a moment to react but turned around to see a burly young tribesman moving off. As it was in full view of several jewellers' shops a few yards off and he must have been seen by several people. I thought that it must be a poor joke until he turned around and realised that I had seen him. He was off in a flash and so was I, without even warning Bob as it was so sudden. I realised instantly that once he disappeared up some tiny side alley all was lost. Doing just that, although bare footed, he slipped a few yards up and bounced to his feet instantly but I was onto him and pulled him down. He was young, heavily built and strong, probably an Afridi, but worst of all my head was inches from a vile open sewer as we struggled on the ground. He managed to break away but in his panic headed back towards the main bazaar. At this point Bob arrived and blocked his escape so that he rushed back towards me at which I got a grip that was not to be broken. Someone in the crowd that had gathered returned my wallet, which had been flung down, and they all gave him a bit of kicking. Our reputation soared from the successful outcome but we strongly suspected that he was well known by shop keepers and probably feared as well.

Heading south once more, we decided to be cheeky and pass through Waziristan again and if possible spend a day or two back in Shaheer village with the helpful teacher. Also we hoped to visit the army library at Miram Shah which was reputed to have a superb collection of books on the Frontier. At Thal we swung in through the arch of the towered gateway that marked the boundary and found all the border guards seated in the middle of the road a few yards ahead. They leapt to safety as we gave a casual, friendly wave and were too late to challenge us. I could see them waving frantically in my mirror but as no rifles were raised we kept going. Half an hour later as we approached Mir Ali, a small militia post well off the road, we saw a figure running desperately up the long avenue of trees leading to the main road in order to intercept us. Clearly our approach had been reported. I accelerated discreetly and we would have won the race had not the strand of barbed wire, half let into a tiny trench in the tarmac, given us a rapid puncture. The officer i/c was charming, we explained our purpose and were entertained for the night.

The next morning he blandly insisted on providing two trucks full of troops as an escort, one in front and one behind. Arriving at a T junction, our leading escort turned left and we were obliged to follow but felt that we should be turning right and began to have doubts about being guided to Miram Shah as given to understand. At a barrier not far ahead our escort left us and we were told to carry on. After a mile or so Bob noticed that by the sun we were heading entirely in the wrong direction. We had been tricked and our return to the barrier was fruitless. Unknowingly we had stirred up the dust. As we headed for Fort Sandeman via Drazinda, we were turned back at Draban by the militia post. From D.G. Khan we crossed the mountains to Ruckni and were again turned back by the militia at Bewatta so the Bolan Pass was our last resort. Obviously telephones had been ringing. As we crossed the Indus at Sukkur, just upstream of the bridge were moored a couple of interesting traditional cargo boats with sails. Upon taking photos of them through the girders of the bridge we were promptly arrested and had to drive our two guards, with fixed bayonets, to their H.Q. nearby. The junior officer there was neither educated nor helpful but when the officer i/c returned an hour later he was quite the opposite and very apologetic after our explanation: and we were free to continue.

That evening we stopped in a tiny 'hotal' in Sibi. Near us sat two middle-aged nomads with small plates of food while the young man with them watched hungrily as they ate. He was probably the son of one and it was clear that they simply did not have enough money to buy him food due to the terrible three-year drought in south-east Afghanistan, so that many of them were virtually destitute. We both found it quite upsetting and discreetly paid for a plate to be sent to him. The logic is simple: the able-bodied men are essential to protect the 'kafila' or caravan so that women, children and youths must come second. They, the grown men, are the defenders of the family group or the migrating village and must be strong enough to act positively if threatened or molested. It's a basic survival strategy. Negotiating the Bolan Pass the next day we saw group after group of nomads on the move, some with smallish flocks, carefully spaced so not to interfere with one another as they travelled eastwards to the plains. We presumed that the Pakistan government had relaxed its closed-border policy (in response to the Pashtunistan movement) for humanitarian reasons when faced with this great Afghan suffering.

Having put so much money and effort into the expedition, we needed to salvage what we could and make contact with Sulaiman Khels in Afghanistan itself, probably near Mukur, rather than at the border in Kakar Khorrasan as originally envisaged. That would be no light undertaking and, to minimise the risks, we decided to enlist Sheikh Rahmat as a guide and go-between. Anticipating that the militia manning the road chain at Hindubagh would be waiting for us, we went to Tarwal by way of the Spera Ghara gravel road which was unguarded. Our priority was to have a word with Sheikh who, let me remind you, spent some years as an outlaw with Sulaiman Khels, fleeing into Afghanistan whenever things got a bit too warm in Baluchistan. When we arrived in Tarwal, Sheikh took a long look at our considerable amount of expensive equipment and shook his head gravely. While it would be easy travel from village to village on foot under the guidance and protection of local 'maliks' and meet his erstwhile partners and friends in Afghanistan, the sight of so much baggage might prove irresistible to some of them. He should have known and we took the hint. The alternative was to hire donkeys and go on foot to the region of Kammaruddin Karez but first there was the cave to explore and a 'karez', one of which was actually in the process of being dredged out by a team of 'karrigur' from Kandahar.

During the evening chat we heard about a Kakar nomad who had taken to living with some Nassers over the border and who migrated to and from Loralai each year with a companion. Foolishly, the previous year one night he and a companion stole a camel belonging to Haji Hayat Khan near his place at Kuli Ghoti well out on the great valley floor. Servants reported this to his brother, Abdur Rahman, who happened to be with Nurullah Khan and Safdar Khan in the Kila Saifulla bazaar that morning. Various exits from the valley were checked and the three Jogezais found footprints heading past Adwal mountain for Loralai. The trio returned to the Loralai turn-off near Kila Saifulla immediately and drove over the hills to Loralai, forty-six miles away, where enquiries among locals revealed that the two men and a camel had been seen heading for Mekhtar. The three Jogezais soon saw the pair some way from the road leading the camel and shouted an order that the two men should abandon the animal but the thieves made no reply and headed for nearby hills. At the second order and warning, the two men broke into a run, leaving the camel.

The three Jogezais followed and returned fire with their .303 rifles when shot at, taking up positions on the rocky slopes. A bullet passed through Safdar's baggy 'partook' and a regular gun battle developed. One of the men managed to escape but the other finally succumbed to a seventh bullet, which determined performance earned the admiration of my friends. However, the encounter had been very near Loralai, long a settled area and so under the jurisdiction of the town and its police, and was thus against the law. There was the possibility of a case being brought but I failed to ascertain the final outcome. No doubt it was settled amicably behind the scenes. The incident soon became common knowledge in Zhob, back over the hills, and there was an intriguing sequel to it about a year later. Safdar Khan, a physically strong, intense and determined young man and one of Jehangir Shah's sons, sold his white mare to a man in Fort Sandeman. For whatever reason the animal would not settle and soon set off for its old home near Kila Saifulla, eighty miles or so back up the great valley. It took several weeks and was seen by dozens of tribesmen, many of whom thought it still belonged to Safdar Khan but no one would catch the beast, just in case it was thought that they were stealing it.

The fast of Ramazan was in progress, when eating or drinking between sunrise and sunset is forbidden, and A.Y.K. was therefore less enthusiastic about exploring the mysterious cave than he had been ten years previously but Bob and I said that we also would observe 'rosa', the fast. With A.Y.K, his brother Mohammad Hassan and Fukhruddin on board, we drove in the Microbus roughly thirty miles along the road towards Fort Sandeman before turning off along a dirt track which led to a vehicle ford through the Zhob River. As we were all armed except Bob and the two Jogezais were of the 'sardar khel' with another eight brothers in reserve as it were, Fukhruddin would be fairly safe in spite of the local enmity that he had mentioned to me ten years earlier. Near our objective, a sharp isolated peak separated from the main Shin Ghar range, we picked up 'malik' Nasser of Spinkai village to act as guide. The peak's name is Batozai Sekei, revealing it to be in that clan's territory. As we approached from higher up the valley, along the north-west side of the river were a number of quite large but scattered sand dunes so for a bit of fun we drove right over several of them and were impressed just how well the vehicle coped, always provided second gear was used.

To my astonishment the cave entrance was about a third way up a broad ridge leading to the summit. Upon reaching the two entrances, our companions were content to sit outside even though there was no talk of 'djins'. Once Bob and I were inside it was soon apparent that a hyaena or hyaenas had been, and possibly still was or were, living in the cave, which was a little worrying even though I had the Colt. Further on, there was evidence of porcupine occupation. Some of the passages were so low that crawling or wriggling was necessary and that was less than comforting for either animal would be a hazard if cornered. Of equal concern was the roof, which had massive slabs of partially detached rock hanging here and there, some looking as if a touch might dislodge them. Surprisingly, one chamber and a passage had stalactites hanging from the roof. However, all visions of Mughal treasure were soon dispelled and, after four hours of wriggling through the maze, thirst began to tell on us while our friends outside were understandably becoming impatient. We left the four separate passages before reaching their ends but we kept our word by observing 'rosa' until nightfall even though released from our promise by A.Y.K. Our map was passed on some years later to a keen caver from Derbyshire and he with friends continued the exploration, again helped by A.Y.K. though I have not seen their findings.

A bit of local excitement at the time of our visit concerned the leading families of two Kakar clans, the Abdullazais and Kibzais. As might be expected young hotheads had lit the flames. No official trade with India existed but in Pakistan there was still a strong demand for betel nut, cardamom and other things; and if I recall correctly, the severe drought made it profitable to take wheat into Afghanistan, giving profit both ways. The spices were flown to Afghanistan then smuggled into Pakistan, where Kammaruddin Karez near the border seems to have been a major route. As told to us, the 'goody' of the piece was Sher Ali Khan Abdullazai of Fort Sandeman, who incidentally had organised an ambush that wiped out a Gurkha platoon under two British officers in 1918. The 'baddy' was Murat Khan Kibzai of Murgha Kibzai village who, before Independence and Partition, had been sentenced to ten years by the British for outlawry and in 1971 was still said to have dubious friends. In the outline history of Zhob, chapter five, Murgha Kibzai featured as a hotbed of lawlessness when the British first moved in and it was not just directed against the British who, after all, were invaders. Two relatives of Sher Ali Khan arrived with a loaded truck at the Lakaband Thana (not the former British post in the region of Murgha Kibzai mentioned in the brief history), near Kammaruddin Karez. There Akhtar Shah and another son of Murat Khan plus a relative, all on Levy service, had been advised of their approach and awaited them. Invited into the Levy post in connection with smuggling, Shah Wazir Abdullazai was promptly beaten about the head with rifle butts and fell to the floor. His companion drew a pistol at this but yet another son of Murat Khan, who happened to be present, shot him dead. Hearing of this, Murat Khan feared retribution, for Sher Ali Khan was a man of strong character, and took several mullahs and 'maliks' and a 'pir' (a purported direct descendant of the

Prophet) to Sher Ali Khan's home where he offered Rs.50,000 and four or five girls in marriage without 'wulwer'. His offer was refused, partly because there was long-standing enmity between the two families, and Sher Ali Khan made a counter demand for the handing over of a good piece of land known as Torra Khulla by the Zhob River. Murat Khan could not hand this over as it belonged to the clan and had been the cause of much bloodshed in the past. Sher Ali Khan then demanded that Murat Khan should exile himself and family to Loralai and never visit Zhob. In short, his patience was ended and he was deliberately making unacceptable demands: it was to be blood for blood. To emphasise the point he publicly offered Rs.10 for every Kibzai shot and suggested that Murat Khan should do the same with his clan. Akhtar Shah, the instigator of the trouble, then went to Nawab Sahib to seek his help, which was rather hopeful as the Jogezais and Abdullazais have inter-married. But Sher Ali Khan also went to Tarwal and asked the chief not to intervene, to make sure.

Six or eight months later a group of Abdullazais secretly rented a suitably sited upstairs room in the bazaar in preparation for the day when a quasi 'jirga' sponsored by government officials ('quazi' because the system had been abolished officially by the central government) was to discus the matter. As hoped, Akhtar Shah happened to pass the clandestine house on his way to the Kibzais' second home in Fort Sandeman ready for the 'jirga' and was shot dead. A Kibzai servant sent then to reconnoitre the house was also shot, after which there was a gun battle for two or three hours until the Levies under Abdul Aziz Luni restored order and arrested the assailants. At the time of our visit the Abdullazais involved were out on bail and everyone was watching to see what Murat Khan would do. He was in a bit of a spot for if he failed to take action he would lose face, especially as he had six surviving sons against Sher Ali Khan's four, but neither Sher Ali nor his sons were to be trifled with. The Kibzai faction were still visiting Fort Sandeman whilst Bob and I were there but in large groups and all heavily armed. Unfortunately, when visiting Zhob several times since then I have always forgotten to ask the outcome.

Back to more mundane and peaceful matters, a team of three Ghalzais of the Shamalzai clan of the Tokhi tribe were busy on Nowi Kashmir Karez and we joined them. They were from Kandahar. Their crude, traditional wooden winch was quite sturdy but the rope of plaited electric wires was less inviting so we brought the VW near and I went down by the winch but relayed from the vehicle, just in case. After all, the twelve-year-old boy digging out the mud thirty feet below weighed considerably less than I. Underground, the very stony soil gave confidence and, while narrow, there was ample height in which to stand. The 'karez' had four branches in all and at the lowest junction the roof was ten feet high, the animal population including rock pigeons and a few bats. Other 'karez' had fish also, though how they got there is anybody's guess. Having the VW by the shaft was our undoing as it was easily visible from the road. The P.A. chanced to drive by on the third day and we gathered that there was urgent consultation with the Nawab as we were the Nawab's guests and no doubt the P.A. had been warned of our presence, putting both men in a difficult situation. We surmised that a compromise was reached, whereby the P.A. would turn a blind eye if given the opportunity to do so. We were promptly transferred from Tarwal to the redundant but serviceable Akhtarzai Thana or militia post a couple of miles away, parking the vehicle out of sight within its high walls and covering it with a tarpaulin. For our comfort Mullah Sohfi had been deputed to cook for us, a gentle old man with a shock of white hair. He also spoke Urdu, to eke out my rusty Pashtu.

We also surveyed two large graveyards to get some idea as to child mortality, bearing in mind what I had learnt from several Jogezais in the early 1960s. This was not easy as the graves are simply mounds of gravel which are eroded by the occasional but violent storms so that it was often impossible to decide whether a grave was a fairly recent one of a child or the old one of an adult. Apart from aligning the body north and south with the head facing west, local custom was to decorate a new grave with a narrow length of white cotton cloth or bandage, suspended between two sticks or two natural headstones. Therefore we decided to count only those graves that had shreds of cloth remaining, probably meaning that they were less than five years old. If we were right this showed that over the period sixty-three to sixty four per cent of the graves were of children and later we found that this was the figure given by the U.N. for third world countries.

While on our way to spend a night at Badderwal Kila with the four sons of the late Azim Khan we discovered a fine crop of hashish growing discreetly within the walls of a small ruin but when we returned the next day to get photographs it seems that our interest had been noted for it had all been harvested. Eid ul Fitr, to celebrate end of the fast of Ramazan, arrived and we were invited to the ceremony at Tarwal. Although non-Muslim we were made to feel welcome and the atmosphere was very much like our Christmas gatherings. It really was delightful and villagers poured in from miles around to greet the chief. We had been planning a visit to Kakar Khorrasan with Sheikh using a couple of pack donkeys but his application for leave from his job on the road was refused. Before we could do more, a minion of the Assistant District Commissioner suddenly arrived late one afternoon and we were hustled to the rest house in Kila Saifulla. Mir Sahib, as addressed by his assistants, was an officious and offensive little man, semi-educated, rather disgusting in fact, and very derogatory about the Jogezais – behind their backs of course. The next morning we had to drive to Quetta with an escort in the Microbus.

Quetta had its share of hippies at that time and they had

earned a low reputation, some of the girls offering themselves for the equivalent of five shillings (25p to those who do not remember), even some of the males joining in. My friends were deeply shocked, elderly men in particular remembering and discussing the integrity, courage and fairness of political officers such as Sir Henry McMahon and Major Barnes, to mention just two. In fact my instant acceptance when I first arrived on the scene in 1958 sprang in large measure from the respect and goodwill created by such predecessors. The sight of young Europeans offering themselves thus or simply begging for money in a poor country such as Pakistan was beyond understanding, and such tales were not entirely hearsay. In Quetta one day, I was approached by a French couple who were begging and were prepared to settle for one rupee so they could not have wanted it for food, and on Lahore railway station I had earlier seen a barefoot European hippy embarrass Pakistani passengers by begging. And all this was in addition to cheating hotels by slipping away in the early hours without paying or falsely reporting the theft of travellers' cheques that had been cashed in some bazaar so that the recipient would not be paid by the issuing agency. Yet, after being repatriated at Embassy expense, some at least were still allowed to retain their passports without having to repay the fare. Near our home, in Street one such traveller had been repatriated twice in this fashion yet was planning yet another trip to India.

December was upon us, four months had passed and we had nothing to show for all our efforts. Our options were very few now but I had an invitation to visit friends among the Luni tribe in the village of Manzai near Duki, a few miles from which many nomads spend the winter. Also Bob had to go to Karachi for a week to meet his wife, Bettina, and bring her up to Quetta. They were to drive the VW leisurely to England and I was to return home by Christmas if possible, by whatever means. As we walked in the bazaar shortly after our enforced return from Zhob I suddenly noted that the same man had passed us three times within a fairly short period. A careful watch showed that he was in fact tailing us and, now alerted, we later discovered him squatting near our hotel when we were inside. To visit my Luni friends and the nomads encamped on the flat land abutting Ghabar Ghar (mountain), it was essential not only to escape his surveillance but to avoid the militia check points here and there. Even the unguarded Spera Ghrara road would still mean passing through Loralai, where I would certainly be detained. Then I had a stroke of luck: quite by chance in the Grindlays bank I saw a map on a wall revealing a little used jeep track over the mountains, through Ziarat and on to Duki. I promptly arranged to take Zaffarullah Khan, a son of the Luni Sardar and studying in Quetta at that time, to his brother's home in Manzai village a few miles beyond Duki.

At our hotel we quietly packed everything into the vehicle, unobserved by the spy squatting on the pavement a few yards from the hotel, paid our bill at the last minute as that intelligence might be passed on quickly, and strolled into the bazaar. After a few minutes, without warning Bob and I then separated, to the confusion of our following sleuth. I immediately jumped into a passing scooter rickshaw, made a long and tortuous run back to the hotel, collected the Microbus a few minutes later and was off, meeting Zaffarullah on the way as arranged. This was done as dusk fell so that we would not be seen crossing the open stretch of gravel desert before the hills but there would be just enough remaining light to drive without lights. It worked perfectly and we reached Manzai around midnight but the jeep track had been extremely bad, as a result of which another tyre had a blister in its wall and I had no spare. Politically, Loralai and Duki were not classed as tribal areas, unlike Zhob, and in theory I was not banned from either but what little trust in authority that we may have started out with had long since faded.

In the morning I took a look at some Dotani nomads grazing the flock in the immediate vicinity of Manzai. Like most nomads they tend to stick with tradition more than most settled tribes people and the shepherd wore a long smock over his 'partook' or baggy trousers instead of the shorter 'camise', modern versions of which are little more than long-tailed shirts buttoned down the middle. Also his smock was buttoned at the shoulder to one side while the Afghan 'camise' around Kandahar is buttoned on both sides of the neck, thus permitting a central panel of exquisite embroidery. Zaffarullah's brother, Nasserullah Khan, took me to Malik Pir Mohammad, a fine Kharoti 'malik' camped nearby. We spent some time with him and his lively male relatives, taking lunch in his large 'kuzhdei'. After that we moved on to an obviously poor Dotani family not far off where I was allowed to photograph the women and girls as they repaired and embroidered dresses. Possessing only twenty-five sheep, seventeen goats and seven donkeys, Mohammad Alum Dotani could barely support his family yet the women and girls sitting in the winter sun beside their worn 'kuzhdei' chatted and laughed as if they had not a care in the world.

At long last I was beginning to gather the material we so anxiously sought, even though Bob was not present to enjoy it all. I have always had a soft spot for nomads and these fully justified it. They squeeze a meagre living from a harsh, grudging land and have so little in the material sense yet they walk with a spring in the step and are so out-going, sharing what little they have with anyone in need who passes by. Sadly, few governments, apart from the Afghan one, have much sympathy for them. Possibly it is because they are inconvenient for statistics and perhaps seem to be an anachronism to third world officials, being regarded as not quite respectable and best hidden from the eyes of any visiting Europeans. Whatever the reason they, just like aboriginals, have a poor deal from we affluent ones who so often treat them as hostiles who must be suppressed and settled to destroy their blatant independence. That tragic book, *The Last Migration* by Vincent Cronin about the Falqani tribe in Iran is the saddest, most upsetting book that I ever read. On his land Nasserullah Khan had a Mahsud working for him, a refugee from Shaheer village in Waziristan, the one which Bob and I had passed earlier on our way north, but he was a very different type from that wild driver at Tarwal in 1960. Mair Jan was very dark for a Pakhtun, open, cheerful and thoroughly likeable – a man one could trust. His story was an interesting one, though far from unique. About four years before we met he had two brothers, Akbar Shah and Zaffar Shah, but the family was in dispute over land with a neighbouring family of seven brothers. Things came to a head when one of his brothers came upon one of the others grazing animals on what Mair Jan's family considered to be their land. Hot words let to hotter deeds and his brother shot dead the alleged trespasser. Retaliation was certain but, in spite of his two brothers' vigilance, a month later the other family mounted an ambush that killed both of them. Although he could not let the loss go un-avenged, he faced six surviving brothers. Further, his opponents family could raise sixty fighting men, whereas his own could muster only forty. Therefore to involve his extended family in the feud was likely to be disastrous. And it was such heavy odds that led to the alleged trespass in the first place, the other side simply not expecting Mair Jan or his brothers to fight.

But what are friends for? Mair Jan's must be exceptional for one joined him two months later in setting an ambush that accounted for two more of the other side. He had now reduced his prime enemies to four but as a realist knew that he had no hope whatsoever of surviving for long so he and his wife fled to Manzai, and even as he worked there he kept his .303 at hand. Needless to say his friend also fled though I do not know to where. A tenant then farmed the family's land and paid the rent to the two widows and their four young sons. Until those boys grew beyond wearing smocks and put on 'partook' they were not legitimate targets in pursuance of a feud and what has happened since I do not know. If he or his brothers' widows were able to offer two or more daughters without dowry all may have ended well. Slightly puzzled, I asked Mair Jan why his enemies did not just take over his family's land when there were no men to defend it. His reply was chillingly simple: the four vengeful brothers knew that if they did that, whatever the odds, he would return and take some of them before he was killed. Small wonder that seventeen years later the Russians failed in Afghanistan.

On a wide plain a mile or two from Manzai is a smallish, isolated mound known as Dilera. It is said to be the site of an ancient fort and a brief look revealed masses of pottery shards, some quite finely patterned. After the occasional heavy storm locals go there to see what may have been washed out from the earth, rumour stating that gems have been exposed from time to time. It is crying out for a proper archaeological excavation and by a team that will not simply plunder whatever is found. Likewise the immense Thal Shaghullai a few miles away and the four huge, ancient 'ghundei' in Zhob and its adjoining hills are being steadily plundered and history lost. A day later Nasserullah Khan took me to the traditional camping ground at Ghabar Ghar, thirty-three miles away, where numbers of nomads, mostly Shinwaris from Kirman near Chagchalan in Afghanistan over-winter each year. Their camels were Bactrian or two-humped animals, stocky, shaggy beasts with a mass of long hair at the neck that can withstand the cold well unlike the single-humped Arabian camels preferred south of the Gomal. When we arrived there a certain air of tension and excitement lingered, and we soon learnt why.

Two days earlier a party of Baluchis, said to be Marris but thought to include Bugtis as well and even some Kosas from the mountains to the east, had run off a flock of two hundred sheep belonging to another Shinwari, Haji Bejaur, whose camp was near Chamanlang, ten miles away. Upon hearing of the raid, 'Malik' Wali Jan Urmanzai, his four brothers, other relatives and friends had rushed to the aid of their fellow tribesmen who had managed to intercept the rustlers' rearguard, for sheep move slowly. In the ensuing gun battle they had helped kill two of the raiders, losing one Shinwari in the encounter. The loss of the flock was a severe blow but in a way they could claim a victory and honour had been upheld, so they were not entirely dissatisfied with the outcome.

Scattered over many miles, Wali Jan's village was a large one comprising fifty two 'kuzhdei'. His was the largest but he shared it with his four brothers. He had one hundred sheep, thirty goats, ten camels and one donkey to support his wife and three children. The sheep and goats would provide a poor living but the camels could be used to transport firewood to the nearest bazaar or hired out to carry materials for road work. I failed to ask the extent of his brothers' livestock but without any they would barely survive if relying upon his. While we chatted the womenfolk spun wool by hand, using a simple cruciform device, or embroidered clothes in the sun. Being 'powinda' or nomads, purdah was not important for them and in any case it was a luxury they could scarcely afford. After the introductions, the men were delighted to fire my .357 magnum, a calibre they had not met before, and my stock probably rose a little as a result. Among most Pashtuns and not a few Afghans, to carry a gun is almost as much a sign of manhood as a wife and family, even if circumstances do not demand it quite so much nowadays. This is not overstating it and even today no unarmed nomad group would risk travelling across Waziristan or camping near Marri-Bugti territory.

Taking photographs of such people takes time for, if it involves women and teenage girls, the trust and confidence of their men folk must first be slowly gained, but non-nomads usually object angrily to their womenfolk being photographed and it is extremely foolish to ignore such objection. Even if and when that hurdle is crossed the females themselves are naturally shy so that much patience is needed and a telephoto lens virtually essential. As to the men, most positively enjoy being photographed but invariably adopt what they consider to be a martial pose: erect, stiff as a board and staring without the hint of a smile straight at the camera. To obtain a relaxed, natural shot may take hours, usually while they are talking with someone else and have begun to ignore one's presence. Unable to get all the shots that I wanted that day, we set off before dawn the next morning across a semi-desert white with deep frost for another session among the Shinwaris. After a mile or two, in the pitch black ahead we saw the reflections from dozens of sheep's eyes and as we drew near the shepherd guarding the flock rose from the shelter of a boulder. In our headlights we saw that he wore only cotton clothes and a shawl in that intense cold.

Back in Manzai that evening I became very worried at an ominous bulge in the side wall of the one remaining original tyre caused by the dreadful jeep track through the mountains. I had no spare and it was clear that the tyre was very unlikely to survive a return journey over the rocky jeep track, leaving me helplessly stranded miles from any help. However, Zaffarullah Khan had a friend, a very good friend, at the barrier in Hindubagh who would be helpful and let us through in the dark. In any case I had virtually no choice. Unable to avoid passing through Loralai on the way to Quetta we bumped into Ahmad Yar Khan in the bazaar. He was clearly excited about something and during the course of our conversation I asked him what he was doing. He was buying up all the cartridges he could get he said, with a glint in his eye and a faint smile on his face. Puzzled, as he usually had sufficient ammunition, I asked why when the war was so far away and Baluchistan was the last place likely to be invaded. He then explained the attack on Fort Sandeman by Waziris and Mahsuds in 1919 as related in Chapter Four, going on to say that he and his brothers had learnt that the more experienced Pakistani officers had been transferred to the border with India and Kashmir – as Bob and I had discovered earlier. The current situation was similar and should the Mahsuds move southwards again, he did not wish to be short of ammunition. He was born in 1927 or thereabouts, years after that incident, but memories endure along the border.

Returning to my situation, the best laid plans of mice and men go oft awry. When we reached Hindubagh in the dark, the trusted friend was on short leave. Briefly questioned, we continued to Quetta but with an escort of two militia men aboard. Upon arriving there quite late, Zaffarullah was dropped off following which I was told to go to a Special Branch officer's house, my escort waking him with difficulty. We then drove to the main police 'thana' in Liaquat Bazaar 'to answer a few questions'. The Microbus was parked safely within the roomy compound and, assuming that all would be over within an hour, I blithely answered my interrogators' questions,. One of these priceless gems was, "Do you know Indhira Gandhi?" and many more which I forget but which were almost as absurd. Even when told that I must 'remain there for the night' I made no protest as I was clearly given to understand that the nonsense would be over by mid-morning at the latest.

The cell had one narrow window facing the road outside, fairly high up, with a steeply sloping sill so that it was impossible to see out by hauling one's self up. There was a massive inner door of steel bars; outside of which was a wooden one rather well past its prime, which later allowed me to extract a large screw to use as a tool. There was neither bed nor chair and the cell reeked of urine, but a filthy blanket that stank to high heaven was provided and a large rusty Dalda tin in an ominously damp corner served as a urinal. Fortunately I was allowed to get my sleeping bag and a tarpaulin from the vehicle. Quite contrary to my usual practice, especially when travelling at night, I was not carrying my .357 magnum revolver, now properly licensed and without payment of a bribe, in its shoulder holster when stopped and virtually arrested. As I was not searched at the police 'thana', to have been locked up while armed would have been quite bizarre and not a little ludicrous. It would have added to the Alice in Wonderland situation. My diary of events is as follows.

Day 1:

At one in the morning another person was put in with me. Our brief exchange of c.v. revealed that he was an Iranian mechanic, Reza Fahti, who had fled his country to escape the unwanted attentions of the SAVAK secret police. Nor had they endeared themselves seven or eight years earlier by shooting his father, who was a Communist. Reza had entered Pakistan some eight months previously on a forged passport that cost the family no less than Rials 100,000, but the theft of that in Peshawar had led to his arrest and he had been brought down to Quetta by two Pakhtun escorts, a Khalil and a Mohmand, pending an appeal he believed. His initial cell, which was next to mine, was suddenly needed for a poor, completely crazed bazaar creature that had just been arrested. I did not see her until later, when the rest of us were allowed out to the toilets at about ten, but she had matted hair, was in rags and leapt around her cell stark naked much of the time, gibbering and muttering wildly, her eyes like those of some cornered beast. She was not an inspiring sight, well past her prime and much in need of a good bath. When the opportunity arose I asked one of the 'thana' police why she had been arrested. "Judas," he replied. So she was a spy, presumably for India with whom an undeclared war was now in progress. Upon what she was supposed to be spying and how she was getting her messages through to the enemy seemed to

276

be of no importance and the lack of any material evidence, so far as I could make out, was equally irrelevant. I presumed that someone had made the allegation because she was being a nuisance and wanted to get her out of the way – and that was that. I could not imagine the finest actress in the world putting on such a convincing and sustained performance of utter, raving madness.

It was almost ten in the morning before the outer door was opened and we joined the other prisoners to use the indescribably clogged toilets, about which the least said the better, following which we were all returned to our cells. It soon dawned on me that my residence might last longer than I had been given to understand and I decided to keep a diary each day. No tea was brought, which was felt a little as I had neither eaten nor drunk anything since two o'clock the previous afternoon, given the freezing air, but at around one in the afternoon a boy from the bazaar came around for orders for food, courtesy of the police. I had very little cash on me and decided to accept their menu rather than pay for fancy stuff. When it arrived the 'naan' was folded around some severely rationed and rather dry vegetable curry whose main ingredient seemed to be red chillies but thankfully I have never been very fussy. Somewhat aggrieved, as this seemed a rather heavy-handed response to my going up the wrong road twice and as all answers to my questions through the bars were evasive, morale had to be maintained. Bob would not be returning for several days and while I had already made out legal documents for him and his wife to take over the VW and drive to Europe, there was no guarantee that I would also be released when he did return to Quetta. I tried to give a written note to the officer i/c addressed to the U.K. High Commission but he declined to take it. Next, a note for friends in Quetta discreetly proffered to the 'tiffin' boy for delivery, in return for payment, resulted in a frightened look on his face.

The outer wooden door had served for many years, was partly

rotted and one of its large screws was loose. Extracting that screw I set to work on the holes in the concrete floor and concrete lintel overhead that held the hinging lugs of the massive, barred, inner door that probably weighed a hundred kilos. It is surprising how something done under the very nose of authority can go undetected, providing it is done blatantly. All that day I dug at the concrete forming the top and bottom hinge sockets until the barred door could be lifted away from the bolt socket by over an inch, beyond which even one of the torpid staff in the compound was likely to notice were I to dig out more. So the padlocked bolt was the next target. As it was I was satisfied with my day's work, morale was rising and it kept me warm. Reza, who had also been a professional part-time wrestler, took no part in this but did frequent exercises to ward off the considerable frost, deepened by the altitude. On the pretext of getting some soap I managed to slip a file from the VW into my sock, ready for the morrow.

A weakly little street vendor was brought in with his rickety wooden stall on four bicycle wheels and several police tried bargaining with him in an aggressive way but he resisted. Finally, one typical bully-boy held the poor man by his shirt while slapping him around his head and alternately kicking the side of his buttocks. After a time he tired of this and then violently jerked his victim backwards and forwards. Having at length satisfied his brutal instincts, while the other six or seven police present watched, the luckless vendor's stall was dismantled. Apparently the man was taken to court the next day and was brought back in the afternoon by the two-pip station commander, carrying eight cartons (not packets) of K2 cigarettes which were then given to that upholder of the law and taken inside. Some time later the man was allowed to leave but an hour of so afterwards a woman, whom I presumed was his wife, courageously came in and complained bitterly about the poor man's treatment, at which our bully-boy laughed at her. It was the sort of thing that one has to witness to comprehend fully the enormity of it all.

Reza had a car in Peshawar being looked after by a friend and expected to return there, having been told that everything would be arranged in Quetta, but I guessed that he was for deportation and said so, sure that it was the usual ploy to lull suspicion and forestall any attempt to escape should an opportunity arise. We both had a little money and could buy tea, my companion taking his black as they do in Iran, though sometimes he had the raw yolk of an egg in his: Iranis seeming to have a predilection for raw egg. He rejected the station ration and paid the young hotel boy to bring a special milk preparation called 'malva'. While the two-pip buffoon was away the pleasant sergeant allowed us to stand in the sun for twenty minutes, telling us that a full scale war was in progress. That meant that Bettina would probably fly on from Karachi to Kandahar or Kabul instead of coming to Quetta with Bob.

Day 2:

After the morning toilets ordeal, which would only be remedied when they actually overflowed and degraded, poverty stricken Christian sweepers would be called in, Reza and I had tea brought. Also I had a pot of tea and a 'naan' sent to the neglected mad woman in the next cell. However, she refused to return the pot and cup to the young 'tiffin' boy afterwards so I tried to regain it, having been let out of our cell for a few minutes, but the stench from her cell and the sight of her prancing around proved too much. Eventually one of the station's police retrieved it, though not without difficulty, to the considerable relief of the young tea boy who was probably aged only twelve or so. Having yesterday done as much to enlarge the hinge sockets as I safely could without being discovered, my next task was to file down the end of the bolt, lifting the door towards the steel plate that received it so that its tip protruded beyond.

All day, as the station officer lazed in the sun and as others wandered in and out, I filed down the tip of the bolt, taking good care to look at them through the bars as I worked.

By the end of the afternoon, having carefully dirtied the newly gleaming tip of the bolt, the removal of two rivets that held an extra plate to take the bolt should then allow me to open the door. That work might have taken an hour but I did not intend doing it unless I was still imprisoned after Bob had returned and left again with the VW. Only if that were to happen would I break out, climb up the low roof onto the top of the high compound wall and walk carefully around to the far side where a telegraph pole stood only three or so feet away and outside it. I would of course ask Bob to wait for me just over the Afghan border for two nights, which time should be enough for me to cover the seventy or so miles in the dark to Chaman on the border. Having for the moment achieved all that was necessary was extremely satisfying. Morale was maintained and I had not involved Reza, whose problems were far more serious than mine.

I tried unsuccessfully to send a telegram to the U.K.H.C. again. Then a chained man was brought in through the large, arched gateway. In full view of us all, the two-pip officer beat him with a swagger stick around the head, on the arms and around the knees for perhaps four minutes. The man made no sound although it must have been very painful. He was then taken from the veranda into a room, after which his cries became quite dreadful, interspersed with 'Allah, Allah'. This sickening treatment and cries of pain continued for ten minutes or more, finally subsiding into a low sobbing. Half an hour later the poor fellow was led out, limping and shuffling like an old man, his eyes red, his face worn. A European hippy entered the compound just after the beating ended and sat outside the same room, causing me to wonder if he were somehow connected with the incident. When he left he studiously ignored me, dashing my hopes of getting a letter out.

Day 3:

Being the 7th December, I should have been on my way homeward if hoping to arrive for Christmas with Sheila and our two young boys and that was very upsetting. The 'thana' officer i/c agreed to accept a telegram but declined money, saying that the government would pay. I was not fooled by this apparent generosity and at last I really began to understand something of the plight of those in South Africa held under the Ninety Day Detention Act and others in totalitarian countries. Later several senior officers visited the place and all the usual loungers disappeared. Reza's two Pakhtun escorts, both very nice, dignified, straight fellows, came two or three times each day to report on what progress was being made. They were genuinely concerned about his future and disliked the Panjabi crowd in the 'thana', referring to them as 'nimai Musselman', meaning 'half Muslims', when talking to us The one-pip officer came to our cell in the evening and asked if he 'could be of any service': I thanked him with equal hypocrisy.

As usual it was essential to exercise to keep warm and we jumped on the spot, ran up the dirty wall or arm-wrestled. Reza was very short but sturdy and of course had done weight training in pursuance of his wrestling with the result that we were fairly well matched. He was lively, aggressive but not stupidly so, and intelligent so that his company was much missed when he was deported four days later. Like my local Afghan friends in Quetta, he related similar tales about degenerate hippies, such as in Peshawar where one European offered his girl companion for the princely sum of Rs.10, Similarly, in Tehran the previous year he had seen a French couple surrounded by several local men and had stopped in case help were needed but found that they were merely bargaining over the price for the girl, offered at two hundred rials. On a more uplifting note, for three penniless Italian smugglers he had repaired the crankcase of their car, little expecting ever to see the money but two months later on their way back to Afghanistan they returned to Mashed and paid an extra five hundred rials as a thank you. Similarly an Italian couple returned after going thirty kilometres in case they had forgotten to pay him for a puncture repair when leaving.

Day 4:

During the morning a pathetic woman with a babe-in-arms and a young child that was crying came to ask about her husband who was in one of the other cells. She was dressed in near-rags and so utterly helpless that it was quite upsetting. Then 'two-pip' appeared and came to our cell, for some reason wanting to shake hands with me but I refused. At this snub he vented his anger on some other civilians who were in the compound. Next a simple-looking tribesman from another cell was taken out for questioning as a spy and Reza told me that I was considered to be a spy as well, so paranoia was much in fashion. Noting the tendency to beat people who were manacled and therefore relatively defenceless, when anyone carrying handcuffs came near our cell I got ready to fight so that at least one or two of them would know what it was like to be on equal terms. In the afternoon a well-dressed man in a British registered car turned up with a family of dark Tanzanians who were immaculately dressed, in contrast to most of those around us, and he said that he would pass on the word. My money was now finished, having blown my last rupee on some delicious carrot 'halva' at midday by way of lunch, and Reza kindly bought me an evening meal so that I could dispense with the grisly station ration.

December is a windy month in Quetta, particularly in the afternoon, and the kite flying season was at its height. The sky was literally full of flimsy, little diamond-shaped paper kites swooping here and there endlessly, their invisible owners stationed on dozens of flat roofs around the bazaar. Almost all were brightly coloured and some engaged in duels, though whether they used string with glass powder glued to it like those in Kabul I did not know, but watching them from our cell helped pass the time. Most of the telephone wires and power cables around the town seemed to hold one or two of these crumpled wrecks. Often the thin cotton cord would break when the breeze became too strong and one such kite fluttered down into our compound as the little 'tiffin' boy came in. He was no doubt very poor, his meagre earnings going to his family, so that his face lit up at the prospect of a free kite but as he hurried forwards one of the police, probably 'bully-boy' but I am far from sure, immediately stamped on it and the poor lad's face fell. It may not have been personally spiteful but it was so utterly thoughtless.

Day 5:

Reza left with his escort this morning at seven-thirty, though for where neither of us was told. I feared the worst for him and will miss his lively company. Without any word from Bob, who should have arrived by now, I violently shook the barred door until the good sergeant came. He, poor man, looked worried at the disturbance I was creating, commenting in Urdu, "Barra tacliffe hojaiga," meaning 'there will be big trouble'. Upon asking who was responsible for my being held I was told by the three-pip officer that it was the C.I.D. but the fat one-pip officer said that it was the P.A. of Zhob. It could easily have been either as the former must have been nearly frantic when I eluded their man and disappeared completely for five days, while the latter was probably miffed because I had ignored his ban on Zhob. During the afternoon some oranges brought in for another prisoner were stolen quite openly by the bully-boy sergeant. Upon asking 'three-pip' to leave a message for Bob in the Spinzar Hotel that we used, he assured me that he would. He also said that Bob had not yet returned from Karachi.

Day 6:

The air was full of rumour: two British ships were said to have been sunk during the bombing of Karachi, trains were taking four days from there to Quetta, a Boeing 747 bound from Quetta to Karachi had turned back the day before and so on. Outside the 'thana' I could hear a march by the bazaar 'boyos' chanting in Urdu: 'Pakistan zindabad, Hindustan murdabad', 'long live Pakistan and death to India'. Just after midday I was abruptly released from the cell and Bob strolled in through the gate with none other than our 'Shadowy Sam the C.I.D. Man' who had been tailing us earlier. What a relief it was to see him after the uncertainty and isolation. The condition for my release was that we both left the country within one week. Bob had in fact arrived the previous day but no message had been left at the hotel by 'three-pip' and he heard of my whereabouts from others. My release had been expedited by S. Abdul Hamid, head of Special Branch, after Bob had been passed on to him by the Superintendent of Police for Quetta, Mr. Welsh. Back at the hotel to my surprise, in view of all the ridiculous suspicion surrounding me if not both of us, I was warmly welcomed by the Pashtun staff and even embraced by one. They would have known of my detention and somehow their sympathy meant quite a lot as it showed that there were still sane, decent people around, unaffected by all the hysteria. A good wash and shave completed this return to what passed for normality.

While arranging the release of the vehicle so that we might leave on the morrow, the 12th December 1971, it was unofficially admitted that the Jogezais were very much out of favour, for whatever reason. I had strongly suspected all along that it may have been a factor in our treatment – an oblique way of getting at them without being too confrontational. Anyway we were no longer tailed but the bank could not change travellers' cheques as the pound sterling was being re-valued upwards. However, we managed to sell some of our expedition equipment to the

University of Baluchistan at a price fair to both parties and were thus marginally solvent once more. For my part, the hopeful thing was that it was just possible to reach the U.K. by road and train in ten days, though only if connections happened to be perfect.

The next day Mohammad Hassan from Tarwal and his nephew Nadir Shah of Quetta helped in buying three kilims which I still treasure, in paying our hotel bill and tanking up with petrol, all on credit to be repaid later from Somerset. Upon visiting a very ambitious member of a different branch of the Jogezai family, Bob was effusively greeted but I was obviously less than a social asset. We then rushed via Kandahar to Kabul where I met Bettina for the first time and left the VW with them to follow at leisure. I promptly flew to Herat in a small Russian Yak jet, whose trainee pilot or his instructor made a brief but violent manoeuvre that made me at least feel very sick for an instant. From there it was by buses to Mashed, beneath its thin layer of wet snow, and thence by train to Tehran. A second train took me to Lake Van where a steamer takes one across to a connection on the far side. The bitter cold had jelled the diesel oil for two days so that the train had been immobile and without heating but they had now managed to start the engine and could return to Istanbul. My clothing was quite unsuited to such conditions and I felt the intense cold.

In Istanbul I savoured the luxury of the ancient 'hamam' or Turkish bath after being in my clothes for four days and three nights. During the three nights and two days to Paris, the train's heating failed among extensive snowfields and I was forced to drink one of the two bottles of Turkish wine that I had bought as presents, neither food nor drink being available on the train. Fortunately I had also bought a small loaf before leaving, just in case. Another train, then the ferry carried me to Newhaven from where a lorry gave me a lift to Brighton where Sheila and our two young sons were staying with her mother while I was abroad. I had been away for over five months and no one knew where I was. My phone call was a complete surprise and brought her and two boys in a taxi to pick me up. As the taxi stopped in the dark all I could see in the back were two rows of small, gleaming white teeth against the window. Christmas was over but suddenly it no longer mattered.

Chapter Nine

Zhob Again Thanks to Rugs

1978 The death of my father bequeathed us a modest capital for the first time in our married lives, though his careful savings had dwindled to very little with the collapse of British Leyland as a result of weak management and the destructive ambitions of the notorious Red Robbo. During my wanderings in the late 'fifties and early 'sixties, and again during the abortive expedition with Bob Chambers in 1971, I had dearly wanted one of those knotted masterpieces offered in dingy little shops or draped over the shoulders of tribesmen walking hopefully around bazaars but all I could afford were one or two felt rugs and kilims or flat-weaves. What are generally but erroneously called 'Afghan rugs' are Turkoman rugs to be precise, for many of the Baluch tribes in Afghanistan as well as in Iran also knot fine rugs, though the Baluch tribes in Pakistan do not. With two sons shortly to educate, money was short and visits to friends in Quetta and Zhob were largely out of the question but, if we set up a small business, the buying of rugs in Quetta would also permit visits at intervals.

1979 In 1978 an overland drive to Afghanistan in our Microbus was arranged make a tentative start in the business and, to avoid wasting so much space in a large vehicle and to help defray expenses by charging a nominal sum, I was accompanied by another member of staff, Ted Birnberg, two senior boys, Sean and Simon, and two senior girls, Brigitte and Julie, plus our older son James, then approaching eleven years of age. Outward bound, in eastern Turkey James and I left the other five with the Microbus and trailer a mile or two from a largish village while we hitch-hiked back the seventy miles back to Yozgat to search for our lost tailgate. On the second day of our absence, two men appeared and showed an unhealthy interest in the group, toying with a pistol as they lounged against a fence nearby. That had been going on for three hours before our fortuitous return in the afternoon and we drove off almost immediately, keeping a wary eye on the two as we left.

Further on we were stopped one night by a gendarme, immaculately dressed and speaking good English: a far cry from the ordinary constables. He explained that a coach full of Asians had been hijacked, driven into the hills and one passenger was reported to have been killed. For the time being night travel was banned. A day or two later we arrived in Tehran at the end of a serious riot in the old bazaar. The atmosphere was tense and it turned out to be the start of the downfall of the Shah. Leaving the capital and heading south-west for Zahedan, we dropped off Ted in Isfahan, to be picked up in Tehran on our return journey. In Kerman, where every house had a wind tower, the people in the fine traditional bazaar were as dignified and quiet as the Tehranis were the opposite but, beyond the oasis and palms of Bam, in Nasratabad the virulent, unconcealed hostility of people, police and soldiers alike was such that we hurried on after re-fuelling without taking a hoped-for meal. As usual we later bivouaced out in the desert on a large tarpaulin, leaving the road at dusk when it was just possible to drive without lights into a secluded hollow or valley where the headlights of any passing vehicles would not reach. Presuming that any attack would start at one end of our row of six, I always slept in the middle of the group with the Colt .357 magnum strapped to me inside my sleeping bag just in case the worst happened. Such precautions were not a bit of melodrama but in response to accounts of several attacks upon travellers driving in Turkey, Iran and Afghanistan.

Unknown to us until back in England, as we continued eastwards after leaving him, Ted was stoned once or twice by hostile mobs but he managed to flee on the last coach from Tehran to Istanbul. Without us being told, our visas stated that we would leave Iran via Tayyebad, far to the north, whereas we had driven to the border near Zahedan. We could not cross the border. I left the four pupils in the protection of the border post while James and I returned the seventy miles to Zahedan to have the six visas varied. Too late to change a traveller's cheque we had only enough money for a light snack, after which we slept secluded in a dry fountain on the outskirts of the town. Rejoining the others next morning, to the south the smoking summit of Kuh-i-Taftan could be clearly seen as we headed across the Makran desert in south-west Baluchistan. The dirt road was overwhelmed by deep sand in one or two places, blown from a wall of immense dunes, perhaps five hundred feet high, just three or four miles south of the road, making short detours across virgin desert necessary. An ordinary saloon car would be unlikely to get through and it was obvious why so many of Alexander the Great's men died as they returned westwards along the coast. Stopping briefly in Nokundi, the water from the well there had an ominous smell but we had no choice but to drink it. Further on, a modern concrete bridge has been shifted a yard or two by a tremendous storm several weeks earlier but we reached Quetta in two days. The sons of the late Usman Khan Jogezai laid on the sort of meal that most of our group had been dreaming about for a fortnight and Jehandar Shah's son Humayun generously drove James and me to Tarwal in his jeep for a lightning visit to introduce James to the aging chief, in whose honour James's third name is Jogezai. We found the Nawab beneath the great Mulberry tree in front of his house surrounded by a large cluster of grandchildren. He was in the very twilight of his life, roughly ninety-three years of age and very frail but fully compos mentis. It was just as well that we took the opportunity for he was gone just four months later.

When we arrived at Spin Boldak the next day it was discovered that our Afghan visas were for entry via Islam Qala, west of Herat. Again we had no inkling of this so, once again, James and I left the four with the vehicle and trailer in the care of the Customs post while we returned the eighty or ninety miles to Quetta to have the visas varied, paying for lifts in pick-ups and the like. The Afghan consulate was closed by the time we arrived but all was made well the following morning and we promptly returned to Spin Boldak, where the Afghan officials had been extremely hospitable to the pupils, or perhaps I should say ex-pupils as all had finished their A levels. As we headed for Kabul via Kandahar, the Nokundi water began taking its revenge and, one after the other, all four succumbed to dysentery, fairly briefly and not too seriously so that they could look after one another and leave me free to drive but James seemed fortunate.

In 1973 Mohammad Daud deposed his reformist uncle Zahir Shah, bloodlessly by way of a change. However, in April 1978, Nur Mohammad Tarraki had violently deposed Daud, reportedly killing thirty members of his family as well. Since then the country had been quiet and we set out in mid-July with no concern for the situation in Afghanistan. When we reached Kabul in the second week of August all was calm, publicly at least. A brief pause in the city resulted in a couple of rugs from a pleasant shopkeeper whose wife was a school teacher, which factor clinched a faltering deal However, after we had left Kabul for Mazar-i-Sharif, unknown to us Babrak Karmal tried to return to the country, complete with a bit of gunfire at the airport, and was sent abroad again The descent in the dark from the Salang Pass and its tunnel over the Hindu Kush at over 10,000 feet gave me a severe fright when the brakes failed just before the first hairpin bend. Fortunately they responded in the nick of time to my frantic pumping of the foot pedal – just as I prepared to steer into the rock wall to our left. The five with me remained sleeping soundly, happily unaware of the crisis.

While choosing fine rugs from the scores of mediocre ones offered is fairly logical and straightforward – colour quality, no colour run, complexity of design, greasiness of wool, number of knots, smooth clipping, etc. – discovering the proper local price is a very, very tricky business and without hard bargaining one is doomed. My only hope was patiently to play off the dealers against one another until a price would drop no more. In a couple of days I had five more good pieces. However, upon trying to cash £1,500 in travellers' cheques at the one bank, the cashier pointed out that only £400 per day was allowed and went on to ask why I wanted so much anyway. Upon explaining that I was buying a few rugs, he replied that his wife and two daughters had just completed two pieces. The price he quoted seemed unduly low, even to my rudimentary knowledge, but he would show them to me in our little hotel. He failed to appear and was such a patently honest and open man that I presume his wife refused to sell at the prices he had quoted and he was too embarrassed to see me. The encashment problem was then solved by the group cashing some of their cheques on my behalf, to be repaid later.

I was thinking seriously of taking the northern route through Maimana to Herat as it is roughly a third of the distance via Kabul, Kandahar and Daulatabad. However, the dirt road was of unknown quality, petrol supplies were uncertain and border areas are often smuggling areas that may host some rough characters. With two teenage girls to consider, the right choice was essential. All four pupils had suffered and recovered from dysentery but at that point and days after the others, young James suddenly succumbed and decided the issue for me. Three bad road accidents along the quiet route as we headed south-east showed the strain of Ramazan when it happens to be summer. Now forewarned of the effect of altitude on brake cylinders, the Salang Pass gave no more shocks. While James's stoicism when vomiting and suffering diarrhoea every half hour throughout the night was impressive, he was on the point of collapse as we approached Kabul just before dawn.

We were still unaware of the airport fracas between Babrak Karmal and supporters and Tarraki's minions, let alone the serious tensions between Tarraki and his sidekick Hafizullah Amin. As we approached the city before dawn, three times edgy soldiers leapt into the road with levelled AK47s to challenge us but, in fairness to them, upon explaining why we were travelling at night we were soon on our way each time. In less than a month Amin would survive an ambush set up by Tarraki and wound his enemy who, it is said, was shortly strangled with Russian connivance. "Uneasy lies the head that wears the crown" sums up the history of Kabul, hence the tensions we had encountered, but one is almost forced to admire the sublime optimism of those who have grabbed the big chair in turn since Zahir Shah was exiled.

My remedies based upon long experience had failed and by now James was causing me serious concern, breathing with difficulty and barely able to walk into the hospital when we arrived. A further twenty-four hours without professional medical attention and he would probably have died: the northern route therefore would very likely have proven fatal. Fortunately the Afghan woman doctor was as competent as she was helpful and charming. Did I want a free public bed or a private one, she asked me? Told that the cross infection rate was fifty per cent among the two or three children that usually shared public beds, my decision took a micro-second though I was less impressed when told reassuringly that the hospital had the deepest well in the city. When leaving him there on a physio-drip while the Microbus was serviced I felt awful, almost as if I were abandoning him and my eyes moistened, prompting him to ask what was wrong. I hurried out.

The Indian boy in the next bed was about James's age and regaled him with his first-hand account of jets strafing the Presidential Palace, while tanks pounded it at close range during the April coup. Unbeknown to me as I left James there, the hospital did not provide food to patients but in fact they did give him some HT milk and dry bread, and that evening the Indian family kindly gave him some curry. After collecting James the next morning and doing some shopping, I thought nothing of the distant lightning to the south as we left the city at sunset. Two hours later when, crossing what appeared in the dark to be a high and level plateau, without warning I saw a deep mass of mud, stones and boulders across the tar road ahead. It was so sudden that all l I could do was to leave the accelerator and brake gently lest we jack-knife until we hit the deep mass at about forty miles per hour. As the under-body of the vehicle tobogganed over the debris the noise was deafening and woke the five with a terrible fright. Frantically wrenching the steering wheel left and right to prevent the trailer from jack-knifing as the V.W. tried to slew one way or the other, the front wheels just cleared the mass as the engine stalled so that the rear ones would just be able to grip. I hate to think what could have happened had we left Kabul earlier and come upon the flash flood in progress. The following day, in the middle of nowhere a man flagged us down for water and turned out to be a Kakar of the Taimani clan, the clan separated from their kith and kin some four hundred and fifty miles to the east, as discussed later.

At the Iranian border post I was told to post on my rugs. That was a daunting prospect to say the least but, after prolonged protest, lead seals were wired onto each piece. Although it was a "one donkey" post in the midst of the desert, the vehicle was minutely searched for drugs and the man in charge was alarmingly smart and wide awake: alarmingly because I had my magnum .357 in a shoulder holster beneath my dark red shirt, worn for the purpose, the discovery of which would have created a considerable problem. As he and I chatted for an hour while his assistants did their bit, he watched me like a hawk but I had already primed James to say, "I wonder if its raining in Butleigh," were the weapon to jut out behind, should I happen to lean forwards or move carelessly. Needless to say, James loved that Bond 007 bit and possibly even saved the day.

The final nerve wrack came when one of the assistants frisked the two senior boys just two or three yards from me in a slick, professional way that spelt instant danger. I promptly stepped forwards a pace and raised my arms invitingly, at which the man shook his head and I secretly breathed again. Why did I carry an un-authorised revolver, covered only by a British and Pakistan permit? There had been several ugly accounts of travellers being molested, such as two German groups in minibuses being robbed and beaten in Iran, Winant the American and his Swedish woman companion disappearing in Afghanistan, the married couple in Turkey that had escaped by the skin of their teeth and two German women near Bamian who were raped by a group of soldiers, whom they asked for help following their car crash a while later. That I had two teenage girls in my care should answer the question. Driving at night through Iran was tiresome as the Irani truck drivers appeared not know how to dip headlights and so they drove with full beam until they approached another vehicle, at which point they switched their lights off then on again at intervals of four or five seconds.

In Tehran there was no word from Ted at the British Consulate and I became deeply concerned, fearing that he might have been harmed until we discovered that he had called at one of the banks. The last serious challenge of the journey was at the Turkish border post of Gürbulak where the Customs held and threatened us for four and a half days because I would not donate one of my seven precious rugs, though, in fairness to that evil crowd, they treated all other travellers and truck drivers in like vein. We could only sleep in the vehicle and trailer, while toilet facilities 'left something to be desired'. Desperately frustrated and bored, after walking to ancient lava flows from Mount Ararat out across the plain, James and I climbed the high hill behind the post, hugging the cliff near the summit and talking in whispers in case of a border patrol above. When down again I told the four what we had done, stressing the precautions to take as such border areas are always very sensitive; and off they went. Nightfall came and there was no sign of the four. I became very worried and was considering what to do when an official came and beckoned me. Following him into a room, I was relieved to see all four, somewhat downcast but that was all. They had been detected and arrested but upon my explanation all was well within a minute or two. To their great credit the two boys had firmly refused to allow the girls to be interrogated in a separate room. Not every school provides such a broad education I'm sure.

On our fifth day, word quietly went around that a senior official from Ankara, over six hundred miles away, was soon to arrive at which I immediately spread out the rugs in front of the main office to cause maximum embarrassment. In no time lead seals were wired onto the rugs and we were free to leave, which we did within minutes lest the official visit were delayed or cancelled and allowed someone change their mind. The central road across the country was in some chaos from extensive improvement work and I was advised that the new military road along the Russian border and the regular road along the Black Sea coast were excellent. Crossing the great mountains in the dark, at one place the gradient was around one in three so that when I happened to miss first gear I was forced to stop and the rear driving wheels simply could not grip for us to continue, making it necessary to wake the group to get out and push, then jump in through the sliding door one by one once we crawled up the steep incline. Fearing to miss our Channel ferry booking,

I stopped to sleep for an hour in the mountains before continuing towards the Russian border. On the way we stopped at a tiny isolated shop, hoping that we might enjoy some tea but all it seemed to offer was a severed goat's head just outside the door. Along the border, clearly visible across the valley, a high wire fence went up hill and down dale, with watch towers at kilometre intervals. The coast, with its neat little towns and long swathes of hazel nuts drying on pavements, was a delight and the Greek border was reached in two and a half days, the driver enjoying another hour's sleep during the second night as we neared Ankara. In Switzerland we had to stop at a border post late at night, where my careless mention that we had come from Afghanistan aroused instant suspicion and the man with a sniffer dog had to be roused from his bed at home. That delay possibly contributed to missing our booking but I did not have to pay again for a later crossing after all. It had been a hectic six weeks.

In 1982 I decided to go out to Baluchistan in an attempt to set up a small safari business in partnership with a Kakar friend, the idea being to take small, exclusive groups along nomad routes across the mountains and desert in traditional black 'kuzhdei'. Although letters to A.Y.K. and others had brought lukewarm responses, I took Richard our youngest son and aged ten, with me. After landing at Karachi, where Aftab Adamji, an Old Boy, helped by installing us in a hotel, I wrestled for four days with officialdom to obtain a firearm permit for the rifle I had with me, a Ruger .270. This was a curious business as I was shunted back and forth several times by the man in charge of the Home Department, Sinde Secretariat. Mr. Mazhar Rafi claimed that it was the responsibility of the Deputy Commissioner's office in the City Court to issue such a permit but, when I arrived there, a Mr. Nur Mohammad insisted that it was the responsibility of the Home Department to authorise it. Karachi is a horrifically crowded city, dreadfully polluted by thousands of scooter rickshaws belching blue smoke, while mid-summer temperatures combined with high humidity do not help. At the end of four days I had had enough, and refused to budge from Mr. Rafi's office on yet another fool's errand and suddenly a document was made out. Presented to the D.C's. office, back in the City Court yet again, the permit was ready within an hour or so. All was well, or so I thought.

Aftab then kindly arranged for a family car to take us to the airport, twelve miles away, to collect the bonded rifle so that we could catch the Bolan Mail to Quetta at the city's Cantonment Station in the evening. There we met yet another official hoping to augment his income by being obstructive. Although presented with a brand new firearm licence, he refused to release the weapon. I forget his pretext but it was nonsense. The train was forgotten and yet another series of office visits had to be undergone: it was maddening, but the following morning the 'reeshwat wallah', as Urdu so aptly describes him, had to capitulate. Such everyday incidents help to explain why so many third world countries tend to remain as third world countries. Advance booking for a sleeping berth on the Bolan Mail to Quetta from Karachi is a tricky business for those unaccustomed to its wiles. The reason for this strange situation I do not know: but such a booking can only be done at an obscure office tucked away in the City Station yet the train can only be boarded at the Cantonment Station two miles away.

Apart from that, the journey is an extremely enjoyable one, going up the Sinde as far as Rohri, over the Indus to Sukkur, through John Jacob's town and across the vast, dreary expanse of the Kachi plain until an abrupt wall of tremendous mountains announces that one is about to enter the Afghan and Baluchi highlands. True, Sibi has to be traversed first, where shade temperatures have been known to top 126°F / 52°C in summer but the beckoning mountains beyond are simply majestic and the sixty-mile-long Bolan Pass through them is awesome in places.

There is no restaurant car on the train but at any station along the line an order given out of the window to one of the 'khana wallahs' has the telegraph clicking away so that a meal is waiting at the next station along the line and even though the chicken legs seem to have come from starved bantams they are worth eating. However, this arrangement was unnecessary for us as the large man sharing our sleeping compartment not only shared his deliciously cooked chicken with us but invited us to spend a few days in his Sindi village. Unfortunately we were on business, had limited time and could not dally.

Once in Quetta, in one or two offices I began to snatch bits of quiet conversation between officials regarding an Afghan gang to the north that was creating mayhem and it dawned on me that this was probably the reason for the lack of enthusiasm among my friends. After visiting several government offices we went up to Tarwal where, after a couple of days while they cautiously sized up one another, Richard was off with Jogezai boys of his own age most of the time. However, one day I decided to take a look at the Zhob River four or five miles out across the wide valley floor. As I had been compelled to leave all my rifle ammunition at Heathrow because it was not packed according to somewhat archaic regulations, I did not carry the rifle for to carry an empty weapon is a dangerous bluff and for the first time in over twenty years of travel in desert, mountain and jungle I was unarmed. As we neared the river we met three men crossing our path and after the usual greetings continued on our way. Familiarity not only breeds contempt but also dispels caution and I failed to look back after a few minutes as I used to do in the old days. Shortly afterwards, at the water's edge, when I chanced to look back from the river I noticed two of the men on the lip of desert we had just left, two or three hundred yards away. They had changed course and followed us.

I sensed trouble instantly and had nasty visions of having our throats cut, and our bodies thrown into the water to roll or float downstream. Richard and I immediately descended the last sheer face of five or so feet near the water's edge and I ducked down to be out of sight. Richard had been training hard before we left England and was both fast and fit for his years, so that we covered perhaps three hundred yards upstream unseen and around a slight bend before the three reached the river proper and began to ford it. Eventually we were forced to climb the high bank to the level desert and were then detected but once over the lip we ran flat out for perhaps two or three hundred yards then slowed to a walk before the first of the men also reached the level desert. It had the desired effect, for the three were well separated as they still pursued us. The first and largest caught up with us but, being now alone, as I turned to face him he realised that he was likely to be worsted and held back so that we got away.

An hour or so later and in a completely different direction, we were passing through a small collection of little mud huts when the weedy little man of the original trio suddenly came out from one of them, having seen us. He greeted us normally and instinctively I accepted his handshake. Almost immediately the biggish one hurriedly appeared from one of the small huts and, as he approached, the weedy one held tightly onto my right hand with both of his as I prepared to face the newcomer. I punched him twice with my left but, being held and off balance, I failed to put him down. In desperation I managed to wrench my right hand free as he rushed in again but with his head stupidly down. There was no time to put in a good punch but it allowed me to get a firm lock under his neck with both arms so that he was completely powerless. By now another man was coming up as I lifted the biggish fellow partly off the ground to choke him unconscious and in a moment the two other men were grappling with me as I hung on grimly. The weedy one then took hold of Richard instead, at which I went into a fury and roared at him so fiercely that he let him go and, urged by me to run to chief Temur Shah's house a mile or so away, Richard slipped away through the nearby thicket of tamarisk saplings un-noticed. Somehow, one of the attackers discovered the sheath knife beneath my long tribal shirt, although it was out of sight as I thought, and withdrew it, cutting me very slightly. At this I stopped fighting instantly, fearing that it might be used against me otherwise.

With Richard more or less safely gone, I felt less worried even though a fourth man appeared waving a rifle, at which point it was easy to ensure that one of my three attackers was between us. My Pashtu had become very rusty since my last visit eleven years earlier but a chance comment by one of men revealed that the isolated house and orchard, supported by a 'karez' just half a mile or so away belonged to old friends, the four sons of dear old Azim Khan, now dead. Simply, as we had approached it from behind I had failed to recognise it. At that I took the initiative, demanding that we see Hashim Khan and his brothers and walked towards the property. Unsure now, the original three followed warily but one by one fell out so that I reached the house alone but desperately worried about Richard. Only a servant was at the house and as I talked with him an obviously educated young man appeared with our tearful son whom he had come upon. He turned out to be a son of the third brother, Munir Khan, spoke good English and was now a doctor.

Later, when all the three brothers had returned, we were about to leave when a fierce storm broke and the fine white soil of the desert became a quagmire. A return to Tarwal, only four or so miles away, was out of the question even though I guessed that A.Y.K. would be extremely worried at our failure to return and we were forced to spend the night there. Before leaving the next morning on two motorcycles, I was invited to return that evening and guessed the reason. When we reached Tarwal, A.Y.K. was out of countenance for the first time in our long friendship until I explained what had happened. Later that day, on a borrowed a motorcycle I drove to Badderwal Karez, where we had spent the previous night. Richard was understandably reluctant but I insisted as it would dispel any long-term apprehension or hang-up. It transpired that two of the men, Sulaiman Khels, had fled to Quetta but one of the Jogezai sons, Najib, a truly fine lad, had brought in the remaining two at pistol point. An improvised court was held there and then. I wanted to fight the biggish fellow one to one but the brothers said that I could hit him but he was not allowed to hit back. That was unacceptable to me and we argued for a while but then the fellow said something out of place and Najib promptly gave him a heavy beating. Sadly, Najib was accidentally shot and killed eight or ten years ago.

However, it was the weedy one, the one who had held Richard captive for a moment or two, that I really loathed. Also he has been treacherous and I decided to treat him in like vein, shaking his hand as we met. As we did so, I twisted his right arm and raised it so that his wrist was being bent backwards and he was powerless, using my right arm only to emphasize the point. I think I nearly broke his wrist for the others, seeing his pain and desperation, called on me to release him. It was then spelt out to him, one of the Jogezais translating, that I would get my rifle to pursue him and shoot him if he ever dared to touch my son again. Moreover I could out-run, out-walk and out-shoot him. It was not an idle threat and his expression showed he knew it. As for Richard, he had seen basic justice done and any lingering fears that might have followed such a frightening incident were dispelled. Indeed, upon our landing at Heathrow he ran ahead to his mother waiting at the barrier to tell her excitedly that we had been attacked by bandits, that I had been cut and so on. On the other hand, since then, upon encountering two or three men when alone I have to confess to becoming cautious: the innocence of my younger days is no longer. I now make sure to look over my shoulder at intervals and there is no question of travelling unarmed again in such places: if I'm going to be killed at least I want the chance to take one or more of my assailants with me.

Upon returning to Quetta and recognising that any small tour business was out of the question for the time being at least, I bought a small consignment of Turkoman rugs, having with me a modest sum of money for the purpose. I had always yearned for a good tribal rug but never had the money. To buy some now would make up for the safari disappointment and at least pay for our air fares but other difficulties soon presented themselves. The Assistant Controller of Imports and Exports was not the sort of person that honest people want to know but he had the power to grant or to refuse export permits according to the whim of the moment or, far more likely, the amount of money offered to facilitate such things. Fortunately there were many others in Quetta and along the Frontier in general of an entirely different nature, such as the shopkeeper selling the cord needed to secure our three large sacks containing my purchases. Richard was with me, with large blue eyes and a mop of blond hair, and the shopkeeper was so taken by him that he said impulsively: "Sta zoi zma zoi deh," meaning literally "Your son is my son", implying that he would treat and protect Richard as if he were his own. It typified the out-going, warm, protective attitude towards children of so many, probably most, tribesmen. Tribal childhood tends to be total but brief, the very earliest teens becoming adulthood with all its implications though increasing education is changing this.

Similarly on another visit to Quetta and Zhob a year later, Jehandar Shah's second son, Humayun, had noticed the look of longing on the face of Newman, our middle son then aged fourteen, when I returned with an old tribal sword from the bazaar for use as decor when selling rugs back home. Without saying a word, Humayun slipped off to the bazaar and bought him one. Humayun has an almost boyish innocence about him which reflects his honesty but belies his toughness and courage. He was badly wounded during Pakistan's war in what is now Bangladesh, was captured and imprisoned, and still suffers from the bullet wound which severed a major nerve in his arm. His Bangladeshi cook of the war days left his homeland to remain with him. Humayun was in the Quetta police for several years and someone else told me of an occasion when the driver of a lorry that he had stopped during a routine check slipped Rs.200 inside his documents when handing them over for inspection. Humayun saw the bribe, turned his back to the man, took out Rs.200 of his own, added it to the money inside the document he had just been given and, without a word, handed bask the documents and told the driver to go. Glancing at his documents, the driver was utterly bewildered. The Quetta bazaar laughed about the incident for days as news travels fast. Since then Humayun has built a house a few miles from Kila Saifulla, planted orchards sustained by a borehole and set up a motel-cum-filling station a healthy distance from the bazaar but has recently rejoined the police I believe.

Back to our rug clearance: we were now a newly registered company, Afghan Tribal Rugs and a clearing agent was hired in Quetta. As Richard and I enjoyed cheap 'bucket shop' tickets for our flights, it also meant that to miss a booked flight would entail the forfeiture of the return ticket. This made me very vulnerable and at one stage my pent up anger at to the stalling tactics of the all-powerful Assistant Controller very nearly exploded. After four days our situation was critical and, still without the essential permit, we stormed out of his office, collected our rugs and baggage and were driven to the station by Mohammad Hassan and a friend of his. There the Bolan Mail's departure for Karachi was delayed for ten minutes so that we could be introduced by our friend to the Station Master and take a cup of tea with him. It was 'the other side of the coin' and well meant though I did feel a little embarrassed that several hundred other passengers should have to wait while I sipped tea.

In Karachi bluff was my only hope so I breezed into the PIA cargo office and blandly presented our rugs. It was a forlorn hope if ever there were but, to my utter astonishment and enormous relief, it worked and all was well. Back home again but still aggrieved I typed out a detailed two-page dossier on our treatment in Quetta and posted copies to five different government departments in Pakistan including the Martial Law Administration, more in hope than in any expectation of a positive response. However, my troubles were not over. The clearing agent engaged at Heathrow was unable to clear the consignment because the origin of the rugs had not been certified in Pakistan and it was only after letters and pleas here and there that a Customs exemption was made. I had yet to learn that official business by a foreigner was only allowed in Pakistan if in partnership with a local person. That stipulation was simply avoided on subsequent visits by buying rugs as a private person without a whisper of our company but such purchases were limited to a maximum total value of Rs.40,000, raised to Rs.70,000 a year or two later so some careful juggling with receipts was essential but at least the certification of 'third world origin' (e.g. made in Afghanistan) no longer applied upon our return but duty had increased.

In 1983, the following year, I took son Newman, aged just fifteen, with me to Baluchistan to see the tribal area and meet the Jogezais while I bought some more rugs from Turkoman dealers still coming over from Afghanistan in spite of the war. The main benefit really of Afghan Tribal Rugs, as it was part-time and very small, apart from an income tax necessity was that I could then afford to visit Quetta and Zhob at intervals. An added benefit was that we could at last afford a rug or two for ourselves and have a little profit left over. At the Damascus stop-over, our plane was delayed for four hours while an engine was replaced and, whilst waiting, we fell into conversation with another passenger who turned out to be Andy Skrzypkowiak, a freelance photographer and correspondent on his way to Afghanistan and the Mujahuddin. He was the rugged, open, good-natured sort of person one wants to meet again and I suggested that we get in touch after his assignment in Afghanistan with view to making a film together on nomad migration. A month or two later, when back in the U.K., I wrote to him only to learn from his wife that he had been brutally murdered. The reason for that savage and squalid act may have been because, understanding Farsi, he had overheard that the group thought to be responsible for his murder had earlier robbed an Aid team of some $30,000. Another opinion was that it was because the group felt that he was giving some other Mujahuddin group greater coverage and publicity. In any event it was a treacherous waste of a resourceful, talented and creative life carried out by smashing his head with a rock while he slept somewhere in the mountains. Ghulbudin Hekmatyar's men were suspected of being the killers and what is believed to have been his body was found hidden in a rock crevice months later. He left a young daughter.

Newman and I set out on a tribal bus from Karachi for Quetta at four in the afternoon but after three or four hours it had to turn back because floods had cut the road near Las Bela. Undaunted, our driver decided to go to via the only alternative route, returning to the city and continuing up through the Sinde to Shikarpur and on through Sibi and the Bolan Pass. We arrived at around four-thirty two mornings later, after some thirty-six hours of almost non-stop travel and roughly nine hundred miles, for the princely equivalent of £4-50 each. Rather than disturb Jehandar Shah and his family we signed into a cheap hotel in Jinnah Road for a few hours of rest. Later that day, when he discovered what we had done, Jehandar Shah slapped the hotelier for accepting us and not telephoning him of our arrival. During my brief stop-overs in Quetta before going to Zhob I usually delivered a bottle of Scotch to another member of the extended family who had been hospitable over the years, always a discreet and private business. While greeting one or two other friends in Quetta, we saw a protest march along Liaquat Bazaar hot up into a mini-riot and got our first taste of tear gas. The cause of that minor disturbance was said to be a shoot-out between rival Baluch and Kakar transport groups plying the Quetta-Khuzdar-Las Bela to Karachi route, which left, if I recall correctly, thirteen dead. Later, after a meal at his house, as a curfew had been declared, our Tajik friend, Mohammad Anwar, led us through the back streets and alleys to the start of the cantonment

The Sulaiman Khel gang masquerading as Afghan refugees that I had heard about the previous year was still raising the dust in northern Baluchistan, particularly in the Districts of Zhob and of neighbouring Loralai. Yet again in Quetta I overheard officials discussing the problem, unaware that I understood much of their conversations. The notoriety of the gang was such that on a subsequent visit, Jehandar Shah and I were travelling to Tarwal by car when he stopped in the hills shortly before Khan Metarzai to check that the magazine of his pistol tucked away in the glove compartment was full and make sure that there was a round in the barrel. My revolver was in a discreet shoulder holster and its cylinder was full as always. A little over two years later, in 1986, in cold blood the gang murdered Ahmad Yar Khan's son-in-law, Shahin Khan, and the three friends with him. By all accounts he was an unusually upright, outspoken and brave young man. It appears that the four came upon a line of trucks stopped and being looted on the road from Kila Saifulla to Loralai. Shahin Khan, with more honour and courage than caution, had remonstrated with the gang. The full details are not known but it ended with the four being bound, put back into their vehicle and then almost ripped apart with Kalashnikovs. Sheila met his sad widow in 1990 when we were again in Tarwal.

1) Breaking camp shortly after dawn with the peak, Yau Harsk, looming behind.

2) Above: Bibi Ruziamat
milking a sheep while
Ziauddin holds it, plus one
or two others.

3) Left: Ruziamat filling our
water bags at a spring as the
next camp further on wss a
dry one.

4) Right: The family threading its way up and out of a deep gorge.

5) Below: Border post at Ghazluna by the frontier with Afghanistan.

6) *A cool early morning and Ruziamat and Malanga warm themselves by the meagre fire.*

7) *Part of the main bazaar at Badani on the Afghan border as locals warm themselves in the early morning sun. The place is not marked on any map.*

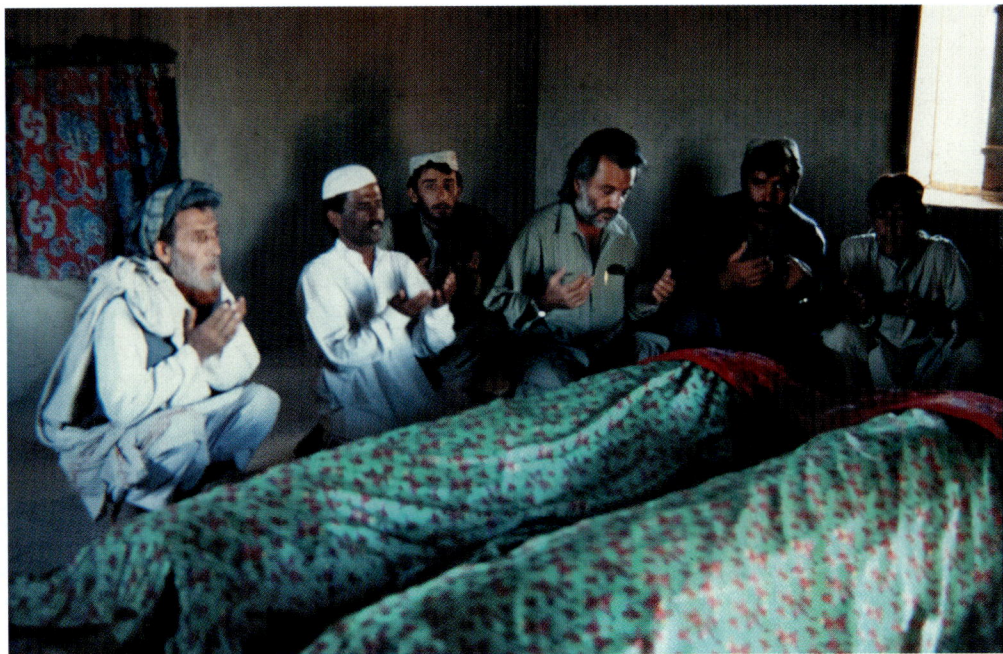

8) *Humayun et al praying in the small Sanzar Nika Ziarat, near Kot. Sanzar is the putative ancestor of the largest and dominant section, the Sanzar Khel, of the Kakars.*

9) *The main street in Kila Saifulla, now tarred, looking east towards the small strong point built during the last war, presumably against the axis party that eluded the British to gain entry into Afghanistan.*

10) *The baker at work in Kila Saifulla, his oven being a bee-hive shaped cavity in the earthen plinth. He is shown hooking out a nan at lunchtime.*

11) The huge ancient mound situated ten miles east of Duki, called Dubbr Kot or the Thal Shahghullai. Note the small figure of a man on the slope to the right of centre. Although visited around 1923 by Sir Aurel Stein, the mound has never been properly excavated.

12) *The way we travelled in 1959 and the 'sixties.*

Again it became all too clear that while potential safari clients might like a whiff of adventure, the current situation was a different matter. In Tarwal it was good to see old friends again and among other invitations, Fukhruddin insisted that we take tea with him. At some stage during our visit he had to leave the tiny living room for a moment and we heard a tiny noise from beneath a crumpled old sack in the corner. Curious, I lifted it cautiously and was astonished to find a baby beneath it, perfectly healthy and contented. This was the occasion when, only half jokingly I suspect, Newman was offered a daughter without 'wulwer' when she came of age. Then aged about twelve, she had strong features like her father and had been with us earlier. I pointed out to Newman that, given a good scrub and her matted hair combed, she had to be a winner genetically.

If there can be a happy ending to the murder of Shahin Khan and his friends after our visit, it was when five years later the same gang waylaid a lone militia man travelling one night on his little motorcycle along the road north-east of Tarwal towards Fort Sandeman. The gang had laid rocks across the road, and while the gang leader and one of his henchmen were dealing with our hero, other members of the gang hiding among nearby rocks as a back-up called out to those on the road. While the two villains were momentarily distracted, the militia man drew his revolver, shot the ring-leader through the heart and severely wounded the other bandit before escaping into the dark amid a fusillade of bullets. Almost miraculously he escaped unharmed, to raise the hue and cry that followed, as a result of which the rest of the gang were captured after a chase involving several vehicles. I failed to ask later what happened to them after their arrival in Mach Gaol but doubt if Community Service was felt to be the answer.

One afternoon while we were chatting on the veranda in front of his house A.Y.K. produced a Russian 9mm Tommy gun that he had just bought, presumably from some visiting 'mujahuddin'.

It took us a while to fathom how to load the drum magazine, after which we tried out the new 'toy', using an empty tin in the garden as a target. The weapon juddered so much that neither of us managed a single hit although our target was only fifteen or twenty yards away. When Newman and I left Tarwal A.Y.K. presented me with a pair of what Afghans call 'Gardeena' bowls from Iran, maroon on the outside with two white panels filled with a posy of flowers. They are treasured by Afghans much as English gypsies regarded Crown Derby plates and there is also a blue version. I discovered later that the design originated from an English potter named Gardener, who went to Russia and either worked in or set up a factory producing this ware and such bowls from Russia are valued more highly than the Persian copies. They are duly treasured by us.

After seeing Newman on to his flight in Karachi, I returned to Quetta to set about buying a few rugs, a protracted and tiring business involving long hours of searching then bargaining in the dust and heat, eased only by countless 'bottals', meaning Coca Cola, Fanta or Sprite but I liked the Turkoman dealers and we got on well. In particular they were trusting and would let me take away a piece on the promise of payment within a few days. Alternatively I would reserve a piece and a handshake with them was as good as any legal document in Britain, sometimes better. However, they had to scratch a meagre living to support themselves in Quetta and their families remaining far away in northern Afghanistan and they needed every extra rupee that they could squeeze from the unwary or the uninitiated. Many of them did not trade from shops but from tiny, dark rooms around the small, secluded courtyard of the so-called Panjab Hotal in the bustling Suraj Gang bazaar. Those traders cooked on little paraffin pressure stoves in the courtyard, literally sleeping, eating and working on heaps of their wares. Far from their villages and families, theirs was a hard, dreary existence. Nearby was a slightly more modern place with two floors and around a more distant corner was the marginally 'more up-market' but equally gloomy Gul Market that boasted a basement, both holding similar treasures. They had taken some finding initially.

I would have happily rented a room in one of the cheap hotels along Jinnah Road for this part of my visit but Jehandar Shah would not hear of it and patiently tolerated my coming and going in noisy scooter rickshaws belching blue smoke. When all was packed and ready in two enormous tin trunks, bureaucracy had to be braved. Some of my receipts were a little quaint as they bore the thumb print of the illiterate vendor instead of a signature but someone could always be found to write the receipts in Urdu, which language few of the Turkoman or Hazaras could speak and which I could not write, our dealings being conducted in Dari, which was virtually Farsi. Next I needed to engage one of the scribes sitting at little desks outside the law courts to type a list of my purchases. After my experiences of the previous year, I then embarked on the hazardous phase with the dubious Assistant Controller of Imports and Exports, who was not the only potential obstacle, with a mixture of anger and trepidation. Before seeking his blessing a No Objection Certificate from the State Bank was essential as evidence that the purchases were with foreign currency. That too should have been a simple routine but vague objections and mysterious delays might arise that took stamina to wear down the 'enemy'. No official ever asks for a bribe but negotiations are cleverly manipulated so that the person seeking this or that permit is virtually cornered into offering a 'tip'. I hate bribes on principal but fighting the system makes a rod for one's own back and I can understand why so many people acquiesce, Thus, in my case, what should take two or three hours might take four days, at the same time raising one's blood pressure.

Upon presenting myself at the Assistant Controller's office, I was both surprised and pleased to see that Sheikh Manzur Hussain, whom I had documented and reported to five departments the previous year, was no longer in charge. Instead, the name above the door was 'Pir Mohammad Bangash'. Recognising the humble 'chaprassi' or messenger, I asked him where was my former tormentor. He gave a significant smile, mumbled briefly and obviously knew something that I didn't know. Looking back, I recall that I was blunt and rather rude when admitted to the new man but mitigated that by praising his tribe, whose valour had long been recognised by British officers and officials of the 'Raj'. Upon giving him my name he said that he had heard of me and I became curious. I responded by asking where was the devious one of the previous year. He had been transferred, and after only nine months instead of the normal tour of three years I was told. A warm glow suffused me as I realised that my painstaking dossier about the previous obstruction had borne fruit. There had not been the briefest acknowledgement from any of the five departments circulated but someone had acted. His successor was a completely different species, confirming my affection for the border tribes, and I left his office as if walking on air. Revenge is not only sweet but it lasts forever.

The last 'minefield' was inspection and clearance by the Customs, to which dingy office just outside the railway station a rickety donkey cart carried my two large tin trunks. A glance at the venal crowd lounging inside made me feel as a pigeon might feel upon seeing a peregrine falcon circling overhead, and with good reason. Soon things were going badly, until I was asked to give my address in Quetta. Almost unbelievably they misread Jehandar Shah's name as that of his older brother, Jahangir Shah, who happened to be a senator in the government at the time and a forthright one at that. I did not disabuse them. I had been saved by semi-literacy. Grudgingly the consignment was examined and cleared and my last call was to the P.I.A. cargo office, always an oasis of honesty and efficiency. The exercise had taken less than two days.

It was 1984 when I flew to Karachi again, then bussed to Quetta, this time alone. After a day or two in the city, Jehandar Shah decided to visit Tarwal and we went there in his car. The notorious gang of robbers was still at large so as we approached Khan Metarzai atop the pass into Zhob, he stopped his car to check over his pistol in the glove compartment. He was not the sort to suffer robbers easily so probably it was just as well that they were elsewhere during our journey. Beyond Hindubagh a violent storm sent a wild flood across one of the concrete fords in the tarred road, stopping several vehicles while another ford behind us prevented any of the vehicles stranded from going back as well. However, the flood was over in less than an hour. A day or two later, while sipping 'poi chai' on the veranda in Tarwal one morning, Ahmad Yar Khan appeared very angry from having just read a newspaper report about a blind woman being given forty lashes for alleged adultery in the Panjab. She was a household servant and had been raped by both her employer and his son, becoming pregnant as a result. Being unmarried she was hauled before a Sharia 'court' in the village where she explained what had happened but, as she was blind, she had been unable to point out her two attackers when asked to identify them whereupon she was pronounced guilty of adultery. His reaction to the above is another reason why we have been close for so long.

Back in Quetta after a couple of weeks in Zhob I set about buying a few rugs. It was all still new to me and so I had to be very careful, not so much with regard to quality, as already explained, but about the price. Moreover, the town was full of mediocre pieces and good rugs were hard to find so that one had to listen for a whisper circulating about some new consignment due to arrive by lorry through Kandahar, having survived the war zones on its way down from Agcha or Mazar-i-Sharif and through Kabul and Ghazni; or across from Bala Murgha, Herat and Daulatabad, to Kandahar then Chaman.

During such visits Jahandar Shah was very tolerant at my comings and goings in smoky scooter rickshaws and the pile of rugs accumulating on the floor of my bedroom in his house. In 1982, on my second venture into the perilous rug market, I had bought two fine pieces from a simple Turkoman from Iran, Turdeh Khull, and his brother. Coming upon him by chance in the bazaar during my 1984 visit we chatted. He had dropped the rug business he told me and was running a tiny restaurant, there and then insisting that I be his guest. The 'pulao' was dreadfully greasy but the gesture so generous. Such genuine Muslims are a far cry from those warped fundamentalists and terrorists who mutilate their religion and currently plague Europe, America, Afghanistan and Pakistan as well as other countries.

During the 1988 visit I had with me a large windscreen in a wooden crate for A.Y.K.'s old blue Chevrolet, no such replacements being available in Pakistan. It didn't make for easy travel but it was good to return one or two of the many favours that I had enjoyed from the Jogezais. Whilst in Tarwal, A.Y.K. related how between the two World Wars two British officers were fishing for mahseer in the Zhob River and recklessly became very drunk. A local man came upon them and cut their throats but whether it was outrage at their condition or simply to rob them is unclear. He was soon identified, captured and duly hanged in Kila Saifulla. At his burial the military padre said prayers over his grave and the mullah presiding laughed openly. At that the officer in charge of the tiny garrison was so incensed that he had the mullah arrested, then made kneel beside the grave all night under a relay of guards who were instructed in front of the mullah to shoot him if he moved so much as an inch. It's perfectly clear that no such sentence would have been carried out but the threat had the desired effect and the chastened mullah was released in the morning.

Invitation after invitation for Sheila to visit Zhob had been made but she had demurred at the prospect of being a woman in such a male dominated society. She changed her mind in 1990 and, recognising that I was unlikely to enter the women's or 'purdah' quarters to help with the language barrier, we took along Helga a relaxed and sociable German friend of many years. Their initial trepidation soon vanished and they were so warmly welcomed that a return visit after two or three years was contemplated but other things intervened until more recently, when the presence of Taliban in Quetta, and even in Loralai, dictates otherwise. As I had anticipated, both became 'honorary men' at meal times and on social occasions, for the tradition is that the men eat first and the women and children are given what remains and separately so. This may be offensive to many Western eyes at first sight but it probably evolved from the former necessity of keeping the men fit and strong in case of attack, as Bob Chambers and I had seen in Sibi when we stopped briefly for a meal.

There was a fascinating situation when we arrived concerning a young married couple, Kabir Batozai and Shakhira, then resident in the A.Y.K. household. Poor Kabir had a cowed look and was a very poor specimen physically, with the suspicion of a poorly healed broken jaw. Although around twenty or twenty-one years of age he resembled a fifteen-year-old English boy but the girl was totally different. She was quite handsome – when her shawl slipped as she brought the breakfast tray – and although possibly only fifteen or sixteen years of age, she had a strong, forthright character. She was also larger and sturdier than her frail husband and not afraid to express her opinions, making their relationship more like that of a mother and son. Theirs was the story of a wicked uncle lurking in a remote, hidden valley in Batozai 'srra' or clan territory forty or so miles to the north-west of Tarwal, where the Shin Ghar continuation of the Spin Ghar along the north-west side of the wide Zhob Valley is much lower than the great crags opposite Tarwal. It is medieval in its savagery and so much so that it might sound fictional to some readers.

Kabir's mother was already dead, though from what cause is unknown, when his uncle, his father's own brother, murdered Kabir's father when the boy was about eight years old. The reason for that horrendous throat-cutting is unknown but it was carried out with the aid of another man so that the actual instigator was unclear. After that the uncle had no choice but to look after his orphaned nephew and the fearful boy then suffered ten or eleven years of beatings and semi-starvation. He was not even allowed to sleep in his uncle's house but forced to sleep outside as best he could, even in winter when the temperature dropped well below zero. Why there was a delay of around nine years before a local 'jirga' ruled in 1987 that the family of the uncle or the family of his accomplice must give a girl in marriage without 'wulwer' as compensation I do not know but Kabir was then seventeen or eighteen or so years of age and the girl only eleven or twelve years old. From that judgement it seems that the uncle and his close relatives may not have had any suitable daughters to offer at the time, and it may be that the accomplice was a distant relative.

Whatever the case, it was simply a betrothal and the couple were kept apart for three or four years and, when presented with these vague times and ages, one must remember that birth certificates do not exist there and calendars were generally not important. Three years or so after the 'jirga' ruling, the uncle's wife died and he plotted to marry the girl himself, probably intending to murder Kabir. Somehow the girl got to hear of it but in any case she noticed that the uncle had his eyes upon her. She told her new husband of her fears and finally persuaded him that they should flee immediately. That they did, crossing the wide Zhob Valley and river at night to reach the road with the intention of finding sanctuary with Ahmad Yar Khan at Tarwal. Having no knowledge of money they simply boarded a bus that came along in the morning and of course were unable to pay the Rs.15 required. However, they had with them a red-legged partridge in a traditional, beehive-shaped bamboo cage and this they sold to a passenger on the bus for Rs.10, which the 'bus wallah' generously accepted as sufficient payment.

The bus driver dropped them off at the small 'hotal' built by one of the Jogezai brothers on the main road a few yards from the drive down to Tarwal village and there the couple learned where Ahmad Yar Khan lived. They had arrived at his house a few days before us, dressed in rags and literally terrified, having guessed what the uncle might do if he managed to intercept them before they had found refuge. In fact, poor Kabir was almost out of his mind from fear, according to A.Y.K., who is not prone to exaggeration. They, or more correctly she, had made the right decision, for A.Y.K. immediately provided them with new clothes and took them on as servants, which is no doubt why bright young Wali, the Afghan refugee of my previous visit, had recently been transferred to Farouk in Quetta. Within a week of our own arrival, Kabir had improved markedly and during the following week, although still looking hurt and timid, he managed to smile and even laugh when coaxed. But memories such as his do not fade overnight and whenever he saw my Beretta .32 pistol in its holster hung on the veranda wall he looked at it like a hungry dog at a bone, no doubt thinking that it could be the answer to all his suffering. Initially A.Y.K. planned to give him a pistol once he became strong and healthy but later on decided against the idea. Even with a pistol, against such a ruthless and cunning uncle, Kabir might not prevail but when the couple left Tarwal for their home village many months later I am fairly certain that a blunt, uncompromising message was sent to the uncle advising what would happen were he to harm them in any way.

During two previous visits one of the younger Jogezais, whose real name will not be used lest it prejudice his job and whom I had first known when he was barely in his teens, showed increasing signs of depression. I suspect that a factor in was that he was scrupulously honest but his boss was corrupt and diverting official finances. It was clear that he was heading for a nervous breakdown and during each visit I had suggested that his father should send him over to us for two or three months, to give him a break. Things came to a head it seems when, following a minor traffic accident in the centre of Quetta, the son drew a pistol though no shots were fired. When I returned from school one evening after the above visit, our youngest son Richard promptly told me that Hassanullah, as I shall call him, had phoned and that a telegram had arrived from Quetta. The telegram said that he was flying to England but it had taken over two days to arrive. I immediately presumed that the phone call was from Quetta but Richard said that Hassanullah was at Heathrow. Faced with an emergency I managed to page him in Terminal 3 and explained that he should take the rail-air coach to Reading Station and from there take a train to Castle Cary where I would meet him. No, he could not do that: he had had a quarrel with three men on the plane and feared leaving the airport in case they attacked him. From the tone of his voice I knew that there was no alternative but to fetch him.

Not wishing to hurry things, he spent that night with us and did not appear unduly upset but the second night was different. He became so agitated that we quickly hid swords and large knives as a precaution. I found it extremely upsetting to see him sitting on his bed repeating over and over, 'Toba Allah', forgive me, God, and we called a local doctor around midnight. He soon phoned the Mendip Hospital in Wells (a psychiatric one and now closed) for an admission and we two set off at two in the morning. In the hospital a check of his suitcase revealed the equivalent of three thousand pounds in sterling, Deutschmark and American dollars – obviously for his treatment. The family must have scoured the bazaars and it was just as well as we were absolutely broke at the time, with little hope of obtaining an overdraft. Anyway, after a month's treatment during which I visited him every evening bar one, he was well enough to return to his family (with three-quarters of the money intact) and resume work. Mild schizophrenia was involved and the consultant who had treated him explained the medication to be used for me to pass on to a member of the family who was a doctor and Hassanullah has not looked back since then. As all the Jogezais had been so welcoming and generous to me, Sheila and our three sons over so many years, the opportunity to repay them a little in that small way was extremely welcome. If only I could have persuaded A.Y.K. to spend a few weeks with us but he could not overcome his fear of flying.

Chapter Ten

Diary of a Shahizai Family's Spring Migration in 1992

Countries such as Iran, Afghanistan and Pakistan have many large, semi-desert regions of good soil but without an adequate and reliable rainfall or, alternatively, an irrigation system based on vertical wells or horizontal 'ghanats / karez'. Therefore such areas are of use only for grazing flocks of sheep and goats and even then it has to be over a wide areas, enforcing a nomadic life. Also many other areas are at an altitude of seven to eight thousand feet and very cold in winter, if not actually snow bound, in Afghanistan necessitating a seasonal move eastwards to lower, milder areas in Pakistan for such tent dwellers. Where there is limited irrigation from a stream or a spring or a 'karez', it may not produce enough food to support a family or a village for the entire year in addition to providing a surplus to sell in order to buy other essentials. Again, seasonal migration is essential. No tribe is wholly nomadic and many settled tribes have sections or clans or even individual families that are nomadic, as in the case of Ruziamat Shahizai with whom I travelled. While the Ghalzai tribes such as the Sulaiman Khel, Kharoti and Nasser in Afghanistan tend to be regarded as the main nomad groups and are predominant, many Afghan tribes such as the Dotani, Shinwari and Zhadran have large nomad sections and even some Pashtun tribes have their share. In the past such nomads belonged to one of three main types:

1) Those with flocks seeking a milder winter and fresh grazing in lower areas, selling wool and surplus animals to buy essentials.
2) Those without flocks seeking winter work as labourers and / or hiring their camels or donkeys for transport on the plains of what was India, mainly to augment inadequate crops in the highlands.
3) Those carrying produce such as kilims, karakul pelts, wool, ghee, dried fruit, almonds, pistacchio nuts, chilghoza pine nuts, liquorice root, asafoetida, etc. in autumn and winter to what was India. They returned from the lowland towns to their highland villages in spring with cotton goods, metal goods, shoes, gurr, sugar, tea, salt and so on to sell in nearby towns. However, since World War Two such trading has virtually been displaced by lorries.
4) A much smaller number moved to 'old' India to become money-lenders during the winter months – and were renowned for their robust treatment of reluctant debtors or those slow to repay – while the small Ut Khel clan of the Nasser tribe went there solely to steal what ever they could, rifles being a 'speciality' it was said.

As to their future, human progress has improved roads along which most of them travel for part of their migrations but that has also meant that their former earnings from carrying goods both ways during their migration has been lost to lorries. Dramatic increases among settled populations and irrigation projects must affect routes as more and more land is permanently cropped and occupied by an ever-increasing population. However, the general increase in prosperity must also make nomads look at settled relatives and begin to compare their own lifestyles unfavourably. Finally, as we shall see shortly, the new availability of relatively cheap, effective medicines leads to larger families so that in the case of pastoralists, the flock may no longer be able support a larger family, however basically, and Ruziamat Shahizai who is detailed below is such an example.

Ever since 1960, when I turned down that offer by three young Sulaiman Khels in Fort Sandeman to join them on their travels through Waziristan I had regretted it. The decision nagged me constantly: it was the opportunity of a lifetime and I had let it slip. However, in 1991 I decided to retire early, even though our financial resources and pension prospects were not conducive to such a move. Personal dissatisfaction and boredom with the grossly diluted G.C.S.E. syllabus and exam compared with the discarded G.C.E., for all its faults, was the main factor but such a move would allow me to experience a nomad migration at long last while I could still cope with what might be its rigours. Correspondence with Zhob friends between late 1991 and early 1992, explaining my plans and seeking information, brought vague and lukewarm replies. Possibly I had been incautious in revealing that I wanted particularly to travel with a Shinwari or Kharoti family or group, having been impressed by them during the abortive expedition of 1971. I soon guessed the reason: it was not laziness or reluctance to help but concern lest I get kidnapped for ransom or be killed – as had been freelance photographer Andy Skrzypkowiak – by some trigger-happy, well-armed band over the border where anarchy and mayhem still prevailed in a number of areas as an aftermath of the Russian intervention. Similarly, when the grandson of the remarkable Eldred Pottinger appeared out of the blue in Quetta in the late 1980s and asked Jehandar Shah for help in tracing the footsteps of his forebear, Jehandar Shah declined for precisely that reason.

My enquiries having achieved nothing, I made hasty preparations and flew out to Karachi in early April, unsure as to when the nomads began to move out from Ghabar Ghar and other winter camping grounds near Manzai or Loralai. The fourteen-hour ride in a tribal covering the four hundred and fifty miles to Quetta was suitably cheap but the word comfort does not come into it: I didn't so much mind the wooden back of the seat hammering my knees as we bumped along or the night cold but the blaring local pop music in front denied all hope of sleep. When pausing briefly in Quetta I heard about the demise of Headarr Kakar as he was known. He was a notorious and ruthless robber who had operated in Karachi for several years, robbing banks and allegedly killing some seventeen men in the process, those no doubt including some of the guards armed with shotguns that are posted at all National Banks of Pakistan. He was of the Taraghara section and, apparently because things were getting too risky in Karachi, he moved back to Quetta.

A police officer whom I know well and like immensely, whom I will refer to as 'Y', heard of Headarr Kakar's return and sent a private warning via the man's father and brother, both of whom lived in Quetta, to leave the area. This unofficial, generous warning and ultimatum to a fellow tribesman brought no response but a second one brought an insolent reply that 'Y' had better look out for himself. The gauntlet had been thrown down. A while later the robber was spotted by a constable who, as instructed, promptly alerted 'Y' who immediately hurried to the street, telling his driver to pull over in such a way that he would be on the same side as the robber and could get out swiftly to confront the man, rightly anticipating that there was little chance of a quiet surrender. Upon being challenged, Haiddr Kakar loosed one shot, which merely hit the police jeep, before he himself was hit in the right arm, causing him to drop his gun. Desperately the gangster reached beneath his 'camise' with his other arm and was promptly shot there also, falling to the ground at that. Approaching the stricken man, it was pointed out that he had been given a fair warning to leave the area, and aware that he might bribe a magistrate or perhaps bribe someone to obtain an early release from gaol, a third shot to the head completed the encounter. Some readers may be horrified at such an outcome but the officer's life and the safety of his family would have been at serious and endless risk otherwise and he knew that all too well. A search of Haiddr's body found Rs.30.000 tied to his right leg, the second pistol, several grenades tied across his chest and an incriminating notebook with plans for future raids. Even better, the notebook contained contact numbers of his gang members in Karachi, most of whom were arrested as a result. Haiddr's next of kin then coolly asked for the money and guns to be turned over to them, which request was refused.

Before heading north to Zhob I went into the Quetta Medical Store to buy some sulphonamides in case of dysentery, these being without any prescription and considerably cheaper than in the U.K. and, fortunately, fake drugs had yet to rear their ugly heads. Unexpectedly I was enrolled in trying to arrange a million rupee order from Brazil by the owner of the pharmacy because the exporter in South America spoke only Spanish and French. However, no telephone line was available at the time but the proprietor generously pressed three different drugs upon me for my travels ahead as thanks for my attempted help. Immediately upon arriving in Tarwal, I button-holed Mohammad Hassan, who was then an Assistant Commissioner in Lorala and it was arranged that I would accompany him to Loralai where he worked. Chatting with A.Y.K. I heard of a tragedy the previous year when, for security, a German couple in a pick-up drove off the road to camp behind a small hill a few miles down the valley. However, the following morning they were spotted by a local militia man who thought he recognised the vehicle as having been stolen recently. Without giving a warning he opened fire but missed, at which the couple drove back to the road as fast as they could. Unfortunately they were then spotted by a group of militia, who also thought they recognised the pick-up and likewise opened fire, but with deadly results that time, killing the women. There was to be a court case over the incident.

Some time during the next few days I called upon Fukhruddin and was concerned to find that his eyesight was failing. This I put down to age coupled with a very poor diet probably low in vitamin A but a search in both Kila Saifulla and Loralai bazaars for suitable vitamin tablets produced only vitamin B complex and vitamin C. I considered sending him some multi-vitamin tablets when I returned home in a few weeks time, though this could run the risk of him overdosing or leaving them within reach of children. Wrongly in hindsight, I did not send any – to my eternal regret. The morning after my arrival in Tarwal another member of the family drove me to Loralai, Mohammad Hassan having already left the village for work. In the Loralai Circuit House he and his colleagues informed me that the Shinwaris and Kharotis had already left for the Afghan border but on the way to Loralai I had spoken with two Kharoti groups only a few miles up the valley as they headed for Kila Saifulla. He is a super chap and we had been close friends for over thirty years and this nonsense was not lying in the sense that we might regard it: simply he wished to protect me without possibly offending me.

It may not be our British way of doing things but when in Rome one has to accept that the Romans are at home and are entitled to do things in their own way, like it or not. Gladly ferrying me back and forth the fifty-three miles between Tarwal and Loralai and allowing me to sleep in the Circuit House for a couple of nights was all very well but it gradually became clear that no one was going to drive me out to the Ghabar Ghar camping grounds where many Shinwari families winter or to Kharoti families around Manzai. Without so saying, my friends were greatly concerned that I might be tempted to continue over the border with the nomads to their lands into Afghanistan were I to travel with them. To be honest I also was a little concerned at the prospect of having to walk a hundred and fifty miles or so back to Zhob alone through areas where various

323

warlords were vying for power, which in turn allowed ordinary robbers a more or less free hand.

Recognising my determination, particularly when I set about hiring a taxi to go to the Ghabar Ghar, some thirty miles away, a compromise was reached. A Kharoti who winters just outside Loralai was enlisted to arrange things for me. However, the fellow insisted that a camel and two bodyguards would have to be hired by me, when all I had with me was a camera and rucsac though food had to be added. Therefore Baz Mohammad was sent away but I disliked him in any case. Two other Kharotis were next supposed to appear but failed to do so. Then a Shinwari from the refugee camp a few miles up the road was expected but he too failed to appear. It was all very frustrating and my impatience increased by the day, if not by the hour, and I was probably beginning to show it as well. I was fully aware of Mohammad Hassan's difficult position for, if I were to come to grief, however indirectly as a result of his help, then he would be placed in a very embarrassing situation that might even threaten his career, as had happened when the American Winant and his female companion vanished in Afghanistan, leading to the resignation of the Minister of the Interior. However, either I had to 'shove' or pack up and go home. Everyone was very hospitable, from the D.C. himself down, but I was making no progress.

21/4/92 On the fourth day there seemed to be a long-awaited breakthrough: two Kakars were going to make some arrangement on my behalf with a Kakar nomad family of the Shahizai clan camped a few miles from Kila Saifulla and already on their way to Kakar Khorrasan. By now I had become sceptical but a long-term acquaintance of the Luni tribe, Nasserullah Khan, lent me a tent – something I had failed to bring in my haste – and I quickly purchased ample supplies of flour, rice, dahl, sugar, tea, cooking oil and an enamelled mug in the bazaar plus some bamboo poles for the tent to replace his heavy iron ones. The following afternoon one of the negotiators, Mir Ahmad, appeared with a pick-up hired on my behalf, though I was not allowed to pay for it, and we were off back to Kila Saifulla. I was still very much in the dark but enquiries were made in the bazaar there and we were soon off again with a recruited guide to the Kakars' camp, said to be a few miles away. Even when we left the tar road for a jeep track I was a shade doubtful but after a mile or two a black dot could just be seen in the distant wastes near the line of low hills that border the south-eastern side of the Zhob valley at that point, behind which were snow clad peaks. It could only be a 'kuzhdei' and a while later I was introduced to my host-to-be, Ruziamat Wali Abdul Hamid Shahizai.

My command of Pashtu is basic and I could only guess at the muffled conversation that took place but can imagine Ruziamat's dismay at the considerable responsibility thrust upon him by the Jogezais but which he could scarcely refuse. If his thoughts could have been read at that moment they would probably have been: "Allah be praised, I am to be burdened with some soft, silly townie and a European one to boot. What have I done to deserve this?" A day or two later I learned that he had been instructed not to let me out of his sight and to guard me with his life if necessary. The second exhortation was superfluous as tribal code puts such a responsibility upon every host to defend a guest in his house or tent. I pitched my tent behind Ruziamat's, a fire was lit and we all had milk tea, sucking it past lumps of brown 'gurr' (solidified molasses) held in our mouths to sweeten it. After that my helpers left in the pick-up while the family and I sized up one another as we sat in the wide entrance of the 'kuzhdei' looking out at the crags of the magnificent Spin Ghar range rising abruptly on the far, north-west side of the great valley.

In this assimilation process both sides were helped by Mullah Akhtar Mohammad, of the Ismailzai clan from Shinkai village thirty miles down the valley who was spending the night there. He also spoke Urdu, his help filling gaps in my Pashtu vocabulary.

To our right, at one end of the 'kuzhdei' dozens of kids and lambs lay patiently, each tethered to cleverly looped ropes set out in rows. After days of tension and mounting frustration I began to relax and look forward to realising an ambition of over thirty years. Apart from his wife, who dutifully held up her 'chadur' all the time, Ruziamat had with him two grown sons, Rahmatullah, who was out with the flock at the time, and Ziauddin who was also in his early twenties but younger; Malanga aged about ten and a toddler Dwardi aged perhaps three years completed the family. In addition he had a married daughter and two other grown sons, Khani Mohammad and Shunshulla forced to work as farm labourers, all three of them further up the Zhob Valley and whom I had yet to meet.

His sheep numbered about one hundred and forty and his goats about thirty, young kids and lambs totalling a further seventy or so. From what Ahmad Yar Khan had told me years earlier this explained why the family has been forced to split and two of the grown sons compelled to do labouring. A small nomad family, meaning one with two or three children, possessing a flock of only a hundred animals is poverty stricken, even by nomad standards. An owner of around two hundred adult animals is more or less comfortably off, which our standards would still class as abject poverty and being on the bread line, while the possessor of three hundred or more is wealthy by nomad standards. Increasing the size of the flock is unlikely to be easy, however, as most of the male animals and possibly some of the females as well must be sold for cash to buy the bare necessities of life – such as clothing, cooking vessels, beakers, flour, tea, salt and 'gurr'. As well as bearing young, the female animals also provide wool for sale and milk as the basis of nomad diet, hence the inclusion of goats which produce more milk per head and whose hair is required to make cloth for the traditional 'kuzhdei'. Further, the sparse grazing over wide areas has to be shared with other flocks and is therefore even more limited, while a larger flock will require more care and guarding, which in turn may necessitate an extra person.

A nomad family man today is therefore frequently faced with something of a contradiction, usually not met earlier when the lack of cheap, efficient medicines strictly limited the size of such families. To rear several sons not only provides better defence against any enemies or would-be rustlers but also ensures better support in old age. At the same time, however, it becomes increasingly difficult, even impossible, for the flock to support them and if there is not a similar number of daughters to bring in 'wulwer' upon marrying then raising money for the sons to marry becomes a severe problem. With only one daughter and six sons, Ruziamat's position in this regard is therefore extremely difficult and most of his sons are unlikely to be able to raise a enough money to gain a bride for many years to come. That was the position for Fukhruddin Khodadzai when, as already related, in order to settle his blood feud two of the family's daughters were given in marriage without any 'wulwer' to the enemy family leaving him high and dry for around twenty-five years, until he was fifty.

However, quite a few nomad clans, such as the Shomalzai for example supplemented their meagre incomes by cleaning 'karez' wells, while their womenfolk produce flat-weave kilims for people who have wool of their own but who either lack the necessary knowledge or the inclination to do all the work involved – washing the wool, carding it, spinning it, dying it, and finally weaving it into a kilim. These women do the work from start to finish. Often their work is very attractive as I have seen many times. Incidentally the Shomalzai are most likely to be a section or clan of the Tokhi tribe but they could be Sohaks. When told about them years ago, I had assumed that the Shomalzai was a tribe in its own right and failed to clarify it with A.Y.K. at the time.

As the sun sank towards the jagged hills there was a distant bleat and in a moment the air was full of the deafening cries of the kids and lambs, having had no milk since early morning and now very hungry. They were on their feet in an instant, many trying frantically to break free from their tethers and the approaching flock replied in full, many breaking into a run to join their young. There was little time to greet Rahmatullah properly as he came in with them for our job was to prevent the mothers from rushing into the 'kuzhdei' before they had been partially milked. This was no easy matter and very difficult without a stick – not to hit them but to ward them off – as some were so persistent in their efforts. What particularly impressed me was that Ruziamat and family knew the lamb or kid of every mother, releasing it only when the mother had been part-milked. Everyone except little Dwardi and the wife, who did the actual milking, but including young Malanga, joined in catching the animals. The wife's name was never used by Ruziamat or by her sons and I never learnt it so I called her 'Bibi Ruziamat'. One or other of the grown sons would hold four mothers, one under each armpit and one with each hand while they were milked by Bibi Ruziamat, the long fleece making this relatively easy. After a few minutes working out the procedures I joined in but at first could not match the catching skill of Ziauddin or young Malanga which required cunning and a sudden lunge. Finally it was all over and the entire flock lay contentedly, mothers and young blissfully reunited, while we drank hot 'poi chai'.

The 'happy hour', as I privately dubbed it, ended at nightfall, when the young animals had to be separated from their mothers for the second time of the day and the adults driven out into the desert for the night. This was an equally lively business as both the mothers and the young desperately resisted the separation so that we were all dashing backwards and forwards constantly to head off this or that animal. After perhaps twenty minutes it was over and Ziauddin, whose turn it was, went off for the next five-hour shift into the chilly night equipped with a flask of warm water to drink, a folded 'pasti' and a cotton quilt to face any fierce storm that might burst upon us. We then tethered the young animals in the smoky gloom of the 'kuzhdei' aided by a small storm lantern. 'Pastis' were then baked on a slightly domed iron griddle, which was placed over a large triangular iron trivet, and I was given a battered aluminium beaker of hot milk with a pinch of salt. After writing up the day's events with the aid of a torch I went to sleep, contented for the first time in days. It would have been better had something more than just my sleeping bag been between me and the numberless stones but one cannot have everything in this world.

22/4/92 I awoke briefly around midnight when the two brothers changed shift in guarding the flock. Rising time was five thirty, at dawn but not sun-up, and I could see the flock in the far distance heading for us. Soon a tremendous bleating advertised its return as the mullah and I chatted while we enjoyed hot 'poi chai', this time made delicious by adding some sugar thanks to my foresight, while the milking was in progress. After that the rest joined us and we ate 'pastis' as they were baked over the tiny fire made from dead desert herbs. When warm I found them very appetising but to the others it seemed to make no difference whether they were hot or cold. The 'kuzhdei' was dismantled at seven o'clock and everything packed into old sacks and loaded onto the eleven adult donkeys, the two half-grown animals being exempt. The kids and lambs were also carried on donkeys, safely loaded into identical mesh panniers made from plaited fronds of the dwarf palm found at lower altitudes. I was surprised at the force used to tie loads onto the donkeys, young animals in their panniers excepted, and wondered why they didn't object but I soon saw the necessity of this when a load flopped to one side in spite of the effort used to secure it earlier. Little Dwardi was tied onto a quilt on top of the four loose panels and poles of the 'kuzhdei', the heavy 'kuzhdei' roof being on another sturdy male with the cockerel tied on top. This tiresome bird resented being tethered on top of the donkey for travelling and evaded us for some minutes each morning. It was simply the family's 'alarm clock', the family possessing no hens.

We were off by nine, joined by an older woman, who was not fussy about 'purdah', and Ruziamat's daughter-in-law who was. To my considerable disappointment we headed up the valley towards Hindubagh, now renamed Muslimbagh, rather then across it towards the Spin Ghar range on the far side, which mountains still fascinate me after all these years. I was surprised, as an ignoramus, when we pitched camp only two hours later, about four hundred yards from the road. I very soon learnt that travel time each day was usually two and a half hours, even three on occasion, the reason for such shorter moves simply being that the rain had been better than usual, resulting in slightly better grazing, a very comparative term.

The gently sloping ground was extremely stony and we passed other nomads on the way. Once camp had been pitched I got a lift in a pickup on the main road nearby back to Kila Saifulla to buy salt, chilli powder and a few sweets for the children. I also enjoyed a chat with A.Y.K. who happened to be there, the bazaar being the social centre for a wide area. As we sipped 'poi chai' from miniature china bowls one of Abdur Rahman's sons, Tahir Khab, passed and A.Y.K. told me that his nickname was Tony, because he so resembled me when a youth. He had not noticed us and I was a little incredulous at this until A.Y.K. called out 'Tony', at which Tahir Khab immediately turned round then came over to greet us. However, apart from his blue eyes any other resemblance is now lacking as he is massively built, probably weighing twenty stones or 125 kilos, and dark haired. Needless to say, I took it as a compliment.

A lift back to our camp in a passing pick-up cost me Rs.5.

With so little to explore or do, boredom was beginning as it is all so civilised these days in the Zhob valley and I longed for the hills opposite. A stranger came to our camp in the evening and was given food and shelter for the night, even though there was a village nearby. It was the typical gesture of a poor nomad such as Ruziamat. I did not bother to set up my tent; no storms threatened, my sleeping bag was warm enough in the open and I assumed that we would move on again in the morning.

23/4/92 We stay put. During the night I was disturbed by a large dung beetle crawling around beneath my groundsheet and had to eject it. In the morning as a result of several fierce storms recently the usually dun-coloured hills not far to the south had a faint flush of green and it was decided not to move on as the grazing in the locality was good – relatively – so I decided to pitch my borrowed tent. I also found that my sunrise mug of tea had already been sweetened with sugar for me, a considerate touch and one of many to follow. A number of casual visitors called during the day including an itinerant pot seller with a sack of cheap, spun aluminium pots, jugs and mugs. In the early 'sixties most such vessels were made of hand beaten copper, traditionally shaped, much finer and often with engraved decoration but the two children were wonderfully excited when Ruziamat bought each a new, shiny beaker. When the family men were away later on the daughter-in-law didn't bother to hold up her veil. The flock was split into two today so that Ziauddin and Rahmatullah were both occupied throughout the day, each missing his quota of sleep.

Ruziamat is not handsome as are so many tribes people and tends to be crotchety but, bearing in mind the strict injunctions of both Mohammad Hassan and Ahmad Yar Khan, he had already resigned himself to my going off alone into nearby hills and makes no protest or effort to dissuade me. Bibi Ruziamat is pleasant looking but receives no affection, sympathy or encouragement either from Ruziamat or her sons and I feel quite sorry for her. Further, she is not free to visit other families on her own as do the men and is virtually tied to the 'kuzhdei'. From time to time she tries to move up a notch in the pecking order by bossing me and, as she has little hope of doing that with her husband or older sons, I let her get away with it once or twice each day. The two eldest brothers, Khani Muhammad and Shunshulla I have yet to meet but Ziauddin, son number four, is already my favourite. Although very short he is quite sturdy, he is always cheerful but above all he gives the impression of being a survivor come what may. That is not to suggest that he is aggressive, selfish or egocentric: simply he exudes a buoyant self-confidence, coupled with obvious intelligence and a tremendous sense of humour. It would be very difficult to dislike him and we already get on famously even though I am old enough to be his grandfather. Rahmatullah, although older, is the opposite: he is very quiet, distinctly serious and reacts to Ziauddin rather like a younger brother when in fact he is the older. He and I, although perfectly friendly, are on a different plane. Young Malanga is a bright boy and excellent at catching the sheep for milking, probably better than most men who are slightly handicapped by having to stoop to grab the animals as they try to bolt. Really he is a miniature man and earns his place in the family.

During the day we had a procession of visitors and late in the afternoon I was called in for black tea. As none of the men were present the daughter-in-law again did not bother about veiling herself and the older woman who came with her quizzed me thoroughly. A young nephew of Ruziamat who called by said that Badani, our eventual destination on the Afghan border, has four hundred houses but I find it hard to believe. Today it was so warm that I had to wear my turban to avoid a sunburnt scalp, the reason for not wearing it always is that it gets in the way when taking photographs – due to the Sanjar Khel style of leaving a length and a long loop hanging freely. When the adult flock returned in the late afternoon some of the goats began chewing the kuzhdei and had to be chased away by me to prevent damage being done. The 'happy hour' lasted seven hours today, for instead of being driven out at around seven p.m., they were kept in camp until almost one a.m., giving the two older brothers some respite.

24/4/92 We are to stay put. There was haze and cloud in the morning and the flock was not brought in until half six. Quite a few of the kids and lambs do not recognise their mothers easily and try to suckle others, only to be butted away roughly, while the mothers often recognise their young only after sniffing their rear ends rather than visually. When the keenest mothers run in ahead of the rest, knowing which are their young, Ruziamat and the two older lads release their young immediately and before the mothers are part-milked to prevent them from desperately barging into the 'kuzhdei'. The 'kuzhdei is aligned north-south to catch the early morning sun, just as A.Y.K. told me years ago, and today the pinned-on rear panel had earth piled on it because storms were hovering over the mountains on both sides of the valley. It being hazy, unsettled weather, the young animals were set loose as they would not overheat away from the shade of the 'kuzhdei'. I went into Kila Saifulla to collect any mail but forgot that it was 'Juma' or Friday, when the post office is closed all day. However, I met several friends there including Mohammad Hassan, Hashim Khan Jogezai (not H. K. Luni from Loralai) and Mohammad Afzal Khan, Jehangir Shah's eldest son who is quiet, refined and speaks beautifully clear Pashtu. I enjoyed the luxury of two cold Cokes and bought some mandarins for my Shahizai companions.

Walking most of the way back to our camp, as I passed one tiny village some young boys threw stones when I declined their offer of hospitality: it was irritating but not serious. I was given lift for the last two or three miles by A.Y.K. who is obviously very concerned at my going to the border in spite of my earlier promise not to cross into Afghanistan. He was on his way to Quetta, accompanied by his grandson Akbar whom he adores. He told me that good land, with water of course, is worth around Rs.35,000 per acre or two jirub and water from a borehole costs about Rs.35 per hour. Unable to just sit around, I later wandered off to some low but rugged hills to our south-east to see if anything deserved photographing, climbing a couple of small isolated peaks. In the torrent beds there were bright yellow miniature pansies with dark brown centres. The flock was not taken out until after one a.m. giving the two grown sons a little added comfort. Back at our camp a small group of men bought some carefully wrapped mica fragments to show me, asking if they were valuable but naturally I had to disappoint them.

25/4/92 Still static as the grazing is good. Awoke late at six a.m., had 'poi chai' and later 'pasti' and hot milk. We are staying here until tomorrow. Saw a large dung beetle with a ball of dung in distance moving so quickly that I thought it was a mouse at first. The cockerel, which has huge spurs, keeps attacking any weak or sickly lambs and kids and frequently has to be chased away with stones or sticks. Ruziamat collected fine gravel from a nearby torrent bed and spread it where the young animals are tethered, one or two showing diarrhoea, another clearly dying. Also one or other of the family is invariably loose or has diarrhoea but that is hardly surprising when one considers the water they drink is from puddles left by rain or pools in torrent beds open to spores carried by the wind.

A motorcyclist came to the tent latish in the afternoon and it turned out to be Asadullah Khan, the eldest son of Temur Shah. He reminded me that his daughter was the bride whose escort I accompanied to Sharan Jogezai village in Khaisor in 1960. He took me to his house in Kila Saifulla for dinner, a hazardous journey perched on the rear of his little machine as I always carry a stick against dog attack, and my camera for its safety because of Ziauddin's irresistible curiosity. On the way a violent storm broke but we were fortunate to be able to shelter in a small school being built near the road. In the bazaar we met Hashim Khan's brothers Munir Khan and Zahir Khan, whose doctor son came upon Richard after we were attacked by Sulaiman Khels in 1983.

Returning to our camp at ten p.m., although Ruziamat had kindly earthed around it as the storm approached I found my tent full of water but fortunately, warned by the clouds then building up, before leaving with Asadullah I had wrapped all my clothing, books and sleeping bag carefully in a small tarpaulin that I carried as a groundsheet.

26/4/92 We stay put for a fourth day. I awoke late again at six a.m., warm but a bit soggy. Ruziamat told me that Ahmad Yar Khan had called yesterday on his way back from Quetta while I was with Asadullah Khan. Shortly after tea three groups of Kharotis with camels marched along the defunct narrow guage railway line not far from us and I took a number of photographs. Two were heading for Ghazni but via Kalat-i-Ghalzai, which seemed an odd route to take. Later another Kharoti, then his wife with four camels, passed along the road and as we chatted he offered me a share of his lump of coarse bread. I told him that I had already eaten, although not true, as his need was greater than mine. They have so little but never fail to share it. Breakfast of 'pasti' and warm milk followed the above interludes. We are to spend yet another night here. Ruziamat's two settled sons live just across the railway line. The daughter-in-law moved out today, back to their tiny mud house. Storms were seen on both sides of the valley but not in it.

I went into Kila Saifulla and met A.Y.K. with brothers Nur Ahmad and Nurullah Khan, accompanying them back to Tarwal where I enjoyed a "real" lunch with meat and the usual salad. I was relieved to get back my Chitrali cap carelessly left at Mohammad Hassan's house in Tarwal. It had been given to me by Abdur Rahman some days previously. Later, back in the bazaar, I was asked to examine with my dichroscope and lens, an 'almas' or diamond, whose badly frayed edges visible to the unaided eye showed instantly that it was not, and a yellow 'pakraj' or topaz was either a citrine or glass. A.Y.K. insisted on lending me his tent (one that I sold him in 1971) as it is much lighter, drove me to our camp site and took away Nasserullah Khan's heavy one. Another kid has died and several still look sickly but when let loose in a few days their infection rate will probably drop. One kid ran across the 'kuzhdei' end to end and both ways today and had to be chased off. The lambs seem never to do this.

27/4/92 We move on at last. I rose at five-thirty and welcomed the sun at five forty-five as we took tea, following which we separated the adult flock from the young animals, as usual a hectic business. I packed my tent and things quickly and the 'kuzhdei' was down by seven o'clock, after which we had breakfast of 'pasti' and hot milk in the open. The cockerel pushed his luck again by evading capture for ten minutes before flying up onto its usual loaded donkey. As we moved off Ziauddin entrusted me to carry his precious .303 Lee Enfield rifle, a good sign, but I was also lumbered with the storm lantern by his mother. The kids and lambs walked to our next camp for the first time, leaving half an hour ahead of the pack animals, the main flock being far away so that they arrived at our new site nearly an hour after us. We travelled for a matter of two and a half hours, perhaps six or seven miles, and had a difficult time crossing a series of steep and quite high 'bunds' (to trap rain water during occasional storms and grow a crop) near one village. It was quite warm and the dun-coloured dog cooled himself in a pool left by a storm but the black and tan bitch didn't join in. Both dogs have cropped ears to help avoid injury during fights. The female is a gentle animal but neither is treated as a pet and seem to enjoy no regular meals, merely surviving somehow on a few scraps. Simply they are essential tools of the pastoral nomad, to warn against possible intruders and to guard the flock against wolves, not that there are many of these left nowadays.

On the way a couple of men from Loralai recognised me and stopped their jeep to ask if all was well. They knew me by name but I could not place them though no doubt they are relatives of Hashim Khan Luni. I got the impression that Ruziamat was rather intrigued that so many people know me. A.Y.K. tooted as he passed on his way to Hindubagh or Quetta yet again and as we travelled I saved a weakly kid on one of the donkeys when a large bag slipped onto its head. Our new camp site is about four hundred yards from the road but between two small peaks, making it seem more private than our previous ones. There was a stiff breeze blowing so that Ruziamat and his wife needed help in setting it up their 'kuzhdei'. After a warm morning, by mid-day clouds were again building up but there was no downpour although tremendous dust storms could be seen at intervals across the great valley. The kids and lambs, or 'junior flock' as I think of them, are loosed each day now but have enough sense to move into the shade of the 'kuzhdei' as the heat increases. Their tails have so fattened up since I have been with the family that they are now broader than their rear ends. A passing pigeon scared them during the day and I saw a fine harrier flying as we travelled. The main flock did not come in until seven p.m., when it was dusk. On a hillside near us are one or two what appear to be very small chrome ore digs, the smallest lumps of white ore looking exactly like python faeces. Later, during supper I was given what was called 'mastah' or yoghurt but it was not sour tasting and had a number of largish, slippery and somewhat un-nerving lumps in it. The lumps could have been the skin from boiled milk which my companions often lift off with a stick, roll up and eat with relish. Anyhow, mercifully perhaps, it was too dark to see the concoction and I had little choice other than to tip it back and think of England.

28/4/92 The main flock was brought in at five-thirty as usual and milked but we did not take tea, packing swiftly instead. Another lamb has died, apparently from some form of gastro-enteritis. I collected the flock from the nearby hillsides and then was burdened with driving them, helped after a while by Rahmatullah. We travelled at perhaps one mile per hour and it was a mentally withering task. On the way a minibus, including Asadullah among its occupants and heading for Quetta, stopped to say hullo. I suspect that everyone thinks my interest in the nomad way of life is decidedly odd and possibly they expect me to drop the idea any day now.

Further on we crossed the road with the flock, after which Ruziamat told me to go ahead with the donkeys that had now caught up with the junior flock and help set up the next camp. In other words, during the morning's travel we were split into three separate groups instead of the usual two: the adult flock, the junior flock and the donkeys with the baggage. It was an enormous relief to be freed from driving the young ones. The new camp was still on gravel, higher up the barely perceptible slope, and as soon as the 'kuzhdei' was up a fire was lit with small dry shrubs dug up with the adze by Ruziamat and 'poi chai' was made. It was the first of the day and very welcome as it was almost noon. After that Ziauddin helped me pitch my tent as it was blowing a stiff breeze. He's always helpful and quick on the uptake.

Having more or less re-united body and soul with several cups of well-sugared tea I explored ahead where the gravel ended and the fine white soil of the wide valley floor asserted itself to find a source of much-needed water. There were only isolated muddy pools and my sterilising tablets did nothing to improve the taste. After showing the spot to Bibi Ruziamat so that she could fill the goatskin water-bags, Ziauddin and I walked a mile or two ahead to the Zhob River. The earth cliffs on either side were at least thirty feet high in places and enclosed a sunken flood plain, perhaps half a mile broad or even more in places and well sprinkled with tamarisk saplings through which the shallow river meandered. We came upon a tortoise among them as we kept a wary eye on a succession of violent thunderstorms over the Spin Ghar three or four miles away. Returning to camp we found hot boiled rice waiting for us and ate it with just sugar and no milk.

Most of the young animals now recognise their own mothers instead of trying to suckle the nearest sheep or goat but one or two mothers actually reject their own young so that Ziauddin has to hold these mothers while the young suckle. I notice that Bibi Ruziamat filters the milk through fine cloth always but otherwise hygiene does not exist. Ruziamat now joins me in taking sugar with the 'poi chai' instead of chewing a lump of 'gurr' but I had to teach him to stir it using a thin piece of stick as a spoon. After a meal of 'pasti' and hot milk with salt, in the evening there was a long discussion as to which route to take through the mountains. We almost escaped the rain but after dark a fierce wind hit us without warning.

29/4/92 We move on. I rose late at six a.m., hurriedly drank tea and packed. Ruziamat and Malanga set off early with the junior flock as it moves so slowly and I helped the two grown lads to load the donkeys. Having done that I hurried on ahead, realising that help would be needed to ferry the kids and lambs across the river although it was shallow and no more than forty or fifty feet wide. It was just as well that I did for the first animals to be carried across became desperate to rejoin the others on the near side and it took a lot of effort to prevent them from dashing into the water, though it was not deep. Similarly, as the numbers on the far side grew so those still to cross became desperate to join those already over the river and meant that I had to stay on the far bank while Malanga had to control those waiting to be ferried over, leaving only Ruziamat to carry animals across two at a time until Ziauddin suddenly appeared.

The main flock and donkeys then arrived and were simply driven across, helped by a Mir Khel Kakar whom we had met the previous day. He was a fine fellow and when his flock arrived, we in turn helped him to drive them across as they too were apprehensive of the water, after which several women and children appeared though I expected that some other men were elsewhere. They were heading for Kakar Khorrasan as well. Rahmatullah left his shoes at the crossing, supposedly by accident but I have a suspicion that, as they were very worn, he perhaps hoped that I might donate the spare pair that he had seen among my things. A Kharoti group with five or six camels also crossed the river about the same time as ourselves but did not need help. To have created its own broad mini valley well below the general level of the great valley indicates there must be tremendous floods at long intervals and flash floods at that. Ziauddin then took charge of the junior flock with Malanga while Ruziamat and I went ahead with the donkeys and Rahmatullah staying with the main flock.

After setting up camp and eating some biscuits that Ruziamat had bought in the tiny hamlet of Nissai, I went back to help Ziauddin, guessing that Malanga would be very tired. The boy was really weary and another group of nomads was giving them a hand. We are camped by a small watercourse and the air is full of the hum of dung beetles. The Spin Ghar rises only a mile or so ahead. Supper was milk tea followed by 'pasti' and yoghurt, which I ate with sugar to the puzzlement of the others. Small portions of 'spin landi' were handed around but, still able to be fussy, I declined the grimy offering without causing offence.

'Landi' is dried meat, a great favourite of mine, but 'spin landi' is made by boiling sheep's fat and pouring it into a sheep's stomach where it hardens and remains edible for weeks if not months.

30/4/92 We stayed put. After I had written up the day's events yesterday evening an extremely violent storm hit us, a hurricane bearing rain and hail. My tent was flooded and almost blown away as I held onto it desperately from within but fortunately I had largely protected my sleeping bag and vulnerable items with the tarpaulin. The small, almost insignificant water course a few yards away became an impassable wild torrent for about an hour while the storm raged and I was none too happy at the possibility of my aluminium V poles being struck by the lightning which flashed almost incessantly. In future, if a thunderstorm threatens I'll place my enamel mug over the spike of the V poles. The swift Fakirzai river a mile away to the south-west must have been deadly while it lasted. The lightning and thunder continued for much of the night but the gale abated and the rain lessened.

Upon waking at five thirty this morning I again baled out the tent as a result of more rain during the night but hot tea revived morale. Hills to the south-east, on the far side of the valley, were white with hail and would have been beautiful in the bright sun had I been less damp. Showers during the day made it difficult to dry things on the stunted shrubs around so that I was very relieved to hear that we are staying put for a second night. I now realise that the main problem with my tent was that the poles sank into the ground as it softened due to the rain so that the guys and cloth become slack and more vulnerable to such fierce winds. That cannot happen easily with a 'kuzhdei' as even the perimeter poles are well protected by the rear and front panels of cloth that are pinned on when necessary and of course Ruziamat had, with his indispensable little adze, dug a small channel uphill of the 'kuzhdei' to divert any water that might flood down from the hillside whenever a storm threatens us, banking the soil over the lower edges of the attached panels to prevent wind from entering and keep away any water that might cross the drainage channel.

Towards evening an itinerant trinket seller came to our camp, bearing a fair-sized tin box of cheap, shiny jewellery. He was an Afghan 'muajjar' or refugee, a rough-looking fellow but Ruziamat put him up for the night. Whether he managed to sell anything to my friends I do not know but at least he was given food and shelter for the night. Had he not met hospitality there was another nomad encampment about a mile to the west of us, near the Fakirzai river where it issues from the hills through the Kazha Tangi, the Kazha gorge. Rahmatullah's toe has been cut so I dressed it properly for him, at which he showed a touching faith in my medical prowess, but it was simply a case of my being a one-eyed man in the land of the blind.

During the afternoon a storm among the nearby peaks sent a small flash flood down the dry water course by our tents, its approach announced by a strange rustling sound, to be followed by the more familiar sound of rushing water as it increased in strength. Without warning Ruziamat called me urgently. Three of the donkeys had sunk up to their bellies in a deep mud hole by a ruined irrigation channel a few hundred yards away. They were already shivering by the time we arrived and were hopelessly trapped, almost to their bellies. As we began to dig them out a sturdy Kharot appeared and gave a hand. Using a short length of rope, the two men tugged so hard that I thought the animal's necks must dislocate but I released one leg after the other and we finally got them out one by one. Ruziamat still tends to regard me as an impractical, inexperienced townie and so was desperately anxious lest I got in too deep and became trapped as well, constantly telling me to be careful. To lose three donkeys would have been a disaster for him, not only immobilising us until replacements were purchased but almost certainly making it necessary to sell off a number of precious ewes to pay for them.

It hasn't been a good day for him in other ways for earlier in the afternoon the main flock went missing; Ziauddin and Rahmatullah who minding it together had fallen asleep. While they anxiously scoured the surrounding desert Ruziamat and I searched with my binoculars. His relief when the two lads hove into sight with the flock was as touching as it was understandable.

1/5/92 We stay put. I rose at five-thirty to find my tent dry but my left foot is sore from yesterday due to chafing by the damp leather of my chaplies. Our trinket seller left after tea and I packed hurriedly but soon learned that we are to remain here until tomorrow. Around the 'kuzhdei' I counted seventy large dung beetles, attracted by the plentiful droppings of the kids and lambs but there were none beyond a twenty yard radius. Shunshulla, Ruziamat's second son, is with us and he with Ziauddin and Rahmatullah went to Nissai bazaar or the far side of the valley. I sent a pre-paid aerogramme with them and it took some time for them to grasp the idea of giving it to the post office there. I also gave them money for sugar. Bibi Ruziamat washed a lot of clothes today, where possible draping them over short shrubs to dry.

After that I went off alone into the nearby hills for five hours to look for any unusual plants and mountain sheep. The main ranges behind are magnificent. Up several of the small valleys there were a number of stumpy though quite large trees yet not a sapling was to be seen so that when the old ones die eventually there will be no more. As all were loaded with young fruit and seeds I surmise that this is the result of heavy grazing by flocks and which ever way one looks across the wide valley floor one or more 'kuzhdei' are to be seen in the distance. To my astonishment I heard a cuckoo in the distance. I was also surprised to come upon a 'kuzhdei' only two or three hundred yards up a small, short valley into these outer hills.

Ruziamat has a cough and produced a bag of assorted medicines for me to identify, having hoarded them from previous times. However, I knew only two-thirds of them and none seemed suitable for his present problem. Both Malanga and I are a bit off colour also. There was a violent and very unpleasant but brief sandstorm in the evening. Just as I was going to sleep the donkeys stampeded and the two dogs went into a frenzy, then Ruziamat came to my tent frantically asking for my sheath knife as a wolf had been, or still was, trying to maraud the flock.

2/5/92 We stay put. I awoke to learn that a sheep had been injured during the wolf attack. The heavy fleece around its neck had prevented it from being killed but although it showed no signs of serious injury it was breathing rapidly and could not walk so we did not move on into the mountains. The Kharotis to the west of us set off at seven forty-five. After the usual 'rodeo' of separating the young animals from their mothers Ruziamat went to fetch a man reputed to be a specialist with sheep from a village two or three miles away. His verdict was not hopeful and the poor animal was sent off on the buyer's horse, to end up on plates no doubt. Rahmatullah had a filthy bandage on his cut toe so I made him throw it away and put on a proper dressing for him.

Because of delay due to the injured sheep we remain here until tomorrow. This being the case, with four rolls of film exposed already, I decided to go to Kila Saifulla, taking about two hours to reach the main road along the other side of the valley. I was soon aboard a pick-up but had to wait for the Post Office to open. Met Nasserullah Khan Luni from Loralai in the bazaar and had tea with him. When the P.O. opened the Postmaster did not have any registered envelopes nor did he know the registration fee and as it was Saturday, a half-day, he could not 'phone Hindubagh or Quetta. I then got a bus to Tarwal and left the rolls of film with Reza Shah, A.Y.K.'s youngest son, as A.Y.K. was away in Quetta. I had no sooner returned to the main road when an acquaintance gave me a lift back to Kila Saifulla. Having located the driver of a bus due to leave for Nissai on my behalf, he then insisted upon giving me a meal of rich stew. Having had only tea and half a cup of sweetened yoghurt in the morning, as it was nearly four in the afternoon by then, it was a meal from paradise.

On the bus back I met an agricultural officer, with an M.Sc. degree, running a model farm project near Nissai growing pomegranates and other fruits plus crops. He said that Baluchistan was becoming warmer but confused the ozone layer as being the cause rather than the greenhouse effect. The Zhob river becomes perennial about here, being greatly reinforced by the Fakirzai river flowing in from the west a bit lower down. Saw several hoopoes, a vulture and a falcon during the two-hour walk across the valley to our camp, fording the Fakirzai at a small rapid. It's a fine stream with a good flow and some deep pools. Ruziamat was alone, apart from his wife and the two small boys. He had had a hard day so he positively beamed when I returned, and he is not greatly given to beaming. He had just returned from some distant village with a goat for the flock, to replace the injured sheep. However, I had a fever and took two chloroquines in the hope that it might inhibit any protozoan infection or fend off malaria, though the cause was unlikely to be the latter but a few cases do occur in Zhob, and went to bed soon after dark.

3/5/92 We move into the hills at last. I heard Ruziamat at four a.m., and was already up at five-thirty when he called me. I had almost packed by the time tea was ready and the 'kuzhdei' was dismantled the moment we had drunk it. As the others loaded the donkeys, I rounded up the flock, which was some way off and in the wrong direction for the valley we were to travel. I had got them to the mouth of the valley when the donkeys caught up and I then left that tiresome work to Rahmatullah. The 'junior' flock had set off earlier with Ruziamat and Malanga at six-thirty.

We were taking a short cut and the going was steep, probably rising to 7,500 feet, so that the donkeys had to be chided much of the way. For some reason, several loads slipped and we had to dash forwards to lift them back into place as the animals continued walking, and where the going was more level the pack animals would wander off course. The track was often narrow when descending the far side and was so steep in places as to be genuinely risky for the laden animals, though not for the two half-grown ones who are not burdened as yet. A man joined us part of the way, a very pleasant fellow. After some three hours we reached our new camp site near the mouth of a valley, just below its junction with another smaller valley that led into a small gorge from which came a good flow of water. However, a strong wind funnels into our valley bearing too much sand and grit for comfort. We can hear the occasional faint murmur of lorries travelling on the road about a mile away and out of sight. It links Nissai with Ghazluna and Badani in Kakar Khorrasan and therefore many of the trucks are probably laden with smuggled goods. The dominant plant here is artemesia, I believe, a highly aromatic dwarf shrub which the flock eats with relish but which makes their breath quite overpowering at close quarters when holding them to be milked. Its name in Pashtu is 'turkha' or 'tirkha', according to dialect.

Ruziamat was uneasy when I pitched my tent on the other side of our little valley, some distance from them, suggesting that there might be robbers about, so later I went to sleep with my pistol strapped to me and with a round in the barrel. I also placed my knife ready in case a quick exit through the back was advisable. The nearby stream, although very shallow, contained many silvery fish up to six inches long, not to mention numerous frogs. I walked some way up the impressive little gorge from which it flowed to scan the surrounding peaks with binoculars in the hope of seeing mountain sheep or even markhor but without luck. Thirty years ago these peaks would have supported dozens of the former and a good few of the latter. The best part about our camp site was that the generous flow of clear water allowed me to wash myself and some clothes. At the bottom end of our valley is a marvellous peak that towers over everything. Its name is 'Yau Harshk', literally meaning 'one peak', and approaches nine thousand feet in altitude. It is needle-sharp and A.Y.K. told me that many years ago an adventurous Jogezai climbed to its summit with a small bundle of sticks to make smoke and so prove his remarkable feat. From the Valley road it is a distinctive landmark.

4/5/92   We move on. Rising at five-thirty I was surprised to see the 'kuzhdei' side panel already detached so I packed immediately and took tea in the open as the 'kuzhdei' itself was dismantled, glad of the fire embers as a cold wind blew from the Hindu Kush far to the north-west. I was told that during the night a wolf, presumably another one, took a sheep by its throat but the thick wool saved it until the wolf was driven off. Ruziamat and Malanga set off with the junior flock at six-fifteen but I had to wait another half an hour until my tent dried out. Being unsure of the route, it was with some relief that I caught up with them on the dirt road. Ruziamat went back when the donkeys came up behind in the sole charge of his wife as both Ziauddin and Rahmatullah were also needed to control the main flock when it reached the road in case a lorry should come. This left me with the junior flock, helped by Malanga. By the Fakirzai, which we had joined, I was intrigued to see the boy pick up a piece of 'pasti' someone had dropped and, without even brushing it, eat it. It was interesting to see that the kids instinctively climbed any nearby bank or rock outcrop while the lambs kept to the road.
  A mile or two on I forded the river to join Ruziamat and his

wife on the old road, Malanga being in sight in case of any emergency. Ruziamat pointed out a colony of beautiful yellow 'shedzenar' lilies (Eremurus stenophyllos) in a hollow in the hillside and I took some photographs. He also pointed out a small bird resembling a redstart so he's warming to me and my interests. Shortly afterwards I stopped to photograph a man with two women ferrying lambs across the river. They were some way below me but he became so angry that I had to desist. We then forded the river again where the old road ended abruptly, having been washed away by the river. The flow was quite swift and Ruziamat actually helped his wife across. After walking for about three hours we set up camp in a delightful spot on an ancient river terrace well above the river, on the other side of which rose a great mountain ridge. About a mile downriver are three 'kuzhdei' belonging to Kakars. Ruziamat lay down in the sun: probably a bit off-colour like me and one of my feet is very sore.

Once camp had been set up we had food: 'pasti', yoghurt and tea but I was longing for dahl or, better still, meat. After that I went ahead three or four miles to some low hills with black dykes jutting out just in case there might be garnets in the rock. Having again heard the cuckoo in the morning, I now saw it fly from a nearby tree. There are two Pashtu names for it: 'kook' and 'kookoi'. When exploring several dry torrent beds leading into the steep, high mountain ridge only half a mile away I saw 4WD vehicle tracks, which could only mean hunters – coupled with the ubiquitous kalashnikov that explains the demise of almost all the game. High on the mountain ridge opposite us, using the binoculars I could see large tufts of brilliant yellow flowers but it would have been a long climb and looked rather tricky. The river is crystal clear and blue in the deeper pools. Late afternoon clouds formed but there was no sign of a storm.

5/5/92 Moving on again. Unusually for me I had a fitful night but rose at the usual time and packed immediately upon hearing the 'kuzhdei' poles being thrown down. I then helped bring in and load the donkeys before 'enduring' a mug of unsweetened tea as the sugar had been packed away. The junior flock left early and kept to the left / near bank of the river but we with the donkeys took a more direct route and forded it twice. Before finally leaving the river, Bibi Ruziamat filled three or four gallons of water into a goatskin bag, telling me that the water ahead was 'trikh' or bitter. At the top of a low pass she prayed briefly at a 'ziarat' or shrine with its bits of rag on poles and a striped banner representing a religious political party. Descending the far side of the pass, on both sides of the tiny stream the ground was white with mineral salts, probably gypsum, as she had warned.

A mile or two on we crossed a flat sandy valley with hundreds of what resembled wild rhubarb plants, each with a single pair of enormous leaves on thick reddish stems lying flat on the ground. No doubt they will re-inflate with water during the night, like the melon leaves in Iran. They were by far the dominant species. However, they were not at all acidic and tasted unpleasantly sulphurous when I cautiously tried one. There were also a few black-eyed poppies and by tamarisk saplings in wet areas grew some obviously parasitic, rather sinister-looking spikes of somewhat fleshy, cream coloured flowers, possibly a species of Orobanche. I had seen them several days ago in the Zhob river flood valley. We finally camped near the junction of two barely perennial streams, each with eight- or nine-inch fish in their small, isolated pools. While collecting heavy slabs of rock to reinforce my tent pegs in case of a storm, I came across six scorpions. A man passing with another small group stopped to help Ruziamat set up the 'kuzhdei'. At this, his dog repeatedly and savagely attacked ours yet no one seemed to notice let alone intervene. I also found an enormous worm-like fossil in a large slab of limestone or lias rock and while we were travelling yesterday I collected a piece of fossil coral about the size of a fist which I will send to the University of Baluchistan in Quetta.

For a people so strictly moral and prudish, their open amusement when our two male donkeys try to mate with the females or even get an erection comes as a surprise. However, when our two long-eared Romeos gallop off in pursuit of the females of another nomad group, all fully loaded, then a mad chase ensues with sticks and stones to head them off before disaster happens. We have one lazy one, one perverse one that always tries to stray and one reliable one onto which baby Dwardi is always tied when travelling. Until this journey I had sympathy for donkeys as being a much abused species but gradually I have come to feel that sticks and donkeys are made for one another. At three p.m. we had boiled rice with a sprinkling of sugar and dahl was promised for the evening. However, an almost apocalyptic storm hit us. Lightning and a sudden wind warned of worse to follow and I got to my tent just in time to wrap up my sleeping bag, clothes and camera before the gale tore out my two main pegs, in spite of boulders to help anchor them, and the rain lashed down. I also placed my tin mug on top of the aluminium inverted V poles so not to attract lightning in such an exposed place.

I was hard put to prevent the tent from being blown away. For almost an hour I knelt in water, using my head and outstretched arms to hold the thing down, the gale driving the water through the cloth. It ended as abruptly as it had started and I now thought of Ziauddin or Rahmatullah who had been guarding the flock with only a cotton quilt as protection. After mopping up I went across to the others to see how they had fared in the onslaught. To my astonishment, as I entered the 'kuzhdei' I kicked up dust from the floor. And this is in spite of the fact that two of the roof panels are so loosely woven that one can clearly see the outline of nearby peaks through them. Long ago A.Y.K. had told me that only goats' hair is of any use as it absorbs water rapidly, swells and thus seals the cloth whereas sheep's wool is too greasy to do this. Now, he is very reliable in all that he says but I had only half-believed him in that detail. He is now fully vindicated. Also I have noticed that the family never refer to their tent as 'kuzhdei' but always as 'korr', meaning house or home. As we slurped our tea, Ruziamat promised me many large flowers in the mountains tomorrow: he's a kind man at heart.

I managed to pick up Indian news on my cheap little radio saying that sixty people had been killed by a rocket attack on Kabul: the work of Ghulbudin Hekmatyar? I had decided eight years ago that he would not be content to share power. My gun belt is coming unstitched and I failed to bring any repair materials with me.

6/5/92 We are to stay put. All of us rose late this morning and Ziauddin thought that we were going to stay put in order to dry out but Ruziamat decided otherwise and we set off at nearly nine o'clock. After two hours we reached the foot of the next high range and are camped by a stream that issues from an impressive gorge. We could now make tea for the first time and eat some 'pastis' from yesterday, both tents having to wait until this essential was over. It was so stony that I carried dozens of spades' full of gravel from the stream to make a satisfactory site for my tent, uncovering a couple of scorpions when collecting boulders to hold down the pegs, but the 'kuzhdei' was erected on an old site that was already cleared of stones. With only a few old home-made felt rugs on which to sit and sleep, a site without stones is virtually essential. I then set about carefully digging up several tuberous roots of the yellow 'shedzenar' lilies for myself, for an ex-Millfield colleague and for Kew if they so wish. The dominant plant now was a shrubby legume with yellow flowers forming large clumps. It also grows along the higher land just over the pass from Kila Saifulla towards Loralai but finished flowering there three weeks ago.

351

When Ziauddin came in he brought a bundle of genuine wild rhubarb which everyone peeled and ate raw. This confirmed that the plants seen yesterday were not wild rhubarb, these leaves being smaller and more shiny, the taste unmistakable. This ritual over, I explored the gorge ahead and saw another cuckoo. As it is clearly too late for them to reach Europe in time they must be breeding here and, as there are so many ground pipits or larks in the wider valleys and on the plains to act as foster parents, this is not entirely surprising. But where would they winter?

Dahl was cooked for the first time in the evening but not long enough to soften it fully. Upon my adding chilli powder to 'pep it up' a bit, Ziauddin decided to try but in spite of my warning was a bit too liberal with it. He paid the price of his incaution but joined in the general laughter. He's a super little chap. Looking into my mirror I saw filthy ears, stubble and a peeled nose: it was not a pretty sight. Before going to sleep I allowed myself the luxury of ten minutes listening to an English language broadcast on the radio. I have no spare batteries so these have to last.

7/5/92 Moving on. Up at five-thirty, a hurried walk to cover was immediately essential. After a quick cup of tea, Ruziamat and Malanga set off with the junior flock, the others loaded the donkeys and I herded the main flock up into the deep gorge until Rahmatullah caught up. I then hurried ahead and upon joining Ruziamat I helped him build a ramp of rock slabs for the donkeys in a tricky spot. The scenery is superb, with jagged peaks on all sides. At one point, where our donkeys were hemmed in by sheer cliffs on either side, there was a magnificent and high pinnacle as a backdrop but by the time I had my camera out the animals had rounded the next bend. It would have made a marvellous shot. Again, there were some sturdy mature trees but no saplings. On the steep zigzag climb to top of the pass we came upon a group with camels. The animals' soft feet suffered from the jagged stones everywhere on the track and were forced to rest every few yards so that we soon left them far behind.

Just over the col was small alp with a fine spring, where we all drank, and juniper trees grew so the altitude must have been around 8,000 feet, maybe more. For the first time I found some brilliant yellow alpine tulips in damp areas, mostly within thorn bushes where they are protected from passing flocks. In the valley beyond, colonies of them grew in the wet sand by small streams but grazing seems to have dwarfed them and they lacked flowers. There we forded a broad torrent, the Kundar River I believe, and set up camp off the trail a mile further on. Ruziamat was not at all well and virtually prostrated with dysentery and fever. Ziauddin soon arrived, at which he, his mother and I set up the 'kuzhdei' and Ruziamat could then lie in shade while tea and 'pasti' were prepared. From his collection of pills I prescribed four Entox tablets but feel sure that he took only one, keeping the rest 'in reserve'.

Bibi Ruziamat pointed out a tortoise by our camp and three magpies flew nearby, two old nests showing that they are resident here and have a local name, 'shin dootee'. Also there was a pair of ptarmigan-like birds on a rocky outcrop above us. After the tea I went off with the spade to collect some tulip bulbs and visited a summer village a little way down the river we had crossed. Some of the dwellings are only half-roofed, the open part to be covered by a 'kuzhdei' when the owners come up from lower areas for the summer. I met the 'chokidar' or watchman, a cheerful man who bravely spends the entire winter there, sometimes cut off from all else by deep snow for weeks at a time. Nearby were small, crudely walled fields of Lucerne with a scattering of fruit trees, irrigated by a leat leading from the river several hundred yards upstream. Also there were several acres of fine soil forming a flat terrace some yards above the river and too high to be irrigated so I guess that it is what is called 'khushk-aba', depending upon trapped rainfall to grow wheat or millet. Protected by a man-made thorn barrier around one house was a colony of beautiful cream-coloured tulips with yellow centres (Tulipa tarda?) that would take the place of honour in any rock garden back in England. There were also blue irises by the river as well as a delicate blue lily seen earlier. If able to stand the wet English climate all have a commercial potential for gardens.

Back in camp several migrating groups passed us and we had a visit by four men. Suddenly it was noticed that the black bitch was missing and Ziauddin walked back a mile or two to look for her but it was almost dark by then. I'll go with him over the pass and down into the gorge in the morning. My tent is on soft sand within a crude enclosure made from sandstone slabs, sheltered and comfortable, and beneath a solitary tree.

8/5/92 We stay put. Because of the altitude I was chilly during the night, in spite of the fact that my sleeping bag is supposed to be a four-season one. Also I had to drive away the donkeys when they tripped over the guy ropes at intervals. As we drank our tea in the morning several kids ran across the 'kuzhdei' at intervals and had to be chased away. Ruziamat is still far from well so we are to remain another night here. For my part: left foot and ankle sore, left big toe sore, right ankle sore, nail of second finger of each hand painful, nose peeling, lower lip cracking, and minor gut rot = having a wonderful time.

After tea Ziauddin and I went back over the col and down into the deep gorge. Near the bottom we found the bitch, desperately pleased to see us but unable to walk and whimpering pathetically. I gave her half of my piece of 'pasti' which she ate ravenously. Ziauddin at first thought that she had cut feet and bandaged them but I immediately realised that both her back legs were either broken or paralysed. However, there was no sign of injury or fracture due to a fall or a fight so the cause is mysterious. Ziauddin was clearly upset, although dogs are never treated as pets, and asked me to return so as to be alone when putting her out of her misery I presumed though I did not hear a shot. Climbing back up the pass I met up with a pleasant man and his wife and stayed with them, helping with their donkeys now and again. The woman was quite open and talkative and, surprisingly, they had no children. After that, during the course of the day three migrating groups passed our camp, the first of which we had seen earlier in the gorge with their camels when seeking the bitch. Ziauddin returned from our search with the second group. The short, fine winter undercoat of the goats is shedding and working its way to the surface of the long hair as strange 'clots' so that at first I wondered what it was. I believe that it is the so-called Angora wool, in which case Ruziamat is losing the opportunity to make a few more rupees.

9/5/92 Moving on again. The cockerel woke me early so that when Ruziamat called me at the usual hour, I was already up. Stomach rather more rebellious than usual and I suspect last night's large cup of yoghurt but who knows? Bibi Ruziamat and I had a troublesome time catching the cockerel after all was loaded onto the donkeys and both flocks had left. Shortly after setting off, a pair of cuckoos flew near us, one – presumably the male – apparently displaying to the other and something I have not seen before. Other families or groups were on the move and the first mile or two was gently downhill, during which Ruziamat suddenly appeared with a largish white dog on a length of rope, having purchased it for Rs.200 to replace the bitch. However, although coaxed with a piece of 'pasti' it somehow escaped later and ran back to its previous owners before we reached our next camping place, an undulating area of soft sand where pitching my tent was very difficult. There is a spring about four hundred yards away but the water is not good and in any case is visited by a host of different animals: namely sheep, goats, donkeys, camels, dogs, presumably jackals and possibly wolves. After only twenty yards or so it disappears into the sand. The area is full of a shrubby composite plant with yellow flowers but the 'shedzenar' lily with tall spikes of yellow flowers seen earlier has yet to bloom here. After he had retrieved the new dog from the other family I offered Ziauddin one rupee for every twenty seeds of the 'shedzenar' collected when ripe in a few weeks time and sent them to Ahmad Yar Khan at Tarwal. Water is near the surface in many places and there are a number of superb miniature blue irises here and there. After some 'pasti' and 'poi chai' I dismantled my pistol, cleaned out fine sand and oiled it thoroughly. It is a .32 Beretta instead of my Colt .357 magnum revolver, which I preferred when buying rugs for being lighter and more compact.

My left foot is so sore that I must wear shoes for a day or two, my chapplis chafing badly at present. Ziauddin says that Badani is only four days ahead but I find that hard to believe. During the afternoon a truck from the road, which is out of sight but not far away, drove up the dry, sandy watercourse near us. This was very puzzling and when I questioned what they might be after, Ziauddin commented 'ghal' or thief though what they might steal is a mystery unless they happen to be rustlers. More likely they were smugglers but I didn't know the Pashtu word.

Bibi Ruziamat muttered to herself and cried quietly after Ruziamat, being feverish and more crotchety than usual, shouted at her in the evening. For the rest of the evening she turned her back on us and maintained a dignified silence. There is no affectionate contact between her and Ruziamat or between her and the sons, including Malanga, and I guess that she is very lonely. In part this is because she is not bright enough or bold enough to improve her situation and of course it would be improper in the eyes of her family for her to visit other nomad families. She doesn't even cuddle little Dwardi or play with him.

Apart from going off to fetch water she is a virtual prisoner in the 'kuzhdei' and I feel quite sorry for her.

10/5/92 We continue west. Perhaps a single Aquaclear tablet was insufficient for the spring water although I managed to reach cover just in time upon rising at five-fifteen. On the other hand perhaps the water from the sad spring contained Epsom salts. We were away by seven-fifteen and soon joined the Nissai-Badani road, a mere track and a rocky, wet one too in a miniature gorge a mile or two on. We came upon two young girls driving a flock of kids and lambs and further on among the low hills there was an isolated, tiny, one-roomed, mud 'hotal' at a spot called Sinzele. Upon entering the undulating plain beyond this range of hills, Ruziamat and I diverted from the road with a couple of donkeys through a series of low, rocky ridges to a fine spring that he knew to fill two goatskin water bags as the intended camping spot ahead was dry. The others kept to the gravel road.

Upon arriving at our camp site Ruziamat again flopped out but only after shouting at his wife who again cried. Then she and I began setting up the 'kuzhdei', to be helped by Ziauddin when he arrived shortly afterwards. While drinking tea at twelve-thirty it suddenly struck me that it was around eight in the morning at home and that Sheila, five or so thousand miles away, might also be drinking tea at that very moment before leaving for work. The chosen site overlooked the nearby road and I had to spend almost three hours preparing a site for my tent, levelling the ground, removing the larger stones and bringing in some sand. As usual the family's 'kuzhdei' was on a regularly used site and almost devoid of stones. Three trucks heading for Badani, whose blaring radios were heard long before we could see the source, saw my tent and stopped to ask who I was. After tea I walked the two miles back to the spring to have a wash and shave, taking care not to pollute its excellent water. On my way back I drank the entire litre from my army water bottle as it was a pleasantly warm day. I met several people during my return and had chats with them, mainly answering questions about myself but I always ask their tribe and clan or section. Along the road large dung beetles were frenziedly rolling balls of dung considerable distances with their back legs, up and over the low roadside bank until they came upon a patch of soil where they would excavate a shallow hole, pull their dung ball into it and continue digging beneath it so that it slowly descends after them until lost from sight. Judging from the way they home in on our camp, or the road when a flock has recently passed, it seems that they have a remarkable sense of smell. The rolling desert here is very stony and the broad torrent bed near our camp is bone dry but the blue lilies seem to like the area and I was astonished to see two quite large white toadstools or types of mushroom. Having already eaten a deliciously warm 'pasti' at around four p.m. I took only milk in the evening but without a pinch of salt like the others.

11/5/92 We continue west. Not-too-serious gut-rot woke me at five o'clock. After packing my own things I helped load the donkeys and we were away at the usual time. The 'night shift' dung beetles, the smaller species, were about in numbers as we took our morning tea so perhaps the supply of fresh dung is not quite up to demand here. For the first mile or two when setting off, if Ziauddin is with the donkeys he is always exuberant, singing away and exhorting the donkeys to greater speed in a strange and characteristic way. His good nature and enthusiasm are quite infectious. On the way we passed through the tiny village of Surr, supported by a small stream and unusual because of the relatively enormous headstones in the graveyard there – large, un-hewn, unmarked, natural splinters, some six feet tall. Beyond there, along a particularly uneven stretch of road, a Shinwari group with a swaying trailer piled high with tents and other possessions passed us, towed by a tractor Their speed was only twice our own pace. They were shortly followed by a Kharoti family travelling similarly, with the women and children sitting on top of everything. Ziauddin identified them, not I, though I don't know how.

We are camped four hundred yards short of the tiny hamlet of Spinkai near a river bed with isolated pools of water where white patches of mineral deposit on the sand and gravel show it to be undrinkable. We therefore took a couple of donkeys to fill two goatskin water bags from a small sweet-water spring just above the hamlet, both hidden from us by a low ridge of sandstone. We then had some black tea. Spinkai boasts a tiny 'hotal' and a tiny shop. I again spread sand and gravel from the river bed before pitching my tent, the ground being very stony. When shaving in one of the pools it was almost impossible to create a lather as there was so much calcium or magnesium in the water.

It was surprisingly warm today and I drank a litre of water, after duly treating it with a double dose of Aquaclear, before exploring a low escarpment two or so miles south of our camp. I notice that both children have diarrhoea, as has Ruziamat. For my part an encouraging sign today was that after the usual 'dawn dash', which was less urgent than for some days past, there was no second call during the entire day. Behind the lip of the escarpment a desolate plateau extended to a range of mountains perhaps eight miles away to the south-east. There was not a tree to be seen anywhere. The new dog ran away yet again, driven by the constant bullying of the family dog and perhaps further encouraged by hunger, for it seemed to be rarely fed. I doubt whether it will be retrieved this time.

In the 'kuzhdei' after dark I brought out my cheap radio-cassette, thanks to Esso 'tiger' tokens back in England, and recorded both Ruziamat and Ziauddin singing traditional songs. This created great excitement and they all listened with rapt attention when I played it all back to them. There are promises of a full repertoire tomorrow. Their pleasure at hearing their own voices was wonderful. I wish I had a good recorder as many, if not most of these traditional songs will be lost in the not-too-distant future on account of the cheap Japanese portables seen and heard in so many places as they churn out the trashy, nasal, Urdu pop music that blights so many bazaars. The Pashtun and Afghan music from Peshawar and Kabul tends to be raucous and is only marginally better. Further, while the 'rebab' is still generally used as an accompaniment, with or without the 'dole' or large drum, there is a trend to use the harmonium and even weird electronic sounds as well.

12/5/92 Rising at five-fifteen I could actually stroll to cover so by nightfall all should be well internally and the yoghurt I again ate last night is exonerated. There are numerous low ridges of vertically outcropping sandstone around us, all swarming with quite large lizards that bob their heads much of the time. Ziauddin says that their name is 'ghadam' as they appear to be praying: I counted six in as many metres along one ridge. Small skinks also abound but shun the rocky outcrops. To my surprise there are few birds other than larks or pipits, whose nests have eggs or young now. We have not seen a bird of prey since leaving Zhob while the cuckoos and magpies also seem to shun this area but as there is hardly a tree that is not surprising.

My gun belt stitching was so frayed and loose that in the morning I borrowed a needle and thread from Bibi R. to repair it temporarily. Later Ziauddin came to my tent for a chat while I was thoroughly cleaning my camera and patiently answered my endless questions. His father's sheep he calls Pakistani, saying that they are not of the Karakuli, Kandahari or Ghalzai breed. As they are fat-tailed I suspect that he is mistaken. A good animal is worth around Rs.1,000 or roughly £25 sterling at that time while a poor one might fetch only half that sum. He reckoned that Badani is only thirty miles ahead but is not so warm. He says that the only road to and from Badani is the Nissai one which we have followed at intervals and that there is no connection with Kammaruddin Karez, Palezgir Karez or Fort Sandeman.

Ruziamat has a slight fever and insists on smoking although he is coughing. He complains of aches in his legs and of stomach trouble but refuses to take full dose of Entox, just as before. These days he often prepares an enamel pot of tea for the two of us in the afternoon, which we sip from 'pialas', small bowls without handles, and he has grasped the idea of stirring it with a small twig when using sugar. With lumps of 'gurr' of course this would be pointless as one chews it while drinking, and if put into a bowl of tea it would hardly dissolve in any case. Both he and his wife are really very considerate and now when we take tea they present me with a small twig which we jokingly call a 'chamcha' or spoon. Also Bibi R. calls me whenever she is baking 'pasties', knowing that I prefer them when they are warm from the griddle. When they are cold I dunk them in my tea. I shall be quite sorry when we have to part. Another idea I introduced was hanging the little storm lantern from one of the central poles when tethering the kids and lambs after dark to provide more light. Previously it was simply placed on the ground in the 'kuzhdei' so that it was of limited help. In the afternoon I again recorded Ziauddin singing but he seems rather anxious and, unlike his father, he tends to sing much too fast. Rahmatullah does not want to be recorded, from shyness I think. A thunder storm threatened in the evening and we dug trenches to protect both our tents, made earth banks and weighed down the 'kuzhdei' rear panel and my tent pegs with small boulders as the usual precaution but in the end it virtually missed us. The local shopkeeper called in the evening, an alert, largish man.

13/5/92 We stay put. It was raining lightly and I did not awake until six a.m. and as my gut is almost normal I could remain

361

in my sleeping bag for another half an hour. After that I enjoyed half a hot 'pasti' and 'poi chai', the shopkeeper being with us still. The flock came in late and I helped catch and hold them for milking as usual. Because of the abundance of artemesia here their breath is quite overpowering at close quarters. Separating the junior flock from the main flock afterwards has become an easier business, both groups having more or less learnt to accept the separation each day. However, the junior flock also go out during the day now for a nibble.

Another man dropped in and shared a breakfast of torn 'pasti' soaked in yoghurt with Ruziamat and the shopkeeper. The latter was said by Ziauddin to be a good singer but would not oblige me. The cockerel was sold to the Spinkai 'hotal' today, having more or less completed his role now that the mornings are lighter. As the kids and lambs have doubled in size he could no longer be spiteful towards them but he was becoming more and more obstinate when it came to flying up onto his donkey whenever we moved on and that sealed his fate. The two or three 'lead sheep' in the flock wear a bell so that the flock can be more easily located in hilly country, while others have two or three bits of bright cloth tied to their tails for good luck. One has a bright woollen tassel at its neck and another has a tiny tortoise shell hung around its neck: the latter to ensure the well-being of the flock I was told. The two children wear little leather triangles containing prayers written by a mullah for the same reason. In such a dry landscape I would not expect liver flukes or other parasites but several sheep are coughing frequently and so may have lung worms.

Bibi Ruziamat undid her plaits today to wash her hair so I gave her a small nylon comb from the airline although she has a large comb already. She carried a water bag all the way from the spring so, as they must hold six gallons give or take, then she must have been carrying something like sixty pounds or twenty-eight kilos and I wondered how she managed alone to get it up onto her back. For lunch we had rice boiled in water, which the others ate with a sprinkling of sugar but I ate my helping with chilli powder and salt. In the afternoon I came upon what appeared to be a genuine mushroom but Rahmatullah kicked it before I could get a photograph. Returning to our camp I was dismayed to hear that the shop has no sugar and ours is almost finished, nor has it any tea or biscuits – not that we indulge in many of these and in any case they are generally so sweet as to be sickly.

For the evening meal the sheep's stomach, blackened by smoke and containing 'spin landi' was brought down from its 'kuzhdei' pole and its contents smeared on the 'pasties' as they baked. My previous reservation was forgotten and I found the result was delicious, so much so that I ate one and a half 'pasties' whereas half or sometimes a whole one is usually sufficient. After food I recorded more songs: on tape I have 'Kakarai', the 'Uttan', 'Sher Jan' whom we already know and one about Nawab Jogezai. There was a tremendous display of lightning from three simultaneous storms but all missed us.

14/5/92 We travel on. I was woken very early by donkeys near my tent and got up to chase them away as they often fail to see the thin nylon guy cords. I am pleased when Ruziamat calls me for it means that we are moving on. After our usual 'poi chai' we packed and were soon off. Passing the 'hotal', I bought and shared a couple of cold 'pastis'. In filling a couple of water bags for our next camp one skin split beyond repair. Lifting them onto donkeys needs two men so Bibi Ruziamat's solo performance is impressive. After that I was left with Malanga to bring along the junior flock, a slow and unbelievably tedious chore. On the way we saw a baby tortoise the size of a small bar of soap and a thin snake that shot off at impressive speed but about which I kept quiet, knowing what would happen to it otherwise. Everywhere in the sand were lizard tracks. Eventually we saw a group with donkeys far to our right, heading in more or less in the opposite direction to us until they shortly stopped but Malanga said that it was ours. As our party's tracks led straight ahead I argued with him but finally realised that our 'korr', as he put it, was there. It transpired that they had missed the site initially and had been forced to do a U-turn.

As I pitched my tent within a small dilapidated compound of vertical slabs of sandstone let into the ground, another storm threatened. Ziauddin showed me a magnificent specimen of the two-leaved plant resembling rhubarb in full flower after which I photographed other plants also in flower, one of which was almost certainly a type of chive. After dark I had just settled down for the night when distant shouting was heard, followed moments later by a loud shot. Instantly Ruziamat called me but I was already getting dressed again. This done I quickly filled the pistol magazine, as I usually keep only four cartridges in it to preserve the spring, and ran off silently into the dark towards the disturbance in case there was trouble with rustlers. In the cold, still night air it was easy to locate the flock and the two lads about three-quarters of a mile away. All was well by then but a wolf had attacked the flock and had been driven off without any real damage on either side. Where wolves manage to hide in such open country, when every hand is against them and so many men have rifles, is a mystery to me. Anyway it added a bit of sparkle to the journey so far as I was concerned. With the mountain sheep and antelope virtually wiped out, I have considerable sympathy for the wolves but such a view is less than fashionable here.

15/5/92 The family stays put. The morning was bleak, a cold, fierce wind bringing light rain when Ruziamat and I set off at a brisk pace for Ghazlunawar on the border. I soon found that we were camped on a slightly raised plateau and after an hour or so we passed the hamlet of Mirza Khan Sahib set in the middle of nowhere on the plain below. The Ghazluna Police Thana on its solitary hill was just visible on the far side of the plain and to its left was a long and quite impressive mountain ridge that lay just within Afghanistan. Another hour and a half brought us to Ghazlunawar, at least ten miles from our camp. The police 'thana' also houses the Customs post, is quite large and built of mud, resembling a Beau Geste fort. I guess that it was built by some chief initially but do not know. The tiny shop did not have the flour urgently needed, nor did it have any sugar but a friend of Ruziamat nearby prepared black tea for us, enlivened by sucking some fruit drop sweets with it. Although the weather was now fine, it became clear that the wet state of the road would probably halt for a time all lorries heading for Badani whereupon Ruziamat decided to press on to his brother's village 'two miles away'. For the next two hours or so we crossed a parallel series of low, jagged sandstone ridges, by which time I was entertaining all sorts of wild notions, until suddenly we came upon a small gorge where we chanced upon a young nephew of his. He joined us and less than a mile further on we reached the tiny village, Jabbar Kuli, set in a deep hollow amid the hills and with tiny plots of wheat containing scattered fruit trees, all watered by an ingenious system of leats. There were twelve houses and eight 'kuzhdei' there, all up a small side valley.

His cousin, Haji Nazur Mohammad, was clearly doing well by local standards and we were installed in his guest room where he had one of the largest and finest kilims or flat weaves that I have ever seen, beautifully patterned and further decorated by rows of small cowry shells, so loved by many Afghans and Pashtuns but especially by nomads. Told that it had been made by Afghan weavers in the village, I asked to meet them, hoping to place an order and happy to pay for their superb artistry and workmanship: however, they were not in the village now but back in Afghanistan. Anxious to photograph such an interesting village and its surroundings, the older teenage son was deputed to show me around, together with a friend. He insisted that we first climb a nearby peak and foolishly I agreed. We were no sooner near the summit than a violent storm struck and we had to shelter beneath a huge boulder for half an hour. Pulling out a matchbox containing a scorpion they amused themselves as we waited by tormenting it. Everywhere was awash and as I was wearing my one good pair of suede shoes instead of more robust chapplis I was none too pleased. Back down in the narrow valley the gentle stream that Ruziamat and I had followed earlier was now a brown torrent, to be forded carefully in view of the expensive camera with me.

In the evening we enjoyed some excellent 'shorwa'. The 'landi' that followed was wonderful and satisfied a long-felt desire for something more substantial than bread and 'poi chai' or yoghurt or hot milk. Ruziamat clearly enjoyed seeing his relatives again but even a cursory glance at their far more comfortable condition must at least make his sons think long and hard about continuing a nomadic life. In the evening we were joined by Ruziamat's brother, mullah Baki Shahizai, whom I found to be ego-centric, bigoted and arrogant beyond words: the very antithesis of mullah Rehmat Tan in Kila Saifulla. For reasons better known to him he was distinctly hostile towards me and tried to belittle me. Perhaps he regarded me as a threat to his monopoly of 'superior knowledge' as he clearly considered himself to be the intellectual leader of the village, and maybe beyond the village. I was therefore glad when it was time to sleep, especially as my clothes were still quite damp and I felt none too warm.

16/5/92 Ruziamat and I visit Badani. We had tea before dawn and I was given hot water to wash my face: what indescribably luxury. As Ruziamat and I waited by the little 'madrassa' or school at the lower end of the village for a jeep to Badani, the noxious mullah joined us and demanded that I take his photograph. The sun had not yet reached this secluded valley and the light too poor as my film was only 25 ASA and I was happy for this excuse to refuse him in a way that brooked no argument. The jeep was late and, when we went to the house of its owner, we discovered that its battery was flat but it roared into life quickly enough when pushed down the steep slope. For the first mile or so the valley was a little broader and we followed the bed of its stream, now returned to its more usual trickle, rather than the rough jeep track until forced to head away from it for Badani. Several side valleys were full of the golden spikes of 'shedzenar' lilies and I hope that Ziauddin can be persuaded to collect ripe seeds for payment. Further on, we crossed innumerable low ridges until we arrived in Badani after some eight or ten miles.

Few shops were open as yet so I had ample time to explore the three main bazaars that form a triangle, all the buildings being single-storied. I was surprised how large the place was so Ruziamat's nephew met in Zhob was correct after all. It also has a small hospital and apparently has some Europeans among its staff. The large lorry park contained several Afghan trucks, their bodywork being much lower and barely decorated so that one could easily distinguish them from the high, ornate Pakistani ones with their prow over the cab shaped like the stern of an old galleon. Down the centre of one of the bazaars ran a stream and when I came upon some men sacking up dried apricots from a huge pile brought over the border from Afghanistan (just a mile or two away I was told) I was promptly given a generous handful, my obvious enjoyment of which pleased my benefactors. The thing that really signified the proximity of Afghanistan were the red-legged partridges here and there kept in little conical cages made of split bamboo, a practice rarely seen elsewhere Pakistan. Their distinctive call during the heat of the day always reminds me of Afghan bazaars.

Returning to where I had left Ruziamat chatting, shops were opening and men squatted in the sun to enjoy its warmth. As souvenirs for friends in England I sought to buy a quantity of 'spurrkhai', the blacksmith-made iron pins used to attach the rear, front and end panels on 'kuzhdei' but we could find only four and they were rather poor specimens so Ruziamat told me to leave them, though unable to comprehend why on earth I should want such things as presents for my friends. I have decided to get some made in Kila Saifulla or Loralai when I leave my Shahizai friends. We stocked up with five kilos of flour, five of sugar and half a kilo of tea, for which I naturally paid, each of us carrying a share in a small sacks over our shoulders. Ruziamat also bought some vermicide so I was right about lung worms infesting some of the flock.

Essential business over, enquiries suggested that no lorries were leaving for Ghazluna that day so we headed out into some low hills nearby to visit yet more relatives not seen for six months or more. Bor Mohammad was his cousin, a bright-looking chap who had already quit his mud house nearby to spend the summer as usual in a 'kuzhdei' pitched on top of a low, permanent, walled enclosure made of smallish slabs of stone. This way he and his family can enjoy the freedom and warmth of summer but when winter returns, with bitter winds sometimes sweeping down from the Hindu Kush, they can retreat into the gloom, their house once more, glass windows being almost unknown here. Thus they enjoy the best of both worlds. Needing to return with supplies to our camp, we ate a hurried meal, were shown a short cut to the winding road and briskly headed for Ghazlunawar, perhaps twenty-five or thirty miles away by the road which has to make considerable detours around the low but rugged hills we had crossed yesterday. We took one or two short cuts until I suggested that we generally keep to the road in case we missed a lorry. Having been passed by one lorry as it was packed, an hour and a half later we were in luck. Further on, at a 'hotal' about halfway, the driver stopped for lunch and we came upon more of Ruziamat's relatives. We had 'pasti' and sweet green tea then boarded another vehicle that was about to leave.

Hitherto the road had been tolerably good but from now on it was second gear for the next two hours, apart from three or four hundred yards in third gear. So poor was the road, a rather grandiose description for such a track, that first gear was necessary in places.

As we stopped at Ghazlunawar village eventually, a figure stepped forward to meet us. It was Ruziamat's eldest son, Khani Mohammad, who had been sent by Ahmad Yar Khan to deliver a letter from my wife. I immediately asked to pay his lorry fares but apparently that had been seen to by A.Y.K. It seems that A.Y.K. thinks I may be tempted to cross the border, in spite of having given my word, and wants me to return to Zhob but our journey is not yet completed. The finer points of the language quite elude me but I suspect that I am almost being ordered back to Kila Saifulla and that Khani Mohammad is a worried about being impolite in delivering an order from A.Y.K. He also is a very shy, diffident character like his brother Rahmatullah and when I wrote a brief note to A.Y.K. for him to take back he was visibly relieved. A policeman from the 'thana' on the hillock then came to the lorry and I saw the driver pass a small brick of hashish to him as a sort of 'toll' I presume.

Returning through Mirza Khan Sahib hamlet an hour and a half later, the three of us were invited in by Mohammad Nawaz Khan Jogezai and revived with hard boiled eggs, biscuits and 'poi chai'. At first I could not place him but he seemed to know me and finally it came out that he was the grandson of Musa Khan of Sharan Jogezai with whom I had spent many pleasant hours over thirty years earlier. At that time our host was a young boy and, a 'Ferangai' being a rare species in those parts, he had remembered me and no doubt had been told of my presence in the area. He recalled far more than I could as we reminisced haltingly but there, I have travelled a great deal since then. Time was not on our side and after we had left my two companions were beginning to tire so I asked their permission to go ahead, if only to keep warm in the cold wind. Kakar Khorrasan is renowned for its persistent and chilling winds and at over 8,000 feet they are rather fresh at the best of times. Arriving back at our camp, I was welcomed like a long-lost brother and was equally glad to see them. Also present as a guest was a small, wiry, almost pixyish man, by name Sattar Baburkazai. Extraordinarily, though far from young, he was a bachelor, an itinerant singer and quite a character. It seems that he travels from family to family, enjoying their hospitality, in return entertaining them; an altogether novel way of life in such a poor, desolate land. One could almost call him a hippy but I guess that his parents were unable to provide a 'wulwer' and he could not save enough to gain a bride. Our 'new' dog was back in camp once more, though for how long is anyone's guess.

Footnote: after my return to the U.K. I was puzzled at being unable to locate Badani on any of my other maps, Kashatu being the only place of any size shown not far from the border in that part of Kakar Khorrasan but by no means virtually on it. Enquiries by mail to A.Y.K. revealed that it was established in the early sixties as a "trading centre" by one, Loghuni, in all probability the rich and ancient nomad whom I met when he came steaming out of the desert from his camp in the Torr Ghar into Rod Jogezai while I was staying with Nasserullah Jan. Clearly it has thrived since then, largely as a smuggling centre from what I saw and heard.

17/5/92 A short forward move. After the usual morning tea with some pasti Sattar Baburkazai left us, having been too shy to let me record him. The rest of us set off in the direction of Ghazlunawar while Ruziamat set off back to Spinkai with a donkey to buy a large bag of flour, the five kilos we brought back yesterday merely being a stop-gap measure. We were away rather late, at eight o'clock, and to my surprise went only a couple of miles, down onto the wide plain bordering Afghanistan, perhaps only a hundred feet lower than the plateau we have just left. This new camp is atop a slight rise on the south-east edge of the plain and we can clearly see a village and fort to the north-west, just over the Afghan border from Ghazlunawar and perhaps ten or eleven miles distant. Widely separated black 'kuzhdei' are to be seen in every direction. The wind is chilly in spite of the sun, coming from the west and is quite strong, which made it difficult to pitch my tent but not the heavy and squat 'kuzhdei'. Little Dwardi is wearing nothing but a thin cotton smock yet seems oblivious to the cold. He is a sturdy little chap if ever and quite sweet at times. I must ask how many of their babies died within a year of birth.

Once the 'kuzhdei' was up, the usual shallow hearth was excavated, small dead and dry shrubs dug up and a fire lit so that tea could be prepared. Thus fortified I went off to locate two quite large pools that I had noted yesterday. They were about a mile away and I was surprised to find one of them murky, its outlet being full of tadpoles until it disappeared into the sandy soil after about twenty yards but the other, only a short distance away, was crystal clear. Both must be fed by springs. After collecting some dirty clothes from my tent, I washed them at the clear water hole, as usual taking care not to pollute it. Back in camp after this chore, when going to play some of my recordings to Shunshulla and a visitor later in the afternoon, I found the radio to be switched on and the tape reversed so I can guess who could not resist the temptation. Ziauddin covets the radio-cassette beyond words so I told him that it was his if he would collect two small 'piala' of ripe 'shedzenar' seeds in due course, an easy matter from what I saw near Jabbar Kuli, and deliver them to Ahmad Yar Khan in Kila Saifulla – with whom I would leave the thing. It's very relaxing sitting just within the wide open front of the 'kuzhdei' with a splendid panorama stretched out before us but sheltered from the incessant wind which starts up at around seven each day and continues until evening. The 'kuzhdei' gives a unique feeling of freedom combined with one of security as anyone approaching from the side or rear can easily be seen through the loosely woven cloth, while we inside are invisible to those approaching. Ruziamat called me to see a slender snake he had just killed at another old camp site a little way off. Its partner had escaped down a hole and certainly was not a dangerous saw scaled viper.

18/5/92 Disaster with donkey. One's priority in open, gently undulating country such as this is to find a sheltered spot to act as toilet when nature makes her urgent call as she will, sooner rather than later. I anticipate that there is no word for constipation in Pashtu. I was already awake at 5.30 when Ruziamat called me for we move on to Mirza Khan Sahib today, perhaps four or so miles away. The biting wind then induced me to eat an entire 'pasti' with the morning tea as we watched the sun rise. Shortly after tea it was decided not to move on today after all. Khani Mohammad left for Ghazlunawar at about eight-forty with a short letter from me to A.Y.K., obviously much relieved to have such a letter in his hand. He had been very insistent about having a note from me, though whether to confirm that Sheila's letter was delivered safely or to explain why I was not returning just yet I could not tell.

A while later Bibi Ruziamat asked me to show her the water hole in order to fill a goatskin water bag but, as the distance is considerable and the donkeys have nothing to do but eat and frolic, I got another water bag, plus a pannier net and back cloth, and suggested that we take a donkey. This was easier said than done as the donkeys had other ideas. After a fruitless ten minutes chasing the beasts, which finally sealed the fate of the two increasingly wayward males, Ziauddin arrived and swayed the balance in our favour. Going to the clear pool, Bibi Ruziamat tasted the water and declared it to be 'trikh' and it was, so we returned to the murky pool to fill our bags. Presumably the clear pool is thus simply because few if any animals or humans use it so that it is not disturbed.

During the morning Bibi Ruziamat mixed yoghurt and water in a goat skin suspended from a bamboo tripod, rocking it vigorously to make 'shlombai' to drink but when she poured it out there was a strong fermenting smell that was far from enticing. In any case I have bad memories of 'shlombai'. A clever little trick she has when baking 'pastis' is to smear the underside of the domed pan with mud just beforehand in order to prevent it sooting up. Around midday there was a sudden furore, with Rahmatullah wildly waving the adze in the air and shouting 'mar, mar' or snake. Just frantically I shouted 'sabbr, sabbr', meaning 'wait, wait' as I wanted to get a photograph but the snake was fast and went down a hole before I could get a shot. It was a magnificent specimen, a little under three feet long and quite plump, unlike the other pair. From its markings I wondered if it were a saw scaled viper although it seemed rather long for that. Anyhow, I blocked the hole with a large rock just in case.

As the two adult male donkeys were becoming increasingly bloody-minded, Ruziamat called in a man said to specialise in their castration. The entire family attended the operation, each animal in turn being immobilised with ropes around its legs and thrown to the ground. As a biologist I am not a particularly squeamish person but the way this 'specialist' carried out his work horrified me. He slit the scrotum neatly enough, with relatively little pain it seemed, but then he simply ripped out each testis in turn without troubling to cut the tubes and ligaments so that internal damage seemed a likely consequence. It was such a callous and ghastly business that I stopped taking photographs. There was no attempt to stitch them up afterwards and post-operative treatment consisted of throwing a few handfuls of water at the gaping wounds. The brown donkey walked off to join the others straight away but the white one refused to join the rest and was clearly in deep shock. In the evening it came to the 'kuzhdei', something it has never done before, finally entering it and having to be pushed out forcibly. I suggested giving it a 'pasti' to fortify it if possible but Ruziamat would not. I don't give much for its chances.

Both lads came to my tent this afternoon to ask me to get A.Y.K. to send a sack of flour by lorry from Kila Saifulla. My second contribution of flour has been only five kilos and probably my presence had caused the current shortage so I gladly agreed but upon offering Ruziamat Rs.400 for the purpose when he joined us shortly afterwards he flatly refused. After that some 'poza' was made in a bowl, though they called it 'posa' in their dialect. Milk that had been put aside in the morning was warmed then curdled into junket by stirring it with the equivalent of a spoonful of the dry, spherical seed capsules of the small 'khamazoogha' shrub (Withania coagulans) wrapped in a small piece of cotton cloth. As first I presumed that we would pour this into beakers to eat or drink, as we had no spoons, but Ruziamat and his wife then proceeded to press the junket repeatedly with their hands (unwashed for a day or two). Gradually, a whitish solid formed, leaving a yellowish green liquid. It was a bit of nomad luxury and I enjoyed my portion with sugar.

During the day we can see occasional lorries crawling across the plain from our side, where the track is about a mile and a half from our camp, to Ghazluna. The total distance is about ten miles and they take just over an hour to cover that distance if conditions are dry. For two or three days after rain it is impassable.

19/5/92 Seeking a lift. My first act this morning after the usual journey to cover, as dosing with Flagyl was helping but not curing fully, was to look for the white donkey and, sure enough, it lay dead a few yards from the 'kuzhdei'. In spite of its maddening behaviour over the past week or so I felt some sympathy for it. Moreover it is a serious financial loss to the family and also means that they are virtually stranded until a replacement can be purchased. After tea and 'pasti' three of us struggled to drag the corpse a couple of hundred yards away from our camp before the sun could bloat it.

Ruziamat had to go to Mirza Khan Sahib to buy flour if possible so I accompanied him. Two builders there were mixing mud for a new house with their bare feet but, perhaps not surprisingly in such a tiny hamlet, there was no flour available so we hurried on to Ghazlunawar, being joined on the way by the shopkeeper. In his tiny, windowless shop I bought tea, batteries and matches among other things but flour had not arrived yet. His arithmetic was as interesting as it was innocent. After being charged Rs.12 for half a kilo of boiled sweets I learnt that the price was Rs.14 per kilo, so I pointed out that the cost should have been Rs.7. At this he promptly refunded Rs.7 whereupon I returned Rs.2 to him.

We returned much of the way along the so-called Nissai road which split into several tracks here and there when the ruts and potholes became too hazardous for the occasional lorry. The road crossed several large dunes also, a laden lorry negotiating one just after us, jolting and swaying as it sent up a huge yellow cloud. Pashtun and Afghan men take uninhibited pleasure in pleasant smells and along the way we met a man sniffing a small sprig of artemesia as he walked. When we stopped to chat with him he promptly thrust it up one nostril so that he could talk without his hand being in the way yet still enjoy its scent. Not wishing to be intrusive I erred by failing to photograph this entertaining incident. Eventually we had to cut across the desert for our camp and in so doing saw two hares. I was astonished at the speed which they could maintain speed when crossing a patch or ridge of sand and there was the odd tortoise at intervals. Ruziamat began to tire towards the end and is clearly less than one hundred per cent health-wise but when considering the untreated water they drink every day and their poor diet this is hardly surprising. In camp tea, 'pasti' and 'shlombai revived us though the last was rather sour and I shall probably pay a price for this recklessness.

Clearly, without a replacement donkey, there is little chance of moving on for a day or two and my airline booking gets closer. Having a concession ticket, to miss my flight would mean its complete forfeiture so, although I very much wish to complete the journey with the family and see their summer quarters, this now seems so risky as to be virtually out of the question and I have decided to return to Zhob tomorrow. I explained this to the family as best I could and gave each a farewell present, pointedly and repeatedly saying that the money I was giving to Bibi R. was entirely hers to spend as she chose. I doubt very much is she has ever had any money of her own before and can only hope that they respect my wishes when I'm gone: but, with a donkey to replace, I am far from confident of that. I also gave her a new comb and soap box but they were trivial things. To Ziauddin I presented my stainless steel Norwegian knife, to Rahmatullah my Bannuchi chapplis and money to Ruziamat and the two young boys.

20/5/92 Hoping to go to Zhob. I rose at five a.m. and, as anticipated, the 'shlombai' made its mark. After the usual breakfast I packed everything ready for when a suitable lorry should be seen setting out from Ghazlunawar village or Ghazluna Thana on its hill and said farewell to Rahmatullah, whose turn it was to take out the flock after breakfast. To my surprise, as he always seems so non-committal and diffident, he displayed remarkable warmth for once and seemed quite upset at my departure. In turn I felt our impending separation far more than I had anticipated although secretly determined to see them all again within a few years.

During the day I counted sixteen trucks leaving Ghazlunawar but they all headed slowly left or south along the foot of the long mountain just over the border, bound for Quetta via Pishin according to Ruziamat, but nothing came heading south-east for Nissai. However, Ruziamat managed to intercept a lorry going to Badani along 'our' road and it turned out to belong to some relative so that he was able to order a sack of flour to be brought back within a day or two rather than go with it.

Being static allows a little culinary variety and Bibi Ruziamat prepared some butter by rocking a suspended goatskin of milk. Not only that but the addition of powder prepared from the root of that strange two-leaved plant that we see in places resulted in a brilliant yellow colour. However, the butter had a sour taste and I politely declined a second helping. With more time on their hands than usual, Ruziamat and his wife pulled out some dry but greenish tobacco leaves and ground them to powder on a slab of rock, finally adding some lime to make 'naswar', not to be smoked but taken in the mouth. What rather surprised me was that no one played either Katal or Roghmat, two 'board' games requiring merely a handful of small stones or short bits of stick to act as pieces and a patch of hard soil in which to mark out the lines of play.

In the afternoon everyone else slept in the 'kuzhdei' so I slipped across to the hole down which the snake had escaped two days ago. My attempt to block its hole had been futile for I found the animal basking beneath a small shrub. After taking several photographs while moving ever closer, I chased it down its hole but more for its own safety than anything else. Obviously it was a diurnal species and so would not crawl into the 'kuzhdei' during the night and possibly harm anyone, apart from which the nights are almost certainly too cold still. By evening it was clear that no lorry would be heading for Nissai so, rather than pitch my tent again, I made a low stone wall of rock slabs to act as a wind break for a bivouac. Such an arrangement would allow a dash to the road at dawn if necessary.

21/5/92 Leaving at last. Waiting and watching for eleven hours from our camp yesterday was both frustrating and worrying but an hour or so after breakfast this morning a truck was seen to leave the tiny hamlet of Mirza Khan Sahib and head for the Ghazlunawar-Nissai road, upon meeting which it turned left towards us. With Ziauddin I rushed to the road and as I was so burdened he went ahead to stop the vehicle. To my considerable disappointment it was going to Sharan Jogezai and not to Nissai, and to travel from there to Kila Saifulla would be even more difficult.

The family's new white dog had also positioned itself by the road though some way off, driven out yet again by the constant bullying of the established family dog, and was howling mournfully. Three or four hundred yards away another nomad family was encamped near the road and Ziauddin told me that one of the daughters was very beautiful but the dowry asked was a huge sum for most people around here let alone nomads. We waited there for almost three hours until a passer-by told us that the road to Nissai had been closed to traffic for five days. Apparently this had been done by the Customs in response to smuggling, in all probability meaning that the Customs were not getting a satisfactory cut of the profits. Obviously there was nothing for it but to hurry to the Ghazluna Thana, at which decision Ziauddin suggested that I leave my heavy rucsac at his friends 'kuzhdei' down the road and stop any lorry I was in to collect it in passing. In the event it was lucky that I turned down this tempting suggestion.

Walking flat out, I reached the road heading south-west some three hours later and just in time to intercept a small pick-up coming down from the Ghazluna Thana. However the driver was going to Hindubagh, not Nissai. I was not in a position to be choosey but I asked him if he were going via Afghanistan and pointed out that I did not have a visa. He was a little vague, perhaps even a little evasive in his reply and wanted Rs.200 for the journey. I offered Rs.100 and, after a brief attempt to extract more from me, he agreed and I climbed into the open back though a little uneasy as to our precise route. After perhaps two miles we passed a village with a small mud fort that flew the Afghan national flag but there was no turning back now. I'm fairly sure that it was Allah Jirga. A few miles further on we halted at a tiny place called Mobarez which boasted both a clinic and a 'hotal'. Upon entering the 'hotal' my camera gave me away and my presence aroused considerable curiosity but I was not quizzed as I ate my rice.

Until this point I had travelled in the open back, though squatting rather than sitting as the road was so rough. The driver and his two companions now decided that there was enough room in the cab for me also. All three were Turrakis from Afghanistan but were living and doing business in Kuchlagh, between Quetta and Chaman. One of them sang at intervals and had a superb voice, far superior to the traditional singers in Peshawar and Kabul, and I hoped to record him when we reached Hindubagh. I have no idea how successful was his business but it seemed a waste of enormous talent not to make commercial recordings of his voice. For a couple of hours we travelled along the foot of the mountain range that I had been admiring for the past week and at one point I was surprised to see what appeared to be the construction of a new 'karez' until I realised that, unlike Zhob, there was no electricity supply there to permit the use of boreholes so that the ancient method was the only one suitable. Finally the road veered due south at or near Loeband to cross the river and its swampy thickets of tamarisk that seemed to form the border.

Upon reaching the high ranges to the south we stopped once more at a little 'hotal' for tea. Whilst there a goat was grabbed and cheerfully slaughtered just across the road, to be ready for the evening meal. We had been travelling for about three hours so far and naively I thought that once over the range looming above us we would be in Hindubagh. As is so often the case, beyond that range was another and another and another so that it took us almost five more hours to reach Hindubagh. Juniper trees revealed the altitude to be over eight thousand feet and later a map showed the highest peak, Sakir, to be 10,931 feet / 3332 metres but the road surface was remarkably good and obviously recent. Even so care was needed in places and by one such drop we came upon two grossly overloaded pick-ups with a crowd of Hazaras, stranded because of a puncture. They were a rough lot and I could not follow what was said but it became abundantly clear that, very reluctantly, the Turrakis were coerced into lending their one and only spare wheel. The ringleader of the crowd opened my door and spoke to me but I was unable to understand him, if he was in fact speaking Pashtu, at which he made a sign of cutting a throat. It was one of those occasions when a pistol quietly tucked away out of sight becomes quite comforting. We also passed a number of nomad groups heading for Afghanistan, some with camels but most with tractors and trailers, this being a traditional migration route.

Sadly, it was evening when we reached Hindubagh and my companions were in a hurry to press on so that a recording was impossible. However, as the journey had been far longer than I had expected, I donated an extra Rs.25 as a token of thanks, having in any case bought them a meal at the second 'hotal'. Before parting I wrote down the driver's name and shop address in the Madina Market of Kuchlagh in the hope of tracing the singer at some future date. In the bazaar I wolfed down a plate of stew, my second in three weeks and the stuff that dreams are made of. A second plate followed immediately. When I had finished eating I was offered a bed for the night by one Khan Mohammad Durrani, but I explained that I hoped to reach Kila

Saifulla that night if possible. Enquiries soon convinced me that it was out of the question and I then accepted his kind offer. At his house, even though he had watched me eating a substantial meal, more food was set before me and my protests ignored, such is the tradition of hospitality. We spent a pleasant evening before the luxury of my first bed in weeks but I gained the impression that he was not enamoured of the Jogezais although he made no open criticism of them. From behind a curtain across the room's inner door, faint whispers revealed that I was being scrutinised by the women of the house.

22/5/92 Return to Tarwal. The driver of the first bus to arrive in the morning said that he was going to Fort Sandeman, which would mean passing Tarwal. On the way, at his request, I photographed him and his assistant in front of their gaudy little bus but at Kila Saifulla it was admitted that Loralai was his destination. A.Y.K. was not in the bazaar but my luck held for there was a pick-up heading for Fort Sandeman very soon. However, before it left I was invited into a large white tent beside the road and asked to sign a petition in support of the strike then in progress. Of course I knew nothing about it and having long ago wrong-footed myself by making political comments in Quetta I declined politely and no one seemed any the worse for it. Unwilling to take off my huge (100 litres) and heavy rucsac I elected to sit on the tailgate of the pick-up but had to hold on like grim death until disembarking by Tarwal seven miles on. Ahmad Yar Khan was relieved to see me and it felt good to be 'home' again. Thirty years of regret had been mitigated and perhaps I'll manage to join some Shinwaris or Kharotis in a year or two to fill in a few gaps.

Back in Quetta I was installed in Kakar House for the week or so before flying to Karachi and it was time to buy the usual batch of rugs although I was feeling far from well. A visit to a doctor friend of Dr. Tariq, A.Y.K.'s second son, suggested that it could from carelessly and heavily over-dosing on Flagyl against a suspected dose of Giardia just before I quit the Shahizais. Mohammad Anwar, Jehandar Shah's long time Tajik friend from Kandahar, went with me around the Gul Market one day to look for Persian rugs, all smuggled over the border south of Zahedan to avoid a heavy Iranian export tax, for his shop in Dubai; and I chanced to come upon a new but superb little Baluch piece, destined to become a family treasure. Four years later he sold me a well-used but dazzling Kazak, to become yet another family heirloom, also telling me of a small-time Turkoman trader in a small dingy flat tucked away in a squalid back street who had a large and truly magnificent Salor carpet, the sort of piece I had sought for years. Whenever sitting in his tiny jeweller's shop in the Liaquat Bazaar, I am always impressed at the way he could do some business over the phone in Baluchi, talk to one of his many casual visitors in Pakhtu or to me in English at the same time, while writing out a receipt in Urdu. Also, because of his reputation for fair dealing, unsophisticated tribesmen with hope in their eyes sometimes drop in to show crystals found in distant hills, no doubt having heard of the fine gems frequently discovered in Afghanistan's Panjshir Valley and Pakistan's Karakorum mountains far to the north. To date, Baluchistan has revealed no such treasures and he will patiently explain that quartz crystals are not diamonds or topaz, that fragments of mica are worthless or that the multitude of flaws in more hopeful finds make them valueless. He always found time to deal with them gently.

Sheila and I were going to arrange schooling in Somerset for his very presentable and able teenage son, Manuwer Ali, and also be the boy's guardians but M.A.J.'s honest and gentle manager of many years, Haq Nawaz, was suddenly offered a job as Manager in a Quetta branch of the Bolan Bank a year or so later and left. As a result young Manuwer Ali had to take his place in the shop and remain in Quetta. Upon leaving Quetta for Karachi, Anwar Jan, as I usually address him now that we have got to know one another, insisted that I stay in his Karachi house rather that a grubby hotel in Saddar until my flight to London where his two other sons would look after me. Clearly obeying strict orders from Father, they were so desperately attentive that I was forced to rebel at times. Some years earlier I was in Quetta over Christmas for some reason or another. Being away from my family at that time was quite hard and, as compensation for this, Jehandar Shah and Anwar Jan laid on their version of a Christmas dinner, scouring the bazaar for 'landi', the local dried meat that I so love. It was a typical gesture. Sadly Jehandar Shah and Anwar Jan after a long illness are no more. Back in England once more, both family and friends were shocked at my appearance. For my part I have never bothered about scales but a fair guess is that I was between six and eight kilos lighter, most if not all of it muscle loss since I carried little fat to start with. But millions of others have survived far worse and it had been fascinating insight into another and shrinking world.

Chapter Eleven

Epilogue

In 1996 James our eldest son was thirty years of age and had only visited Zhob for a few hours at the age of twelve. As I was going out to buy rugs, he felt that he would like a proper look at Tarwal. We were accompanied by Marc Bye, a Royal Navy officer-friend of his whom he met just after graduating, and the two had only a week in the Valley. A day or so after arriving in Tarwal, I took them across the village to call on Fukhruddin as I always did. He was sitting against the wall in his gloomy little front room and as we stooped to enter it became clear that he was blind. The son with him shouted into his ear, "Tony larreh," and, at a second attempt, Fukhruddin registered that I had come to see him. As I down sat beside him, he cried out my name in surprise and pleasure that he was not forgotten, feeling my head to make sure that it really was me. It was so very sad to see such a tough little chap shrunken to little more than skin and bone and reduced to a dark, almost silent world. A lump entered my throat and I could not speak for a few moments as I draped my arm across his frail shoulders.

He had been so different only six years earlier when I went there with Sheila and Helga and I felt almost guilty at not having sent out a regular supply of vitamin tablets that included vitamin A. It might have made his last few years so much better and my regret lingers. The other incident of note was when the three of us climbed Seerzha, the small but dramatic peak topped by a jagged, vertical ridge only two or three miles from the village where I had seen mountain sheep and nearly bumped into a magnificent wolf that was stalking them in the early days, but guns have done their work and even the pair of lammergeyers that used it as their lair are all a distant memory. On our way up I saw what appeared to be a small Stapelia growing in the wide scree slope below the vertical ridge but could not find it among the rocks and stones on our way down in order to take a photograph. The failure nagged me but, three years later, accompanied by Newman, against all odds I found it, following which the Kew Herbarium identified it as Caralluma tuberculata, a related genus. For a number of years before my retirement Ahmad Yar Khan and I used to talk of building two homes at the foot of Seerzha's twin though unequal peaks but the advent of electricity and the hordes of trucks trundling through the Valley have destroyed the remoteness and serenity of the great valley. Strangely, after all these years A.Y.K. still calls me 'Mister Tony' in spite of my repeated corrections. The habit is engrained and I just don't bother about it any more.

After the two had left I decided to take a look at two huge ancient earth mounds reported in the Zhob Gazetteer of 1907 to be near Fort Sandeman. In all the months that I had stayed with the Jogezai brothers, such mounds had never been mentioned and it was thanks to A.Y.K.'s brother in Quetta, Jehandar Shah, who quite un-asked had kindly photocopied large tracts of the Gazetteer, that the mounds came to my notice. The first of the two, listed as Kodan, is known today as Kakar Kaudan and is a mere three hundred or four hundred yards from Pokha Malawar village, listed simply as Malawar in the Gazetteer. The visit was by courtesy of Humayun Jogezai, one of Jehandar Shah's four sons, with what appeared to be a bodyguard in his two 4WDs while we were on our way via Fort Sandeman to the shrine of Sanjar Nika at Kot, the putative founder of the dominant Sanjar Khel section of the Kakars. Therefore I was on the lookout for such a mound as we sped along and, although about a mile and a half from the main road, it was easily seen. Humayun was obliging and diverted from the main road.

At first the seven or eight others of our group were tolerantly indifferent to this small and un-planned diversion but gradually my enthusiasm warmed them to the search. Using turbans to collect items, in half an hour we gathered a considerable and interesting pile of pottery shards plus a small stone ball and a small clay one, from which I selected the best and most varied bits, later presenting the best items to the Antiquities Department of Baluchistan in Quetta. After that diversion we continued to Kot, having an excellent picnic on the way prepared by Humayun's Bangladeshi cook. Our pilgrimage to the 'ziarat', where all prayed at the two tombs inside the small stone building, was quite moving, and for me also as it meant so much to them. The day was somewhat marred when, largely at my suggestion (having covered the road in 1971) our return was to be via Murgha Kibzai and Loralai rather that Fort Sandeman. However, with no one to ask the way in Murgha Kibzai as it was late by then, we took the wrong turning onto a dreadful track with enormous potholes that lead us to Mekhtar and a number of miles out of our way.

A day or two later I decided to investigate the second huge mound that I had noted from the summit of Kakar Kaudan when with Humayun. As I left to take a bus to Fort Sandeman from the top of the Tarwal road, A.Y.K. slipped his small .22 pistol into my pocket. The bus driver obligingly put me down a couple of miles beyond Kaudan, opposite the second ancient mound that was three or so miles from the road. It turned out to be situated half a mile from Apozai village, in Mando Khel territory, and is larger than Kaudan, being known locally as Pariana I was reliably told by an educated passer-by but there is not even a similar name in the Gazetteer. Unlike Kaudan, thousands of tons of soil had been removed from Pariana to build houses and orchard walls nearby. The 1907 Gazetteer spoke of ruins being visible but only a small portion of mud brick wall was visible, while small exposed faces showed the usual layers of ash and carbon. As might be expected, in addition to builders, pits here and there showed that treasure seekers were also at work. This time I collected shards with designs not noted on Kaudan. Later a selection of shards collected from both mounds was given to the British Museum and appear to be contemporary with material found by a professional team that excavated a similar mound over a period of ten years in Waziristan called Sheri Khan Tarakai and situated some ten miles from Bannu. If so, the Zhob mounds probably date from the last quarter of 5th millennium B.C. which would make them around 6,250 years old. The Waziristan excavation was under armed escort when in progress and since then has been discontinued on the grounds of safety. The Gazetteer briefly mentions two more ancient mounds near Fort Sandeman but I was unable to see them from the summits of Kaudan or Pariana though one was located three years later.

At my request Omar Khayyam, son of Nur Ahmad, was deputed to drive me the ninety-five or so miles far over the hills from Tarwal, past Loralai and ten or twelve miles beyond Duki, to an immense mound known locally as the Thal Shaghullai. It is a truly gigantic, dwarfing those mentioned above, about a mile or so off the Nana Sahib Ziarat road and clearly within sight of Duki. Its height was estimated at eighty feet in the Loralai Gazetteer of 1907 but a report in 1929 puts it at one hundred and thirteen feet and I suspect that to be a considerable underestimate. As we drove to it across 'khushk-aba' land, a patchwork of small plots and low banks, I got out to ask for directions from a youth shepherding a few sheep but could get no response until Omar Khayyam came across and realised that the lad was a Murri Baluch and did not understand Pashtu. Children in particular rush to the mound after each rare downpour, we were told, to see if anything valuable has been washed out from the fine soil and a year or two before our visit one boy is reputed to have found a chipped plate there that netted Rs. 80,000, the equivalent of seven years earnings for a village farmer at that time. Sir Aurel Stein visited the mound in 1904 but called it Dubbr Kot and shortly before his visit an earthen pot containing two hundred silver coins had been found, while a few years previously near the village of Aghbarg in Sherani territory of northern Zhob, some boys found a pot containing fifteen (at least) primitive squares or oblongs of silver stamped with symbols. They are the so-called punch-marked coins that were used throughout India and are thought by the British Museum to date from the fourth century B.C., if not earlier. However, it seems that a site known as Monastary Hill just three miles from Loralai impressed Stein more than his Dubbr Kot but it slipped my mind and I failed to visit it.

To realise that humans had created such a gigantic mound by hand was astonishing, Silbury Hill in Wiltshire being a mere 'molehill' by comparison. After exploring the mound and photographing various stone and clay artefacts, we returned to Duki and called upon Omar Khayyam's in-laws. Upon examining and discussing the bits and pieces that we had gathered, someone mentioned 'rock carvings' not very far away, stating that one was of a hand. At the time I was a little sceptical but it was too late to take a look at the site. However, his in-laws were soon proven to be right by a site over a hundred and twenty miles away near the village of Anderbez in the area of Hindubagh. Eight or so miles north from Duki is the village of Manzai, where I stayed briefly in 1971, and just a mile or two across the plain from there is yet another but much smaller mound or 'ghundei', as they are often called locally, known as Dilera. That probably was little more than an ancient fort and I had visited it briefly but likewise it is littered with shards and storms are said to have exposed jewellery. There is also an ancient graveyard near Manzai with the graves aligned east-west instead of north-south indicating that they are pre-Muslim. Erosion is slowly exposing some of the graves, and jewellery is then sometimes found. Nur Ahmad presented me with an engraved seal and some semi-precious beads from one such grave, duly passed on to the British Museum, while many years ago A.Y.K. was given a pair of gold earrings from there. Unfortunately no one so far has undertaken a proper archaeological excavation of any of these tantalising sites except that one in Waziristan.

Another archaeological mention in the Gazetteer refers to 'rock carvings' near Andrebiezh although the name of the village has changed since then or was incorrectly written in the Gazetteer. During this visit I located Anderbez, as it is now called, without difficulty as it is famed locally for its fine apples. It lies just off the road to Murgha Fakirzai that leads off the main Valley road only two or three miles north of Hindubagh and is perhaps fifteen miles into the hills. For this visit I hired a pick-up to take me there, not wishing to burden my friends too much. My driver was a cheerful sort of chap convinced of his own infallibility and immortality, a frightening combination when negotiating blind bends on a dirt road teetering over fearsome drops, with only one of his hands on the steering wheel while his other explored each nostril in turn – usually a rewarding and satisfying occupation in such a dry, dusty land. But he was punctual, nothing was too much trouble and at the end of our day-long expedition he made no attempt to push up the modest fee originally agreed so that I was content to add a little to the original price. The tangle of multi-hued mountains was both awesome and beautiful but rather lost upon me as we hurtled over bedrock and gravel and I offered silent prayers as we approached each bend.

Upon arriving at the village, a youth volunteered to be our guide, from goodwill and not for payment, and we had to negotiate the long, very narrow lane to the torrent bed with great care. We examined two clusters of the rock chippings, or petroglyphs as they turned out to be. They consist of thousands of tiny indentations apparently made with some pointed metal tool. The first were on a very small, isolated and almost vertical outcrop of nearly black rock but were so poor that I almost felt our hazardous journey to have been wasted. That was until a curious passer-by stopped and mentioned that there were better 'tessui', as they call them, on a large almost black boulder perched above the almost dry torrent bed a mile downstream. He was right and they also turned out to be far more numerous, much clearer and more varied. Later on, while busy on the boulder, some other passers-by told us that there were many more such sites in nearby gullies but we lacked the time to visit them. So far no one seems prepared to hazard a guess as to their date but presumably they are pre-Muslim as they depict human figures and hands as well as animals such as dogs, ibex and possibly even a rhinoceros, in addition to abstracts. Even allowing for the hardness of the rock, they were quite naive and child-like, a 'match stick' man with a sword and shield shown standing rather than sitting on a horse for example. They were well worth the time and stress involved.

In Quetta, when preparing to return home, Nur Ahmad suddenly turned up at Jehandar Shah's and asked if I would like to join him on a visit to Vesh, three or so miles over the Afghan border, as he wanted to look at vehicles there. In Chaman we called on a friend of his and changed from his 4WD to that of the friend. I had no passport with me but at the border we were casually waved through by both the Pakistani officials and the Afghan ones. Across the desert, Vesh turned out to be a large collection of steel shipping containers of every size and colour with doorways cut into them arranged along both sides of the road. There were no normal, mud-walled buildings visible and the steel "shops" were stacked high with vehicle accessories such as tyres in their bright wrappers, National Oil, Duckhams Oil and so on. Perhaps the most intriguing thing was a lofty steel arch over the dirt road about halfway along the street. We approached it driving along the left hand, as in Pakistan, but as we passed beneath it we swung over to the right hand as in Afghanistan. It was the regular procedure.

Upon stopping we were promptly warned to behave discreetly as the Taliban had suffered a military reverse in the north and were said to be edgy. As I was not wearing a Chitrali cap let alone full tribal dress, I felt distinctly conspicuous and did not wander far. In addition to us there was a trio of flashy young town men, probably from Karachi, looking around. Behind the lines of containers were large, mud-walled compounds, each containing hundreds, some possibly thousands of Toyota, Nissan & Mitsubishi vehicles up to small truck size. All had blue number plates with Arabic writing in white that showed the ports of export in the Persian Gulf, such as AJ, SHJ, UAQ in Roman letters. Customers pay in cash, documents are forged and the vehicles are driven across the border in a quiet area to be collected at an arranged rendezvous. The whole thing is so obvious that government officials must be aware of what is going on and such a vehicle is referred to in northern Baluchistan as a 'Kabuli motorr'. One had to assume that the Taliban were being paid and others as well. Told that import duty in Pakistan was 250 per cent currently I could understand the temptation. Shortly afterwards several local men in Zhob who had 'Kabuli' vehicles suddenly stopped driving into Kila Saifulla for a few days, following newspaper reports that the army was checking such vehicles and extracting the unpaid duty from those owners unlucky enough to be caught.

In 1999, apart from needing a few more rugs for our small business, after three years of dull routine, like an Australian aborigine, I also needed a 'walk-about' and our middle son Newman felt like joining me. He had been there previously some sixteen years earlier when he was just fourteen. Fog delayed our plane in Dubai so that we had no hope of catching a connection to Quetta shortly after landing at Karachi. As usual my revolver in its padlocked green box came through on the carousel with all the other baggage in spite of all the P.I.A. security fuss at Heathrow and an attached label stating 'Security'. A steaming night in Saddar was not welcome and had we but known it we could have enjoyed transit accommodation near the airport courtesy of P.I.A. but as a result we chanced to meet a very pleasant Sulaiman Khel businessman in the bazaar who took us to a jewellery exhibition in the modern part of city. There were guards armed with shotguns at the door and on the stairs, some of the fabulous displays showing the reason why, when one emerald earring and pendant set consisted of three magnificent stones, and weighed around forty-five carats each.

When we landed at Quetta the next morning, at 5,000 feet the cool, crisp dry air was simply wonderful. However, we were seriously over-burdened with baggage and packages and I almost dreaded the anticipated argument over the taxi fare into town. Moreover, since Jahandar Shah was no more, it seemed rather unfair to impose ourselves on his son Aurangzeb who had taken over the house and I was unsure where to go without possibly causing offence, as had happened years earlier when with Newman. Generally I had made it my practice not to tell my time of arrival as they would then feel obliged to drop everything and drive to the airport to meet me but, having thoughtlessly mentioned the day of our arrival, Ahmad Yar Khan had instructed number one son, Farouk, to meet us. It was a wonderful relief to be collected and taken to his official bungalow in the town but even better was to follow, for Nur Ahmad, A.Y.K.'s younger and ever-cheerful brother planned to drive the one hundred and twenty miles to Tarwal an hour later, after lunch.

Three years earlier I had located two of seven ancient sites reported in the Zhob Gazetteer (Dubbr Kot is mentioned in the Loralai Gazetteer) and was eager to locate the other four so Newman and I braved a Toyota minibus to Fort Sandeman bazaar, aka Zhob now, some eighty miles down the valley. The uncontrolled proliferation of tube wells was causing the water table in many areas to plunge at the rate of a metre a year yet we saw four boring rigs at work on the way but we also saw a young orchard whose every tree was covered with dead, brown leaves for that reason. Stopping at a 'chai khana' in a small gorge that boasted a trickle of water, for some reason the waiter decided to serve only the other passengers, possibly because I addressed him as 'alek' or 'boy' as does A.Y.K. but the man possibly felt too old for such familiarity. A middle-aged Kakar near us noticed this and, without a word, passed us one of his own 'naans'.

In Fort Sandeman we installed ourselves in the Al Marad hotel, for the princely equivalent of £1.20 for the two of us. It was early afternoon so we located a taxi at the central point of the bazaar to seek Sang, our clue being that it was near the village of Dera a few miles from the town. The driver we happened to choose was Nurullah Jan, a Mando Khel, who turned out to be honest, helpful and wide-awake and as his wife was a school teacher we shared common ground. He knew the place but, when we arrived, Sang turned out to be not an earthen mound but an isolated dog-tooth pinnacle of rock, roughly two hundred and fifty feet high, as perhaps I should have guessed from its name which means rock in Farsi. It abutted the left bank of the Zhob River, which at that point had a small flow of water, and I began to think that the journey had been wasted. However, upon walking around to its far side we found a smallish, steep slope of soil against the rock with numerous pottery shards on the surface but the settlement must have been very small and we spent little time there. Another mound listed is Dera, said to be three or four miles from the town and one wonders if there is confusion with Dera. As for Kabdanai, yet another mound allegedly situated two or three miles north of Dera, we saw no sign but orchards may have obscured our view.

We arranged for our helpful driver to meet us at the hotel at eight the following morning. Back in our dingy room that evening, a refined, courteous and pleasant young man from the Special Branch called to check our passports. Afterwards, as we made our way to the Khyber Hotal for a meal, two police officers who were obviously neither Afghan nor Pashtun ignored my protestations in Urdu that we had been checked already and took us to their station to record our details. The bazaar was as dirty and un-inviting as any could be and we quickly agreed that one more night there would have to be enough, come what may. Having said that, the restaurant recommended to us was spotlessly clean and its liberally oiled meat stew very tasty. In the morning the owner of the taxi appeared right on time, after we had breakfasted on warm 'paratas' and 'poi chai' just a few yards from our 'hotal', and drove us across town to collect our driver from his house. Our next clue for another ancient mound, 'Maglia Ghundi nine miles west of Fort Sandeman' in the Gazetteer, was Jhalar village but Nurullah Jan was adamant that no such village existed in the area and we had come to trust his judgement. However, there was a Jalal village five or so miles away and there was a 'ghundei' or ancient earth mound nearby. For whatever reason 'l' and 'r' are sometimes interchanged, so we decided that it was probably the same village. However, the reported name, 'Maglia Ghundi', merely means 'mound of the Mughals' and therefore is rather vague especially when anything more than several generations back tends to be considered Mughal in origin.

After a tortuous journey through a couple of villages with narrow lanes hemmed in by high mud walls, the mound turned out to be Pariana, the one that I had visited three years earlier, our approach being from its other side. From its summit no other mound other than Kakar Kaudan was visible on the wide floor of the valley and therefore it seems likely that the two quite different names refer to the one mound even though the distances appear not to match perfectly. More importantly, in a hole dug by treasure seekers our enterprising driver found several found large fragments of two plates, finely and differently decorated in colour that included the rims and centres so that the missing parts could be replicated. Later the airport Customs at Karachi made no objection to them being taken out by Newman and they were duly delivered to a suitable home. We would have liked to continue the search but our 'hotal' was distinctly cheerless and the bazaar itself squalid beyond words so we fled after two nights there. On our way back to Tarwal we saw that the Zhob river only thirty-five or so miles upstream from Fort Sandeman consisted of isolated pools due to the three-year drought.

Afghan and Pashtun hospitality is legendary among those who know and this visit was no exception. My Pashtu was never good and the gaps of several years between visits make it even worse so that, in one way, invitations to dinner tended to be hard work. Abdur Rahman was a born gentleman and sadly had died ten or so years earlier but his sons invited us to their home at Kuli Ghoti out on the great valley floor. We set off in the dark with Ahmad Yar Khan but his thirteen-year-old and beloved grandson, Akbar Khan, drove the car, being constantly told to slow down or be careful. Three of the four sons are massively built and include Tahir Khab, whose resemblance to me at the age of fourteen when I was that age was quite eerie. The three heavier probably top twenty stones in weight and they are not obviously fat. Our next social round was at the home of Afzal Khan, the eldest son of the late Jahangir Shah whose name read in error had saved me from the villainous Customs some years earlier. As mentioned earlier Afzal Khan is very gentle yet always seems to carry a pistol in his pocket.

For many years, upon hearing of my arrival in Tarwal Sheikh, Rahmat, the riotous old ex-outlaw, would promptly come across to say his salaams. This time he made no appearance so we went across the tiny village to seek him, only to find that he had moved to his sons' compound a couple of miles from Kila Saifulla on the far side. A few days later Akbar Khan drove us there for a touching reunion. He was over eighty-five, a shade deaf and very frail, but the sturdy spirit of old lingered. Amazingly, as we passed an open door we glimpsed an aged woman and it was indeed his wife. In the West wives generally outlive their spouses but in the tribal areas the reverse seems to hold. The sons have done quite well, judging from the high-walled compound with its flower garden surrounded by a number of rooms, and treat him with respect. He was reclined on the floor and as we all talked he kept fingering my most recent Christmas card tucked under his mattress as if it were some talisman. We returned with A.Y.K. several evenings later to find a feast that would have fed fifteen men although with his three sons we totalled a mere seven. For the meal he remained in his room and his sons declined to eat with us out of respect but as we chatted beforehand he threw a gaudy handkerchief to Newman as a small gift and another to me together with a small cotton sachet of cloves – for Afghans love scents.

The Jogezai clan is a large one and many are prosperous but the "inner core", for want of a better word, of those closely related to the old chief had a recognised meeting place in the old days well down the one street that formed the bazaar. It was a simple room with a threadbare carpet of sorts and no furniture of any kind, owned by I know not whom and seemingly with no other function. Entry was by a little sticks-and-earth bridge across the evil open sewer oozing fitfully along the edge of the earthen street just outside. These days the main bazaar has a tar road and the recognised venue has moved to a smaller room but with a desk and chairs next to the P.T.O., as everyone calls the public telephone office. The P.T.O. is in a large courtyard just off the main road to which the bazaar has now spread. A.Y.K. goes there most days and Ayaz Khan, the present chief drops in at intervals. As we chatted there one day, when the group's conversation turned to mounds and ancient things, Dr. Daud Khan, one of

Abdur Rahman's sons, mentioned that villagers were digging up what he called small 'clay statues', meaning figurines, from a 'ghundei' in the territory of the Bharat Khel clan, roughly forty miles down the valley. Indeed, so many were being found and sold that it had come to the ears of the government who then put a ban on the business, though only on paper to be more precise. A day or two later Omar Khayyam took us there, probably having been 'volunteered' by his father, as happened three years earlier when he took me to Dubbr Kot.

The Bharat Khel 'ghundei' was near the village of Nerai, hidden away in a shallow valley among low, barren hills seven miles south-east from the main road. As we were driven to it along the gravel track we saw many nomads, their flocks trying to glean a living from a landscape so arid and devoid of vegetation that it almost seemed that they were feeding upon the stones. The state of their poorly patched 'kuzhdei' showed a new poverty brought about by the severe drought and meant that they could no longer afford the goats' hair cloth from the Ali Khel or the Wardak in Afghanistan. Also their unusual numbers suggested that the drought was as bad in south-eastern Afghanistan as in the late sixties and early seventies. Surprisingly in such an arid area, there was a small stream near Nerai with a substantial pool above a miniature, concrete holding dam; below, dense shoals of fish, four or five inches long, were cramped into rocky pools before the weak flow disappeared beneath the gravel after fifteen yards or so. I was also surprised to see three other apparently thriving villages between the main road and Nerai, surprised because there appeared to be no electricity supply for boreholes, which suggested that the irrigation of their orchards would be either by abundant springs or 'karez' wells out of sight on their far sides. The villages were oases in the semi-desert landscape.

The 'ghundei' turned out to be considerably smaller than either Kaudan or Pariana and from a mile away, as we paused for a drink at the pool, it was visibly pock-marked all over as if hit by a cluster bomb, so busy had the locals been in their search for figurines and any other 'goodies' that might be there. Obviously the clandestine business was thriving. Although it was the third week in October it was too hot for comfort but we did the necessary: taking photographs, collecting pottery shards and carbon samples before returning to Tarwal. The irony is that all these mounds are – or at least were – in a peaceful area and simply waiting for proper archaeological excavations, whereas the dig in Waziristan had involved armed guards throughout and was eventually halted due to a threatening situation. In the meantime, unknown but probably considerable quantities of artefacts are being dug out, sold illegally and virtually lost for all time. Dr. Faizaldad Kakar i/c Antiquities in Quetta not only had a vast area to cover but simply did not have the funds at his disposal to undertake proper investigation.

A day later Nur Ahmad took us duck shooting at a holding dam in the hills a few miles from Tarwal, where a couple of men happened to be target shooting rather unsuccessfully at a small rock. As we approached the dam along the tiny stream that flowed from it, Newman and I saw a snake but kept quiet, knowing what would happen to it otherwise. In any case it clearly was not a Russels viper or cobra and was almost certainly harmless. Neither of us has any interest in hunting but, when we were seated on a low mound overlooking the lake, Nur Ahmad handed Newman his shotgun just before a duck hurtled overhead. It was a difficult, almost vertical shot and his first ever yet almost miraculously Newman downed the bird and so maintained family honour. That afternoon Omar Khayyam and a couple of his friends took our son to climb Kassa, off the road to Loralai and not far from Chinjan village to the west. It is a quite high, isolated mountain that dominates the gently sloping plain around it and has scree slopes leading up to sheer cliffs all round its flat top that show caves here and there. However, there is a precipitous path to the top and Newman wisely opted out of the last few, almost vertical feet, where a slip would mean certain death. The other three made it but later admitted that they were scared and had it not been for Newman's presence I wonder if they would have taken such a risk. When they failed to return until well after dark I became quite worried

Among other things I hoped to meet up with Ruziamat Shahizai and his family who should have arrived from Badani by then. Sure enough, a day or two after our arrival at Tarwal, a Shahizai 'malik' frequenting the Kila Saifulla bazaar reported that the family was camped in an area called Barrg among the mountains about fifty miles away in the Loralai area so Newman and I took a bus over the hills to the bazaar and there hired a taxi out to the area but to no avail. The days had passed and work now called Newman. I decided to go with him to Quetta to help him seek a rug or a kilim prior to flying home but before leaving we made a rapid two-hour hike across the plain to the Zhob River and back, eight or nine miles in all. It was bone dry for the first time in living memory and even some of the young tamarisk saplings along the margin of its sandy bed were turning yellow. When we returned A.Y.K. was away and we were on the point of setting off for the main road when he appeared with Ruziamat, whom he had collected in Kila Saifulla. How Ruziamat came to be in Kila Saifulla I failed to discover but strongly suspect that he had been asked to come from his camp. The family was fine but the flock was struggling. Malanga was then around seventeen or eighteen years of age and as the flock could not possibly support five adults he had replaced one of the two brothers, who was then forced to labour somewhere up the valley. I felt that he was a bit over-awed by having lunch with one of the old chief's prestigious sons but we were able to present him with a stainless steel vacuum flask brought with us to provide a hint of comfort for his two sons during the cold night watches.

Martial Law had been declared shortly after our arrival but, as on two or three previous occasions when there, the army's presence was discreet and it was generally a case of 'business as usual'. After choosing a kilim, Newman flew to Karachi and, for reasons forgotten, I also continued to Karachi, but by tribal bus and endured a cold, bumpy, sleepless journey of twelve hours, finally reaching Anwar Jan's house in Clifton by taxi from some distant suburb. Having completed whatever I had to do, I returned to Quetta by train, the first time for many years as rocket attacks, machine gunning and robberies had been frequently reported for a period previously, allegedly by 'muhajir' or immigrants from Hyderabad in India who were demanding their own state in the Sinde. On the platform in the late afternoon I was approached by friendly young Hotak, who originally was from Kandahar. He had an almost child-like innocence about him and had been to America for five years as an Afghan refugee, where he had worked in a factory with Mexicans so that his Spanish was far better than his English but to his great disappointment he had not been granted a green card and was now resigned to living in Karachi with his family. In the a/c compartment booked, my companion turned out to be a settled Zhadran, many of whom are still nomadic but he was a town-dweller. He was seen off by his daughter-in-law, a determined looking young woman whose strident voice coped well with his deafness, and she had prepared a delicious whole chicken for his journey. Once we were under way he generously shared it with me as he sat cross-legged on the seat opposite. Later, as we settled down for the night with both door fastenings secure, I took out my revolver from the small back-pack that I carried and attached it to my belt prior to sliding into my sleeping bag lining. I am always discreet about firearms, even when legally entitled to carry one but naturally he saw this, at which his only comment in English of 'very good' showed his approval. Although our places had been booked, during the night an inspector tried to move us but we suspected that his attempt was probably in answer to the offer of a bribe by another passenger and we refused to budge. Still later we were joined by two other men who took the top bunk on either side but they were considerate and disturbed us little. Sighting the great hills that rise abruptly from the endless Kachi Plain in the bright morning sun brought a lift to the heart.

When his wife Taj Bibi died, Ahmad Yar Khan missed her greatly. Sheila and Helga had met and truly liked her during their visit with me in 1990. Upon that return to Tarwal from Karachi, A.Y.K. who was then seventy-three, was remarkably candid with me about his re-marriage to a young girl of twenty that had been arranged by his brothers. Because of his age it had been impossible to find a woman or girl of similar social status, and many of the Jogezais in Zhob marry their cousins for that reason, so his brothers had made a fruitful approach to a poor family of the Haiderzai clan some twenty miles down the valley. He and his new wife already had a son aged eighteen months, Shouaib, whom A.Y.K. adores and who is younger than his own grandson Akbar Khan, but A.Y.K. still laments the passing of his wise Taj Bibi. Why produce a child at such an age? It was so that the wife would have something to love and treasure after A.Y.K. was dead. The solemn little boy aged about twelve who brought our tea and meals is his brother-in-law, as was the young man in his late teens hanging about the house, so the new in-laws are being cared for. However, A.Y.K. himself is putting on weight and his legs are beginning to feel the strain so I pointed out that the new son, his fifth, would benefit from his living a few more years, which end would be better served if he cut down on his food and took regular exercise. I expect that his doctor son, Tariq, has said much the same, albeit more tactfully than my attempt. In any case I look upon him as a brother and want him around for as long as possible. He agreed with me but his smile was not reassuring.

Mina Bazaar, seventy miles down the road, is reported in the Gazetteer as being partly built upon a 'ghundei' so I caught a bus and asked the driver to put me down at the turn-off to the village. Having detoured to check two low mounds, after a couple of miles I returned to the gravel track and found that it forked. This was a problem but a motorcyclist chanced along at that moment and I asked him which track to take. However, he told me to get aboard and went out of his way to take me to the village two or three miles further on and thus I failed to call upon a friend of A.Y.K.'s as arranged. With his turban as often as not wrapped around my face and blinding me, it was a trifle nerve-wracking at each little skid, not from risk of injury as we were not travelling fast but because of my precious camera. In Mina Bazaar all the mounds that I could see were entirely natural and composed of shale but the dry-stone-walled houses, a recent innovation in the Valley, were built with dry stone from elsewhere. The one tiny shop was closed and I was already quite thirsty but a glance at the small, dirty, isolated pools in the deep 'nulla' through the village that were the water supply was enough to ensure abstinence. The women filling their containers were left with no choice and I expect that infant mortality is high as a result. As I set off back to the main road five or so miles away, a large group of young boys fighting among themselves decided that it was more fun to send a few stones in my direction, not really at me but to the right and left and just behind. It was a bit of bravado and had I been hit I would have wreaked my own vengeance as of old but all was well. In the early days of the British occupation, this village became known for its belligerence and for sheltering outlaws so this was a faint echo from the past. Within minutes another motorcyclist came along heading for the tar road and, without my asking, I was immediately installed on the pillion seat.

That track had far more stretches of fine gravel and sand than the first one so that we swerved and slid alarmingly at intervals.

Arriving at the tar road, he asked my intention, which was to locate a 'ghundei' named Kanroki, said by the Gazetteer to be in the vicinity. It was possible to see several miles each way along the Valley floor and I could see only a pair of isolated rock bosses, perhaps a hundred feet tall, some three miles away and straight ahead but there was no sign of an earthen mound. They were entirely natural and seemed to offer little hope until, without prompting, he named them Kanokei. It could hardly be a coincidence. At that, he then elected to take me there although it was not his destination. As we approached through orchards and fields of tomatoes being harvested, all fed by a borehole gushing much-needed clean water that we both enjoyed, a large artificial earth mound against one of the rock bosses became clear. Its outer slopes especially were littered with thousands upon thousands of pottery shards and higher up the mound was an intact, ancient stone saddle quern. In an exposed face was a thick carbon layer and in some bedrock protruding from the soil of the upper slope was an extraordinary hole about nine inches in diameter drilled vertically down into it. After taking photographs and carbon samples, helped by two local youths who clambered down from the top of the rock boss, I set off down the Zhob River only a few yards away, for an isolated, dog-toothed pinnacle about four miles distant that rose almost sheer from the valley floor for perhaps five hundred feet. It was Masakhwul.

Along each side of the shallow river, which had a small flow along that stretch, were extensive reed beds through which I threaded warily in case of saw scaled vipers whose venom is both haematoxic and neurotoxic and dangerous but wild boar were almost certainly a thing of the past. Ahmad Yar Khan had been told that the peak had a cave with paintings and carvings and that prior to Partition, Hindu shopkeepers and Muslim tribes people in the area made it a place of pilgrimage. I had eaten nothing other that 'poi chai' and a couple of biscuits since morning, the usual breakfast, not that it mattered much in the warmth, but I was again very thirsty so my enthusiasm was waning. Moreover, there was little more than an hour before darkness so I capitulated when three-quarters up the steep ravine with its sheer sides that reached nearly to the top where it was so over-hanging that it could just be called a cave. After a rapid walk around the rock base to see if there were any petroglyphs visible, I re-crossed the river, this time without removing my shoes, and headed for the road a couple of miles away. I reached it just as the sun set and was soon aboard a Toyota minibus that appeared to be full of mullahs. A little further on we stopped at a 'chai khanna' for prayers and pots of sweet black tea. Two hours later I was back in Tarwal. Dinner with A.Y.K. and six large glasses of water was a blessing.

When returning to Tarwal from Quetta after my brief Karachi trip, at the Pishin Adda bus centre I had been surprised to meet Maboob Ali Khan, the third son of the late Temur Shah, also taking the large, modern coach, and within a few days he sent a dinner invitation. While I never think of food until I am actually hungry I do enjoy good food and that put before us could not have been bettered. As always, meals are not taken at a table but on a cloth spread out on the floor. We numbered around eighteen or so and included the local Political Agent, who happened to be a Baluchi. When finished we all rose but no one left the room and I suddenly became aware that many eyes were upon me. Having few delusions of grandeur it dawned upon me only slowly that I was the guest of honour and was expected to lead the way from the room, washing our hands at the door as we left.

When searching the bazaar for good rugs with Newman earlier I had been worried at the scarcity of good pieces and even Anwar Jan, who had put me onto more than one good source in the past, could not help. I suspected that the Taliban may have been the cause by imposing too many 'duties' or too much 'duty' on such goods on their way to Quetta from the north and west of

Afghanistan with the result that the trade was being re-routed through Peshawar or even across the Oxus River into Turkestan or Uzbekistan. Several well-established shops had closed and the two Turkoman colonies of rug dealers in the upper part of Suraj Ganj were depleted, another colony elsewhere closed entirely. Adding to that, a Special Branch officer who happened to be in Anwar Jan's shop one day quietly told me that Quetta and Karachi were officially regarded as being danger areas for Europeans and especially so for Americans who, together with the I.M.F., seemed to be widely held responsible for all of Pakistan's ills. As I often carried a considerable sum in cash to pay the Turkoman dealers the possibility of a mugging or attempted mugging always had to be considered. Moreover, Europeans are sometimes regarded as soft and easy game, as with the Peshawar incident in 1971. Forewarned is always fore-armed but in any case I always tried to blend in discreetly, wearing a Chitrali cap, fawn trousers that almost pass as baggy 'partook' or 'shalwar' and a similar shirt kept outside the trousers both for coolness and to cover my waist holster. In fact I was earlier surprised and quite flattered another day when a man in Anwar Jan's shop asked if I were a Kashmiri and, after I said that I was English, asked me a second time just to make sure that I wasn't pulling his leg. I only wished that the same could be said regarding Pashtu.

Whilst pausing in Quetta for rugs before departing, I had an extraordinary experience one day as I walked the mile or two down to the city centre from what is now Aurangzeb's house in the Cantonment. Two poor women with a sickly child-in-arms approached me. The mother mumbled something, possibly in Baluchi, so I pulled out some notes. No, that was not what she wanted I managed to understand and then I realised that she wanted me to carry out faith healing. As a biologist I am not a great supporter of that sort of thing although ready to grant that there can be remarkable benefit in some cases, the so-called placebo effect, but that could hardly happen in the case of that poor mite so I was faced with a dilemma. To refuse would be cruel, while to acquiesce would be hypocritical in my own mind. So I duly gave a token spit to the side of the child's head, as I had seen the old chief do, and mumbled a brief prayer. I suspected a protozoan problem such as Giardia or Entamoeba and would gladly have paid for the mother to see a doctor but knew of none, apart from A.Y.K.'s son Tariq who works in University's Opthalmic Department during the day and, by the time I recalled the little hospital established by Dr. Theodore Pennel in Mission Road five minutes later, they were out of sight and it was too late to help. I still regret it.

On that visit I had with me a small, Sony digital tape recorder in the hope of locating the fine Tarraki singer met in 1992 but I failed to trace him in Kuchlagh. Also I hoped to persuade Ahmad Yar Khan to sing some traditional Kakar songs as he had sung for Sheila and Helga six years previously. They both said that he had a good voice but he became bashful in Tarwal when I produced the recorder. In spite of these minor frustrations, shortly before leaving I chanced upon a blind musician playing the traditional tribal violin, the 'chara ka' in Quetta's Jinnah Cloth Market. Imam Baksh had been born just after the terrible earthquake of 1935, in which most if not all the doctors perished so that there was no one to treat the eye infection that he developed shortly afterwards. However, he manages to support himself and family with his music, moving around the bazaars without a guide or regular help. I found his renderings fascinating in a wild, rather plaintive way and recorded him for over an hour. When home once more the tape was transferred onto a compact disc by an ex-colleague and the original sent to the International Music Collection of the British Library complete with photographs. They already had a recording of Ruziamat and Zua Uddin from 1992 but the quality of that must leave much to be desired.